Communications and Briti
Western Front, 1914–1918

C000092491

This is an important new study examining the military operations of the British Expeditionary Force in 1914–18 through the lens of its communications system. Brian Hall charts how new communications technology such as wireless, telephone and telegraph were used alongside visual signalling, carrier pigeons and runners as the British army struggled to develop a communication system adequate to wage modern warfare. He reveals how tenuous communications added to the difficulties of command and control during the War's early years, and examines their role during the major battles of the Somme, Arras, Ypres and Cambrai. It was only in 1918 that the British army would finally develop a flexible and sophisticated communications system capable of effectively coordinating infantry, artillery, tanks and aeroplanes. This is a major contribution to our understanding of British military operations during the First World War, the learning processes of armies and the revolution in military affairs.

BRIAN N. HALL is Lecturer in Contemporary Military History at the University of Salford. He is a councillor for the Army Records Society and was awarded the US Society for Military History Moncado Prize in 2015.

Cambridge Military Histories

Edited by

HEW STRACHAN, Chichele Professor of the History of War, University of Oxford and Fellow of All Souls College, Oxford

GEOFFREY WAWRO, Professor of Military History, and Director of the Military History Center, University of North Texas

The aim of this series is to publish outstanding works of research on warfare throughout the ages and throughout the world. Books in the series take a broad approach to military history, examining war in all its military, strategic, political and economic aspects. The series complements Studies in the Social and Cultural History of Modern Warfare by focusing on the 'hard' military history of armies, tactics, strategy and warfare. Books in the series consist mainly of single author works – academically rigorous and groundbreaking – which are accessible to both academics and the interested general reader.

A full list of titles in the series can be found at:

www.cambridge.org/militaryhistories

Communications and British Operations on the Western Front, 1914–1918

Brian N. Hall

University of Salford

CAMBRIDGE
UNIVERSITY PRESS

CAMBRIDGE
UNIVERSITY PRESS

University Printing House, Cambridge CB2 8BS, United Kingdom

One Liberty Plaza, 20th Floor, New York, NY 10006, USA

477 Williamstown Road, Port Melbourne, VIC 3207, Australia

4843/24, 2nd Floor, Ansari Road, Daryaganj, Delhi – 110002, India

79 Anson Road, #06–04/06, Singapore 079906

Cambridge University Press is part of the University of Cambridge.

It furthers the University's mission by disseminating knowledge in the pursuit of education, learning, and research at the highest international levels of excellence.

www.cambridge.org
Information on this title: www.cambridge.org/9781107170551
DOI: 10.1017/9781316771747

First published 2017

A catalogue record for this publication is available from the British Library.

Library of Congress Cataloging-in-Publication Data
Names: Hall, Brian N., author.
Title: Communications and British operations on the Western Front, 1914–1918 / Brian N. Hall, University of Salford.
Description: New York : University of Salford, [2017] | Series: Cambridge military histories | Includes bibliographical references and index.
Identifiers: LCCN 2016051045 | ISBN 9781107170551 (Hardback : alk. paper)
Subjects: LCSH: Great Britain. Army–History–World War, 1914–1918. | World War, 1914–1918–Campaigns–Western Front. | World War, 1914–1918–Communications. | Great Britain. Army. British Expeditionary Force. | Great Britain. Army.–Communication systems–History–20th century.
Classification: LCC D546 .H38 2017 | DDC 940.4/144–dc23 LC record available at https://lccn.loc.gov/2016051045

ISBN 978-1-107-17055-1 Hardback

To Kathryn

Contents

Plates

Figures

Tables

Acknowledgements

This book is the culmination of a little more than ten years' research, during which time I have incurred many debts. The idea of examining the BEF's communications system was born out of a conversation in 2005 with Nikolas Gardner, who agreed to supervise my doctoral studies. Although Nik left shortly thereafter to teach at the USAF Air War College in Montgomery, Alabama, I am grateful for his initial guidance and encouragement. My next supervisor, Alaric Searle, guided me through to the successful completion of my doctorate and has remained a constant source of inspiration. Without his advice, support and constructive feedback it is doubtful that I would ever have come this far. I am also extremely privileged to have been the beneficiary of the knowledge, expertise and mentorship of Jim Beach. Since my viva his help and enthusiasm towards this project have been invaluable, and I will forever be in his debt for copying documents on my behalf at the Australian War Memorial. Special thanks are also reserved for my external examiner, Timothy Bowman, whose wise and incisive judgements broadened my outlook, forcing me to pursue fresh leads and uncover new evidence. The collective input of these individuals has, I hope, made this a far more rounded and detailed book than would otherwise have been the case.

I would like to acknowledge the financial assistance provided by the University of Salford, which paid my tuition fees during my time as a Ph.D. student and, together with the Royal Historical Society, kindly furnished me with the additional funds to conduct research in the United States. I am also grateful to the Scouloudi Historical Awards Committee for providing the financial assistance to carry out research at the Library and Archives Canada. I would like to thank the following institutions and their staffs for their generous help and assistance in making my research a pleasant and rewarding experience, and for permissions to quote material from their collections: the UK National Archives; the Bodleian Library; the BT Archives; the Trustees of the Imperial War Museum; the Trustees of the Liddell Hart Centre for

Military Archives; the British Library, Department of Manuscripts; the Liddle Collection, Brotherton Library; the Royal Mail Archive; the Manchester Regiment Archive; and the Trustees of the Churchill Archives Centre. I would particularly like to single out the following individuals for going out of their way to help me: Mitchell Yockelson at the US National Archives and Records Administration; Charlotte Hughes at the Royal Engineers Museum Archive; and Tim Stankus at the Royal Signals Museum Archive.

My knowledge and understanding have been shaped considerably by a number of colleagues, friends and acquaintances. For their advice, help and encouragement, I would particularly like to thank Jonathan Boff, Elizabeth Bruton, James Corum, Adam Dighton, Chris Forrest, David French, Simon Godfrey, Paul Harris, Matthew Hughes, Spencer Jones, Dan Lomas, Chris Murphy, Samantha Newbery, Bill Philpott, Andy Powell, Philip Pratley, Adam Prime, James Pugh, Gary Sheffield, Andy Simpson, Dmitri van den Bersselaar and Bruce Vandervort. Special gratitude is reserved for the editors of the Cambridge Military Histories series, Sir Hew Strachan and Geoffrey Wawro, for their support for this project. I am also extremely grateful to Michael Watson and his editorial team at Cambridge University Press for their help, patience and support while guiding me through the somewhat daunting and complex process of publication. I also wish to thank the two anonymous referees who read my manuscript and provided some very useful feedback. Any remaining errors and omissions are mine, and mine alone.

My final expressions of gratitude are reserved for the people who matter most in my life. Researching and writing a project of this nature can sometimes be a rather lonely and frustrating experience. However, I am extremely fortunate to have been surrounded by loving and supportive family and friends. Without them, the completion of this book would not have been possible. In particular, I am eternally grateful to my parents, Nigel and Alison; to Nanna Joan, and to my sisters, Jemima and Naomi, who supported me unfailingly during the course of this project. I am sorry that my other grandparents, Alan, Doreen and Ken, did not live to see this book published. I hope they would have been proud. Heartfelt thanks is reserved for Gwen Walford, who not only afforded me a place to stay during my periodic visits to London, but also provided me with food, drink and friendly conversation after long days spent in the archives. Tim and Karen Harris, Mike and Joe Hermida, Gerry and Craig Thomson, Karl Walford, Trish and Ethan Whyley, Jonathan Peachey and Becky Kilburn have all, at various times, shown an interest in my work and provided much-needed distraction when I needed a break. Last, and most importantly, I wish to thank Oliver and Joshua for their love, patience and understanding when their father was absent, either physically or mentally, and to my wife, Kathryn, who has had to share me with this project for longer than she may have wished. Her love, self-sacrifice and encouragement have inspired and made all my labours worthwhile. This book is dedicated to her with all my love.

Abbreviations

AD Signals	Assistant Director of Army Signals
AEF	American Expeditionary Forces
AG	Adjutant General
AIF	Australian Imperial Force
AIR	Air Ministry
AMIEE	Associate Member of the Institution of Electrical Engineers
ANZAC	Australia and New Zealand Corps
AWM	Australian War Memorial
BEF	British Expeditionary Force
BGGS	Brigadier-General General Staff
BGI	Brigadier-General Intelligence
BGO	Brigadier-General Operations
BGRA	Brigadier-General Royal Artillery
BL	British Library
BLO	Bodleian Library, Oxford
BTA	British Telecom Archives
C^2	Command and Control
C^3	Command, Control and Communications
CAB	Cabinet Office
CAC	Churchill Archives Centre
CEF	Canadian Expeditionary Force
CFA	Canadian Field Artillery
CGS	Chief of the General Staff
CIGS	Chief of the Imperial General Staff
C-in-C	Commander in Chief
CO	Commanding Officer
CRA	Commander Royal Artillery
CRE	Commander Royal Engineers
CW	Continuous Wave (Wireless)
DAA	Deputy Assistant Adjutant

DD Signals	Deputy Director of Army Signals
DMT	Director of Military Training
DRLS	Despatch Rider Letter Service
DSD	Director of Staff Duties
DSO	Distinguished Service Order
FOO	Forward Observation Officer
FSR	*Field Service Regulations*
GHQ	General Headquarters
GOC	General Officer Commanding
GPO	General Post Office
GS	General Staff
GSO	General Staff Officer
HQ	Headquarters
IWM	Imperial War Museum
KCB	Knight Commander of Bath
KCMG	Knight Commander of St Michael and St George
LAC	Library and Archives Canada
LCL	Liddle Collection, Leeds
LHCMA	Liddell Hart Centre for Military Archives
MC	Military Cross
MGGS	Major-General General Staff
MGRA	Major-General Royal Artillery
MRA	Manchester Regiment Archives
MUN	Ministry of Munitions
NARA	National Archives and Records Administration
NCO	Non-Commissioned Officer
OC	Officer Commanding
OP	Observation Post
PRO	Public Record Office
psc	Passed Staff College
QMAAC	Queen Mary's Army Auxiliary Corps
QMG	Quartermaster General
RA	Royal Artillery
RAF	Royal Air Force
R.E.	Royal Engineers
REMA	Royal Engineers Museum Archive
RFA	Royal Field Artillery
RFC	Royal Flying Corps
RMA	Royal Mail Archives
RSMA	Royal Signals Museum Archive

TNA	The National Archives
VC	Victoria Cross
WAAC	Women's Army Auxiliary Corps
WO	War Office
W/T	Wireless Telegraphy

Maps

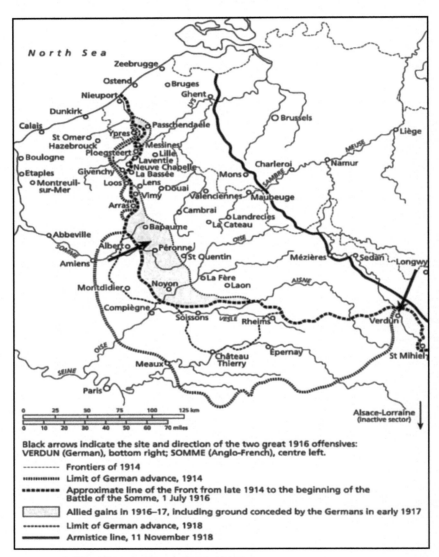

Black arrows indicate the site and direction of the two great 1916 offensives: VERDUN (German), bottom right; SOMME (Anglo-French), centre left.

--------- Frontiers of 1914

••••••••••• Limit of German advance, 1914

▬▬▬▬▬▬ Approximate line of the Front from late 1914 to the beginning of the Battle of the Somme, 1 July 1916

▢ Allied gains in 1916–17, including ground conceded by the Germans in early 1917

--------- Limit of German advance, 1918

▬▬▬▬▬ Armistice line, 11 November 1918

1 The Western Front, 1914–1918

Introduction

Looking back on the events of 1914, Brigadier-General (later Major-General Sir) Edward Spears likened the British Expeditionary Force (BEF) to

a giant with a quick and brilliant brain, but whose nervous system is slow, lethargic, and inadequate. Something goes wrong with one of his distant limbs. Hours pass before he registers it. Once he has done so a counter-move is rapidly devised, but transmission is again slow, and before his arm or leg can receive and obey it, it may have been gnawed to the bone.[1]

Spears' analogy neatly encapsulated the difficulties that tenuous communications posed for British commanders on the Western Front during the First World War as they struggled to exercise efficient command and control over their troops during the heat of battle. Indeed, in October 1932 one of the principal findings of the Committee on the Lessons of the Great War was that 'without communication, command cannot function; it can neither receive information, nor get out its orders. The army is then fighting without a brain; or worse still, with a disordered brain which acts regardless of reality'.[2] Consequently, the end result for many of the BEF's battles, as identified at a staff conference in January 1933, had been 'confusion, huge casualties, [and] failure'.[3] This interpretation of communications has become something of the orthodoxy within the popular and academic literature. Yet, it is a view that has failed

---

[1] Brigadier-General E. L. Spears, *Liaison 1914: A Narrative of the Great Retreat* (London: William Heinemann, 1930), 316. Spears had acted as a liaison officer between the BEF and the French Fifth Army in 1914.

[2] Taking its name from the committee's chairman, Lieutenant-General Walter Kirke, this is usually referred to as the Kirke Report. See 'Report on Operations on the Western Front, by Major-General J. Kennedy', in 'Report of the Committee on the Lessons of the Great War: Appendices, The War Office 1932', WO32/3116, The National Archives, Kew (TNA). A revised version of the report was issued two years later. See 'Notes on Certain Lessons of the Great War', 30 April 1934, WO32/3116, TNA.

[3] 'Report on the Staff Conference Held at the Staff College, Camberley, 9–11 January, 1933', WO32/3116, TNA.

1

to attract a detailed, scholarly enquiry, and thus, in many respects, it cannot be regarded as conclusive. In investigating one of the central challenges for British commanders during the First World War, this book seeks to rectify this curious anomaly, principally by attempting to answer one key question: how, and to what extent, did communications influence British military operations on the Western Front between 1914 and 1918? This book intends, then, to cast new light on British command and control practice and military performance by studying the oft-mentioned but frequently misunderstood role played by communications.

Because of the nature of trench warfare and the unprecedented human cost, issues concerning command and control during the First World War have been part of the debate over British military performance ever since the war ended.[4] In general, much of the early literature falls between two very distinct categories: the 'internal factor' and 'external factor' schools of thought.[5] The former subscribes to the view that the war was little more than 'a murderous nightmare of misdirected heroism and pointless suffering', blame for which rests firmly on the shoulders of the military high command.[6] This 'lions led by donkeys' approach, first laid down by the polemic works of the interwar period and of the 1960s,[7] has now been thoroughly discredited, though it still retains a small number of supporters,[8] whose studies are 'more than an impediment to the exploration of real issues' and do nothing more than 'preserve historical writing about the Great War in its ridiculously protracted adolescence'.[9] The latter school of thought, meanwhile, emphasises the importance played by factors that were outside the control of the generals, such as the lack of artillery shells,

---

[4] Brian Bond (ed.), *The First World War and British Military History* (Oxford: Clarendon Press, 1991), 1–12; Brian Bond, *The Unquiet Western Front: Britain's Role in Literature and History* (Cambridge: Cambridge University Press, 2002), 75–101; Dan Todman, *The Great War: Myth and Memory* (London: Hambledon, 2005), 73–120.

[5] Tim Travers, *The Killing Ground: The British Army, the Western Front and the Emergence of Modern War 1900–1918* (London: Unwin Hyman, 1987), xvii–xviii.

[6] John Bourne, 'Goodbye to All That? Recent Writing on the Great War', *Twentieth Century British History*, 1 (1990), 87–8.

[7] The most notable being: Basil Liddell Hart, *The Real War, 1914–1918* (London: Faber and Faber, 1930); David Lloyd George, *War Memoirs*, 2 Vols. (London: Odhams Press Ltd., 1938); Alan Clark, *The Donkeys* (London: Hutchinson, 1961); and, A. J. P. Taylor, *The First World War: An Illustrated History* (London: Hamish Hamilton, 1963).

[8] John Laffin, *British Butchers and Bunglers of World War One* (London: Bramley Books, 1988); Denis Winter, *Haig's Command: A Reassessment* (London: Viking Press, 1991); and John Mosier, *The Myth of the Great War: A New Military History of World War One* (London: Profile Books, 2001).

[9] Robin Prior and Trevor Wilson, 'Review of *Haig's Command: A Reassessment*, by Denis Winter', *Australian War Memorial Journal*, 23 (1993), 57. See also Jim Beach, 'Mosier's Myths' (review essay of John Mosier, *The Myth of the Great War*, 2001), *British Army Review*, No. 142 (2007), 90–4.

the shortage of trained officers and men and the restrictions imposed by coalition warfare. The most prominent exponent of the 'external factor' view was John Terraine, who did much to defend the reputation of British generalship.[10] Although many historians have since acknowledged the important contribution he made to the debate,[11] Terraine is not without his critics.[12] In particular, by stressing the great extent to which external factors hampered British operations, Terraine tended to ignore the fact that the BEF undoubtedly suffered from its fair share of internal problems as well.[13]

Since the early 1980s, however, 'a new era of scholarship', based largely upon the examination of archival material which had previously been unavailable or neglected, has provided a much more balanced assessment of the BEF.[14] Building upon the pioneering works of historians such as Shelford Bidwell, Dominick Graham, Tim Travers, Robin Prior and Trevor Wilson,[15] scholarly examinations of the BEF at the operational and tactical levels have deepened our understanding of British military conduct during the First World War.[16] More specifically, a

---

[10] For works by John Terraine, see: *Mons: The Retreat to Victory* (first published 1960; new ed., Ware: Wordsworth, 2002); *Douglas Haig: The Educated Soldier* (London: Hutchinson, 1963); *The Road to Passchendaele: The Flanders Offensive of 1917: A Study in Inevitability* (London: Leo Cooper, 1977); *To Win a War: 1918, the Year of Victory* (London: Sidgwick and Jackson, 1978); *White Heat: The New Warfare, 1914–1918* (London: Sidgwick and Jackson, 1982); and, *The Smoke and the Fire: Myths and Anti-Myths of War 1861–1945* (Barnsley: Leo Cooper, 1992).

[11] See, for example, Gary Sheffield, 'John Terraine as a Military Historian', *Journal of the Royal United Services Institute*, 149 (2004), 70–5.

[12] For an overview of the rivalry between Terraine and another famous British military historian, John Keegan, see Alex Danchev, '"Bunking" and Debunking: The Controversies of the 1960's', in Bond (ed.), *The First World War and British Military History*, 273–8.

[13] Bond, *Unquiet Western Front*, 72–3.

[14] Gary Sheffield and John Bourne (eds.), *Douglas Haig: War Diaries and Letters 1914–1918* (London: Weidenfeld and Nicolson, 2005), 1.

[15] Shelford Bidwell and Dominick Graham, *Fire-Power: The British Army Weapons and Theories of War 1904–45* (London: Allen and Unwin, 1982); Travers, *The Killing Ground*; Robin Prior and Trevor Wilson, *Command on the Western Front: The Military Career of Sir Henry Rawlinson, 1914–1918* (Oxford: Blackwell, 1992).

[16] Ian Beckett and Keith Simpson (eds.), *A Nation in Arms*, (Manchester: Manchester University Press, 1985); Peter Simkins, *Kitchener's Army: The Raising of the New Armies 1914–1916* (Manchester: Manchester University Press, 1988); Tim Travers, *How the War Was Won: Command and Technology in the British Army on the Western Front 1917–1918* (London: Routledge, 1992); Martin Samuels, *Command or Control? Command, Training and Tactics in the British and German Armies, 1888–1918* (London: Frank Cass, 1995); William Philpott, *Anglo-French Relations and Strategy on the Western Front, 1914–18* (London: Macmillan, 1996); Robin Prior and Trevor Wilson, *Passchendaele: The Untold Story* (London: Yale University Press, 1996); Brian Bond et al., *'Look to Your Front': Studies in the First World War by The British Commission for Military History* (Staplehurst: Spellmount, 1999); Albert Palazzo, *Seeking Victory on the*

number of works have emerged within the past 20 years arguing that the BEF underwent a 'learning curve'.[17] Far from seeing the war as futile with needlessly heavy casualties for minimal military gain, historians such as Paddy Griffith, Gary Sheffield and Andy Simpson maintain that the British military command consistently analysed the mistakes and lessons of previous battles and began to improve the army's tactical and operational efficiency.[18] Collectively, these works have influenced a growing number of specialist studies, examining the less-glamorous, though crucial, 'support services' such as logistics, intelligence and staff work, which have also shown that by 1918 the BEF had developed into a highly sophisticated and extremely formidable institution.[19] Indeed, it has been

Western Front: The British Army and Chemical Warfare in World War One (Lincoln: University of Nebraska Press, 2000); Nikolas Gardner, *Trial by Fire: Command and the British Expeditionary Force in 1914* (Westport, CT: Praeger, 2003); Robin Prior and Trevor Wilson, *The Somme* (New Haven, CT: Yale University Press, 2005); J. P. Harris, *Douglas Haig and the First World War* (Cambridge: Cambridge University Press, 2008); William Philpott, *Bloody Victory: The Sacrifice on the Somme and the Making of the Twentieth Century* (London: Little, Brown, 2009); William Sanders Marble, 'The Infantry Cannot Do with a Gun Less': The Place of Artillery in the BEF, 1914–1918, an e-version of which can be found at www.gutenberg-e.org/mas01/main.html [Accessed 26 August 2014]; David Kenyon, *Horsemen in No Man's Land: British Cavalry and Trench Warfare 1914–1918* (Barnsley: Pen and Sword, 2011); Jonathan Boff, *Winning and Losing on the Western Front: The British Third Army and the Defeat of Germany in 1918* (Cambridge: Cambridge University Press, 2012).

17 In light of the criticism that this term has generated, 'learning process' is now deemed a more accurate description. For criticism, see: Hew Strachan, 'Back to the Trenches: Why Can't British Historians Be Less Insular about the First World War?' *Times Literary Supplement*, 5 November 2008; and, William Philpott, 'Beyond the "Learning Curve": The British Army's Military Transformation in the First World War', 10 November 2009, www.rusi.org/analysis/commentary/ref:C4AF97CF94AC8B/ [Accessed 27 August 2014]. For additional context, see: Holger Afflerbach and Gary Sheffield, 'Waging Total War: Learning Curve or Bleeding Curve?' in Jay Winter (ed.), *The Legacy of the Great War: Ninety Years On* (Missouri: University of Missouri Press, 2009), 61–90; and, Stephen Badsey, 'Ninety Years On: Recent and Changing Views on the Military History of the First World War', in Ashley Ekins (ed.), *1918 Year of Victory: The End of the Great War and the Shaping of History* (Auckland: Exisle, 2010), 360–86.

18 Paddy Griffith, *Battle Tactics of the Western Front: The British Army's Art of Attack 1916–18* (New Haven, CT: Yale University Press, 1994); Paddy Griffith (ed.), *British Fighting Methods in the Great War* (London: Frank Cass, 1996); J. P. Harris with Niall Barr, *Amiens to the Armistice: The BEF in the One Hundred Days' Campaign, 8 August–11 November 1918* (London: Brassey's, 1998); Gary Sheffield, *Forgotten Victory: The First World War – Myths and Realities* (London: Headline, 2001); Gary Sheffield, *The Somme* (London: Cassell, 2003); Simon Robbins, *British Generalship on the Western Front, 1914–18: Defeat into Victory* (London: Frank Cass, 2004); Gary Sheffield and Dan Todman (eds.), *Command and Control on the Western Front: The British Army's Experience 1914–18* (Staplehurst: Spellmount, 2004); Nick Lloyd, *Loos 1915* (Stroud: Tempus, 2006); and, Andy Simpson, *Directing Operations: British Corps Command on the Western Front 1914–18* (Stroud: Spellmount, 2006).

19 Ian Malcolm Brown, *British Logistics on the Western Front 1914–1919* (Westport, CT: Praeger, 1998); Jim Beach, *Haig's Intelligence: GHQ and the German Army, 1916–1918*

further argued that these changes took place within the context of a 'Revolution in Military Affairs' (RMA), which gave birth to the 'Modern Style of Warfare'.[20]

Yet, despite this copious amount of scholarship there remains a dearth of detailed information on the subject of communications. Virtually all the literature published before Bidwell and Graham's *Fire-Power* is devoid of any detailed reference to communications. The exception to this was John Terraine, who rightly drew attention to the inadequacies of communications technology at the time. Arguing that the First World War was the only conflict in history in which the military commanders on both sides had no direct 'voice control' over their troops in battle, Terraine observed that once the troops went 'over-the-top' and out into 'no-man's-land' and beyond, they passed out of the control of the generals, who 'became quite impotent at the very moment when they would expect and be expected to display their greatest proficiency'.[21] Although he highlighted the negative impact that communications had on command and control, Terraine did not develop his line of argument in any greater depth. This may largely be explained by his use of sources. While he made good use of published memoirs and the official history, he failed to utilize archival material that was made readily available at the end of the 1960s.[22]

With regards to the more recent, archive-based studies of the First World War, analysis of the BEF's communications system has been somewhat patchy. Bidwell and Graham's *Fire-Power* examined the development of artillery in the British Army between 1904 and 1945, yet devoted just three pages to the issue of communications during the Great War.[23] Although Tim Travers' *The Killing Ground* dealt with the BEF's tactical and operational decision-making process, particularly the internal problems within (General Headquarters) GHQ, it had very little to say about the practicalities of communications. The same is also true of his second book, *How the War Was Won*, which focused

(Cambridge: Cambridge University Press, 2013); Paul Harris, 'The Men Who Planned the War: A Study of the Staff of the British Army on the Western Front 1914–1918' (PhD thesis, King's College London, 2013).

[20] Jonathan Bailey, *The First World War and the Birth of the Modern Style of Warfare*, Occasional Papers 22 (Camberley: Strategic and Combat Studies Institute, Staff College, 1996); Jonathan B. A. Bailey, 'The First World War and the Birth of Modern Warfare', in MacGregor Knox and Williamson Murray (eds.), *The Dynamics of Military Revolution 1300–2050* (Cambridge: Cambridge University Press, 2001), 132–53; and, Colin S. Gray, *Strategy for Chaos: Revolutions in Military Affairs and the Evidence of History* (London: Routledge, 2004), 170–221.

[21] Terraine, *Smoke and the Fire*, 118.   [22] Bond, *Unquiet Western Front*, 72–3.

[23] Bidwell and Graham, *Fire-Power*, 141–3.

specifically on the battles of 1917–18.[24] Travers' work is comple-
mented by that of Martin van Creveld and Martin Samuels, who
compare and contrast the British and German command philosophies
during the war.[25] Although both raised the issue of communications,
neither provided a systematic analysis of the BEF's communications
system.[26] Gary Sheffield and Dan Todman's edited collection of
essays, *Command and Control on the Western Front*, did pay more
attention to communications than has been customary, but only to
the extent of providing 'snapshots' of communications at certain
points during the war.[27] Meanwhile, Andy Simpson's *Directing Operations* provided some revealing insights into the practice of command
and control at the corps level of command, but was concerned primarily with the role and functions of corps as a whole, rather than just the
issue of communications. Jonathan Boff's recent study, *Winning and
Losing on the Western Front*, also discusses communications but only
from the point of view of Third Army's operations during the 'Hundred Days' campaign in 1918.[28] In fact, the BEF's communication
problems have received rather short shrift within most general
accounts of individual battles and campaigns.[29]

Notwithstanding Bill Rawling's 1994 journal article, which, although
instructive and well researched, is limited by its narrow focus on the

---

[24] The main criticism of both books, however, is that they rely heavily upon post-war,
anecdotal evidence, particularly the CAB45 files in the National Archives pertaining to
the writing of the British official history. See: John Bourne, 'Haig and the Historians', in
Brian Bond and Nigel Cave (eds.), *Haig: A Reappraisal 70 Years On* (Barnsley: Leo
Cooper, 1999), 6–8; and, Simpson, *Directing Operations*, xix–xxiii.

[25] Martin van Creveld, *Command in War* (Cambridge, MA: Harvard University Press,
1985), 148–88; Martin Samuels, *Command or Control?*

[26] Most disconcerting are their methodologically unsound comparisons of the BEF's
command and control system on 1 July 1916 with the German Army's practice of
command and control during the spring of 1918. No analysis of the BEF's operations
during the last one hundred days of the war is made at all. For criticism of their work,
see: Hew Strachan, 'Review of *Command or Control? Command, Training and Tactics in the
British and German Armies, 1888–1918*, by Martin Samuels', *Journal of Military History*,
60 (1996), 778–9; Brown, *British Logistics*, 9; Richard Bryson, 'The Once and Future
Army', in Bond et al., '*Look to Your Front*', 54; and, Gary Sheffield, 'British High
Command in the First World War: An Overview', in Gary Sheffield and Geoffrey Till
(eds.), *The Challenges of High Command: The British Experience* (London: Palgrave
Macmillan, 2003), 23–4.

[27] Most notably in Niall Barr, 'Command in the Transition from Mobile to Static Warfare,
August 1914 to March 1915', in Sheffield and Todman (eds.), *Command and Control on
the Western Front*, 13–38.

[28] Boff, *Winning and Losing*, 179–91.

[29] See, for example: Peter H. Liddle (ed.), *Passchendaele in Perspective: The Third Battle of
Ypres* (Barnsley: Pen and Sword, 1997); Ian Passingham, *Pillars of Fire: The Battle of
Messines Ridge June 1917* (Stroud: Sutton, 1998); and, Bryn Hammond, *Cambrai 1917:
The Myth of the First Great Tank Battle* (London: Weidenfeld and Nicolson, 2008).

Canadian Corps,[30] there are only two studies that address exclusively the issue of communications on the Western Front. The first is Raymond Priestley's *The Signal Service in the European War of 1914 to 1918 (France)*, published in 1921.[31] Priestley was well qualified to write this history, having served as adjutant to the army's Wireless Training Centre (1914–17) and then as a signal officer in 46 Division on the Western Front in 1918.[32] However, besides predating the Second World War, Priestley's dry and complex narrative has acted as a deterrent to historians wishing to understand communications. As Paddy Griffith opined, although 'revealing and informative', it is 'positively the most impenetrable book ever written on the war'.[33] The second study, Mike Bullock and Laurence A. Lyons' *Missed Signals on the Western Front*, certainly provides a much easier and more understandable narrative than Priestley's.[34] Yet, not only is it hampered by its rather controversial and overly techno-centric counterfactual argument, but it also relies heavily upon Priestley for its source material and, as such, offers little in the way of fresh information about communications.[35] The greatest limitation of both Priestley's and Bullock and Lyons' studies, however, is that they are severely constrained by their attempts to examine communications either solely through the exploits of the Royal Engineers Signal Service, or largely via the medium of communications technology. As important as the Signal Service and communications technologies were, they were but two elements within the confines of a much larger and intricate communications system which also involved the key elements of personnel, training and doctrine, and the integral processes of staff work and command. Thus, a more holistic approach, examining the interaction of all these

---

[30] Bill Rawling, 'Communications in the Canadian Corps, 1915–1918: Wartime Technological Progress Revisited', *Canadian Military History*, 3 (1994), 6–21.

[31] R. E. Priestley, *Work of the Royal Engineers in the European War, 1914–19: The Signal Service (France)* (first published 1921; new ed., Uckfield: The Naval and Military Press, 2006).

[32] Prior to the war, Priestley was appointed as geologist to both Ernest Shackleton's (1907–9) and Robert Falcon Scott's (1910–13) Antarctic expeditions. In 1934, he became the University of Melbourne's first salaried vice-chancellor and in 1938 he was appointed principal and vice-chancellor of the University of Birmingham. See: S. Murray-Smith, 'Priestley, Sir Raymond Edward (1886–1974)', *Australian Dictionary of Biography*, National Centre of Biography, Australian National University, http://adb.anu.edu.au/biography/priestley-sir-raymond-edward-8116/text14173 [Accessed 1 September 2014].

[33] Griffith, *Battle Tactics*, 266.

[34] Mike Bullock and Laurence A. Lyons, *Missed Signals on the Western Front: How the Slow Adoption of Wireless Restricted British Strategy and Operations in World War I* (Jefferson, NC: McFarland, 2010).

[35] For a more detailed critique, see Brian N. Hall, 'Letters to the Editor', *Journal of Military History*, 78 (2014), 1208–13.

factors, is required in order to understand fully the BEF's communications system and its influence upon operations.

Therefore, in order to understand communications in the context of the First World War, it is worth considering at the outset the large body of literature now available on communications in its broadest sense. This material can be viewed as falling into two categories: purely military studies and an ever-increasing body of social science literature. Both provide not simply an awareness of many of the issues surrounding communications, but also a better understanding of the terminology associated with this field. It is, for instance, very difficult to deal with communications without confronting the term *command and control*.[36] Indeed, many scholars, military analysts and social science researchers would treat command, control and communications as one theme.

In laying down the duties of command in battle, the 1909 British Army *Field Service Regulations* stipulated that a commander 'influences the general course of the action by his preliminary dispositions, which determine the direction of the decisive attack, and the force with which it is to be delivered'. He could also influence the battle once it was under way by committing his reserves.[37] With regards to control, the pre-war regulations prescribed the following philosophy:

The command of military forces is exercised on the following principles: the C.-in-C., aided by his Staff, exerts his authority over a limited number of subordinate commanders. These, aided by their staffs and assistants, convey his will to a limited number of subordinate commanders under them, each of whom carries it still down lower, until eventually all ranks are controlled by it.[38]

These definitions do not differ dramatically from those utilized by the modern British Army. According to the 2006 *United Kingdom Glossary of Joint and Multinational Terms and Definitions*, command is 'the authority vested in an individual of the armed forces for the direction, co-ordination, and control of military forces'. Control is defined as 'the

---

[36] This is usually referred to as 'C^2'. Since the late 1970s the simple equation of C^2 has been replaced and expanded by a whole host of acronyms and abbreviations, each of which seeks to emphasise a particular feature within the system. These include C^3 (Command, Control and Communications), C^{3}I (Command, Control, Communications and Intelligence), C4I (Command, Control, Communications, Computers and Intelligence) and C4ISR (Command, Control, Communications, Computers, Intelligence, Surveillance and Reconnaissance). See Thomas P. Coakley, *Command and Control for War and Peace* (Washington, DC: National Defence University Press, 1992), 9.

[37] *Field Service Regulations Part I: Operations (1909)* (Reprinted, with Amendments, October 1914) (London: HMSO, 1914), 111.

[38] *Field Service Regulations Part II: Organisation and Administration (1909)* (Reprinted, with Amendments, October 1914) (London: HMSO, 1914), 25.

process through which a commander, assisted by his Staff, organises, directs and co-ordinates the activities of the force allocated to him'.[39] Put simply, if command is *what* a commander does, then control is *how* he does it.[40] Combined, a *command and control system* is 'an assembly of equipment, methods and procedures and, if necessary, personnel, that enables commanders and their staffs to exercise command and control'.[41] The degree of control that a commander seeks to impose upon his subordinates, however, is a contentious issue, with military historians and modern defence analysts frequently making reference to two contrasting methods: 'restrictive' and 'mission' command.[42] In the former, a commander issues detailed orders to his subordinates which prescribe exactly *what* they are to do and *how* they are to achieve it. If, during the course of carrying out those orders, the plan needs to be amended, subordinates are expected to refer to the commander for official guidance and approval. In the latter, meanwhile, general orders and objectives are issued, but subordinates are given a degree of flexibility in terms of choosing the methods that are to be employed to achieve them.[43] Within the context of the literature on the First World War, the general consensus amongst historians has been that the Germans were the leading practitioners of mission command, while the British favoured restrictive command,[44] though these views have been challenged in recent years.[45]

---

[39] *United Kingdom Glossary of Joint and Multinational Terms and Definitions*, Joint Doctrine Publication 0–01.1 (June 2006), 68, 76.

[40] Dan Todman and Gary Sheffield, 'Command and Control in the British Army on the Western Front', 1.

[41] *United Kingdom Glossary*, 69.

[42] Also referred to as *Befehlstaktik* and *Auftragstaktik*, respectively. For additional context, see Eitan Shamir, *Transforming Command: The Pursuit of Mission Command in the US, British and Israeli Armed Forces* (Stanford, CA: Stanford University Press, 2011).

[43] Mission command, based upon a philosophy of 'centralised intent and decentralised execution', became part of official British Army doctrine in 1989. See *Army Doctrine Publication (ADP). Operations* (2010), www.gov.uk/government/uploads/system/uploads/attachment_data/file/33695/ADPOperationsDec10.pdf [Accessed 28 August 2014]. On the debate concerning the application of mission command in British Army history, see Christopher Pugsley, *We Have Been Here Before: The Evolution of the Doctrine of Decentralised Command in the British Army 1905–1989*, Sandhurst Occasional Papers No. 9 (Camberley: The Royal Military Academy Sandhurst, 2011), www.army.mod .uk/documents/general/rmas_occ_paper_09.pdf [Accessed 15 January 2016].

[44] Travers, *The Killing Ground* and *How the War Was Won*; Samuels, *Command or Control?*; and, van Creveld, *Command in War*.

[45] It has been argued that by 1918 the German Army's command system had become highly centralized under Erich von Ludendorff's leadership. See Boff, *Winning and Losing*, 226–42. Most historians now tend to agree that the BEF was exercising a more decentralized style of command during the summer and autumn of 1918, but they disagree as to how this came about and how consistently it was applied. See: Prior and Wilson, *Command on the Western Front*, 300, 305, 396–7; Harris with Barr, *Amiens to the Armistice*, 149; Peter Simkins, '"Building Blocks": Aspects of Command and Control at

From a multi-disciplinary perspective, however, command and control means different things to different people and, as such, no universally accepted theory has been developed. Quite often, these theories are conveyed through the medium of charts or diagrams, which represent the flow of information within an organizational decision-making cycle.[46] With regards to the military models, three such examples will suffice. The first is Joel Lawson's cybernetic model, which he argued was applicable to any echelon of the military hierarchy. Lawson divided the command and control system into five internal sub-systems or functions (Sense, Process, Compare, Decide, Act) which any military commander would have to go through in order to make 'effective use of resources to deal with an *external* hostile environment'.[47] Two models that further highlight the decision-making process of a commander are J. G. Wohl's 'SHOR' paradigm and John Boyd's 'OODA' loop or 'Boyd Cycle'. Essentially, both 'SHOR' (*S*timulate, *H*ypothesis, *O*ption, *R*esponse) and 'OODA' (*O*bserve, *O*rientate, *D*ecide, *A*ct) amount to the same thing: the commander who goes through his decision cycle fastest is likely to gain the upper hand over his slower opponent.[48] What is significant about all three models is the considerable emphasis that each places upon the receipt of timely and accurate information. In

---

Brigade Level in the BEF's Offensive Operations, 1916–1918', in Sheffield and Todman (eds.), *Command and Control on the Western Front*, 141–72; Simpson, *Directing Operations*, 155–75; and, Boff, *Winning and Losing*, 179–225.

[46] For various concepts, models and theories on command and control, see: Michael Athans, 'Command and Control (C²) Theory: A Challenge to Control Science', *IEEE Transactions on Automatic Control*, 32 (1987), 286–93; C. J. Harris and I. White (eds.), *Advances in Command, Control and Communications Systems* (London: Peter Peregrinus, 1987); C. J. Harris (ed.), *Application of Artificial Intelligence to Command and Control Systems* (London: Peter Peregrinus, 1988); G. Clapp and D. Sworder, 'Command, Control, and Communications (C³)', in Richard C. Dorf (ed.), *The Electrical Engineering Handbook* (London: CRC Press, 1993), 2211–18; Carl H. Builder, Steven C. Bankes, Richard Nordin, *Command Concepts: A Theory Derived From the Practice of Command and Control* (Washington, DC: Rand National Defence Research Institute, 1999); J. Moffat, 'Representing the Command and Control Process in Simulation Models of Conflict', *Journal of the Operational Research Society*, 51 (2000), 431–9; Michael R. Frater and Michael Ryan, *Electronic Warfare for the Digitised Battlefield* (London: Artech House, 2001); J. Moffat and S. Witty, 'Bayesian Decision Making and Military Command and Control', *Journal of the Operational Research Society*, 5 (2002), 709–18; and, David S. Alberts and Richard E. Hayes, *Understanding Command and Control* (Washington: CCRP, 2006).

[47] J. S. Lawson Jr., 'Command Control as a Process', *IEEE Control Systems Magazine*, 1 (1981), 5–11.

[48] Joseph G. Wohl, 'Force Management Decision Requirements for Air Force Tactical Command and Control', *IEEE Transactions on Systems, Man, and Cybernetics*, 11 (September 1981), 618–39; John R. Boyd, 'Organic Design for Command and Control' (US Air Force Academy, 1987), www.ausairpower.net/JRB/c&c.pdf [Accessed 27 August 2014].

other words, communication is at the very heart of a military command and control system. As Lars Skyttner has observed:

The most important quality in a system of command and control is the ability to send, store, present and deliver data and information in the shape of messages... In an organisation, data and information transfer is the main tool to coordinate and control that the goal of the operation is fulfilled.[49]

The literature of business studies and organization theory reinforces the argument that communication is the most pervasive feature of any organization and is paramount in determining its smooth running and overall efficiency.[50] It also suggests that there is much more to communications than just technology. As Martin van Creveld points out, command and control is very much a human activity, where a commander's ideas and decisions are just as integral to the system as are communications and the information processing apparatus: 'No single communications or data processing technology, no single procedure or method, is in itself sufficient to guarantee the successful or even adequate conduct of command in war'.[51] Furthermore, the *practice* of command and control is not as simple or as straightforward as the *theory* of command and control as laid out in models such as 'OODA'.[52] As Clausewitz noted, friction, chance and uncertainty render the simplest things in war very difficult.[53] According to Edward Luttwak, 'errors ... in military command-and-control structures ... are virtually inevitable'.[54] Thus, the use of inter-disciplinary tools and approaches allows us to attempt an analysis of the BEF's communications system in a rather less one-sided manner than has so far been the case, since existing works on British communications have focused

---

[49] Lars Skyttner, 'Systems Theory and the Science of Military Command and Control', *Kybernetes Journal*, 34 (2005), 1253.

[50] See, for example: Dalmar Fisher, *Communication in Organizations* (New York: West, 1993); Derek Torrington and Jane Weightman, *Effective Management: People and Organization* (Hemel Hempstead: Prentice Hall, 1994); Stephen Ackroyd, *The Organisation of Business: Applying Organisational Theory to Contemporary Change* (Oxford: Oxford University Press, 2002); and, Tim Hannagan, *Management Concepts and Practices* (London: FT Prentice Hall, 2005).

[51] van Creveld, *Command in War*, 261. See also: Lieutenant-General William S. Wallace, 'Network-Enabled Battle Command', *RUSI Defence Systems*, 7 (2005), 20–2; and, Air Chief Marshal Sir Glenn Torpy, 'Effective Air Command and Control', *RUSI Defence Systems*, 9 (2006–7), 54–6.

[52] For criticism of 'OODA', see: Colin S. Gray, *Another Bloody Century: Future Warfare* (London: Weidenfeld and Nicolson, 2005), 192.

[53] Carl von Clausewitz, *On War*, ed. and trans. Michael Howard and Peter Paret (Princeton, NJ: Princeton University Press, 1976), 119.

[54] Edward N. Luttwak, *Strategy: The Logic of War and Peace* (Cambridge, MA: Harvard University Press, 2003), 11–12.

predominantly on technology at the expense of an understanding of the wider communications system.

Communications, as can be seen from the foregoing discussion, is a crucial component of command and control, but within the historiography of the First World War one generally taken for granted or viewed simply through the prism of technology. As the relevant social science literature demonstrates, however, there is much more to communications than just technology. It is impossible, for example, to study communications within a military context without making reference to the closely related subjects of *information* and *doctrine*. Considering the role of communications in the BEF, a clear distinction needs to be made between these terms. At the same time, analysing the close relationship among communications, information and doctrine promises new insights into some of the major historiographical controversies surrounding the performance of the BEF. Given their importance for this study, therefore, all three terms – communications, information and doctrine – warrant closer examination and better understanding.

The term which obviously requires definition first is *communications*. In a study of naval warfare, Andrew Gordon argued that the term C^3 is 'dangerously misleading' because it wrongly implies that communications is on the same level of importance as command and control. Seeing communications as 'merely a means to an end', he stated that another way of achieving effective command and control was through doctrine.[55] While Gordon is undoubtedly correct in highlighting the importance of doctrine within a command and control system, he underestimates the significance of communications. Much depends on the definition one uses. For the purpose of this study, communications will be understood to be

the provision and passing of information and instructions which enable ... [an] organisation to function efficiently and employees to be properly informed about developments. It covers information of all kinds which can be provided; the channels along which it passes; and the means of passing it.[56]

This definition allows us to view communications as more than just a mere 'service provider'. It is the interchange of information involving a whole host of technical and non-technical means, without which command and control cannot be accomplished. Indeed, as one signal officer during the interwar period put it, 'Under all conditions of war,

---

[55] Andrew Gordon, 'Rat Catchers and Regulators at the Battle of Jutland', in Sheffield and Till (eds.), *The Challenges of High Command*, 31.
[56] Hannagan, *Management Concepts*, 271.

communication *is* command'.[57] A *communications system*, therefore, is the combination of equipment, methods, procedures and personnel, organised to accomplish the conveyance of information.[58] This implies that there is more than just a simple one-to-one link. The more effective the system is, the more successfully an organisation can interact and function effectively.[59] Thus, an efficient communications system is an essential prerequisite for the successful prosecution of modern war.

Another key term used throughout this study is *information*. According to one writer, information refers to 'the words, numbers, images and voices that are flowing from one point to another in an orderly fashion, that impart meaning, that inform the information consumer, and that have the potential for influencing the future state of affairs'.[60] To place the term within its historical context, Lieutenant-General Sir John Monash, GOC Australian Corps in 1918, noted:

The vital information, which is imperative for the ... Commander to have accurately and rapidly delivered throughout the course of a battle, is that relating to the actual position, at any given moment in time, of our front line troops; showing the locations which they have reached, and whether they are stationary, advancing or retiring.[61]

Thus, in terms of Monash's definition, it can be surmised that information is not the same as intelligence. While information 'refers to the location and activities of friendly troops', intelligence 'is the order of battle, dispositions and possible intentions of the enemy'.[62] Within the context of this book, therefore, it is important that information is not inadvertently equated or confused with intelligence. It is also important to realise that information on its own is meaningless unless

---

[57] Captain F. S. Morgan, 'Modern Communications and Command', *Journal of the Royal United Services Institution*, 76 (1931), 419.

[58] A. Nejat, Cem Evrendilek, Dag Wilhelmsen and Fadil Gezer, *Planning and Architectural Design of Modern Command Control Communications and Information Systems* (London: Kluwer Academic, 1997), 6.

[59] M. A. Rice and A. J. Sammes, *Communications and Information Systems for Battlefield Command and Control* (London: Brassey's, 1989), 3–4. For an interesting comparison with the development of communication systems in the commercial and industrial sectors during the late nineteenth and early twentieth centuries, see JoAnne Yates, *Control through Communication: The Rise of System in American Management* (Baltimore: Johns Hopkins University Press, 1993).

[60] Emily O. Goldman, 'Introduction: Information Resources and Military Performance', *Journal of Strategic Studies*, 27 (2004), 196.

[61] Lieutenant-General Sir John Monash, *The Australian Victories in France in 1918* (first published 1920; new ed., London: Battery Press, 1993), 124.

[62] Dominick Graham and Shelford Bidwell, *Coalitions, Politicians and Generals: Some Aspects of Command in Two World Wars* (London: Brassey's, 1993), 29–30.

an organisation has an efficient system for gathering, processing, storing and disseminating it. For information to be meaningful, it must be analysed and interpreted. Once processed and understood, information becomes knowledge.[63] Organisations can improve their information processing through a combination of training personnel, developing and embracing new processing techniques and reorganising the system.[64] The ability to convert information into knowledge and then knowledge into action accurately and rapidly lies at the very heart of the military decision-making process, and is therefore critical to enhancing military performance.

Given the frequency with which it is used in discussions of communications and information, *doctrine* is the third term which requires clarification. Unfortunately for historians, it has proven a rather difficult concept to define. For example, while Bidwell and Graham identify doctrine as the 'study of weapons and other resources and the lessons of history, leading to the deduction of the correct strategic and tactical principles on which to base both training and the conduct of war',[65] according to Ian Malcolm Brown, doctrine refers to 'a set of rules, regulations, and methods that, taken together, describe how an army will approach battle'.[66] Another definition is that provided by a former US Air Force officer, I. B. Holley Jr., who defines doctrine as 'the "tried and true", the one best way to do the job which has been hammered out by trial and error, officially recognised as such, and then taught as the best way to achieve optimum results'.[67] The search for a correct definition of doctrine also requires an understanding of the doctrinal process – that is, how doctrine within military organisations is developed. According to Holley, there are three essential elements that constitute the doctrinal process: first, the *collection* phase, which involves the gathering of information from a wide variety of sources, based primarily

---

[63] Richard L. Daft and Robert H. Lengel, 'Organisational Information Requirements, Media Richness and Structural Design', *Management Science*, 32 (1986), 554–71; Roy Radner, 'The Organisation of Decentralised Information Processing', *Econometrica*, 61 (1993), 1109–46; Edward Waltz, *Information Warfare: Principles and Operations* (London: Artech House, 1998), 2; Alistair Black and Rodney Brunt, 'Information Management in Business, Libraries and British Military Intelligence: Towards a History of Information Management', *Journal of Documentation* 55, No. 4 (1999), 362; JoAnne Yates and John Van Maanen (eds.), *Information Technology and Organisational Transformation: History, Rhetoric, and Practice* (London: Sage, 2001); and, Matthew Hinton, (ed.), *Introducing Information Management: the Business Approach* (Oxford: Butterworth-Heinemann, 2005), 1–3.

[64] Goldman, 'Introduction', 202.   [65] Bidwell and Graham, *Fire-Power*, 2.

[66] Brown, *British Logistics*, 39.

[67] Major-General I. B. Holley Jr., 'The Doctrinal Process: Some Suggested Steps', *Military Review*, 59 (1979), 4–5.

upon the combat experience of one's own forces; second, the *formulation* phase, whereby doctrinal statements are devised, revised and perfected largely through intellectual processes such as journals and conferences; and, third, the *dissemination* phase, which involves not only the dissemination of doctrine throughout the organisation, but also efforts to ensure that it is properly understood.[68] Thus, despite the difficulties of reaching a clear definition, the process of collection, formulation and dissemination suggests that the end product is often a field manual or similar document.

It is clear, therefore, that the issue of communications is intimately related to a number of historical questions surrounding both information and doctrine in warfare. The interaction among these three factors is even more significant in the light of a number of ongoing historical controversies surrounding the BEF's military performance. In essence, historians have still not resolved a number of issues relating to the gradual improvement of British battlefield performance during the war – these all relate to one central question: was it a result of improved tactical and operational methods, ultimately superior to those of the enemy, or more a combination of superior weight of manpower and matériel against weakening German resistance? The complexity of the communications process means that this study cannot hope to provide new perspectives without posing a series of specific sub-questions relating to a range of contentious issues concerning British operations on the Western Front.

First, an examination of communications draws attention to the flexibility of the BEF's command and control system and, in particular, the extent to which the BEF showed signs of adaptability, one of the chief characteristics of a 'learning organisation'.[69] The increasing professionalism of the Signal Service is of particular significance given that its chief responsibility was to provide and maintain the BEF's 'nervous system'.

---

[68] Ibid., 5–12. See also Lieutenant-Colonel Jack Burkett, 'Dynamic Management of US Army Doctrine', *Military Review*, 71 (1991), 81–4. For the modern British Army's take on doctrine, see *Army Doctrine Publication (ADP). Operations* (2010), www.gov.uk/government/uploads/system/uploads/attachment_data/file/33695/ADPOperationsDec10 .pdf [Accessed 28 August 2014].

[69] For an examination of the problems that military organizations confront when attempting to adapt in war, see Williamson Murray, *Military Adaptation in War: With Fear of Change* (Cambridge: Cambridge University Press, 2011). For additional context on learning organizations, see: Margaret Dale, 'Learning Organisations', in Christopher Mabey and Paul Iles (eds.), *Managing Learning* (London: Cengage Learning EMEA, 1994), 22–33; and, Mark Easterby-Smith, John Burgoyne and Luis Araujo, (eds.), *Organizational Learning and Learning Organizations: Developments in Theory and Practice* (London: Sage, 1999).

A definitive set of criteria, however, must be utilised in order to identify any noticeable improvements. According to M. A. Rice and A. J. Sammes, a successful military communications system must be able to deliver 'real-time' information, preserve the integrity of the information it carries, have the capacity to perform under the stress of battle and ensure that all information is kept secure.[70] Using these criteria – speed, integrity, capacity and security – this study will assess how, and to what extent, there was an identifiable improvement in the BEF's communications system during the course of the war.

Second, an assessment of the BEF's communications system must also engage with the enduring and controversial debate concerning the relationship of the British military command and new technology. Contrary to the views of some historians,[71] recent research has demonstrated convincingly that British commanders at all levels did encourage the development and employment of a range of new technologies, such as tanks, aeroplanes and poison gas.[72] Detailed analysis of the interaction between British commanders and the latest communications technologies, however, has only recently begun to receive the attention it deserves, with opinion divided, in particular, with regards to the BEF's use of wireless.[73] Therefore, in an effort to shed further light and clarification on these issues, this study will assess how successful British commanders were at recognizing the utility of new communication technologies and whether or not they exploited their full military potential.

A third issue that a study of the BEF's communications system raises is that concerning the development of doctrine. While doctrine has proved a difficult concept to define, complicating matters further for historians is the fact that the term 'doctrine' was itself rarely used within British military circles during the First World War. This has led a number of historians to argue that the British Army of the period had no doctrine, at

---

[70] Rice and Sammes, *Communications and Information Systems*, 107–8.
[71] Most notably, Travers, *How the War Was Won*, 179–80; and, Tim Travers, 'Could the Tanks of 1918 Have Been War-Winners for the British Expeditionary Force?' *Journal of Contemporary History*, 27 (1992), 389–406.
[72] See, for example: J. P. Harris, 'The Rise of Armour', in Griffith (ed.), *British Fighting Methods*, 113–37; Harris with Barr, *Amiens to the Armistice*, 287–301; Palazzo, *Seeking Victory*, 191–2; Michael Crawshaw, 'The Impact of Technology on the BEF and its Commander', in Bond and Cave (eds.), *Haig: A Reappraisal*, 155–75; and, Gary Sheffield and David Jordan, 'Douglas Haig and Airpower', in Peter W. Gray and Sebastian Cox, (eds.), *Air Power Leadership: Theory and Practice* (London: The Stationary Office, 2002), 264–82.
[73] Bullock and Lyons, *Missed Signals*; Brian N. Hall, 'The British Army and Wireless Communication, 1896–1918', *War in History*, 19 (2012), 290–321; and, 'Letters to the Editor', *Journal of Military History*, 78 (2014), 1208–13.

least not in the narrow prescriptive sense.[74] For Albert Palazzo, however, the BEF instead relied upon its ethos – 'the characteristic spirit and the prevalent sentiment, taste, or opinion of a people, institution, or system' – which provided its officers with 'the means for interpreting the war and guiding their responses to its challenges'.[75] Palazzo's view is supported by Andy Simpson, who contends that the *Field Service Regulations Part I* (1909), in conjunction with the SS series of training pamphlets produced by GHQ throughout the war, provided the BEF with an effective and flexible set of principles through which it was able to plan and conduct operations on the Western Front.[76] Still, even though the term 'doctrine' was seldom used during the war, the emergence of the SS training manuals, which conforms to the collection–formulation–dissemination model mentioned earlier, makes clear that the concept of doctrine is relevant to the study of the BEF. Hence, a study of communications cannot avoid confronting whether there is evidence which points to an effort to develop a communications doctrine and, if this was the case, asking whether it proved successful. This offers the potential of throwing light on the wider issue of the development of doctrine and its role in the BEF's conduct of war.

Fourth, and finally, when considering the overall influence of communications upon the BEF's military operations, it is difficult to avoid the debate on the 'learning curve'. However, as already noted, although it is a concept that is now firmly rooted within the historiography, historians are divided over its usefulness as a means of evaluating British military performance. One problem in particular with the 'learning curve' concept is that it implies that the BEF as a whole underwent a smooth and steady incremental learning process.[77] As the works of recent historians have highlighted, this was definitely not the case. It appears far more likely that the rate of learning varied across the 'horizontal and vertical dimensions' of the BEF's military activities.[78] Historians have also begun

---

[74] Bidwell and Graham, *Fire-Power*, 2–3; Travers, *The Killing Ground*, 54. Brian Holden Reid goes so far as to argue that the British Army lacked 'a coherent doctrinal philosophy' for much of the twentieth century. See Brian Holden Reid, *A Doctrinal Perspective 1988–98* (The Strategic and Combat Institute: The Occasional, No. 33, May 1998), 12–28.

[75] Palazzo, *Seeking Victory*, 8–10. See, also, Stephen Badsey, *Doctrine and Reform in the British Cavalry 1880–1918* (Aldershot: Ashgate, 2008), 3–4.

[76] Simpson, *Directing Operations*, xvi–xvii.

[77] Todman, *Great War*, 82–3; Boff, *Winning and Losing*, 247–9.

[78] Allan R. Millett, Williamson Murray and Kenneth H. Watman, 'The Effectiveness of Military Organizations', in Allan R. Millett and Williamson Murray (eds.), *Military Effectiveness*, Vol. I: *The First World War New Edition* (Cambridge: Cambridge University Press, 2010), 1–30.

to investigate how the BEF learned, focusing on the processes rather than just the outcomes.[79] Therefore, an examination of communications presents the opportunity to reflect upon the nature of learning within the BEF.

By addressing these four issues, this study will provide fresh insight into how communications influenced the BEF's operations and, in the process, shed new light on some of the key historiographical controversies regarding the BEF's performance. Furthermore, from these issues it is evident that the subject of communications also has implications with regards to much broader academic controversies regarding the role of technology in warfare. In particular, an examination of communications draws attention to the current RMA debate.[80] Over the last three decades, dramatic advances in communications and information processing technology have led a number of commentators to speculate that the armed forces of several Western states are in the midst of an information-based RMA.[81] Historians have sought subsequently not only to uncover past examples of RMAs but also to assess the extent to which these RMAs depended upon their communications components.[82] As yet, however, there has been no detailed and systematic exploration of the role of communications and information in the BEF during the First World War, the conflict which, according to some historians, spawned the most important RMA to date.[83] This study has the opportunity, then, to position the subject of communications within the wider context of the literature on the First World War RMA, asking

---

[79] Robert T. Foley, 'Dumb Donkeys or Cunning Foxes? Learning in the British and German Armies during the Great War', *International Affairs*, 90 (2014), 279–98; Aimée Fox-Godden, '"Putting Knowledge in Power": Learning and Innovation in the British Army of the First World War' (PhD Thesis, University of Birmingham, 2015).

[80] An RMA here is defined as 'a major change in the nature of warfare brought about by the innovative application of new technologies which, combined with dramatic changes in military doctrine and operational and organisational concepts, fundamentally alters the character and conduct of military operations'. See Thierry Gongora and Harald von Riekhoff, 'Introduction: Sizing up the Revolution in Military Affairs', Gongora and von Riekhoff (eds.), *Towards a Revolution in Military Affairs? Defence and Security at the Dawn of the Twenty-First Century* (Westport, CT: Greenwood Press, 2000), 1.

[81] Jeremy Shapiro, 'Information and War: Is It a Revolution?' in Zalmay M. Khalilzad and John P. White (eds.), *Strategic Appraisal: The Changing Role of Information in Warfare* (Washington, DC: RAND Corporation, 1999), 113–53. See also the collection of articles in *The Journal of Strategic Studies* 33 (August 2010), Special Issue: The Information Technology Revolution in Military Affairs.

[82] Emily O. Goldman, (ed.), *Information and Revolutions in Military Affairs* (London: Routledge, 2005).

[83] Bailey, *First World War and the Birth of the Modern Style of Warfare*; and, Gray, *Strategy for Chaos*, 170–221.

to what extent the role and impact of communications and information contributed to the emergence of the 'modern battlefield' in 1918.

This book is based primarily upon the examination of unpublished archival material from across the English-speaking world, particularly the contemporary memoranda, operation orders and post-battle reports contained within the appendices of the unit war diaries held at the National Archives of the United Kingdom.[84] Significant use is especially made of the GHQ, army, corps and divisional signal company war diaries, which have so far remained largely untouched by historians. Although they are generally more reliable than the post-war official history correspondence,[85] the war diaries need to be dealt with carefully. They vary in terms of detail and quality, from the meticulous and concise to the illegible and very poor. Nevertheless, the collective wealth of information contained within them provides an unparalleled glimpse into the realities of command, control and communications on the Western Front. Moreover, as Peter Simkins argues, they demonstrate that 'a continuous process of tactical evaluation, operational analysis and often robust criticism was taking place at all levels of command in the BEF'.[86]

Also invaluable are the training manuals issued by GHQ and printed by the Army Printing and Stationary Service of the BEF during the war.[87] Based on the lessons learnt from battlefield experiences, these manuals were issued by GHQ to the rest of the army as a means of instilling a common set of tactical principles, though they were not prescriptive orders as such. More than 650 training manuals were printed during the course of the war on a variety of subjects, including communications.[88] Since many of the manuals were revised and updated, they provide revealing insights into what GHQ considered 'best practice' at

---

[84] Document series WO95, TNA. Also significant are the correspondence and papers of the BEF's various military headquarters, document series WO158. These contemporary operations files were removed from WO95 by the War Office for instructional purposes. See: Prior and Wilson, *Passchendaele*, 218–9; and, Ian F. W. Beckett, *The First World War: The Essential Guide to Sources in the UK National Archives* (London: Public Record Office, 2002), 55–8.

[85] Document series CAB45, TNA. On the value of the official history, see: David French, '"Official but Not History"? Sir James Edmonds and the Official History of the Great War', *Journal of the Royal United Services Institute for Defence Studies*, 131 (1986), 58–63; and Andrew Green, *Writing the Great War: Sir James Edmonds and the Official Histories 1915–1948* (London: Frank Cass, 2003).

[86] Simkins, '"Building Blocks", 148.

[87] These are known collectively as the SS series of pamphlets. For additional context, see Griffith, *Battle Tactics*, 179–86; and, Jim Beach, 'Issued by the General Staff: Doctrine Writing at British GHQ, 1917–1918', *War in History*, 19 (2012), 464–91.

[88] The two most important being *SS. 148. Forward Inter-Communication in Battle* (March 1917) and *SS. 191. Intercommunication in the Field* (November 1917).

the time they were written, and the extent to which the BEF formulated a 'communications doctrine' during the war.

In addition to the war diaries and training manuals, the unpublished letters, diaries and papers of a number of British officers, such as those held, for example, at the Imperial War Museum, London, Liddell Hart Centre for Military Archives, King's College London, and the Churchill Archives Centre, Cambridge, have also been consulted. The problem for this particular study, however, is that only one of the most senior officers of the Signal Service left any personal papers, correspondence or diaries relating to his wartime experiences.[89] To compensate for this deficiency, not only have the private papers belonging to junior officers, NCOs and other ranks of the Signal Service been utilized, but also the private papers of a substantial number of officers, who were not attached to the Signal Service, have been examined extensively in the search for information pertaining to communications. These sources are supplemented by the material contained in the under-utilized collections of the BT, Royal Mail, Royal Engineers and Royal Signals archives, which have yielded crucial information pertaining to the BEF's communications organisation, personnel and practices.

Finally, although the research for this book has been based upon a comprehensive study of material from government archives and private collections within the United Kingdom, because of the erratic preservation of documents relating to the BEF's communications system in British archives, there are notable gaps in the records. In an effort to overcome this dilemma, the files of the Australian and Canadian Corps, and the American Expeditionary Force (AEF), located, respectively, in the Australian War Memorial, Library and Archives Canada and the National Archives and Records Administration, have been consulted. The AEF files (Record Group 120), in particular, contain detailed reports and correspondence related to the inner workings of the BEF's communications system, which American officers studied and copied to good effect in 1917–18. Since this material has not survived in the British archives, it has made a useful addition to the primary material used in this study.

In order to provide a thorough examination of the BEF's communications system and help establish what influence communications had on British operations, this study has adopted both a thematic and a chronological approach, consisting of seven chapters. Chapters 1–3 will examine

---

[89] This was Brigadier-General Arthur Hildebrand (Deputy Director Signals, Second Army), whose personal diary of the 1914 campaign on the Western Front was published as: 'Second Army Signals, 1914: From the Personal Diary of Brigadier-General A. B. R. Hildebrand', *Royal Signals Quarterly Journal*, 6 (1938), 129–41.

the general components – organizational, personnel and technological – that constituted the British Army's communications system. Combined, these thematic chapters explain how the BEF's communications system functioned and how it evolved during the course of the war. They also provide the necessary foundations from which an investigative analysis of the performance of the BEF's communications system can then be made. Chapters 4–7 assess more specifically how this communications system influenced the nature and conduct of British operations between 1914 and 1918. The Conclusion then draws together the book's main findings, revealing the true extent to which communications shaped the BEF's operations and, more broadly, what this tells us about the BEF as an institution.

1   Organisation

In many respects, the importance of communications to British military operations on the Western Front is revealed by the immense organisational transformation that took place during the course of the war. As the scale and intensity of the fighting increased, and as the BEF grew in both size and complexity, so too were there corresponding changes to the communications establishment. This was particularly the case with regards to the Signal Service, aptly described by Field Marshal Sir Douglas Haig as 'the nervous system to the whole vast organism of our Army', which grew from an establishment of just below 2,400 officers and men in 1914 to a force consisting of nearly 42,000 at the signing of the armistice.[1] This chapter charts the development of the BEF's communications machinery, from its humble composition upon the outbreak of the war through to its maturation in 1918. In the process, it highlights the scale of the BEF's communications effort, as it expanded from an initial body comprising just 29 signal units in 1914 to a force encompassing 443 signal units by the war's end.[2] However, in order to make sense of these developments, it will first be necessary to examine the state of the British Army's communications system immediately prior to the war, and assess the extent to which it was geared for the scale and intensity of the war that lay ahead.

Pre-War Developments

The origins of the Signal Service can be traced back to the formation of the first professional signal unit in the British Army, C Telegraph Troop,

---

[1] Field Marshal Sir Douglas Haig's Final Despatch, 21 March 1919, in Lieutenant-Colonel J. H. Boraston (ed.), *Sir Douglas Haig's Despatches* (London: Dent, 1920), 334. In terms of relative growth, the Signal Service constituted 1.03 per cent of the BEF in August 1914 and 3.1 per cent of the BEF in November 1918. See Major Paul W. Evans, 'Strategic Signal Communication: A Study of Signal Communication as Applied to Large Field Forces, Based upon the Operations of the German Signal Corps During the March on Paris in 1914', *Signal Corps Bulletin*, 82 (1935), 55–6.

[2] War Office, *Statistics of the Military Effort of the British Empire, 1914–1920* (London: HMSO, 1922), 170–1.

R.E., in 1870.[3] In 1880, the first *Manual of Instruction in Army Signalling*
was issued and four years later, C Troop was merged with the 22nd and
34th Telegraph Companies attached to the General Post Office (GPO)
and renamed the Telegraph Battalion, R.E.[4] Despite seeing action in a
number of the British Army's colonial campaigns during the late nineteenth century, including the Nile Expedition of 1884–5 and the Ashanti
Campaign in 1895–6, the Telegraph Battalion's biggest challenge
occurred during the Second South African, or Boer, War (1899–1902).[5]
Up until then, communication practice had often been rudimentary and
extemporised, in part a reflection of the limited scale of the army's
colonial campaigns and its relatively ill-equipped and technically inefficient opponents. The conflict in South Africa, however, provided the
British Army with its first taste of a more modern style of war against an
adversary equipped with some of the most up-to-date French and
German armaments.[6] Subsequently, the army suffered from uncoordinated and clumsy signal organisation and practice, particularly during the
first half of the war. The defective transmission of information throughout
the Battle of Spion Kop (23–4 January 1900), for example, confirmed
'how inherently unreliable and subject to accidents' British communication arrangements were.[7] Issues of interoperability were a particular

---

[3] This consisted originally of 2 officers and 133 other ranks, commanded by Captain
Montague Lambert. See Major-General R. F. H. Nalder, *The Royal Corps of Signals:
A History of Its Antecedents and Development, 1800–1955* (London: Royal Signals Institution,
1958), 21. In 1871, the adjutant of C Troop was Lieutenant (later Field Marshal Lord)
Horatio Herbert Kitchener. See Cliff Lord and Graham Watson, *The Royal Corps of Signals:
Unit Histories of the Corps (1920–2001) and Its Antecedents* (Solihull: Helion, 2004), 16.

[4] 'Proceedings of the Committee on Telegraph Troop and Companies, Royal Engineers,
According to the Recommendations of the Royal Engineers Committee 1880', undated,
WO33/36, TNA; Lord and Watson, *Royal Corps of Signals*, 17.

[5] 'Report on Army Telegraphs, Nile Expedition 1884–1885', undated, WO33/47, TNA;
Major C. F. C. Beresford, R.E., 'The Field Telegraph: Its Use in the War and Its
Employment in the Late Expeditions in the Soudan and South Africa', *Journal of the
Royal United Service Institution*, 30 (1886), 573–601; Nalder, *Royal Corps of Signals*,
26–32. For a discussion of the employment of military telegraph units in earlier
campaigns, see: Major A. W. Mackworth, 'The Field Telegraph Corps in Egypt', *Royal
Engineers Journal*, 12 (1882), 269–72; and, Lieutenant-Colonel A. C. Hamilton, R.E.,
'Our Field Telegraph: Its Work in Recent Campaigns, and Its Present Organisation',
Journal of the Royal United Service Institution, 28 (1884), 329–55.

[6] Edward Spiers, 'The Late Victorian Army 1868–1914', in David Chandler and Ian F. W.
Beckett (eds.), *The Oxford History of the British Army* (Oxford: Oxford University Press,
1996), 187–210; Spencer Jones, *From Boer War to World War: Tactical Reform of the British
Army, 1902–1914* (Norman: University of Oklahoma Press, 2012), 17–36.

[7] Colonel Hubert du Cane (trans.), *The War in South Africa: The Advance to Pretoria after
Paardeberg, the Upper Tugela Campaign, etc. Prepared in the Historical Section of the Great
General Staff, Berlin* (London: John Murray, 1906), 169. See, also, Captain F. S. Morgan,
'The Development of Communication and Command', *Journal of the Royal United Service
Institution*, 76 (1931), 132–4.

concern. In July 1900, a report by Lieutenant-Colonel Tom O'Leary, the Director of Army Signalling noted that, because many signallers within the Royal Artillery were instructed in semaphore only, heliographs and signalling lamps could not be used by infantry units wishing to communicate with their artillery batteries.[8] On the whole, post-war reports concurred that the means of signalling available was thought to be 'poor' and 'insufficient' at worse, and merely 'satisfactory' at best.[9] Although by the end of the war there were 24 officers and 2,424 men responsible for maintaining a little more than 9,300 miles of cable in South Africa, there were strong calls from officers within the Telegraph Battalion for 'a careful analysis of the varying conditions met with on active service', so as to produce an organisation of much greater flexibility and efficiency.[10]

Many of these problems were again exposed during army manoeuvres in the years immediately following the end of the war. Major Edmund Godfrey-Faussett, commanding 2nd Telegraph Company, complained that the 1904 summer training exercises had been hampered by a severe shortage of equipment and draught horses. As a consequence, communications among the various headquarters could not be adequately maintained since telegraph cable could not be laid fast enough.[11] In light of the disastrous experiences of the Second South African War and of the ongoing problems encountered during yearly army manoeuvres, in March 1905 a War Office committee was set up to review the state of the army's telegraph service. Chaired by Major-General Sir Elliott Wood, the army's chief engineer, the committee's aim was to increase the field telegraphic establishment, since

the role in field telegraphy in war has entirely changed. It is now used as a means of communication, not only between the field army and its communications, but also between units which are actually engaged in battle; this much enhances its value, and it is a matter of the highest importance that we should possess sufficient telegraphic establishments to admit of a general being in constant communication with the component parts of his force.[12]

The Telegraph Battalion was subsequently abolished and three telegraph companies formed, one for each army corps and 'K' Telegraph Company

[8] 'Report on Signalling Rendered to the Field-Marshal Commanding-in-Chief by the Director of Signalling, Army Headquarters', July 1900, WO108/256, TNA.
[9] 'Signalling Equipment: Extracts from Reports by Officers Commanding Units in South Africa during 1899–1901', undated, WO108/278, TNA.
[10] Lord and Watson, *Royal Corps of Signals*, 18; Major E. G. Godfrey-Faussett, 'Studies on the Use of Field Telegraphs in South Africa', *Royal Engineers Journal*, 8 (1908), 24.
[11] 'Report on Summer Training, 1904', undated, WO32/6799, TNA.
[12] 'Report of the Wood Committee on Army Telegraph Units, March 1905', WO32/6799, TNA.

for the lines of communication. From 1907, a telegraph company was added to each infantry division of the newly created expeditionary force. Two airline and two cable telegraph companies were formed for army communications, three cable sections for the Cavalry Division and two experimental wireless companies created. Two telegraph companies were also provided for work on the lines of communication.[13]

The Wood Committee was the first of several committees set up between 1905 and 1914 to review and amend the army's signal organisation. Many of the recommendations of these committees, however, were met with considerable opposition from the General Staff, which considered some of the proposals to be too far-reaching.[14] One of the clearest examples of this conflict of interests occurred in 1906–7, following the report of a committee presided over by Field-Marshal Sir Evelyn Wood.[15] Observing the lessons of the Russo-Japanese War of 1904–5, the committee recommended that all means of communication within the British Army should be placed under the control of one overriding authority. The committee also strongly recommended that this 'Communication Service' should take over infantry and artillery signalling as far forward as battalion and battery headquarters.[16] The committee's proposals did not sit well with the General Staff, which voiced its disapproval in January 1907:

The Committee have assumed that the Manchurian Campaign should be taken as a guide to the employment of Engineers in our probable campaigns. This is not accepted by the General Staff as a correct assumption, because the conditions... rendered the Engineer work both in attack and defence quite abnormal... Brigade level of communications should not be done by the Royal Engineers... The Infantry are perfectly capable of doing this themselves.[17]

Because of the objections of the General Staff, the committee's proposals were not implemented. Although the issue of communications was at least receiving some attention, it appears that the General Staff was reluctant to provide the army with anything more than an absolute bare minimum of signal organisation.

---

[13] In 1912 these were amalgamated into 'K' Telegraph Company. See Nalder, *Royal Corps of Signals*, 50–1; Lord and Watson, *Royal Corps of Signals*, 18.

[14] Priestley, *Work of the Royal Engineers*, 5.

[15] Ian F. W. Beckett, 'Wood, Sir (Henry) Evelyn (1838–1919)', *Oxford Dictionary of National Biography*, www.oxforddnb.com/view/article/37000 [accessed 18 December 2015].

[16] 'Report of the Committee Appointed to Inquire into the Organisation of the Corps of Royal Engineers together with Evidence and Appendices, 1906', WO32/6805, TNA.

[17] 'Criticism on R.E. Committee (Sir E. Wood): Employment in the Field and War Organisation', 7 January 1907, WO32/6805, TNA.

However, the increasing complexity of modern warfare, as demonstrated by the Russo-Japanese War, created a growing interest in, and appreciation for, communications.[18] As Lieutenant-Colonel Bernard Dietz, CO 7th Dragoon Guards, observed in January 1908, 'the increased range and great accuracy of modern artillery, machine guns and the magazine rifle have made the transmission of information during field operations more difficult than in the past'.[19] Indeed, as the 1909 *Field Service Regulations* made clear: 'The constant maintenance of communication between the various parts of an army is of urgent importance; it is on this to a great extent that the possibility of co-operation depends'.[20] The issue of whether or not the army should possess one organisation solely responsible for all its communication needs was one of increasing importance, especially since the defects of the present service were becoming ever more noticeable during yearly army manoeuvres.[21] For example, Captain D. H. Blundell, who commanded a small experimental communication company in 2 Division during the 1906 army exercises, noted afterwards:

So long as the telegraphs and the telephones and the Communication Company worked under separate control... co-operation was hard to arrive at... because neither officer in charge knew exactly what the other was doing... To get the best work out of a Communication Company, it must be working *with* the telegraphs; and to ensure this, all methods of communication within a division should be under one control.[22]

Eventually, in April 1909 a War Office committee met to consider whether it was desirable to coordinate all methods of communication in the field in one organisation. Chaired by Brigadier-General (later General Sir) Archibald Murray,[23] the Director of Military Training, the committee had as its primary concern that 'while in certain portions of the field there may be overlapping of work and waste of communication

---

[18] Anon., 'The Service of Communication in the Light of the Experience of the Russo-Japanese War', *Journal of the Royal United Services Institution*, 52 (1908), 968–70; Anon, 'Communication on the Battlefield. Translated by Permission from La Revue d'Infanterie', *Journal of the Royal United Services Institution*, 53 (1909), 357–69; Jones, *From Boer War to World War*, 153.

[19] 'Memorandum on Signalling by Means of Discs', January 1908, History of Military Signalling, 908.2, Royal Signals Museum Archive (RSMA), Blandford.

[20] *Field Service Regulations Part I*, 22.

[21] Captain R. C. Hammond, 'Communication in the Field', *Royal Engineers Journal*, 7 (1908), 139–52.

[22] Quoted in Bat.-Colonel J. E. Capper, 'Information on the Battlefield', *Royal Engineers Journal*, 6 (1907), 34.

[23] J. E. Edmonds, 'Murray, Sir Archibald James (1860–1945)', rev. Martin Bunton, *Oxford Dictionary of National Biography*, www.oxforddnb.com/view/article/35155 [accessed 18 December 2015].

personnel, in other directions the communication service may be so inadequate as to cause a complete breakdown'.[24] The committee argued that the creation of one overriding signal organisation would ensure that all methods of communication, whether telegraph, telephone, wireless, visual or despatch rider, would be used to their best advantage and that their 'economical and scientific employment' would be met. The major question, however, was where this new organisation was going to originate. The committee considered four possible alternatives.

The first proposal called for the formation of an entirely new corps. A separate 'Corps of Signals' would provide the army with all its communication needs. However, there were already objections within the military over the ever-increasing number of new corps being created. Adjutant General Sir Ian Hamilton, in a letter dated 20 April 1909, outlined his misgivings over the possible establishment of a Corps of Signals stating, 'If a separate Corps were formed it might add to the already complicated organisation of our army'.[25] There were also concerns raised over the difficulties affecting the promotion of officers and, perhaps more importantly, problems over economy and finance. In the end, as a result of financial constraints and administrative difficulties, the committee found the idea of raising a separate corps of signals to be impractical.[26]

The second alternative the committee considered was the creation of signal companies from a selection of the most suitable officers and men in any branch of the army. In essence, this would be an improvised corps of sorts. The acceptance of this proposal, however, rested on the necessity for the officers and troops selected to receive Royal Engineer pay. Since Royal Engineers soldiers were some of the highest paid in the British Army, problems of precedent and economy forced the committee to rule out this second proposal.[27]

The third alternative was to provide signal personnel on a non-regular basis. While this was certainly the most economical of the proposals considered, it would not provide the army with a communication service fitting of its size and importance. There was also an additional problem of

---

[24] 'Committee on Coordination of Methods of Communication and Schools of Telegraphy and Signalling', April 1909, WO33/3003, TNA.

[25] 'Remarks of A. G. on Report of Committee on Coordination of Methods of Communication in the Field', 20 April 1909, WO32/6942, TNA.

[26] 'Committee on Coordination of Methods of Communication and Schools of Telegraphy and Signalling', April 1909, WO33/3003, TNA.

[27] For army pay scales, see *Field Service Pocket Book: 1914* (Reprinted, with Amendments, 1916) (London: HMSO, 1917), 179.

the length of training and service of troops of the Territorial Force.[28] The committee agreed that troops selected would require at least three years' training to be of 'the higher standard essential for the personnel of Signal Companies'. Overall, however, the proposal was thought not to be an adequate solution to the problem.[29]

The fourth alternative discussed by the committee was the provision of a limited 'Signal Service' with personnel drawn from a communication branch of an already existing corps. It was agreed that the most suitable established corps would be the Royal Engineers as it already had a pool of highly trained personnel. This, in turn, would prove less costly than forming an entirely new corps. It was decided, therefore, that the Signal Service should be formed as a separate branch of the Royal Engineers.[30] However, the committee upheld the General Staff's earlier decision that signalling within infantry battalions, cavalry regiments and the artillery should remain the responsibility of those units and not the Signal Service. It was felt that the duties of Signal Service personnel 'will be firstly and mainly communication, to which their role as fighting men will be subsidiary only', while regimental signallers were recognised as 'soldiers first and their duties as signallers secondary'. Intercommunication within the artillery, in particular, was to remain the responsibility of the artillery signallers chiefly because artillery messages were deemed 'generally of a highly technical character'.[31] Consequently, the responsibility of the Signal Service would end at the headquarters of infantry battalions and cavalry regiments; the communication requirements of those units were to be fulfilled by signallers provided, trained and controlled by those respective arms, while artillery communications were to remain outside the Signal Service's jurisdiction.[32] This was to prove a major organisational stumbling block during the first half of the war, exposing a significant and highly vulnerable weakness within the army's communications system.[33]

---

[28] On the pre-war Territorial Force, see K. W. Mitchinson, *England's Last Hope: The Territorial Force, 1908–14* (London: Palgrave, 2008); and, Timothy Bowman and Mark Connelly, *The Edwardian Army: Recruiting, Training, and Deploying the British Army, 1902–1914* (Oxford: Oxford University Press, 2012), 106–46.

[29] 'Committee on Coordination of Methods of Communication and Schools of Telegraphy and Signalling', April 1909, WO33/3003, TNA.

[30] Ibid.; Nalder, *Royal Corps of Signals*, 50.

[31] 'Committee on Coordination of Methods of Communication and Schools of Telegraphy and Signalling', April 1909, WO33/3003, TNA.

[32] Priestley, *Work of the Royal Engineers*, 5–6.

[33] Despite the lessons and organisational changes that occurred during the First World War, the Royal Corps of Signals (established in 1920) found itself in a similar predicament during the course of the Second World War, when it also had no official jurisdiction over communications at regimental and battery levels. See Simon Godfrey,

The structure and responsibilities of the Signal Service as laid out by the Murray Committee in 1909 remained virtually unchanged in August 1914. However, it was not until 1912, as a result of the recommendations of a further committee which met in 1911,[34] that the Signal Service was officially recognised and its activities regularised by means of Army Order 309.[35] With the formal recognition of the Signal Service, the old telegraph units were abolished and the term 'telegraph' replaced by 'signal', which was now the recognised term when reference was made to communications in the army.[36]

Control and Direction

Upon the outbreak of the war, within the War Office in London there existed neither a Director of Signals nor one branch that was solely responsible for the direction and coordination of the Signal Service. Instead, responsibility was divided between the various members of the Army Council. Organisation and training fell under the jurisdiction of the Chief of the Imperial General Staff (CIGS), via the Director of Staff Duties and Director of Military Training, respectively. The Adjutant-General dealt with all matters relating to personnel, while the Quartermaster-General was responsible for the design, manufacture and provision of signalling equipment. The former was coordinated by the Director of Staff Duties, while the Director of Fortifications and Works supervised the latter, with assistance from the Royal Engineers Committee.[37]

In 1916, the position of Director of Military Training was abolished and most of his responsibilities passed to S.D.4, a branch under the director of staff duties.[38] Coordination of signal training at home and abroad was handled jointly by S.D.4(d), a section which consisted simply of one GSO3,[39] and the Royal Engineers training and special

British Army Communications in the Second World War: Lifting the Fog of Battle (London: Bloomsbury, 2013), 3.

[34] 'Report of the Committee on Coordination of Methods of Communication and Schools of Telegraphy and Signalling', undated [1911], WO32/6942, TNA; Priestley, *Work of the Royal Engineers*, 5.

[35] 'Army Order 309, Reorganisation of the Intercommunication Services of the Expeditionary Force for War', November 1911, WO123/53, TNA.

[36] 'Report of the Inter-Departmental Committee on Postal and Telegraph Services, 1911', WO32/11396, TNA; Nalder, *Royal Corps of Signals*, 51.

[37] Nalder, *Royal Corps of Signals*, 75.

[38] Charles Messenger, *Call to Arms: The British Army 1914–18* (London: Weidenfeld & Nicolson, 2005), 340.

[39] Captain J. S. Yule, R.E. (GSO3), assisted by a Superintending Clerk and seven additional clerks. H. C. Perrott (comp.), *The War Office List: 1917* (London: HMSO, 1917), 76.

services. In the continuing absence of a senior Signal Service representative at the War Office, the Commandant of the Signal Service
Training Centre, Colonel (later Brigadier-General) Reginald Boys,
was consulted on an ad hoc basis.[40] These arrangements persisted until
February 1918 when, upon the express wishes of the BEF's Director of
Army Signals, a separate signals branch, S.D.6, was formed, at last
giving the Signal Service 'adequate weight and representation at the
War Office'.[41] Headed by Lieutenant-Colonel Llewelyn Evans,[42] and
assisted by one GSO2 and four clerks, S.D.6 was responsible for coordinating and prioritising signal training, personnel and equipment
throughout all theatres of war.[43] Although a marked improvement
compared to the previous War Office arrangements, it was a far cry
from the Signal Directorate established in January 1941, which, by the
end of the Second World War, consisted of 65 staff officers, working in
11 branches and headed by an experienced signal officer, Major-
General Geoffrey Rawson.[44]

The lack of suitable control and direction of the Signal Service's
activities at the War Office was replicated to a similar degree in the field,
and was particularly problematic during the first half of the war.
Although a *Manual of Army Signal Service – War* did exist, not only was
it under revision when the war broke out, but it also did not anticipate the
enormous scale of the challenges the Signal Service was about to face.[45]
Upon mobilisation, the BEF's Signal Service numbered 75 officers and

---

[40] This situation seemed to mirror a trend within the War Office as a whole during this
period. Upon entering the War Office as the new CIGS, General Sir William Robertson
told Haig: 'I found things here even in a greater state of muddle and chaos than I had
feared, and it will take me some time to get them right'. General Sir William Robertson
to General Sir Douglas Haig, 26 December 1915, cited in David R. Woodward (ed.),
*The Military Correspondence of Field-Marshal Sir William Robertson, Chief of the Imperial
General Staff, December 1915-February 1918* (Army Records Society: Bodley Head,
1989), 23. See, also, Sir William Robertson, *Soldiers and Statesmen 1914–1918*, Vol. 1
(London: Cassell, 1926), 164–90.

[41] Priestley, *Work of the Royal Engineers*, 300.

[42] Prior to the war, Evans had commanded the R.E. Wireless Company based at Aldershot,
taking part in the early experiments in wireless communication between aircraft and the
ground. See Walter Raleigh, *The War in the Air*, Vol. 1: *The Part Played in the Great War
by the Royal Air Force* (Oxford: Clarendon Press, 1922), 224.

[43] Captain B. J. M. Bebb, R.E. was the GSO2. J. R. Wade (comp.), *The War Office List:
1918* (London: HMSO, 1918), 87.

[44] Rawson had been AD Signals XII Corps (Salonika) during the First World War.
Between 1932 and 1936 he was Chief Instructor, School of Signals, and in 1944 he
was appointed Colonel Commandant of the Royal Corps of Signals, a post he held until
1950. See: Lord and Watson, *Royal Corps of Signals*, 322–3; Nalder, *Royal Corps of
Signals*, 76, 214, 268.

[45] *Manual of Army Signal Service – War (Provisional): 1914* (London: HMSO, 1914).

Table 1.1 *Signal Service Establishment, BEF, August 1914*

Unit and No. of Personnel	Allotted to	No. of Units in the BEF	Total No. of Personnel
'L' Signal Company (5 Officers, 263 Men)	Inspector General of Communications HQ (Lines of Communication)	1	5 Officers and 263 Men
GHQ Signal Company (5 Officers, 75 Men)	GHQ	1	5 Officers and 75 Men
'Q' Wireless Section (2 Officers, 66 Men)	GHQ	1	2 Officers and 63 Men
Army Corps HQ Signal Company (4 Officers, 63 Men)	Army Corps HQ	2	8 Officers and 126 Men
Airline Section (1 Officer, 57 Men)	Distributed to GHQ and Army Corps HQ	5	5 Officers and 285 Men
Cable Section (1 Officer, 35 Men)	as may be required	8	8 Officers and 280 Men
Divisional Signal Company (5 Officers, 157 Men)	Infantry Division	6	30 Officers and 942 Men
Signal Squadron (8 Officers, 198 Men)	Cavalry Division	1	8 Officers and 198 Men
Signal Troop (1 Officer, 23 Men)	Cavalry Brigade	3	3 Officers and 69 Men
Signal Troop (1 Officer, 42 Men)	Independent Cavalry Brigade	1	1 Officer and 42 Men
Grand Total		29	75 Officers and 2,346 Men

Source: Compiled from Priestley, *Work of the Royal Engineers*, 11; and, *Field Service Pocket Book*: 1914, 60–2.

2,346 other ranks, comprising 29 units in all (Table 1.1).[46] The control and administration of these units were the responsibility of Colonel (later Lieutenant-General Sir) John Fowler, who held the post of Director of Army Signals at GHQ throughout the war.[47] As well as advising the commander-in-chief on all matters pertaining to the Signal Service and

[46] The signal units of the Territorial Force provided a further 103 officers and 2,893 other ranks, which comprised 14 divisional telegraph companies; five army wireless telegraph companies; five army cable telegraph companies; and, five army airline telegraph companies. See Priestley, *Work of the Royal Engineers*, 11–12.

[47] Fowler was promoted to brigadier-general in October 1914 and to major-general in January 1917.

to communications throughout the BEF in general,[48] Fowler's main duties included the 'organisation and maintenance of all means of intercommunication, including visual, electrical, and mechanical, and despatch riders in the theatre of operations', and the 'administration and distribution of the signal troops, and for the employment of those not allotted to subordinate commands'.[49] To help carry out these responsibilities, however, Fowler was afforded an extremely slender staff, consisting initially of only one staff officer and three clerks, which made it virtually impossible for him to exert complete control over the activities of such a diverse array of signal units.[50] This problem was exacerbated by the fact that Fowler had no representative of a similar appointment to himself – in other words, a chief signal officer – at corps, and later army, headquarters. Consequently, although Fowler could issue 'all orders regarding the technical employment of the signal personnel, and for the regulation of signal traffic',[51] the lack of an effective central chain of command within the Signal Service meant that most signal companies tended to work independently of one another and under the direction of their own headquarters' staffs.[52] Since the officers commanding signal companies were responsible not only for commanding their companies but also for advising their staffs, the vast increase in both the scale of the fighting and the size and complexity of the BEF from 1915 meant that close supervision of subordinate signal units during the first half of the war was rarely exercised, resulting in clumsy, ad hoc and uncoordinated signal administration.[53]

The key turning point for improved control and coordination of the Signal Service's activities in the field occurred in 1916: first, in February with the appointment of Deputy Directors of Army Signals (DD Signals), with the rank of colonel, at army headquarters; and, second, in November, with the appointment of Assistant Directors of Army Signals (AD Signals), with the rank of lieutenant-colonel, at corps headquarters. The chief justification for the creation of these new posts was 'to free the Officers Commanding Army and Corps Headquarters Signal Companies from their executive duties in connection with their units, and to enable

---

[48] *Manual of Army Signal Service – War*, 11.   [49] *Field Service Pocket Book: 1914*, 28.

[50] Not only did the size of Fowler's staff remain the same for the first two years of the war, crucially it also lacked a liaison officer until 1916. See Priestley, *Work of the Royal Engineers*, 340.

[51] Major G. R. N. Collins, *Military Organization and Administration* (London: Hugh Rees, 1918), 352.

[52] Nalder, *Royal Corps of Signals*, 77.

[53] Colonel R. S. Curtis, 'The Work of Signal Units in War', *Royal Engineers Journal*, 18 (1913), 270; *Manual of Army Signal Service – War*, 16; Priestley, *Work of the Royal Engineers*, 92.

them to deal with the larger questions affecting the general scheme of inter-communication throughout their respective areas'.[54] Thus, there now existed a chief signal officer at each army and corps headquarters in addition to the officers commanding the army and corps signal companies.[55] These were to prove inspired appointments, since not only did they gradually improve the coordination and overall efficiency of the Signal Service, but they also helped mend the somewhat strained relationship between the Signal Service and the General Staff.[56]

Indeed, the DD Signals were accountable to the army commander, through the General Staff, for the efficiency of the methods of communication within the army area, the training of signal units and personnel, and were responsible for the provision of signal stores and their distribution. They had to cultivate good working relationships with the army staff on the one hand and with the AD Signals on the other. The importance of the relationship between the DD Signals and the army staff was particularly emphasised in a memorandum by Godfrey-Faussett, now DD Signals Fifth Army, in early 1918. He stressed that 'it is much more important for his [DD Signals] office to be close to the "G" Staff Office than the Signal Office, and when important operations are in progress he should be in and out of the "G" Office every 2 or 3 hours'.[57] As Table 1.2 shows, given that nearly all the DD Signals appointed in early 1916 retained their posts until the end of the war, it may be deduced that the working relationships between them and the army staff were almost certainly productive – a reflection of the overall improvement in signal–staff relations and coordination during the last two years of the war, which greatly facilitated the overall performance of the BEF's communications system.

Though specific to the corps level of command, the duties and responsibilities of the AD Signals were almost identical to those of the DD Signals. Besides maintaining close contact with commanders and staffs of all formations within the corps, the AD Signals were responsible for the planning and supervision of the general scheme of communications

---

[54] 'Signal Service – Officers', 25 February 1916, AWM25/463/1, Australian War Memorial (AWM), Canberra.

[55] In late 1917, a Deputy Assistant Director of Army Signals (DAD Signals) was added to the staff of the dd signals, with the rank of major. Priestley, *Work of the Royal Engineers*, 192–3, 253, 337.

[56] Nalder, *Royal Corps of Signals*, 109; Paul Harris, 'The Men Who Planned the War' 137, 140–1.

[57] 'Organisation of the Signals of an Army When Holding a Sector of Line (Siege Warfare)', 3 March 1918, Organisation and Work of Signals in WW1 – Papers on Various Subjects, M1599, Royal Engineers Museum Archive (REMA), Gillingham.

Table 1.2 *DD Signals, BEF, 1916–1918*

	First Army	Second Army	Third Army	Fourth Army	Reserve/Fifth Army
1916					
February	Edmund Godfrey-Faussett	Arthur Hildebrand	William Newbigging	Robert Earle	
May					Lionel Sadleir-Jackson
June	Herbert Moore				Edmund Godfrey-Faussett
1918					
May					Frederick Iles
October		Hubert Clementi-Smith			

Note: All colonels, with the exception of Sadleir-Jackson, who was a major at the time.
Source: Compiled from Major A. F. Becke (Comp.), *History of the Great War: Order of Battle of Divisions, Part 4* (London: HMSO, 1945), 71–111; and, Nalder, *Royal Corps of Signals*, 503–80. It should be noted that there existed from the beginning of the war a DD Signals (Lines of Communication). This position was held by Major (later Major-General) Ernest Turner.

within the corps area, as well as with neighbouring corps; the preparation and issuing of general and technical signal instructions; control over the issue of signal stores; the formation and supervision of the Corps Signal School; and the selection and recommendation of signal officer appointments.[58] However, unlike the DD Signals, who were afforded the assistance of a GSO2 and two clerks, the AD Signals had no staff of their own, having to borrow from the corps signal company as a result.[59] As Appendix 1 shows, there was a higher turnover of AD Signals than DD Signals, though the degree of continuity varied considerably. Although only two of the AD Signals originally appointed in November 1916 (Danielsen and Harrison) retained their positions within the same corps until the armistice, seven (Stevenson, Bald, Walsh, Mair, Dobbs, Yeats-Brown and Smith) served as AD Signals in two corps, while one (Carey) served as AD Signals with three different corps. Overall, the permanent establishment of AD Signals from 1916 onwards should be viewed not only as an important milestone in the development and increased status of the Signal Service, but also as a significant indicator of the growing

---

[58] 'Allocation of Duties to Officers – Corps Signals', 2 January 1918, RG9-III-C-5/4443/7/6, Library and Archives Canada (LAC), Ottawa.
[59] Nalder, *Royal Corps of Signals*, 85.

importance of corps in the planning and execution of the BEF's operations. As Andy Simpson has argued: 'From 1916 onwards, corps was
the highest level of command... concerned with the detail of operations
and success was crucially dependent on the planning of corps staffs'.[60]

Aside from the Director of Army Signals, DD Signals and AD Signals,
the signal unit of each formation down to, but not including, infantry
battalion headquarters was commanded by a Signal Service officer.
Typically, the OC GHQ Signal Company and the OC Army Signal
Company were afforded the rank of major, while the OC Corps Signal
Company and OC Divisional Signal Company were appointed majors or
captains.[61] The principal duties of these officers were largely administrative in nature and included 'the co-ordination and supervision of the
Signal work not only of the Signal Service, but also of all Artillery,
Infantry and other units under the command of his GOC'.[62] However,
as an American observer reported in 1917, the OC divisional signal
company was also instructed to 'keep in the closest communication with
the [divisional] General Staff... and be prepared to proffer advice as to
communications'.[63] As such, most of the administrative details and
arrangements concerning the divisional signal company, such as signal
office routine, the provision of stores and writing the company war diary,
were carried out by the OC divisional signal company's second in command, typically a captain or a lieutenant.[64] In all of the duties, pre-war
doctrine dictated that the provision and maintenance of communication
between two headquarters were the responsibility of the higher commander and organisation.[65] However, it was also stressed that this did
not lessen the responsibility of a subordinate commander in keeping his
superior 'regularly informed of the progress of events and of important
changes in the situation as they occur'.[66]

Arguably the most important, yet equally the most challenging,
position within the Signal Service's chain of command was that of the
brigade signalling officer. Since he commanded one of the four sections

---

[60] Simpson, *Directing Operations*, 226.
[61] 'Signal Service – Officers', 25 February 1916, AWM25/463/1, AWM.
[62] 'Signal Service – Summary of Instructions', 31 December 1916, AWM25/425/
47, AWM.
[63] 'Detailed Instructions for the Headquarters Staff of a Division', undated [late 1917],
AEF General Staff Library Files, RG120/279/35, National Archives and Records
Administration (NARA), Maryland.
[64] 'Divisional Signal Company: Allocation of Duties to Officers', undated [early 1918],
AWM25/425/3, AWM.
[65] 'Report of a Conference of General Staff Officers at the Staff College, 15th to 18th
January, 1912', 16, WO279/45, TNA; Collins, *Military Organization*, 353.
[66] *Field Service Regulations Part I*, 22.

Plate 1.1 Interior of the New Zealand signal office, 1 August 1917
(Henry Armytage Sanders: Alexander Turnbull Library, Wellington,
1/2-012884-G)

that comprised the divisional signal company, he owed his allegiance to
the OC divisional signal company. However, because he spent the majority of his time at brigade headquarters, it was crucial that he also lived on
good terms with the brigadier-general and his staff.[67] Typically a subaltern, the brigade signal officer had the principal task of providing and
maintaining communications with neighbouring brigades and, crucially,
between brigade and battalion headquarters.[68] Officially, it was at the
latter headquarters where the brigade signal officer's, and thus the Signal
Service's, jurisdiction ended. Yet, as one signal officer observed after the

---

[67] J. B. Scrivenor, *Brigade Signals* (Oxford: Basil Blackwell, 1932), 48–50; Austin Patrick
Corcoran, *The Daredevil of the Army: A Motorcycle Despatch Rider and 'Buzzer' in the
British Army during the First World War* (first published 1919; new ed., Milton Keynes:
Leonaur, 2011), 61.

[68] 'Notes on Signal Communication within a Division When Holding a Defensive Line',
April 1915, AWM27/311/32, AWM; 'Lectures: 47th Canadian Infantry Battalion',
undated [1917], Sir Arthur Currie Papers, MG30, E100/35/161, LAC.

war, 'it was also clearly laid down that the brigade signalling officer was responsible for the supervision and coordination of all communications in the brigade area, which of course included the battalion areas, though the battalion signalling officers were not under his direct control'.[69] The *Trench Standing Orders* of the 124th Infantry Brigade in late 1915 also stipulated quite clearly that the 'Brigade Signalling Officer is responsible for communications within the battalions'.[70] In light of the fact that the battalion signal officer could refuse to carry out a verbal order or instruction by the brigade signal officer on the grounds that he was answerable only to the battalion commander, the importance of getting his battalion counterpart 'to do what you wanted them to do without any friction' was impressed upon the brigade signal officer. In this respect, cohesion of personnel and the efficient working of communications forward of brigade headquarters 'were not the result of the organisation, but depended on the ability of all concerned to pull together amicably'.[71] One brigade signal officer, for example, recalled how in early 1917 he was 'most flattered at being addressed as "Sir" one day by two Battalion Signal Officers!'[72]

Indeed, one of the major organisational concerns for the Signal Service was also where the BEF's communications system was at its most vulnerable – the battalion level.[73] Because of the ruling made by the General Staff before the war, communications forward of battalion headquarters were to remain the responsibility of the regimental signallers, not the Signal Service. In 1914, an infantry battalion's signal section was made up of a sergeant and 16 men, typically under the nominal supervision of the battalion adjutant.[74] Some, more fortunate, battalions managed to retain a signal officer, usually of subaltern rank, though such a position had been officially abolished before the war. Communications within these battalions were generally more efficient and better organised than in those battalions that could not spare an

---

[69] Scrivenor, *Brigade Signals*, 49.

[70] 'Trench Standing Orders, 1915–16. 124th Infantry Brigade', in Stephen Bull (comp.), *An Officer's Manual of the Western Front 1914–1918* (London: Conway, 2008), 80.

[71] Scrivenor, *Brigade Signals*, 50.

[72] Archibald Gordon MacGregor and Anna Welti (ed.), *Signals from the Great War: The Experiences of a Signals Officer on the Western Front as Told through His War Diaries 1917–1919* (Brighton: Reveille Press, 2014), 34.

[73] Anon., 'Trench Signaling [sic] Becomes a Fine Art: British Officer Writes of Difficulties Overcome on the Western Front', *New York Times*, 12 August 1917, 5.

[74] *Field Service Manual, 1914 Infantry Battalion, Expeditionary Force* (London, HMSO, 1914), 8–9; Chris McCarthy, 'Queen of the Battlefield: The Development of Command, Organisation and Tactics in the British Infantry Battalion during the Great War', in Sheffield and Todman (eds.), *Command and Control on the Western Front*, 173.

officer to focus exclusively on communications. However, since in the vast majority of cases the adjutant assumed responsibility for the battalion signallers, not only could he not devote enough attention to the task, since he had an array of other duties to perform, but he also knew very little about the practicalities of signalling.[75] It was not until December 1917 that the post of battalion signal officer was officially reinstated, though by that time most battalions had found it necessary to appoint an unofficial signal officer.[76] According to John Staniforth, the battalion signal officer was 'responsible for maintaining communication at all times from his Bn. Hdqrs. to the Brigade, to the component companies of his battalion, and to the units on either flank, and to establish the necessary stations accordingly'.[77] Since such officers were under strict instructions to 'devote the whole of [their] attention to [their] lines' and to 'work in the closest cooperation with the Brigade Signal Officer', they were not 'to undertake any other duties whatsoever'.[78]

Unsurprisingly, given the lack of adequate coordination and supervision during the first half of the war, the state of battalion communications quickly deteriorated.[79] The high number of casualties amongst regimental signallers,[80] as well as the decision in early 1915 to extend cable communications beyond battalion headquarters and up to the frontline trenches, a task that was beyond the ability of the typical regimental signaller who was trained almost exclusively in visual methods of communication, further exacerbated the state of affairs within battalion signals.[81] Consequently, as early as December 1914 it was noted that 'duties are being thrown on Divisional Signal Companies which are not included in any manuals, but which require to be recognised'.[82] Essentially, the Signal Service was compelled to step in to coordinate and supervise the provision and maintenance of communications right up to the frontline. Although it was never officially sanctioned by the high command, largely as a result of objections raised concerning practicality

---

[75] 'Organisation of Battalion Signallers', 18 January 1916, Guards Division Signal Company War Diary, WO95/1205, TNA.

[76] Priestley, *Work of the Royal Engineers*, 15, 146.

[77] J. H. M. Staniforth and Richard S. Grayson (ed.), *At War with the 16th Irish Division 1914–1918: The Staniforth Letters* (Barnsley: Pen and Sword, 2012), 34.

[78] 'Major-General H. A. Williams to 1st ANZAC Corps, 30 April 1916, AWM25/425/26, AWM.

[79] 'Communication within a Battalion in the Trenches', 25 December 1914, 5 Division War Diary, WO95/1510, TNA.

[80] Major F. S. Garwood (OC 7 Division Signal Company), diary entry, 8 November 1914, Garwood Papers 91/23/1, Imperial War Museum (IWM), London.

[81] Priestley, *Work of the Royal Engineers*, 146.

[82] 'Director of Army Signals. Circular Memorandum No. 29', December 1914, Director of Army Signals War Diary, WO95/57, TNA.

and economy, gradually 'commanders of divisional signal companies acquired through their brigade signal officers a definite measure of control over battalion communications'.[83] As one brigade signal officer noted after the war, since he 'exercised general supervision' over the regimental signallers, he practically 'ran his own Signals show forward of Bde. H.Q.'.[84] This tacit acknowledgement of Signal Service control was strengthened further by the fact that battalion signallers received their equipment directly from the Signal Service's stores and that the training of regimental signallers became the responsibility of the OC divisional signal company, initially via classes arranged at brigade level, and from 1916 under the more centralised direction of the Divisional Signal Schools.[85] Thus, gradually Signal Service equipment and methods permeated down to the lowest levels of the BEF, giving the Signal Service far greater control and direction over the communications system than had been the case in 1914.

Specialist Communications

The growing demand for greater and more efficient communications from 1915 onwards meant that not only was the BEF's communications system extended to support the functions of a whole range of specialist arms and formations, but also new organisational structures were created to enable the effective use of some of the more innovative means of communication that were developed and employed during the course of the war. With regards to the former, the three most significant arms were undoubtedly the artillery, the Royal Flying Corps (RFC) and the Tank Corps. In the case of the latter, the growing importance of wireless communication necessitated profound changes to the way in which it was controlled and coordinated. All provided unique challenges for the BEF's communications establishment to contend with, particularly for the Signal Service, which was increasingly called upon to extend the scope of its jurisdiction into areas that had either been excluded from its remit at the start of the war, or into areas that were entirely novel.

With the commencement of trench warfare, the increasing dominance of artillery over the battlefield, coupled with the insatiable needs of the arm, brought about some of the most fundamental changes to signal

---

[83] Nalder, *Royal Corps of Signals*, 97.
[84] MacGregor and Welti (ed.), *Signals from the Great War*, 34, 115.
[85] 'Organisation of Battalion Signallers', 18 January 1916, Guards Division Signal Company War Diary, WO95/1205, TNA; Scrivenor, *Brigade Signals*, 49; Priestley, *Work of the Royal Engineers*, 45, 133.

practice and organisation.[86] At first, however, the General Staff's pre-war decision to separate artillery communications from the Signal Service's sphere of influence had a detrimental impact upon the efficiency of artillery signals. Artillery–infantry cooperation, for instance, was very ad hoc, relying largely upon a primitive system of liaison during the first months of the war. Although this worked reasonably well during the initial period of mobility, it quickly became apparent with the onset of trench warfare that drastic reorganisation was required. Hampered by inadequate numbers of personnel and by the fact that most artillery signallers in 1914 lacked suitable training in handling telephones and laying and repairing lines,[87] it soon became standard practice for the Signal Service to lay the initial telephone lines of a newly arrived artillery unit. Although the artillery signallers would operate the line thereafter, often the Signal Service was called upon to repair faults and resolve any technical problems that occurred.[88] In this way, the Signal Service gained its first foothold in the realm of artillery communications, a process that was further extended in April 1915 when a small signal office detachment for the Commander Royal Artillery (CRA) was added to the divisional signal company, and a cable detachment created for the sole purpose of laying artillery lines. Although artillery brigade signal officers, who were drawn from the Royal Artillery, were made responsible for all communications within their area, including the links between observation posts and their batteries, and for liaison with the infantry,[89] the OC divisional signal company, via his brigade signalling officer and representative with the CRA, gradually assumed control over all lines in the brigade area.[90]

Throughout 1916, the increasing demands by the artillery and its associated services – anti-aircraft batteries, flash-spotting, sound ranging, kite balloons and trench mortar batteries – became too much for the Signal Service to meet adequately under the restrictions of the existing organisation. Not only were the majority of cable circuits in forward areas required for the artillery, but they were becoming increasingly complex. Thus, during the winter of 1916–17 the decision was made to transfer all

---

[86] On the significance of artillery at the tactical and operational levels, see Bailey, *First World War*; and, Marble, 'The Infantry Cannot Do with a Gun Less'.

[87] 'Further Notes on Artillery in the Present War', November 1914, AIR1/2251/209/54/19, TNA.

[88] See, for example, 4 Division Signal Company War Diary, 4 October 1914, WO95/1471, TNA.

[89] 'Notes on Signal Communication within a Division When Holding a Defensive Line', April 1915, AWM27/311/32, AWM.

[90] Priestley, *Work of the Royal Engineers*, 57.

Plate 1.2 A New Zealand battery receiving communications on a field
telephone, Beaussart, France, 23 May 1918 (Henry Armytage Sanders:
Alexander Turnbull Library, Wellington, 1/2-013220-G)

artillery signallers into the Signal Service and to give the latter complete
control over all artillery communications down to, but not including,
battery level.[91] Five new units were added to the Signal Service's establishment just in time for the opening of the 1917 campaign (Table 1.3),
remedying one of the greatest organisational shortcomings in the BEF's
communications system.

In contrast to the artillery, from the outset of the war the planning,
direction and control of the ground communications of the RFC, along
with its related branches, the anti-aircraft and kite balloon sections and
field survey companies, was the responsibility of the GHQ and army
signal companies. While the RFC was responsible for air-to-ground
communications, the headquarters of RFC brigades, wings and squadrons were connected via a 'self-contained and self-sufficient' exchange
system, which formed part of the larger Signal Service network, though
RFC operators manned the telephone switchboards and operated the

---

[91] Nalder, *Royal Corps of Signals*, 118–19; 'History of the Development and Work of the
Directorate of Organisation. August, 1914-December, 1918', 494, WO162/6, TNA.

Table 1.3 *New Signal Units, Winter 1916–17*

Unit	Allotted To	No. of Personnel
Signal Construction Company	1 per Army	3 Officers and 116 Men
Area Signal Detachment	8 per Army	1 Officer and 15 Men
Corps Heavy Artillery Section	1 per Corps	1 Officer and 36 Men
Heavy Artillery Group, Sig. Section	1 per Group	1 Officer and 36 Men
RFA Brigade Signal Sub-section	1 per Brigade	1 Officer and 19 Men

Source: Taken from Priestley, *Work of the Royal Engineers*, 160.

telegraph instruments.[92] The formation of the RAF on 1 April 1918,[93] however, necessitated much tighter control and administration of what was to become known as Air Formation Signals, a task that was given to the newly appointed AD Signals, RAF, Lieutenant-Colonel (later Colonel) Jacob Waley-Cohen.[94] In addition, the Independent Force – the RAF's strategic bombing component – was afforded an AD Signals in July and an establishment of 7 officers and 229 men to oversee its ground communications system.[95] By the end of the war, 80 RAF ground stations were in operation, linked via an intricate wireless system.[96]

The organisation of communications for the Tank Corps[97] was particularly unique, since it was impossible to allocate a permanent system of telegraph and telephone lines to link tank formation headquarters to the rest of the BEF until it was known where and when an offensive would take place.[98] Both on the Somme in the autumn of 1916 and at Arras in April 1917, tank formation headquarters were simply

---

[92] Ibid., 188, 295; Lord and Watson, *Royal Corps of Signals*, 310; 'Lessons from Recent Operations', undated, Cambrai Lessons, WO158/316, TNA.

[93] Peter Gray, 'The Air Ministry and the Formation of the Royal Air Force', in Gary Sheffield and Peter Gray (eds.), *Changing War: The Hundred Days Campaign and the Birth of the Royal Air Force, 1918* (London: Bloomsbury, 2013), 135–48.

[94] Commissioned into the Queen's Westminster Rifle Volunteers in 1893, Waley-Cohen had served as a signal officer in the Second South African War and as OC 18th Infantry Brigade Signal Section, 1915–18. Nalder, *Royal Corps of Signals*, 580.

[95] Priestley, *Work of the Royal Engineers*, 295–6; Nalder, *Royal Corps of Signals*, 153.

[96] 'Wireless Telegraphy in the RAF from the Outbreak of the War by Colonel A. M. Grenfell', 1918, AIR1/109/15/27, TNA.

[97] Known until July 1917 as the Heavy Branch Machine Gun Corps. J. P. Harris, *Men, Ideas, and Tanks: British Military Thought and Armoured Forces, 1903–1939* (Manchester: Manchester University Press, 1995), 57.

[98] For additional context on tank communications, see Brian N. Hall, 'The Development of Tank Communications in the British Expeditionary Force, 1916–1918', in Alaric Searle (ed.), *Genesis, Employment, Aftermath: First World War Tanks and the New Warfare, 1900–1945* (Solihull: Helion, 2015), 136–62.

connected to the lines already provided, operated and maintained by
the infantry signal companies.[99] Tank units had only a very small
number of linesmen to maintain and repair their own lines, and as a
result faults were commonplace and communication between headquarters severely impaired.[100] Consequently, beginning in May
1917 three tank brigade signal companies, each consisting of a mixture
of tank and Signal Service personnel, were formed in order to facilitate
communications for and between Tank Corps, brigade and battalion
headquarters.[101] Although that was a notable improvement, one of the
principal lessons to emerge from the Battle of Cambrai in November
was the necessity for even closer liaison between the Tank Corps and
the Signal Service.[102] Thus, in late 1917 Lieutenant-Colonel John
Molesworth was appointed AD Signals, Tank Corps, a move that led
to improved signal training and tighter Tank Corps–Signal Service
coordination, the first notable fruition of which was the creation of
the 4th Tank Brigade Signal Company, the first to consist entirely of
Signal Service personnel.[103]

Finally, technological advances also led to the formation of specialist
organisations tasked with coordinating newer methods of communication, the most noteworthy of which was wireless. In January 1915, 'Q'
Wireless Section at GHQ was expanded into the GHQ Wireless
Company and a separate wireless headquarters was established, responsible for the activities of both wireless communication and intelligence.
In September, a wireless officer was attached to each army headquarters,
charged with advising the OC Army Signal Company on all wireless-
related matters and responsible for arranging experiments with new and
existing wireless equipment, and for overseeing the training of wireless
operators. This training arrangement persisted until the creation of the
Wireless Depot at Abbeville and the Central Wireless School, based at
Montreuil, in April 1916.[104] Two months prior to the school's opening,

---

[99] Priestley, *Work of the Royal Engineers*, 245–6.

[100] See, for example, 'Summary of Tank Operations 1st Brigade, Heavy Branch. 9th April–
3rd May 1917', 17 May 1917, Tank Corps War Diary, WO95/91, TNA.

[101] J. F. C. Fuller, *Tanks in the Great War 1914–1918* (New York: E. P. Dutton, 1920), 180.

[102] 'IV Corps Report on Telephone and Telegraph Communications During Operations
Commencing 20th November 1917', undated, WO158/383, TNA.

[103] Fuller, *Tanks in the Great War*, 182; Priestley, *Work of the Royal Engineers*, 246; Becke,
Order of Battle of Divisions, 268; *Instructions for the Training of the Tank Corps in France*
(Tank Corps Headquarters, December 1917), 24.

[104] Priestley, *Work of the Royal Engineers*, 161–2. The chief wireless instructor at GHQ was
Major Rupert Stanley, previously Professor of Electrical Engineering at Queen's
University, Belfast. Brian Austin, *Schonland: Scientist and Soldier: From Lightning on
the Veld to Nuclear Power at Harwell: the Life of Field Marshal Montgomery's Scientific
Adviser* (London: IOP Press, 2001), 48; Major Rupert Stanley, WO339/10841, TNA.

the OC Wireless, GHQ, Lieutenant-Colonel Lyster Blandy,[105] was officially charged with coordinating all wireless throughout the BEF, and in July, 'in view of the increasing importance of wireless telegraphy as a means of communication in the field',[106] army wireless companies were formed. Although these wireless companies were independent of the army signal companies, because they were under the control of the OC Wireless, GHQ, they composed sections for each corps and sub-sections for each division, thus representing an important step in the decentralisation of wireless in the BEF.[107]

This process of decentralisation was furthered in June 1917 when the post of OC Wireless, GHQ, was abolished and coordination of the BEF's wireless activities transferred to the newly created AD Signals, Wireless, who served on the Director of Army Signals' staff.[108] Thereafter, GHQ's wireless activities were limited to the Wireless Observation Groups, whose primary function was to intercept German wireless communication, a formation which was subsequently duplicated and passed to army control.[109] Meanwhile, the wireless sections and subsections in each army, corps and division were absorbed into the respective signal companies, ending the semi-autonomy and separation of wireless from the Signal Service,[110] and sparking greater interest in wireless communication within divisional signal companies and brigade signal sections.[111]

Growth of the Communications Establishment

The exponential growth of the BEF, from six infantry divisions and one cavalry division totalling approximately 150,000 men in 1914, to a peak force of 66 divisions numbering more than two million men in 1918,[112] generated a dramatic increase in the communication needs of the army. This in turn necessitated a substantial growth in the size of the Signal Service as it sought to provide communications 'on an immense and

---

[105] 'Colonel/Air Commodore L. F. Blandy, CB, DSO', *Royal Engineers Journal*, 78 (1964), 340.

[106] 'General Staff Circular No. 21. Wireless Telegraphy', 23 September 1916, AWM25/425/3, AWM.

[107] Nalder, *Royal Corps of Signals*, 121.   [108] Priestley, *Work of the Royal Engineers*, 164.

[109] Beach, *Haig's Intelligence*, 160–1.

[110] 'O.B./242', 17 June 1917, AWM25/425/3, AWM.

[111] 'General Report on Wireless Telegraph Communication in the Canadian Corps, Feb. 1915–Dec. 1918', 16 April 1919, RG9-III-D-3/5058/968, LAC.

[112] Richard Bryson, 'The Once and Future Army', in Brian Bond et al., *'Look to Your Front': Studies in the First World War by the British Commission for Military History* (Staplehurst: Spellmount, 1999), 28.

elaborate scale'.[113] The most dramatic areas of expansion occurred within the GHQ and Lines of Communication ('L') signal companies. In 1914, GHQ Signal Company consisted of 5 officers and 75 other ranks, while 'L' Signal Company numbered 5 officers and 263 other ranks. They also consituted three airline and six cable sections, totalling an additional 9 officers and 381 other ranks. By October 1916, GHQ Signal Company alone had expanded to 6 officers and 129 other ranks, and in April 1918 numbered 13 officers and 315 men.[114] In 1918, the two signal companies were amalgamated into the GHQ Signal Battalion, which totalled 40 officers and 1,784 other ranks. Combined with the five telegraph construction and six railway telegraph companies that worked behind the army areas, the grand total working on the lines of communication at the end of the war amounted to an incredible 73 officers and 3,232 other ranks (Figure 1.1).[115]

Upon their creation in late 1914, the army signal companies each consisted of 7 officers and 142 other ranks. By 1916, this number had increased to 10 officers and 224 men, and by the end of the war an army signal company boasted 15 officers and 340 other ranks. During this period of growth a wireless section, consisting initially of 1 officer and 23 other ranks, had been added in 1917, the army artillery sub-sections taken over in the same year, and a wireless observation group and light railway signal company, totalling 3 officers and 116 men, established in 1918. In addition, one signal construction company, three motor airline and two cable sections had been added by 1918, and an army signal school of four officers and 10 NCO instructors established (Figure 1.2).[116] Taken as a whole, and notwithstanding corps and divisional signal units and artillery signal sub-sections, by the end of the war a DD Signals commanded approximately 32 officers and 815 other ranks.[117]

A corps signal company at the beginning of the war consisted of just 4 officers and 63 other ranks, which included 18 motorcycle despatch riders and 20 signal office staff.[118] Although gradual increases to the number of personnel were made during the first half of the war, it was not until 1917 that major changes in corps signal company organisation occurred. Again, this was in many respects a reflection of the growing

---

[113] General Sir Douglas Haig's Official Despatch, 23 December 1916, in Boraston (ed.), *Sir Douglas Haig's Despatches*, 56.

[114] 'History of the Development and Work of the Directorate of Organisation. August, 1914–December, 1918', 487, WO162/6, TNA.

[115] Priestley, *Work of the Royal Engineers*, 340–2.

[116] Ibid., 337–40; Collins, *Military Organization*, 355–6.

[117] Nalder, *Royal Corps of Signals*, 84.   [118] *Field Service Pocket Book. 1914*, 61.

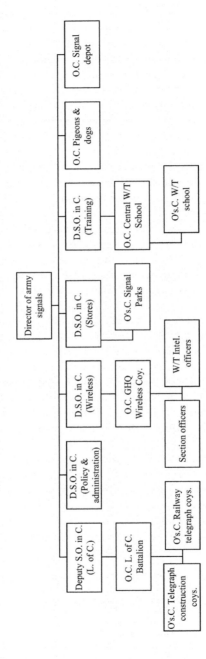

Figure 1.1 Signal Service organisation (GHQ), November 1918

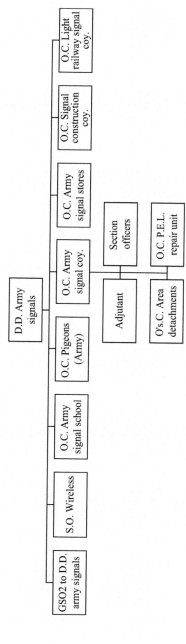

Figure 1.2 Signal Service organisation (Army), November 1918

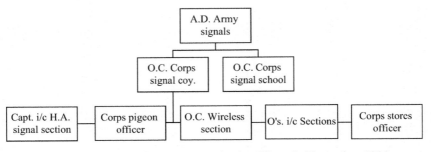

Figure 1.3 Signal Service organisation (Corps), November 1918

importance of the role and responsibilities of corps during the war.[119] Not only was a Wireless Section, consisting of 3 NCOs and 24 men, added to the corps signal company, but a Corps Heavy Artillery Signal Section, comprising 1 officer and 36 other ranks, was also created. In addition, corps signal schools were established in the same year, comprising 1 officer and 5 NCO instructors. Arguably the most important development, however, was the creation of permanent area signal detachments, each initially comprising 1 officer and 8 men (8 per army), responsible for ensuring continuity in line construction, maintenance and operation when reliefs took place.[120] Thus, at the end of the war a corps signal company numbered 8 officers and 191 other ranks, in addition to two motor airline and two cable sections (Figure 1.3).[121] The exception to this, however, was the Canadian Corps, which, by virtue of its larger size, possessed four cable sections in 1918.[122]

In 1914, a divisional signal company consisted of a headquarters and four sections.[123] No. 1 Section was made up of three cable detachments, each possessing 10 miles of cable and capable of establishing three telegraph offices ('base', 'intermediate' and 'travelling'),[124] as well as the staff which manned the divisional signal office. Also possessing four mounted orderlies, eight cyclists and nine motorcycle despatch riders, No. 1 Section had the primary responsibility of establishing communications between divisional and brigade headquarters, and between

[119] Simpson, *Directing Operations*, passim.   [120] Nalder, *Royal Corps of Signals*, 84, 110.
[121] Priestley, *Work of the Royal Engineers*, 336–7.
[122] Brigadier-General Sir J. E. Edmonds, *Military Operations, France and Belgium, 1918*, Vol. V (London: HMSO, 1947), appendix III, 624; Shane B. Schreiber, *Shock Army of the British Empire: The Canadian Corps in the Last 100 Days of the Great War* (Westport, CT: Praeger, 1997), 20–2.
[123] *Manual of Army Signal Service – War*, 22.
[124] Colonel F. J. Davies, C.B., 'The Communications of a Division in the Field', *Journal of the Royal United Service Institution*, 53 (1909), 888.

neighbouring divisions.[125] Sections 2, 3 and 4 were each allocated to the infantry brigades, charged principally with connecting brigade and battalion headquarters to one another, and each comprising 1 officer and 26 other ranks. In all, the divisional signal company totalled 5 officers and 170 other ranks. By 1918, this number had expanded to 15 officers and 400 other ranks.[126] In the process, a fourth cable detachment had been added in 1915 for the purpose of laying artillery communications, before the headquarters of the Royal Artillery Signal Section and the field brigade artillery sub-sections were absorbed in early 1917. Finally, in 1918 No. 5 (Machine Gun) Section was added, which consisted of 1 officer and 20 other ranks drawn largely from the Machine Gun Corps, and the personnel within the divisional signal company headquarters increased from 1 officer and 44 men in 1914 to 3 officers and 173 men in 1918 (Figure 1.4).[127] On paper, the establishment of the infantry brigade signal section remained largely unchanged until the last year of the war, when a second officer and three 'pigeoneers' were added. In reality, the creation of 'brigade pools' in 1917, which consisted of eight specially trained signallers drawn from each battalion in the brigade, significantly reinforced the brigade signal section's manpower, though there was never a shortage of complaints about the inadequate number of sufficiently trained reinforcements amongst forward signal units.[128]

Finally, with regards to cavalry communications, in 1914 the Cavalry Division was served by a signal squadron, organised into four troops: 'A' Troop consisted of two wagon wireless detachments responsible for communication with GHQ; 'B' Troop was made up of two cable detachments, having 28 miles of cable in total, and employed to facilitate communication between cavalry division headquarters and the wireless stations of the squadron, or to connect the former to the civil telegraph system; 'C' Troop consisted of one wagon and three pack wireless detachments, charged with establishing communications between cavalry division and brigade headquarters; and, 'D' Troop, which comprised 12 mounted men, 28 cyclists, 6 motorcycle despatch riders and two motorcars, was responsible for an array of communication duties throughout the division. The signal troop of a cavalry brigade consisted of an officer and 23 other ranks capable of laying and operating 7.5 miles of cable, with eight portable telephones, and augmented by a wireless detachment comprising two pack sets. Its primary responsibilities were communication within the brigade and connecting with the permanent

[125] *Field Service Pocket Book: 1914*, 60; Curtis, 'Work of Signal Units in War', 268.
[126] Priestley, *Work of the Royal Engineers*, 334–5.   [127] Nalder, *Royal Corps of Signals*, 83.
[128] Priestley, *Work of the Royal Engineers*, 146, 296–9; Scrivenor, *Brigade Signals*, 86.

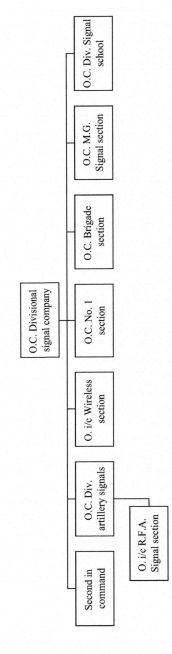

Figure 1.4 Signal Service organisation (Division), November 1918

telecommunications network of the country.[129] When the Cavalry Corps was formed in October 1914,[130] a signal squadron consisting of 4 officers and 101 men was added, though little change occurred thereafter in the size of the squadron, or indeed in the cavalry communications establishment as a whole, until 1918, when the most notable addition was the Cavalry Wireless Squadron, comprising 3 officers and 136 men, which replaced the wireless troops of the divisional signal squadron.[131]

Signal Research, Design and Supply

The enlargement of the BEF's communications establishment resulted inevitably in the huge demand for signal equipment. Throughout the war, responsibility for the supply of signal stores rested with F.W.9, a branch of the Director of Fortifications and Works. Headed by Major Algernon Dumaresq, the chief electrical engineer, and with the help of just two officers and six other ranks in August 1914, F.W.9 grew to comprise 12 officers and 34 subordinates by the end of the war. However, the pressure of the job took its toll on Dumaresq, who died suddenly in his office in May 1917.[132] His successor, Lieutenant-Colonel Edwin Seaman, also succumbed to a similar fate, dying of a stroke in May 1919.[133] Throughout this period, F.W.9 was assisted by the Chief Inspector of R. E. Stores at Woolwich, Captain (later Colonel) Frederick Robertson, whose staff grew from 4 officers and 165 other ranks upon mobilisation, to 30 officers and 1,620 subordinates by October 1918. The stores F.W.9 supplied the BEF included 11,000 telegraph sets, 120,000 telephone instruments, 100,000 signalling lamps and 600,000 miles of telephone cable. It was also responsible for supplying wireless sets to the RFC.[134]

In September 1916 a Signals Experimental Establishment was set up on Woolwich Common, under the initial command of Chief Experimental Officer Colonel Arthur Bagnold.[135] As the precursor of

---

[129] *Field Service Pocket Book: 1914*, 60; Curtis, 'Work of Signal Units in War', 268; *Manual of Army Signal Service – War*, 20; Collins, *Military Organization*, 356–7.

[130] Becke (Comp.), *Order of Battle of Divisions*, 123.

[131] Priestley, *Work of the Royal Engineers*, 332, 343; Nalder, *Royal Corps of Signals*, 83.

[132] Brigadier-General W. Baker Brown, 'Hints from History (Part II). The Supply of Engineer Stores and Equipment', *Royal Engineers Journal*, 56 (1942), 282–3.

[133] Anon., 'Memoir: Col. E. C. Seaman', *Royal Engineers Journal*, 30 (1919), 139–42.

[134] Major-General H. L. Pritchard (ed.), *History of the Corps of Royal Engineers*, Vol. V: *the Home Front, France, Flanders and Italy in the First World War* (Chatham: Institution of Royal Engineers, 1952), 82–4.

[135] 'Obituary Notices: Arthur Henry Bagnold', *Monthly Notices of the Royal Astronomical Society*, 104 (1944), 86; W. B. B., 'Memoir: Colonel A. H. Bagnold', *Royal Engineers Journal*, 58 (1944), 131–2.

the Signals Research and Development Establishment, it employed 17 officers and 267 other ranks, and was charged with designing, adapting and testing specialist signalling equipment that could not be obtained from other sources. Also in 1916, at the request of the Director of Army Signals a Signal Service Committee was established and a separate branch of the War Office, F.W.7, was subsequently formed, responsible for coordinating the activities of the many contractors, departments and organisations involved in signal equipment research, design and experimentation. These included, amongst others, the Munitions and Inventions Committee, the Marconi Company, the GPO, the RFC Wireless Telegraphy School and the R.E. Wireless Training Centre.[136]

The system of supply on the Western Front was, from the outset, firmly under Signal Service control.[137] All signalling equipment was held at a Signal Park, which opened at the Advanced Base at Amiens in mid-August 1914 under the administration of the DD Signals, Lines of Communication.[138] In light of the BEF's situation, however, the park was relocated at the end of the month to Le Mans, where it remained until the end of the year, when it was moved to its final location at Le Havre. A second park was opened at Calais later in the war and smaller parks established within army areas shortly before the war's end.[139] Strict control of signal stores meant that all requests had to receive approval from the office of the Director of Army Signals before being sanctioned. Naturally, priority was given to requests made by signal units either about to take part in a large-scale offensive, or residing in a sector of the front that was facing an imminent enemy attack.[140] Maintenance of signal equipment, meanwhile, was the responsibility of individual signal companies, although each army also set up repair workshops. In February 1917, official Signal Repair Workshops were built at Le Havre, dealing mainly with equipment too badly damaged for the army workshops to repair. Although personnel from 'L' Signal

[136] Nalder, *Royal Corps of Signals*, 86–7; Pritchard (ed.), *History of the Corps of Royal Engineers*, 83; Baker Brown, 'Hints from History, Part II', 283; Lieutenant-Colonel A. G. T. Cusins, R.E., 'Development of Army Wireless During the War: Lecture Delivered before the Wireless Section of the (London Wireless) Institution, 3 April, 1919', *Journal of the Institution of Electrical Engineers*, 59 (1921), 766–7, Sir Henry Norman Papers, 01/15/3, IWM.
[137] *Manual of Army Signal Service – War*, 37.
[138] 'Director of Army Signals, Circular Memorandum No. 10', 19 August 1914, Director of Army Signals War Diary, WO95/57, TNA.
[139] Priestley, *Work of the Royal Engineers*, 49–50.
[140] See, for example, 'Director of Army Signals, Circular Memorandum No. 220', 19 December 1917, Director of Army Signals War Diary, WO95/57, TNA.

Company supervised the workshops, the majority of the technical main-tenance workers were German POWs.[141]

Overall, the growth in both the size and complexity of the BEF's communications establishment conformed to the overall pattern of expansion experienced by the army as a whole during the course of the war. In 1914, the Signal Service was marked by its diminutive size and the absence of a central chain of command, as well as being handicapped by restrictions imposed upon its sphere of influence, most notably within the artillery and infantry battalions. Humble, ad hoc and inadequate coordination and supervision during the first half of the war, however, gradually gave way to a far larger, more influential and more proficient organisation, though it was not until 1916–17, first with the appoint-ments of DD Signals and AD Signals for armies and corps, and second with the absorption of artillery communications into the Signal Service's jurisdiction, that the control, direction, scale and provision of the BEF's communications machinery began to mature. Even then, problems remained, most notably at the strategic level with the inadequate control and direction exercised by the War Office until the establishment of S.D.6 in early 1918. Nevertheless, through an evolutionary process of trial and error, by the end of the war the BEF had in the Signal Service an organisation more than capable of meeting the insatiable communication needs of the army.

---

[141] Priestley, *Work of the Royal Engineers*, 295. For more information on the BEF's use of German labour companies, see Heather Jones, *Violence against Prisoners of War in the First World War: Britain, France and Germany, 1914–1920* (Cambridge: Cambridge University Press, 2011), 137–40.

2   Personnel, Recruitment and Training

> The signallers, privileged people, have a secret life of their own and maintain endless conversations full of technicalities and private jokes, with an occupational hazard of no small seriousness. Very often their conversation stops dead. 'Dis-' says the signaller, and goes out alone into the night, presumably under fire, to follow his line across the fields until he finds, and mends, the break, perhaps disconnected by a shell-burst, perhaps by the carrying party ... stumbling against it.[1]

Charles Carrington's description of one of the many tasks performed by the BEF's signallers during the First World War captures neatly the manner in which the signallers were regarded by the rest of the army; a view shared by one historian who described them as 'a somewhat alien group of specialists who observed their own chain of command and their own black arts'.[2] Although the effectiveness of the BEF's communications system was, broadly speaking, dependent upon the calibre of the technology employed and upon the way in which it was organised, the quality of its personnel was also of crucial importance. In fact, any organisation and the technology it employs are only as good as the people who compose and operate it.[3] Studies of the BEF's communications system, however, tend to say very little about the personnel dimension, preferring instead to concentrate on the organisational or technological facets.[4] As pointed out in the Introduction, this anomaly

---

[1] Charles Carrington, *Soldier from the Wars Returning* (London: Hutchinson, 1965), 93. For additional context on Carrington's wartime experiences and subsequent writings, see Brian Bond, *Survivors of a Kind: Memoirs of the Western Front* (London: Continuum, 2008), 13–26.

[2] Paddy Griffith, 'The Extent of Tactical Reform in the British Army', in Griffith (ed.), *British Fighting Methods*, 8.

[3] This is often referred to as an organisation's 'human capital asset', defined as 'the collective sum of the attributes, life experience, knowledge, inventiveness, energy, and enthusiasm' of its personnel. See Leslie A. Weatherly, *Human Capital – the Elusive Asset: Measuring and Managing Human Capital: A Strategic Imperative for HR* (Alexandria: Society for Human Resource Management, 2003), 1.

[4] Priestley, *Work of the Royal Engineers*; Rawling, 'Communications in the Canadian Corps'; Bullock and Lyons, *Missed Signals*.

54

can partly be explained by the dearth of personal papers, correspondence and diaries belonging to senior Signal Service officers. However, a number of historians have begun to utilise army personnel files, amongst other sources, to shed new light on our understanding of individual formations within the BEF.[5] Using a similar socio-military approach, it is possible to piece together a more detailed picture of the officers and men who constituted the BEF's communications system than has so far been the case, and in the process provide an illuminating example of the way in which the army sought to harness the skills of its citizen soldiers in a modern 'total war'. This chapter, therefore, seeks to provide answers to three crucial questions: First, who were the BEF's signallers? Second, how were they perceived by the rest of the army? Third, and finally, what training did they undergo? Because of the availability of sources and the remit of their work, the officer cadre of the Signal Service will form the primary focus of the subsequent analysis, though not to the complete exclusion of the other ranks of the Signal Service, or indeed signallers within other arms.

The Directors

The most senior Signal Service officer on the Western Front was John Fowler, who held the post of Director of Army Signals continuously from August 1914 until the armistice.[6] The fact that he did so immediately suggests that Fowler was the right man for the right job. Having received a direct commission into the Royal Engineers in 1886, Fowler was 25 years old when he joined the Telegraph Battalion 3 years later. Obtaining engineering qualifications alongside certificates from the Army Veterinary School and the Hythe School of Musketry, he saw

---

[5] See, for example: Jim Beach, '"Intelligent Civilians in Uniform": The British Expeditionary Force's Intelligence Corps Officers, 1914–1918', *War & Society*, 27 (2008), 1–22; and, Timothy Bowman, 'Officering Kitchener's Armies: A Case Study of the 36th (Ulster) Division', *War in History*, 16 (2009), 189–212. For additional context, see Richard S. Grayson, 'Military History from the Street: New Methods for Researching First World War Service in the British Military', *War in History*, 21 (2014), 465–95.

[6] Unless stated otherwise, this section is based upon the following biographical sources: 'Naval and Military: Official Appointments and Notices', *Times*, 5 November 1923, 24; 'Obituaries: Lieut.-Gen. Sir John Fowler. Development of Army "Signals"', *Times*, 21 September 1939, 10; Anon., 'Memoir: Lieutenant-General Sir John Fowler', *Royal Engineers Journal*, 53 (1939), 580–83; Nalder, *Royal Corps of Signals*, 526; R.M.A., 'Esto Pernox: A Story of Lieutenant-General Sir John Fowler, KCB, KCMG, DSO', *Journal of the Royal Signals Institution*, 7 (1966), 177–84; and, Alan Harfield, 'Lieutenant-General Sir John Sharman Fowler, KCB, KCMG, DSO', *Journal of the Society for Army Historical Research*, 70 (1992), 67–70.

service in India during the 1890s and received the DSO.[7] Fowler entered the Staff College at Camberley on a nomination in January 1898, successfully completing the course at the end of the following year alongside fellow graduates George Milne, Walter Braithwaite and Aylmer Hunter-Weston.[8] After serving as Director of Telegraphs in the Orange River Colony during the Boer War, Fowler then spent the decade prior to 1914 serving in a variety of staff and command posts, most notably DAA and QMG, 2 Division (1905–9); instructor at the Staff College, Camberley (1911–13) and Commandant of the Army Signal School at Aldershot (1913–14).[9] This wealth of practical experience led to his appointment as Director of Army Signals upon mobilisation in 1914.

Mentioned eight times in despatches, Fowler ended the war a major-general and was knighted for his services in 1918.[10] Sir John French praised Fowler's 'skill and energy' during the retreat from Mons in 1914, while Sir Douglas Haig acknowledged Fowler's 'heavy and responsible duties' during the course of the German offensives in 1918, which were 'discharged... with most commendable smoothness and efficiency'.[11] According to one anonymous eulogist, Fowler 'was very far-seeing – leaving the execution of work and the examination of new ideas to experts. He was, in fact, an ideal Director, a charming personality, accessible, receptive, valued by those in authority senior to him, and able without pressure to get the best work out of his subordinates'.[12] Two

---

[7] He was captured and wounded during the Chitral campaign (1895), which subsequently won him promotion to captain and awarding of the DSO. Letters and papers relating to Fowler's experience can be viewed at the National Army Museum, London.

[8] Later Field Marshal Lord Milne, CIGS (1926–1933); General Sir Walter Braithwaite, adjutant-general to the forces (1927–31) and Lieutenant-General Sir Aylmer Hunter-Weston, GOC VIII Corps (1915–18). *New Annual Army List, Militia List, and Yeomanry Cavalry List, for 1900* (London: John Murray, 1900), 121. On the pre-war Staff College, see Brian Bond, *The Victorian Army and the Staff College 1854–1914* (London: Eyre Methuen, 1972); and, Harris, 'Men Who Planned the War', 44–75.

[9] He was promoted lieutenant-colonel in January 1911. *Hart's Annual Army List, Special Reserve List, and Territorial Force List, for 1914* (London: John Murray, 1914), 41; Brigadier-General W. Baker Brown, *History of the Corps of Royal Engineers*, Vol. 4 (Chatham: Institute of Royal Engineers, 1952), 307.

[10] After the war, Fowler was appointed the first commandant of the newly created Royal Corps of Signals in September 1923, retaining the position until 1934. Between 1922 and 1925 he was GOC British Forces in China. Promoted lieutenant-general in 1926, Fowler retired in 1928 and died on 20 September 1939.

[11] 'The Aisne', 8 October 1914, in Field-Marshal Viscount French, *The Despatches of Lord French* (London: Chapman and Hall, 1917), 61; 'The Great German Offensive', 20 July 1918, in Boraston (ed.), *Sir Douglas Haig's Despatches*, 240.

[12] Anon., 'Memoir', 582.

Plate 2.1 Sir John Sharman Fowler, Director of Army Signals, BEF, 1914–1918 (Walter Stoneman, 1921, National Portrait Gallery, NPG x67268)

examples, in particular, highlight Fowler's willingness to seek civilian expertise and to implement new ideas in order to improve the BEF's communications system. Both occurred in the spring and early summer of 1915. In the first instance, Fowler was called upon to settle a minor disagreement between the Director of Army Signals, Home Forces, Colonel Andrew Ogilvie and the Postal Telegraph Clerks' Association concerning the employment of over-age GPO men deemed unfit for service in divisional signal companies. The association's suggestion that men between the ages of 38 and 45 would be best suited to office telegraphy work along the lines of communication was then referred to the commandant of the Signal Service Training Centre, Reginald Boys, who in turn passed the matter on to Fowler to resolve. Fowler's response was unequivocally enthusiastic, asking Boys immediately to make the necessary arrangements to draft 100 such men to lines of communication offices.[13]

Clearly, Fowler was receptive to new ideas if it meant that the Signal Service would benefit as a result. The second example, however, demonstrated Fowler's capacity to seek the assistance of civilian experts and had even greater ramifications for both the Signal Service and the BEF as a whole. Reacting to the Signal Service's dwindling supplies of reliable technical equipment,[14] in early 1915 Fowler called upon the assistance of Colonel Thomas Purves, head of the Design Section of the GPO,[15] to travel to France and make 'a systematic study of war conditions, with a view to replacing the many instruments developed by local ingenuity by standard and improved designs'.[16] This was the beginning of an extremely important and fruitful wartime relationship, which saw the GPO supply the Signal Service with stores to the value of £6.5 million. This included 90,000 telegraph/telephone poles, 400,000 miles of copper, bronze and iron wire and 47,000 miles of specially designed trench cable. The GPO also provided new and specialist equipment designed to meet the requirements of trench warfare, including 40,000 trench telephone sets, 36,000 telephone switchboards and 10,000 portable exchanges.[17] Although the GPO was not the sole provider of the Signal Service's stores,[18] according to one signal officer, by the end of the war 'Post Office methods and Post Office material were adopted as standard' in the Signal Service, while the training of its personnel was 'very largely based on Post Office practice'.[19] The relationship between

---

[13] Ogilvie to Sutton, 17 April 1915, Qualifications for Enlistment in the Army Signal Service, POST30/4061B/12/4, Boys to Ogilvie, 5 June 1915, POST30/4061B/12/13, BT Archives (BTA), London.

[14] Captain Basil Williams, *Raising and Training the New Armies* (London: Constable, 1918), 77. The effect this shortage of equipment had upon signal training will be discussed later in this chapter.

[15] Later, Colonel Sir Thomas F. Purves, Engineer-in-Chief of the GPO. *Nature: International Weekly Journal of Science*, 130 (10 December 1932), 874.

[16] Purves subsequently became the chief liaison officer between the Signal Service and the GPO for the remainder of the war. Brigadier-General Sir J. E. Edmonds, *Military Operations, France and Belgium, 1916*, Vol. 1 (London: HMSO, 1932), 72–3. See also: Priestley, *Work of the Royal Engineers*, 167.

[17] Lieutenant W. J. Gwilliam, R.E., 'A Signal Master on Active Service', *Post Office Electrical Engineers' Journal*, 8 (1915–16), 262–63; Anon., 'Complimentary Dinner to Sir Andrew Ogilvie', *Post Office Electrical Engineers' Journal*, 13 (1920–21), 70–71; Pritchard (ed.), *History of the Corps of Royal Engineers*, Vol. V, 35.

[18] The Marconi Company, for example, supplied much of the BEF's wireless equipment. W. J. Baker, *A History of the Marconi Company* (London: Routledge, 1970), 164–8. See, also, Chapter 1.

[19] Captain J. G. Hines, R.E., 'The Training of Permanent Linemen in the Army Signal Service', *Post Office Electrical Engineers' Journal*, 12 (1919–20), 21.

the Signal Service and the GPO highlights an important aspect of the way in which the BEF sought to resolve one of the major challenges of waging modern, industrialised war; a relationship which owed a great deal to Fowler's initial foresight and pragmatic initiative, itself a reflection of a wider cultural trait within the British Army at the time.[20]

Equally astute and adept were Fowler's immediate subordinates, the Deputy Directors of Army Signals (DD Signals). Just nine men occupied these important posts (one per army) from their inception in February 1916 until the armistice, two of whom, William Newbigging (Third Army) and Robert Earle (Fourth Army), in their entirety. All were either pre-war Regular or Territorial officers who had had distinguished military careers.[21] Newbigging, for instance, was remembered by Sir Gerald Hurst as 'an impressive figure' with 'inspiring energy' who, whilst a battalion adjutant, had won the DSO for leading the attack of the 1/Manchester Regiment at Elandslaagte in October 1899.[22] Newbigging remained with the Manchesters until July 1912, when he became chief instructor of the Army Signal School at Aldershot, and upon the outbreak of the war he was appointed OC III Corps Signal Company.[23] His intellectual prowess was noted by Randall Davidson, the Archbishop of Canterbury,[24] who, having visited Third Army headquarters at St. Pol on 19 May 1916, recorded in his diary how Newbigging had given him 'an amazing explanation' of the army's signal arrangements, which was 'bewildering in extent and elaboration'.[25]

---

[20] According to one historian, the outcome of the fighting on the Western Front demonstrated that 'British pragmatism trumped German rationalism'. Boff, *Winning and Losing on the Western Front*, 249. On the pragmatic nature of the British officer corps, see: Brown, *British Logistics*, 231–40; and, David French, 'Doctrine and Organization in the British Army, 1919–1932', *Historical Journal*, 44 (2001), 497–515.

[21] Sir O'Moore Creagh and E. M. Humphris (eds.), *The V.C. and D.S.O.*, Vol. 2 (London: Standard Art, 1924), 367, 389–90, 398; ibid., Vol. 3, 362.

[22] Gerald B. Hurst, *With Manchesters in the East* (Manchester: Manchester University Press, 1918), 2; Sir Gerald Hurst, K.C., *Closed Chapters* (Manchester: Manchester University Press, 1942), 51. Having served as an officer in 7/Manchesters in South Africa and during the First World War, Hurst became the MP for Manchester Moss Side (1918–35) and later served as a county court judge.

[23] *Hart's Annual Army List, 1914*, 120; Becke (Comp.), *History of the Great War*, 146.

[24] Randall Thomas Davidson, Archbishop of Canterbury between 1903 and 1928. Stuart Mews, 'Davidson, Randall Thomas, Baron Davidson of Lambeth (1848–1930)', *Oxford Dictionary of National Biography*, www.oxforddnb.com/view/article/32733 [accessed 19 February 2015].

[25] Michael Snape (ed.), 'Archbishop Davidson's Visit to the Western Front, May 1916', in Melanie Barber and Stephen Taylor, with Gabriel Sewell (eds.), *From the Reformation to the Permissive Society: A Miscellany in Celebration of the 400th Anniversary of Lambeth Palace Library* (Woodbridge: Church of England Record Society, 2010), 488.

The personal attributes of these men also bore a striking resemblance to those displayed by Fowler. For example, while General Sir Horace Smith-Dorrien described Arthur Hildebrand (Second Army) as 'that most resourceful of men',[26] who 'never failed us for an instant',[27] Major-General Geoffrey Rawson remembered Edmund Godfrey-Faussett (Fifth Army) as 'a Commander who inspired affection, loyalty and enthusiasm in his Officers, NCOs and men, and who possessed the great attribute that while being master of every detail of his job, he would decentralise and trust his subordinates and stand by them in cases of trouble'.[28] In addition, further evidence of the Signal Service's close affiliation with the GPO is revealed in the case of Ernest Turner, who was the GPO's chief engineer in Ireland before the war. As the DD Signals of the BEF's Lines of Communication, he was, in effect, Fowler's second in command throughout the war.[29]

Finally, Assistant Directors of Army Signals (AD Signals) were appointed to corps headquarters from November 1916. Notwithstanding those who assumed the role in an acting capacity, a total of 42 officers served as AD Signals during the war.[30] Using medal rolls, *Army Lists* and other sources, it has been possible to establish that, as with the DD Signals, all of the AD Signals were either pre-war Regular or Territorial officers, highly skilled and experienced. Frederick Stratton, for example, who in later life would become Professor of Astrophysics at the University of Cambridge and President of the Royal Astronomical Society, had organised a signal company in the Cambridge University Officers' Training Corps prior to the war which conducted important early experiments with wireless telegraphy.[31] Commissioned into the Territorial Army in 1910, he was appointed OC 20 Division Signal Company in 1915, and in June 1917 he was promoted to AD Signals XIX Corps. Mentioned five times in Despatches, 'Chubby' Stratton was admired by his subordinates for his cheerfulness,

---

[26] General Sir Horace Smith-Dorrien, *Memories of Forty-Eight Years' Service* (London: John Murray, 1925), 398.

[27] Smith-Dorrien Diary, 10 September 1914, CAB45/206, TNA.

[28] G.G.R., 'Memoirs: Brigadier-General E. G. Godfrey-Faussett', *Royal Engineers Journal*, 56 (1942), 331.

[29] *Post Office Circular*. Tuesday, 26 June 1917, No. 2357, 255; *Manual of Army Signal Service – War*, 14–15; Nalder, *The Royal Corps of Signals*, 566.

[30] Becke (Comp.), *History of the Great War*, 123–268.

[31] R. O. Redman, 'Stratton, Frederick John Marrian (1881–1960)', *Oxford Dictionary of National Biography*, www.oxforddnb.com/view/article/36346 [accessed 20 February 2015].

displaying remarkable energy and proficiency even when having gone days without sufficient sleep.[32]

As with the DD Signals, some of the AD Signals also had strong connections to the GPO. Both Wilfred Carey (XVIII Corps, 1917–18) and James Day (II Corps, 1916–17) had been employed as executive engineers of the GPO in Ireland before the war, while Ralph Chenevix-Trench (Cavalry Corps, 1917–18) had been the Assistant Director of Posts and Telegraphs in Sudan between 1913 and 1916.[33] Furthermore, while two AD Signals, Hubert Clementi-Smith (XXII Corps, 1918) and Frederick Iles (X Corps, 1916–18), ended the war as DD Signals (Second and Fifth Armies, respectively),[34] other AD Signals rose to hold positions of considerable influence in the British Army after the war. Lionel Sadleir-Jackson (Cavalry Corps, 1916–17), who was appointed GOC 54th Infantry Brigade in late 1917 and wounded in August 1918 during the capture of Albert,[35] commanded the North Russian Relief Force in Archangel in 1919–20.[36] During the Second World War, Chenevix-Trench served as the Signal Officer-in-Chief of the BEF, 1939–40, while Robert Naylor (X Corps, 1918) was appointed GOC lines of communication, 21st Army Group, in 1944.[37]

Taken as a whole, the directors of the BEF's Signal Service shared a number of intrinsic characteristics, the most notable of which was that they were all either Regular or Territorial officers. This finding would seem to support Tim Travers' view of an insular, 'personalised system' of command operating within the British Army.[38] Despite the influx of volunteer signal officers during the war, it would appear that none progressed far up the career ladder to infiltrate the senior ranks of the Signal Service. However, the BEF had in the directors of the Signal Service some of the most experienced, qualified and forward-thinking

[32] Donald Portway, *Memoirs of an Academic Old Contemptible* (London: Leo Cooper, 1971), 141; James Chadwick, 'Frederick John Marrian Stratton, 1880–1960', *Biographical Memoirs of Fellows of the Royal Society*, 7 (1961), 288.

[33] *Post Office Circular.* Tuesday, 16 January 1916, No. 2332, 21; *Post Office Circular.* Tuesday, 13 February 1917, No. 2337, 61; Nalder, *Royal Corps of Signals*, 517.

[34] Creagh and Humphris (eds.), *V.C. and D.S.O.*, Vol. 2, 389–90.

[35] Frank Davies and Graham Maddocks, *Bloody Red Tabs: General Officer Casualties of the Great War, 1914–1918* (London: Leo Cooper, 1995), 190.

[36] G. R. Singleton-Gates, *Bolos and Barishynas: Being an Account of the Doings of the Sadleir-Jackson Brigade, and Altham Flotilla, on the North Dvina during the Summer, 1919* (Aldershot: Gale & Polden, 1920); Brigadier R. Chenevix-Trench, 'A Signal Officer in North Russia, 1918–1919', *Journal of the Royal United Services Institution*, 104 (1959), 341–48.

[37] Nalder, *Royal Corps of Signals*, 547; Godfrey, *British Army Communications*, 73–4.

[38] Travers, *Killing Ground*, 26.

individuals in the army. Their personal and professional connections to the GPO, in particular, were exploited brilliantly, providing the Signal Service not only with invaluable technical and material assistance, but also, as will be shown, with a ready supply of skilled employees who would form the basis of the Signal Service's manpower.

Signal Officers

While the appointment of well-trained and experienced officers at the highest echelons of the Signal Service did not appear to create any major headaches or concerns, as the war progressed the appointment of middle-ranking and junior officers did. Although the original cadre of Signal Service officers (75 Regular and 103 Territorial) contained a number of prominent individuals who would go on to have either long and distinguished military careers, such as Edmund Osborne[39] and Ronald Penney,[40] or hold important positions in post-war civilian life, such as Stanley Angwin,[41] they and the men they commanded were simply too few in number, a problem compounded by the heavy casualties they sustained during the opening months of the war and the implications of the British government's decision to raise a mass citizen army to fight on the Continent.[42] As early as March 1915, a memorandum issued by GHQ acknowledged 'the deficiency of trained men for telegraphic and telephonic communication in the field' and the 'lack of

[39] Lieutenant-General Edmund Osborne (1885–1969), OC 7 Division Signal Company, 1914–15, and later GOC 44 Division, 1938–40, and GOC II Corps, 1940–1. See: C. T. Atkinson, *The Seventh Division 1914–1918* (first published 1926; new ed., Uckfield: Naval and Military Press, 2012), 507; Nalder, *Royal Corps of Signals*, 550; and, David French, *Raising Churchill's Army: The British Army and the War against Germany 1919–1945* (Oxford: Oxford University Press, 2000), 183, 202.

[40] Major General Sir (William) Ronald Penney (1896–1964), attended the Royal Military Academy, Woolwich, before being commissioned into the Signal Service in 1914, reaching the rank of captain by the end of the war. During the Second World War he served as Signal Officer-in-Chief, Middle East, 1941–3; GOC 1 Division, Italy, 1943–4; and, Director of Intelligence, HQ Supreme Allied Commander, South East Asia, 1944–5. See: Nalder, *Royal Corps of Signals*, 552; and, Godfrey, *British Army Communications*, 95, 127, 134–9, 151–3.

[41] Colonel Sir (Arthur) Stanley Angwin (1883–1959) was employed in the Engineering Department of the GPO from 1906 and from 1908 raised the Lowland Division Telegraph Company, T.F. He was OC 52 (Lowland) Division Signal Company, 1915–18; Engineer-in-Chief, GPO, 1939–46; and, Chairman of Cable and Wireless, Ltd., 1947–51. See 'Obituary. Colonel Sir (Arthur) Stanley Angwin, KCMG, KBE, DSO, MC, 1883–1959', *ICE Proceedings*, 14 (1959), 224–5; and, Gordon Radley, 'Angwin, Sir (Arthur) Stanley (1883–1959)', *Oxford Dictionary of National Biography*, www.oxforddnb.com/view/article/30421 [accessed 6 March 2015].

[42] Clive Hughes, 'The New Armies', in Beckett and Simpson (eds.), *A Nation in Arms* 99–126; Simkins, *Kitchener's Army*.

available linemen' for laying and maintaining cable communications within the infantry and artillery.[43] Similarly, a set of instructions issued by 2 Division in October 1915 noted that the supply of trained signallers in the army 'has apparently now been exhausted'.[44] As Major R. M. Powell (OC X Corps Signal Company) informed an audience of Third Army officers in early 1916, the chief problem of providing communications 'in Fortress Warfare on an intense scale' was the 'lack of trained personnel inherent in the rapid expansion of our armies'.[45] Although the raising of the New Armies was a formidable achievement, it produced officers who did 'not initially possess that military knowledge arising from a long and high state of training which enables them to act instinctively and promptly on sound lines in unexpected situations'.[46]

The problem was particularly acute for technical branches of the BEF such as the Signal Service, since its officers required 'something more than the general education of a public school'.[47] Applicants for all temporary R.E. officer appointments during the war had to possess 'technical qualifications of sufficient quality'. Applicants over the age of 30 were also required to have had 'experience in the execution of engineering, constructive or scientific work'. Provided that these criteria were met, and he was of good health and physique, a candidate 'already possesse[d] four-fifths of the qualifications required by an engineer officer in war'. All that was needed was the additional officer tuition, such as weapons training, horsemanship and a thorough knowledge of military discipline and law.[48] The selection of such officers was the responsibility of the office of the A.A.G., R.E. at the War Office (A.G.7),[49] and was

---

[43] 'Signal Communication within a Division. Issued by General Staff, GHQ', 7 March 1915, Correspondence and Papers of 2 Division Signal Company in WW1, 1915–18, A231.52, REMA.

[44] '2nd Division Instructions No. 85', 9 October 1915, Orders, Maps and Papers Relating to the Service of Signal Companies of 2nd and 20th Division During the Great War, IWM.

[45] 'Lecture Given to the Senior Officer's Class. 3rd Army. On Communications (a) During Trench Warfare (b) During an Attack', 31 January 1916, X Corps Signal Company War Diary, WO95/875, TNA.

[46] 'Fourth Army. Tactical Notes' (May 1916), 3, Field Marshal Sir Archibald Montgomery-Massingberd Papers 7/33, Liddell Hart Centre for Military Archives (LHCMA), King's College London; SS. 109. Training of Divisions for Offensive Action (May 1916), 2.

[47] Williams, Raising and Training, 66. See also: Keith Simpson, 'Officers', in Beckett and Simpson (eds.), Nation in Arms, 72–4.

[48] Pritchard (ed.), History of the Corps of Royal Engineers, Vol. V, 31–2.

[49] From August 1914 until January 1917 the A.A.G., R.E. was Colonel [later Major-General Sir] Reginald Curtis, formerly Commandant of the Army Signal School, 1912–13. See 'Obituary. Major-General Sir R. S. Curtis', Times, 12 January 1922. A.G.7 grew from just two officers and 9 other ranks at the start of the war to nine

aided by the recommendations of the president of the Institution of Civil Engineers and from the commanders of university and public school Officers' Training Corps. Following the introduction of the Military Service Act in January 1916, NCOs wishing to obtain a commission in the R.E. were interviewed by a CRE.[50]

The signal officers recruited by this system came from diverse backgrounds, though as the results from a consolidated sample of 40 officers' service files show (Table 2.1), the majority were aged between 20 and 29 and had been employed in engineering-related occupations before the war. Again, like some of the original cadre, several volunteer signal officers would rise to notable prominence in their chosen professions after the war, such as Joshua Burn, Emeritus Professor of Pharmacology at the University of Oxford (1937–59); Basil Schonland, Director of the UK Atomic Energy Research Establishment (1958–61); Philip Strong, Archbishop of Brisbane (1962–70); Howard Hands, co-founder of the oilfield engineering company Hands-England; and Owen Morshead, Royal Librarian and Assistant Keeper of the Royal Archives (1926–58).[51] However, although they were not R.E. men, arguably the most famous British signal officers of the First World War were the writer and poet J. R. R. Tolkien, author of *The Hobbit* and *The Lord of the Rings*,[52] and the children's writer, poet and playwright A. A. Milne, best known for the *Winnie-the-Pooh* stories.[53]

officers and 37 other ranks and civilians by January 1919. See Pritchard (ed.), *History of the Corps of Royal Engineers, Vol. V*, 30.

[50] Ibid., 34; Williams, *Raising and Training*, 66.

[51] Lieutenant J. H. Burn, WO339/132511, TNA; 'Typescript Recollections', undated, J. H. Burn Papers, GS0240, Liddle Collection, Brotherton Library, University of Leeds (LCL); T. E. Allibone, 'Schonland, Sir Basil Ferdinand Jamieson (1896–1972)', *Oxford Dictionary of National Biography*, www.oxforddnb.com/view/article/31659 [accessed 6 March 2015]; Austin, *Schonland: Scientist and Soldier*; Lieutenant Philip Strong, WO339/120744, TNA; David Wetherell, 'Strong, Philip Nigel (1899–1983)', *Australian Dictionary of Biography*, National Centre of Biography, Australian National University, http://adb.anu.edu.au/biography/strong-philip-nigel-15782/text26974 [accessed 7 March 2015]; 2/Lieutenant Howard George Hands, WO339/121995, TNA; Oliver Everett, 'Morshead, Sir Owen Frederick (1893–1977)', *Oxford Dictionary of National Biography*, www.oxforddnb.com/view/article/66332 [accessed 4 January 2016]; Major Owen Frederick Morshead, WO339/64295, TNA.

[52] Tolkien served as a signal officer in the 11th Battalion, Lancashire Fusiliers, June–October 1916. See John Garth, *Tolkien and the Great War: The Threshold of Middle-Earth* (London: HarperCollins, 2004); and, Lieutenant John Ronald Reuel Tolkien, WO339/34423, TNA.

[53] Milne served as a signal officer in the 4th Battalion, Royal Warwickshire Regiment, July–November 1916. See A. A. Milne, *It's Too Late Now: The Autobiography of a Writer* (London: Methuen, 1939), 211–23.

Table 2.1 *Signal Service Officers from Personnel Files*

Year Joined Signal Service (Number)		Age upon Joining (Number)		Occupation (Number)	
1914	6	20–29	25	Accountant	1
1915	6	30–39	12	Barrister	1
1916	11	40–49	3	Business	3
1917	12			Clerk	3
1918	5			Engineer	19
				Farmer	1
				Scientist	4
				Student	5
				Unknown/None	3

Source: WO339/139, 9930, 14387, 16155, 25245, 32272, 32513, 33427, 39549, 46392, 57800, 60843, 62546, 67674, 68692, 74525, 81997, 85100, 85101, 94652, 104905, 104964, 106030, 114485, 115504, 116172, 116212, 118687, 120744, 121995, 122869, 132511; WO374/182, 1613, 4620, 6564, 14864, 15340, 44201, 59803, TNA. Only R.E. Signal Service officers have been sampled.

In many respects, the civilian backgrounds of these men made them eminently suitable for the work and responsibilities entailed in their new roles as a 'technical officer[s] in the field', broadly defined by one signal officer after the war as

one who fights in the second degree. Normally he leads no troops in battle and he directs the fire of no batteries, but he helps his brother officers who do these things, and makes their task possible. He is a combatant, because he may be killed, but he overlaps the division between fighting troops and administrative services... He [is], as it were, the expert called in to help.[54]

There are several colourful descriptions of signal officers that echo this stereotype, and they help reveal the manner in which the signallers and their work were regarded by the rest of the army. Captain Wyn Griffith, for example, described Emlyn Davies, his brigade signal officer, as

a man of forty, quietly carrying about him a reserved air of authority and competence, unhurried in movement and in speech. The technical nature of his work preserved him from interference, and he ruled over his kingdom of men with a certainty of control denied to an infantry officer. No Brigadier could dispute with him concerning the wisdom or unwisdom [*sic*] of his dispositions of

[54] Lieutenant-Colonel R. Chenevix-Trench, 'The Technical Officer in the Field', *RUSI Journal*, 75 (1930), 516, 519.

men or material. His duty was to give others a means of speech, and as he never failed in his task, his competency was obvious to all.[55]

Similarly, signaller Jack Martin regarded his CO, Fletcher Buchanan, as 'a good officer – he keeps us all up to scratch and he won't let any other officers interfere with us and that's something to be thankful for. Even the Staff Captain and the Brigade Major are afraid to give us any orders without his permission'.[56] Indeed, A. A. Milne called signalling 'much the most interesting work in the infantry, with the great advantage that one is the only officer in the Battalion who knows anything about it, and is consequently one's own master – a great thing to a civilian in the Army'.[57] He elaborated upon this point in an article that appeared in the *Evening Post* towards the end of the war:

The advantage of the signalling officer's position is that he has a free hand. As long as things go well, nobody can dispute with him. Colonels and adjutants doubtless have authority over him, but they have little technical knowledge of his craft. The disadvantage of his position is that, if things go wrong, there is nobody but him to blame. Sometimes, of course, he will deserve the blame; but even if he does not, it will be useless for him to try to explain, for there will be nobody to understand... If, then, you happen to like as much freedom from routine as you can get; and if you are not afraid of responsibility, signalling may safely be recommended to you as much the most interesting work open to an infantry officer.[58]

Most signal officers regarded their role as important but at the same time unglamorous and certainly not heroic.[59] As one brigade signal officer put it, unlike an infantry officer leading his men in an attack 'there was nothing whatever dashing about a signal officer with a telephone and coils of cable. Maintaining telephone and other kinds of communication... was an occupation that might have been winning merit for us to be reaped in an afterlife, but in this life there was nothing distinguished about it'.[60]

---

[55] 115th Infantry Brigade (38 Division). Llewelyn Wyn Griffith, *Up to Mametz and Beyond* (first published 1931; new ed., Barnsley: Pen & Sword, 2010), 97–8.

[56] Richard van Emden (ed.), *Sapper Martin: The Secret Great War Diary of Jack Martin* (London: Bloomsbury, 2010), 32. Buchanan was a 27-year-old lieutenant from Glasgow, commanding the 122nd Infantry Brigade Signal Section (41 Division) in 1916–17. He was later promoted captain and transferred to 39 Division Signal Company, but was forced to resign his commission at the end of the war on the grounds of ill health.

[57] Quoted in Ann Thwaite, *A. A. Milne: His Life* (London: Faber and Faber, 1990), 167.

[58] Lieutenant A. A. Milne, 'Communications: Signalling Officer's Work', *Evening Post*, 11 September 1918, 8.

[59] Captain A. P. Corcoran, 'Wireless in the Trenches', *Popular Science Monthly* (May 1917), 795.

[60] Scrivenor, *Brigade Signals*, 43.

Many drew comparisons to their work in civilian life before the war and so simply got on with the job.[61] During the chaos and confusion at Zillebeke on 31 July 1917, for instance, 'one calm man. . . was Lieutenant Lepper of the 18th Divisional Signal Company, a plump, rosy-cheeked, soft-voiced officer, who kept his head and responded with optimistic pleasantness to urgent, sometimes angry, demands that smashed wires should be repaired'. Later, upon the eve of the Battle of Amiens on 8 August 1918, an officer who had spoken to Lepper that day, said "'I believe you were the most unflurried man among that seething crowd"', to which Lepper replied: '"Well, I had a good training for it. You see, I was once a night sub-editor on the *Daily Mail*".[62]

According to the *History of the Corps of Royal Engineers*, the ratio of Regular R.E. officers to volunteer and Territorial R.E. officers during the war was approximately 1:8 and that this 'very strong and appropriate' amalgam 'succeeded in "delivering the goods"'.[63] However, throughout the war the supply of signal officers often struggled to meet demand. Part of the reason for this was that many suitably qualified candidates were employed in 'reserved' or 'protected' occupations, which made it difficult for them to be released for military service.[64] For instance, Clifford Chaster, an electrical engineer working for British Insulated and Helsby Cables Ltd., was refused permission to enlist by his employer until May 1916, owing to 'important contracts with various government departments'.[65] Nevertheless, even when experienced and well-qualified candidates were released, it was found that not all volunteer signal officers were suited to the rigours of military service. In a letter to the editor of the *Post Office Electrical Engineers' Journal* in late 1915, for instance, one former GPO executive engineer-turned-subaltern admitted finding it 'somewhat difficult to settle down under the existing military conditions', chiefly because 'modern warfare is beyond the imagination unless you are actually on the spot'.[66] While this particular officer managed to adjust to the dangers and hardships of

[61] See, for example: 'A Signaller in France 1914–1918', 40, Captain J. C. Craven Papers, 92.1 CRAVEN, REMA. Craven had worked as a telegraphist at the post office in Hull before the war. See Captain John Clayton Craven, WO339/115504, TNA.

[62] G. H. F. Nichols, *The 18th Division in the Great War* (Edinburgh: Blackwood, 1922), 203.

[63] Pritchard (ed.), *History of the Corps of Royal Engineers, Vol. V*, 33.

[64] Hew Strachan, *The First World War*, Vol. 1: *To Arms* (Oxford: Oxford University Press, 2001), 1038; Adrian Gregory, *The Last Great War: British Society and the First World War* (Cambridge: Cambridge University Press, 2008), 210, 289.

[65] Letter dated 23 May 1916, Lieutenant Clifford Chaster, WO339/116212, TNA.

[66] Gwilliam, 'Signal Master on Active Service', 262–3.

modern trench warfare, others were not so fortunate.[67] Both Tolkien and Milne, for example, were invalided out of the Battle of the Somme, each succumbing to trench fever after serving four months in the frontline.[68] There were also other signal officers who were clearly unsuited temperamentally to the role. Having attempted to enlist twice before, but failing on account of his poor eyesight, Edmund Ponting finally managed to obtain a commission into the Signal Service in 1918, only for his superiors quickly to identify his shortcomings and begin proceedings to have him demobilised. According to Major (later Lieutenant-Colonel) Miles Reid, OC 62 Division Signal Company, although Ponting's technical qualifications were good, 'he is however lacking in powers of leadership and is not a good disciplinarian. His chief failing lies in the apparent lack of energy with which he conducts his work... [and] he is handicapped by bad eyesight'.[69] Throughout the war, problems with the supply of suitable and sufficient numbers of reinforcements affected the recruitment of signal officers and other ranks alike, but perhaps more so the latter.

Other Ranks

The demand for new signallers increased in particular during the second half of 1916 and became ever more urgent in 1917, partly as a result of the heavy casualties incurred on the Western Front, but also partly due to faults and inconsistencies with recruitment procedures.[70] This was particularly the case with regards to the enlistment of skilled GPO workers into the Signal Service. Since it was recognised that the telegraphists, telephonists and engineers of the GPO formed 'practically the sole source of supply' for the Signal Service,[71] the signal units of the Special Reservists and Territorial Force had developed strong working

---

[67] Gwilliam was mentioned in despatches in January 1917 and ended the war a captain. See: *Post Office Circular*. Tuesday, 22 January 1917, No. 2333, 31; *Quarterly Army List for the Quarter Ending 31st December 1919*, Vol. 2 (London: HMSO, 1920), 704; Captain W. J. Gwilliam, R. E., 'Transmission of Messages by Carrier Pigeons', *Post Office Electrical Engineers' Journal*, 11 (1918–19), 203–6.

[68] Garth, *Tolkien and the Great War*, 200–1; Milne, *It's Too Late Now*, 222–3.

[69] Letter dated 26 December 1918, WO339/104964, TNA. Reid would later act as liaison officer between British GHQ and the French First Army in 1940 before commanding the GHQ Liaison Squadron in Greece the following year. He was subsequently captured and spent the rest of the war as a POW, most notably inside Colditz between September 1943 and January 1945. See Miles Reid, *Into Colditz* (London: Michael Russell, 1983).

[70] Boys to Ogilvie, 5 August 1916, POST30/4061B/19/8, BTA; Pritchard (ed.), *History of the Corps of Royal Engineers, Vol. V*, 568.

[71] 'Secretary of the Army Council to HM Treasury', 15 November 1912, Postal and Signal (Telegraph) Reserves of the Expeditionary Force, 1912–13, T1/11519, TNA.

relationships with the GPO before the war.[72] However, as James Dart, a GPO telegraphist in Bristol and later a divisional signal company NCO, commented after the war, 'the loss of the services of Royal Engineer Army Operators who were seconded to the Post Office by arrangement with the Army' severely depleted the number of trained telegraphists within the GPO in the autumn of 1914. Consequently, 'Post Office operators were not permitted to apply to join a unit in Lord Kitchener's Army until official notification that they could do so had appeared in the Post Office Weekly Circular'.[73] Indeed, the *Post Office Circular* of 26 August stated clearly that 'in view of the particular importance at the present time of maintaining the Telegraph and Telephone services in an efficient state, Post Office servants engaged on Telegraph or Telephone work cannot be released for military service unless they propose to serve in Signal Units of the Territorial Force'.[74]

Not until late September, with the Reserve Signal Company at Aldershot having been 'squeezed dry',[75] did GPO officials grant permission for their employees even to begin applying to enlist in the signal units of the New Armies, but even then this was dependent upon the individual's first gaining the consent of his branch or district manager.[76] In many cases, there was a great reluctance on the part of managers and postmasters to release skilled engineers and telegraphists for fear of the disruption and loss of efficiency that might occur as a result.[77] As the Director of Army Signals, Home Forces, noted in April 1915: 'The main difficulty at the present time is not so much to obtain willing recruits as to arrange for the work of telegraph offices if the required number of men are withdrawn for military work'.[78] This left many men who were keen to enlist extremely frustrated and having to take matters into their own hands. Emlyn Davies, for example, who had had numerous applications to be released for military service rejected by his employer, the Post Office at Oswestry, finally took it upon himself to quit his job in July 1915 to join

---

[72] 'Number of Telegraphists Working in Territorial Forces, 1913', POST47/13, Royal Mail Archive (RMA), London. On the relationship between the army and the GPO before 1914, see Nalder, *Royal Corps of Signals*, 21–53.

[73] Typescript Memoirs, 2–3, Sergeant J. C. Dart Papers, GALL025, LCL.

[74] Thus, as Territorials they were only liable to serve within the United Kingdom and not abroad. *Post Office Circular*. Wednesday, 26 August 1914. No. 2178, 442.

[75] Colonel R. R. Ward [Officer i/c R.E. Records] to the War Office, 23 September 1914, POST30/4061B/3/18, BTA.

[76] *Post Office Circular*. Tuesday, 29 September, 1914, No. 2187, 509; Simkins, *Kitchener's Army*, 170.

[77] Ogilvie to Kirkwood, 23 April 1915, POST30/4061B/10/20, BTA; Hughes, 'New Armies', 102.

[78] Ogilvie to Sutton, 17 April 1915, POST30/4061B/12/4, BTA.

the infantry, much to the annoyance of his head postmaster, who was 'very angry, not to say nasty'.[79] Eventually, in response to the implementation of the Derby Scheme in October 1915,[80] authority was given for local GPO officials and district managers to begin replacing skilled telegraphists and engineers of military age with female and casual labour.[81] Nevertheless, Herbert Samuel, the Postmaster General, still stressed that 'a very large number of Telegraphists must be retained to do indispensable civil work at home, and cannot be released even to serve in the Royal Engineers' Signal Service'.[82]

Ultimately, these restrictions had a negative effect upon Signal Service recruitment, a situation that was further compounded by the fact that pre-war trade testing of R.E. recruits at Woolwich and Chatham had been abandoned at the beginning of the war, largely because of an inability to cope with the influx of volunteers, and not reintroduced until November 1916.[83] Thus, either as a consequence of their desperation to enlist in the army or because of restrictions and inconsistencies in recruitment procedures, many skilled GPO employees found themselves being posted either to infantry units or to technical branches of the army other than the Signal Service.[84] When the demand for qualified telegraphists, telephonists and linesmen became urgent in 1917,[85] the decision was made to allocate a special recruiting liaison officer of the Signal Service to the Woolwich Trade Testing Centre in order to form a pool of recruit telegraphists, as well as initiate plans to draw out highly skilled GPO workers from non–Signal Service units at home and abroad. Through these initiatives, as Ogilvie informed the War Office in September 1917, 'I think we shall have combed out a certain number of Telegraphists who in the early days got into Units other than the Signal Service'.[86] In addition, those who had

---

[79] Quoted in Simkins, *Kitchener's Army*, 170.

[80] Gerard J. DeGroot, *Blighty: British Society in the Era of the Great War* (London: Longman, 1996), 93–5.

[81] 'Postmaster General's Recruiting Letter of 25th October, 1915', 6 November 1915, 'Employment of Women at Night', 10 November 1915, Letters for Volunteers, 1915, POST56/103, RMA; Duncan Campbell-Smith, *Masters of the Post: The Authorised History of the Royal Mail* (London: Penguin Books, 2012), 237.

[82] 'Recruitment for War Service. P.M.G.'s Letters to Staff, 29 October 1915', POST56/102, RMA.

[83] Pritchard (ed.), *History of the Corps of Royal Engineers, Vol. V*, 135; K. W. Mitchinson, *Pioneer Battalions in the Great War: Organised and Intelligent Labour* (Barnsley: Pen and Sword, 2013), 196.

[84] War Office to the Secretary, GPO, 9 August 1916, POST30/4061B/20/2, J. K. Alexandre to Director of Recruiting, 16 May 1917, POST30/4061B/22/2, BTA.

[85] Ogilvie to Director of Recruiting, War Office, 22 May 1917, POST30/4061B/22/6, BTA.

[86] Ogilvie to War Office, 5 September 1917, POST30/4061B/22/28, BTA.

previously been rejected for military service on medical grounds were to be re-examined.[87] Once identified at Woolwich, nominated men would then be sent to the Signal Service Training Centre at Bedford, where they were specially tested and graded as either pioneers or sappers according to their results.[88] Finally, the Signal Service's recruitment problems were also partially eased by the employment of female telegraphists and telephone switchboard operators from the Women's Army Auxiliary Corps (WAAC).[89] From April 1917, these women, many of whom were already engaged in similar work on the home front, were employed at lines of communication signal offices, replacing highly skilled men, who were released for duty at the frontline.[90]

In terms of the technical proficiencies required to become a signaller, an office telegraphist in the Signal Service had to be able to read and receive messages of at least 25 words per minute, which was the standard GPO rate at the time, while 20 words per minute was the requirement of a Territorial signaller.[91] At the battalion level, 20 words per minute was expected of signal officers, while the other ranks had to be able to 'buzz' messages at a rate of 14 words per minute.[92] Furthermore, besides having good eyesight for visual signalling, excellent hearing and memory for telegraph and telephone work and being physically fit to lay cable or act as runners, regimental signallers 'when first assembled for instruction, must be examined by dictation as to their capabilities of writing well and quickly and spelling correctly, and those men should be rejected who are unable to meet the necessary requirements'.[93] Unsurprisingly, this usually meant that 'the most intelligent of the company [were] chosen for the job'.[94] Above all, as Fletcher Buchanan informed Jack Martin, 'the duties of a signaller demand resource and initiative, and... there are

---

[87] Messenger, *Call to Arms*, 152.

[88] Ogilvie to Lieutenant-Colonel George Scovell, 3 September 1917, POST30/4061B/22/26, BTA.

[89] Later renamed Queen Mary's Army Auxiliary Corps (QMAAC). See Diana Shaw, 'The Forgotten Army of Women: The Overseas Service of Queen Mary's Army Auxiliary Corps with the British Forces, 1917–1921', in Hugh Cecil and Peter H. Liddle (eds.), *Facing Armageddon: The First World War Experienced* (London: Leo Cooper, 1996), 365–79; and, Lucy Noakes, *Women in the British Army: War and the Gentle Sex, 1907–1948* (London: Routledge, 2006), 61–81.

[90] Priestley, *Work of the Royal Engineers*, 160–1; Gertrude Eaton and Marion Gates Waddell (ed.), *With the Signallers in France: The Diary of a WAAC* (London: First Choice Books, 2010).

[91] Ogilvie to Kirkwood, 23 April 1915, POST30/4061B/10/20, BTA.

[92] Staniforth and Grayson (ed.), *At War with the 16th Irish Division*, 33.

[93] *Training Manual – Signalling: Part II* (London: HMSO, 1914), 95.

[94] Corcoran, *Daredevil of the Army*, 61.

times when he must act on his own and not be bound by the rigidity of Army Rules and Regulations'.[95]

Although not as technical as telegraphic communication, despatch riders also had to possess a number of key attributes, including good memory and map reading skills, linguistic attainments so as to be able to speak with the local population, mechanical knowledge of their motorcycle and the initiative and ability to think for themselves in times of crisis.[96] Such qualities required men of a high intellectual standard, and as such, the University Officers' Training Corps provided the most suitable recruits.[97] James Dunn noted that the original cohort of despatch riders he came into contact with 'were, for the most part, University students and young schoolmasters, with a sprinkling of young businessmen'.[98] According to Austin Corcoran, of the 20 other despatch riders who accompanied him to France in 1914, 'not more than two had failed to graduate from either Oxford or Cambridge, and they were professional men of high standing in their own line, far above the type that might be deemed suitable for a competent "regular"'.[99] Financially, these men were well off, taking their newly bought motorcycles with them,[100] and all were automatically given the rank of corporal so as to enable them to approach and speak directly to commissioned officers.[101]

But who exactly were the individuals recruited by this system and what were their occupations in civilian life? According to one signal officer in late 1914, the BEF's original signallers were 'drawn from T. S., the London Postal District, and from Provincial offices, and while excellent soldiers they are no less expert telegraphists'.[102] Commenting upon the new drafts that his battalion received in the spring of 1917, Frank Richards noted that 'we now had on the signallers a schoolmaster, two

---

[95] van Emden (ed.), *Sapper Martin*, 51.
[96] *Signalling: Imperial Army Series, Based on Training Manual – Signalling: Part II. 1914* (London: John Murray, 1914), 123–4.
[97] Priestley, *Work of the Royal Engineers*, 16.
[98] Captain J. C. Dunn, *The War the Infantry Knew 1914–1919* (first published 1938; new ed., London: Abacus, 1998), 15.
[99] Corcoran, *Daredevil*, 21. For a discussion of the misemployment of the Intelligence Corps in this role in 1914, see Beach, *Haig's Intelligence*, 69–70.
[100] Captain W. H. L. Watson, *Adventures of a Motorcycle Despatch Rider during the First World War* (first published 1915; new ed., Liskeard: Diggory Press, 2006), 5.
[101] Corcoran, *Daredevil*, 20; David Venner (ed.), *Despatch Rider on the Western Front: The Diary of Sergeant Albert Simpkin MM* (Barnsley: Pen and Sword, 2015), 4; W. George Mead, 'Forty Thousand Hours of War', Typescript Memoirs (1971–2), 20, GALL194/1, LCL.
[102] Lieutenant A. A. Jayne, R.E., 'Telegraphing in the Field: Arrangements at Headquarters', *Times*, 31 December 1914.

Table 2.2 *Signal Service Other Ranks*

Year Enlisted (Number)		Age upon Enlistment (Number)		Occupation (Number)	
1914	2	18–19	5	Blacksmith	1
1915	73	20–29	41	Business	2
1916	8	30–39	44	Carpenter	2
1917	5	40–49	10	Clerk	15
1918	12			Driver	1
				Electrician	9
				Engineer	10
				Farmer	2
				Joiner	1
				Labourer	6
				Lawyer	1
				Linesmen	6
				Miner	2
				Plumber	1
				Postman	1
				Skilled Workman	3
				Telegraphist	29
				Telephonist	4
				Unknown/None	4

Source: Sample taken from the 'British Army WW1 Service Records, 1914–1920', accessed via Ancestry.co.uk [30 January 2015]. In total, the search brought up the names of 1,691 individuals. The sample took 10 names each from surnames beginning A–J. Only those whose enlistment forms stated clearly a R.E. Signal Service unit are included.

school teachers, two bank clerks and a young architect'.[103] Similarly, John Scrivenor recalled that the brigade signallers under his command in mid-1918 'were mostly Lancashire men, but we had a few from other parts: Edinburgh, Kent, Hatfield, Suffolk, Tipperary, and even one whose home address was Brooklyn, NY... One was a lawyer's clerk. Others were glass workers. Others again were post-office operators'.[104] However, these are merely snapshots. A consolidated sample of 100 enlistment forms paints a more detailed picture of the backgrounds of those who served in the Signal Service during the war. As Table 2.2 suggests, the typical new signaller enlisted during the first half of the war, was in his thirties and was employed in an electronic communications, or engineering-related occupation. A further breakdown of these findings reveals that 41 of those sampled were employees of the GPO and that of the 73 who enlisted in 1915, 44 did so between mid-October and mid-December.

[103] Frank Richards, *Old Soldiers Never Die* (Eastbourne: Antony Rowe, 1933), 219.
[104] Scrivenor, *Brigade Signals*, 89.

Three key observations can be drawn from these results. First, it is clear that, in comparison with the findings in Table 2.1, the other ranks that joined the Signal Service during the course of the war were, generally speaking, older than their officer counterparts: 54 per cent of the other ranks sampled were aged 30 or above, compared to 38 per cent of the officers. This can be explained to some extent both by the official R.E. temporary officer recruitment preference for men in their twenties and by the granting of a special extension in April 1916 to men up to the age of 45 wishing to serve as office telegraphists in the Signal Service.[105] Thus, as one officer observed: 'He is a seasoned vessel, the Buzzer of today, and a person of marked individuality. He is above all things a man of the world'.[106] Donald Portway, for example, described his second in command, George Whitchurch, as 'quite a character. He was a good deal older than I and had been working outdoors putting up telegraph and telephone lines all his life, and, as I knew little or nothing about post-office construction and general routine, he was invaluable'.[107] This impression of the mature and level-headed signaller is perhaps best encapsulated in the depiction given by Lord Gorell, a former infantry battalion adjutant:

Of the failure of office life to affect the nerves let another story speak. In a certain signal section a little robin of a man lives and has his being; he is middle-aged, and before the war had passed more years inside the walls of the Post Office than most soldiers can boast at all. For over 20 years he lived a life of entirely regular and uneventful routine. The war came, and the telegraphist became a signaller and continued to "buzz" messages of orders as placidly as he had sent messages of business and pleasure. During a certain battle this little man, who had hitherto been employed well behind the line, was picked as one of the most efficient operators to serve an important advanced signal station... He went, and as he sat "buzzing" a shell struck the upper part of the house, passed through without exploding, and, after an interesting skate-dance, came to rest in the road not many yards away. There it remained and the operator "buzzed"... It was the first time he had been under fire, and he found it full of interest; he had picked up a trophy to send home to his wife, and was simply beaming as he related how he had kept an eye on the "dud" all day. At the close of the action an officer intimated a desire that it should be removed; "I didn't offer to do it", naively ended the little man amidst the laughter and chaff of his friends.[108]

[105] Pritchard (ed.), *History of the Corps of Royal Engineers: Vol. V*, 31; Ogilvie to Mr G. L. Harding, 20 April 1916, Requirement of Telegraphists for Royal Engineers Signal Service, POST30/3498A, RMA.

[106] Ian Hay [John Hay Beith], *Carrying On – after the First Hundred Thousand* (Edinburgh: William Blackwood and Sons, 1917), 134.

[107] Portway, *Memoirs*, 112.

[108] Ronald Gorell Barnes, 'A Citizen Army from Within, II - Ease and Unconcern', *The Times*, 1 December 1916.

Second, the large proportion of other ranks who enlisted in the autumn of 1915 can be attributed mainly to the Derby Scheme, in which men aged 18 to 41 across Britain were encouraged to attest a willingness to volunteer based upon the understanding that young unmarried men would be called up first.[109] Within the GPO, the Postmaster General's recruiting letter of 29 October, urging those who could be spared by their employer to comply with the scheme,[110] was sent to 2,461 'skilled telegraphists' across 60 GPO offices, of whom 1,256 (51 per cent) responded and agreed to enlist.[111] That 49 per cent did not respond or agree to enlist can be seen as indicative of the disappointing general response rate to Lord Derby's scheme, in which almost half of the two million single men and 40 per cent of the near three million married men on the UK National Register failed to attest.[112] It is worth noting, however, that part of the reason why so many GPO employees did not respond to the Postmaster General's letter is that it was suspected that many did not receive it in the first place; the suggestion was that some local GPO officials and district managers had deliberately not circulated the letter for fear of the inconvenience that would result from the loss of their skilled telegraphists.[113]

Nevertheless, in spite of these problems, the third, and final, observation that can be drawn from surveying Table 2.2 is that the GPO did form a very important manpower pool into which the Signal Service could dip.[114] That 41 per cent of those sampled were employed by the GPO is reinforced by the figures given by the GPO shortly after the war. Accordingly, between 1914 and 1918 the GPO provided the Signal Service with 531 officers and 17,355 other ranks. Leaving aside the additional 73 officers and 1,174 men who joined the RFC/RAF, and the 5 officers and 688 men who enlisted in the Royal Navy, GPO employees constituted 43 per cent of the Signal Service's total personnel.[115]

---

[109] Messenger, *Call to Arms*, 131–2.

[110] 'Recruitment for War Service. P.M.G.'s Letters to Staff, 29 October 1915', POST56/102, RMA.

[111] 'Postmaster General's Replies to Letter to Telegraphists of 29th October 1915', POST30/3498A, RMA.

[112] Simkins, *Kitchener's Army*, 156; Keith Grieves, *The Politics of Manpower, 1914–18* (Manchester: Manchester University Press, 1988), 22.

[113] 'Postmaster General's Recruiting Letter of 29th October, 1915', 6 November 1915, POST56/103, RMA.

[114] Indeed, the GPO employed just over 250,000 people in 1914 of whom 75,000 were released for military service during the course of the war. Of these, roughly 36,000 enlisted with local regiments, approximately 12,000 served in the Post Office Rifles and a further 8,000 in the Royal Engineers Postal Service. See Campbell-Smith, *Masters of the Post*, 235.

[115] Anon., 'Complimentary Dinner to Sir Andrew Ogilvie', 70.

Of those who did enlist during the course of the war, what motivated them to become a signaller? Apart from the obvious point that most of those who became signallers did so because they had a specific skill that the army needed, particularly the ability to send and receive messages in Morse code, there appear to be three other main influences, and understanding these helps shed further light on the way in which the signallers were regarded by the wider army. First, there was a financial incentive. This applied specifically to those wishing to join the Signal Service, which, as a branch of the R.E., was amongst the best-paid posts in the army.[116] Officers, in addition to their basic daily rate of pay, were awarded 'Engineer Pay', which, depending upon their rank, was between 33 and 67 per cent of their basic wage. NCOs and Sappers were also better paid than their infantry counterparts and could draw additional 'Engineer Pay' as well, depending upon their level of qualification.[117] Naturally, this extra pay was a source of resentment to many infantrymen, who expressed their professional jealousy in one such humorous way:

> God made the bees,
> The bees make the honey;
> The Glosters do the work
> And the R.E.s get the money.[118]

With specific reference to the signallers, 'tersely described by the rank and file as "The Buzzers", or the "Iddy-Umpties"',[119] one infantry corporal remembered that during a route march: 'We approached a signaller… repairing a broken line, and a voice cried: "Some say 'Good old Signals!'", to which a second voice replied: "Others say '— old Signals!'"'.[120] All joking aside, the additional pay that R.E. personnel received was stressed repeatedly in GPO recruitment letters and official correspondence, and may go some way in explaining the allure of the Signal Service to many of its employees.[121]

---

[116] David French, *Military Identities: The Regimental System, the British Army, and the British People c. 1870–2000* (Oxford: Oxford University Press, 2005), 53.

[117] 'British Army Rates of Pay: As Defined by War Office Instruction 166 (1914)', The Long, Long Trail: The British Army in the Great War of 1914–1918, www.1914-1918.net/pay_1914.html [Accessed 26 March 2015].

[118] *Fifth Gloucester Gazette*, no. 15 (October 1916), quoted in Vivien Noakes, *Voices of Silence: The Alternative Book of First World War Poetry* (Stroud: Sutton, 2006), 286.

[119] Hay, *Carrying On*, 130. Other names for signallers included 'sigs', 'flag-waggers' and 'tic-tacs'.

[120] Anthony French, quoted in Paul Fussell, *The Great War and Modern Memory* (Oxford: Oxford University Press, 1977), 180.

[121] *Post Office Circular*. Tuesday, 22 December, 1914. No. 2203, 685–6; 'Office Telegraphists and Line Telegraphists in the Royal Engineers', 31 October 1914, POST30/4061B/4/6, 'Notice for Post Office Circular of 13 April 1915', POST30/4061B/9/5, BTA; 'Interview between Director of Army Signals and Representatives of Postal and Telegraph Clerks' Association – 20 January 1916', POST30/3498A, RMA.

A second motivation for becoming a signaller was that, particularly for those not in the Signal Service, it provided them with an opportunity to learn new skills. Upon joining the Signal Section whilst undergoing training at the Bettisfield Park Artillery Training Camp in 1917, for example, Ivor Hanson was approached by a sergeant who said: 'You've made a good move, for among other things you'll be taught a trade – telegraphy. What use will a knowledge of gunnery be to you after the war?'[122] Similarly, whilst undertaking a six-week officers' signalling course in 1915, John Staniforth informed his parents: 'There's one thing – I shall always be able to get a job as a telegraphist when the war is over'.[123] Indeed, for many signallers, including Lionel Harris, Eisenhower's Chief of Telecommunications in 1944–5,[124] and the future Nobel Prize winner John Cockroft,[125] their experiences during the war paved the way for their future careers.

Third, and perhaps most significant, was the seemingly 'attractive life' that signallers led.[126] As one linesman on the Somme in 1916 put it, 'If this job is not so cushy as generally supposed, it is a very great improvement on the fire step life of the ordinary soldier'.[127] According to John Lucy, the signallers 'regarded themselves as privileged because their job was important, and they took advantage of this. They "won" hand-carts

---

[122] J. Ivor Hanson and Alan Wakefield (ed.), *Plough & Scatter: The Diary-Journal of a First World War Gunner* (Yeovil: Haynes, 2009), 79.

[123] Staniforth and Grayson (ed.), *At War with the 16th Irish Division*, 34.

[124] Brigadier Sir Lionel Harris (1897–1971) emigrated from England to Australia in 1914 following the death of his mother and served as a linesman in 5 Australian Division Signal Company, 1915–18. He held a series of senior appointments in the Post Office Engineering Department in the United Kingdom during the interwar period, becoming superintending engineer of the North Midland District in 1938. Commissioned into the Territorial Army in 1926, he started the Second World War as a company commander and ended it as Chief of Telecommunications, SHAEF, 1944–45. He was later Engineer-in-Chief of the GPO, 1954–60. See: Brigadier L. H. Harris, *Signal Venture* (Aldershot: Gale and Polden, 1951); Nalder, *Royal Corps of Signals*, 531; and, 'Profile: Sir Lionel Harris: Leader of the Post Office's Engineers', *New Scientist*, 4 (1958), 856–7.

[125] Sir John Cockroft (1897–1967) served as a signaller in the Royal Field Artillery, 1915–18. After the war he became Jacksonian Professor of Natural Philosophy, University of Cambridge, 1939–46; Director of the Atomic Energy Research Establishment, Harwell, 1946–58; and, was awarded the Nobel Prize for physics, 1951. See: T. E. Allibone, 'Cockroft, Sir John Douglas (1897–1967)', *Oxford Dictionary of National Biography*, www.oxforddnb.com/view/article/32473 [accessed 20 March 2015].

[126] William G. Ogilvie, *Umty-Iddy-Umty: The Story of a Canadian Signaller in the First World War* (Ontario: Boston Mills Press, 1982), 10.

[127] 'Blue Chevrons: An Infantry Private's Great War Diary' (c. 1962), 37, Arthur Surfleet Papers, P.126, IWM. For a similar reference to the 'cushy if somewhat tiring job' of a signaller, see Felicity Jane Laws (ed.), *War on Two Wheels: A Diary of Overseas Service British Expeditionary Force France, 1915–1918, David Winder Small, Royal Engineers Signals* (Raleigh, NC: Lulu Press, 2010), 24.

and perambulators to take their kit to the front line, and they moved independently like gypsies. They carried all kinds of kit forbidden to the ordinary troops, and built up a fine comfort service for themselves'.[128] Indeed, there was a collective perception among both signallers and non-signallers alike that the signaller's was generally 'a safe job', though as John Staniforth pointed out, 'Occasionally, of course, it emerges from a kind of underground safety and obscurity right into the limelight; then it's "some job", and gets thrills enough to satisfy the most reckless glory-hunters'.[129] Signallers certainly suffered casualties, the most high-profile being George Dobbs (AD Signals XVIII Corps), who died of shrapnel wounds received while inspecting a new cable trench in the frontline near Poperinge in June 1917.[130] Although this was a rather exceptional case, it highlights the obvious point that the closer to the frontline a signaller was employed, the greater were the risks his job entailed. As a battalion signaller, for instance, Victor Wheeler described how 'the dangerous assignment of finding, stringing, testing and repairing several lines along the trenches under continuous gunfire was utterly comfortless... It required nerves steeled against constant peril coupled with technical skill and exceptional courage'. Yet, Wheeler would also be assigned to work at brigade head-quarters from time to time, 'under very different conditions than those with which we were familiar in the front line', in 'the unfamiliar and rather stuffy and haughty atmosphere of Staff Officialdom'.[131] As Archibald MacGregor later noted, 'Any risks and discomforts I experienced as a Brigade Signal Officer were in no way comparable to the constant dangers and hardships endured by officers and men of infantry battalions'.[132]

In training, signallers were excused from most fatigues,[133] while in the frontline:

Signallers had to do no trench work or patrols and were the only men in the trench that were exempt from stand-to... A signaller could wander around the front line and no questions were asked... Signallers also got to know when something important was coming off, in many instances before the company commanders did... A signaller's life on the whole was far more pleasant than a rifle-and-bayonet man's.[134]

---

[128] J. F. Lucy, *There's a Devil in the Drum* (London: Faber and Faber, 1938), 301–2.

[129] Staniforth and Grayson (ed.), *At War with the 16th Irish Division*, 35.

[130] Lieutenant-Colonel G. E. B. Dobbs, WO339/5948, TNA. Dobbs had played rugby union for both the army and England before the war. See: Nigel McCrery, *Into Touch: Rugby Internationals Killed in the Great War* (Barnsley: Pen and Sword, 2014), 29–30.

[131] Victor W. Wheeler, *The 50th Battalion in No Man's Land* (Ontario: CEF Books, 2000), 22, 109.

[132] MacGregor and Welti (ed.), *Signals from the Great War*, 115.

[133] Ogilvie, *Umty-Iddy-Umty*, 10; Hanson and Wakefield (ed.), *Plough & Scatter*, 80.

[134] Richards, *Old Soldiers*, 108–9.

Many of these privileges had been enshrined in the army's pre-war doctrine. For instance, the 1909 *Field Service Regulations* stipulated that 'no signal unit exists solely for the formation to which it is allotted'.[135] Consequently, signallers were routinely called upon to provide and maintain communications for units other than their own.[136] As Frank Richards recalled: 'When going in the line we were not always posted to our own companies, and although I belonged to A [Company], I would sometimes be in the line with B, C, or D, or Battalion Headquarters'.[137] Similarly, with regards to the reliefs of signal units in the frontline, a memorandum by the Director of Army Signals in July 1916 stated that 'in the present form of warfare, it is inadvisable to treat the Brigade Signal Section as an integral part of the brigade'. The chief explanation for this was because if the communications system in a particular sector was either very complicated or in the process of being repaired, it was 'better for the personnel to remain in the sector they know' than move out with their own brigades upon being relieved.[138] It was also the case that signallers would move up to the frontline trenches and take over their posts 24 hours before their battalions.[139] Once there, the signallers further alienated themselves from their fellow soldiers by spending 'most of their time sitting down in dugouts, buzzing their telephones, disappearing occasionally down a trench with one finger on a wire, following that wire round corners, across ditches and over fields'.[140] Not only did his blue and white armband further disstinguish him from others,[141] but the signaller also spoke a language of his own. As one 'outsider' related:

His one task in life is to prevent the letter B from sounding like C, or D, or P, or T, or V, over the telephone; so he has perverted the English language to his own uses. He calls B "Beer", and D "Don", and so on. He salutes the rosy dawn as "Akk Emma", and eventide as "Pip Emma". He refers to the letter S as "Esses", in order to distinguish it from F. He has no respect for the most majestic military titles. To him the Deputy Assistant Director of Mobile Veterinary Section is merely a lifeless formula, entitled Don Akk Don Emma Vic Esses.

---

[135] *Field Service Regulations Part I*, 39. See also, *Manual of Army Signal Service – War*, 18.
[136] 'Organisation of Battalion Signallers', 18 January 1916, Guards Division Signal Company War Diary, WO95/1205, TNA.
[137] Richards, *Old Soldiers*, 108.
[138] 'Director of Army Signals Circular Memorandum No. 118. Notes on Signal Service from Operations in the Ypres Salient, June 1916', 13 July 1916, AWM 25/425/47, AWM.
[139] 'Trench Standing Orders, 1915–16. 124th Infantry Brigade', in Bull (comp.), *Officer's Manual*, 67.
[140] Griffith, *Up to Mametz*, 78.
[141] 'Director of Army Signals. Circular Memorandum No. 175. Blue and White Armbands', 20 December 1916, Director of Army Signals War Diary, WO95/57, TNA.

It is therefore not surprising that many soldiers came to view the signaller as 'a troglodyte, of sedentary habits and caustic temperament'.[142] Although some signal officers did their best to ensure that they and their men were not regarded as 'merely an attached party of specialists',[143] because of the specialist nature of their work many within the BEF, including Wyn Griffith, came to regard the signallers as 'always with the company, but never of it. . . They were a clan within our tribe'.[144]

Training

Before the war, prospective signal officers underwent their initial training alongside fellow R.E. cadets at the Royal Military Academy, Woolwich. Following the completion of this two-year course, they then undertook a further two-year programme of study at the Royal School of Military Engineering, Chatham, specialising in electrical engineering and telegraphy.[145] The training of non-R.E. signallers took place at the Army Signal School, Aldershot, where recruits were taught visual signalling only. However, in 1913 Aldershot assumed responsibility for the training of all signallers in both electrical and visual methods of communication.[146]

Upon the outbreak of the war, a Reserve Signal Depot under the initial command of Captain A. B. Cunningham, R.E., was formed at Aldershot to cater for the training of non-regular reinforcements. However, it was soon realised that something much larger would be required to accommodate the training of the signallers of the New Armies. Accordingly, in April 1915 the Reserve Signal Depot, the Army Signal School and the Signal Service Training Centres of the Territorial Force were amalgamated to form the Signal Service Training Centre, based in Bedfordshire.[147] Under the direction of Reginald Boys,[148] the Signal Service Training Centre consisted of a headquarters, originally based in Ridgmont but relocated to Bedford in October 1917, and a number of nearby depots, each specialising in a particular activity: Bedford (recruit training), Hitchin and Stevenage (holding and drafting), Baldock (unit formation), Houghton Regis (Army Signal School), Haynes Park

---

[142] Hay, *Carrying On*, 134, 156.   [143] Scrivenor, *Brigade Signals*, 149.
[144] Griffith, *Up to Mametz*, 78.   [145] Bowman and Connelly, *Edwardian Army*, 15.
[146] Nalder, *Royal Corps of Signals*, 19, 52.
[147] 'Historical Record of Headquarters. Signal Training Centre, Vol. 1, 1914–1949', WO305/2088, TNA.
[148] Commandant of the Signal Service Training Centre until his appointment as DD Signals, GHQ Home Forces, in May 1918. He was succeeded by Edmund Godfrey-Faussett. See: Becke (Comp.), *History of the Great War*, 8.

(riding instruction and cable laying) and Fenny Stratford (Wireless Training Centre).[149] Combined, these depots were responsible for the technical training of officers and other ranks, as well as the formation and training of non-divisional signal units.[150]

Compared to the general training schemes adopted elsewhere in the army, the system in place at the Signal Service Training Centre appears to have been somewhat different, as John Scrivenor later recalled:

The depot was not comfortable. The cadets' mess was overcrowded, no less than a hundred cadets being there for training. The procedure also in the depot was, to my strict ideas, odd. Parades were sloppy, and labour-men who waited in the mess also appeared on guard at the gate... If such a thing had happened in the Inns of Court – it was unthinkable – the orderly officer and N.C.O.'s would have thrown fits... In the infantry cadet schools at Berkhamsted, the cadets were encouraged to regard themselves as officers as soon as they entered the school and were treated as such. In the signal service the cadets were told bluntly that until they passed their examination and 'learned their trade' they were not considered as even the equals of pioneers.[151]

The course itself was long, intensive and 'difficult to pass unless one started with a good grounding'.[152] 'We hardly get a breathing time', Harry Lamb noted in his diary in late 1914.[153] Similarly, reflecting on the training he received in 1917, Captain W. G. Wallace, a signals liaison officer with the French Army in 1918, stated: 'The course was splendidly conceived and laid out and embraced an immense range of fascinatingly interesting subjects... How hard we used to work, out all day or else at lectures and then in the evenings writing up notes, revising and cramming'.[154] Scrivenor's experience is perhaps best illustrative of the training undertaken by aspirant signal officers during the second half of the war. Between 9 June 1917 and 8 January 1918 (approximately 30 weeks), Scrivenor rotated in and out of the various depots, beginning with a 2-week visual signalling course at Houghton Regis, before moving on to a month's instruction in elementary electricity, telegraphy and airline drill at Fenny Stratford. The next part of the training involved an 8-week stint at Haynes Park, learning how to ride, laying field cable and working on telephone exchanges, followed by a further 8 weeks' instruction at Bedford, at the end of which Scrivenor, alongside his

---

[149] Nalder, *Royal Corps of Signals*, 81–2.
[150] Lord and Watson, *Royal Corps of Signals*, 327.   [151] Scrivenor, *Brigade Signals*, 22–3.
[152] Ibid., 24. See also: Austin, *Schonland*, 29.
[153] 'First World War Diary', 11 October 1914, Second-Lieutenant H. A. J. Lamb Papers, PP/MCR/187, IWM.
[154] 'Memoirs of 1914–1918' (1935), 69, Captain W. G. Wallace Papers, 86/9/1, IWM.

fellow recruits, undertook the 'board-scheme' – a week of examinations consisting of written papers, practical tests and interviews with the examiners and the Commandant of the Training Centre. Whilst awaiting the results of their examinations, the recruits undertook a week's administrative course, dealing with military law, pay and other routine matters. A final interview with the Commandant then took place and the successful candidates received their commissions whilst undertaking a further month-long course in wireless at the Fenny Stratford depot. According to Scrivenor, there were roughly 300 cadets at the Training Centre at any one time, with classes numbering between 25 and 30 'passing out' approximately every fortnight.[155]

Meanwhile, the RMA, Woolwich, continued to award regular commissions to R.E. officers, though the course was initially reduced from two years to just 6 months. This was extended to 9 months in 1916 and then to 12 months in January 1917. In all, however, just 407 regular commissions were awarded to R.E. officers between August 1914 and June 1918.[156] Signal Service officers with regular commissions went from Woolwich to Chatham, where they undertook 3 months' general training, after which they were transferred to the Signal Service Training Centre, where they completed their technical instruction.[157] Short, formal refresher or 'polishing up' courses in signalling were also established in theatre.[158] A considerable amount of training was carried out at the Signal Service Depot in Abbeville, where reinforcements were initially sent before being posted to their units.[159] The GHQ Wireless, and the Army and Corps Signal Training Schools, however, became permanent establishments from 1916 onwards, whose primary purpose was to train instructors, while 'classes of instruction' were more temporary arrangements at division, brigade and battalion levels, dealing predominantly with the training of personnel. Both the Army and Corps Training Schools provided six-week instructor courses for regimental signallers (Syllabus A) and five-week instructor courses for Signal Service personnel (Syllabus B).[160] Typically, the artillery and infantry officers and NCOs who completed these courses would then train the signallers in

[155] Scrivenor, *Brigade Signals*, 24–42. See also: 'Historical Record of Headquarters. Signal Training Centre, Vol. 1, 1914–1949', WO305/2088, TNA.

[156] 'Remarks on Training at the Royal Military Academy, Woolwich. August 1914 to June 1918', 12 June 1918, WO314/1, TNA.

[157] Nalder, *Royal Corps of Signals*, 80; Pritchard (ed.), *History of the Corps of Royal Engineers*, Vol. V, 34–5.

[158] Priestley, *Work of the Royal Engineers*, 169.   [159] Ibid., 48.

[160] SS. 152. *Instructions for the Training of the British Armies in France* (January, 1918), 6–7, 43, 56.

their units at the division, brigade or battalion classes.[161] But how efficient and realistic were these various training schemes?

During the first year of the war, the training of new signallers suffered from the want of technical equipment.[162] Buzzer telephones and wireless sets, in particular, were in very short supply. As a result, many signallers who underwent their training during this period recalled after the war that the bulk of their time was spent on mastering visual methods of communication.[163] According to Lionel Harris, the time spent on 'flag wagging' during training was completely wasted. 'The retention of semaphore', he sceptically remarked, 'can only have been due to some old die-hard who probably still thought it a pity that we had abandoned red jackets for khaki'.[164] Yet, it would appear that the army's love affair with training recruits in visual signalling persisted well into the war. For instance, shortly after the opening of a new Corps Signal School in early 1918, a group of Canadian battalion signal officers complained that 'they did too much visual, and had not nearly enough work on other instruments'.[165] One officer found this preoccupation with visual signalling puzzling since 'the Buzzer's first proceeding upon entering the field of active hostilities is to get under-ground, and stay there'.[166] Some cadets also discovered that despite receiving special lectures from recently returned signal officers regarding their experiences at the front, their training could only prepare them so much for the realities of the conditions on the Western Front.[167] Shortly after arriving in France in May 1917, for example, Archibald MacGregor was sent out to repair a broken telephone line, only to be 'rather shocked at the tangled mass of variously coloured telephone cable that came out of the signal office – *so* different from the orderly array we had been taught to deal with at Training Depots in England!'[168]

Despite these incidents, the doctrinal framework for communications underwent a significant development in March 1917 with the publication of *SS. 148. Forward Inter-Communication in Battle*,[169] the BEF's first

---

[161] 'Fourth Army. Courses of Instruction during the Winter. 1 November 1916, to 1 April 1917', 8 January 1917, Montgomery-Massingberd Papers 7/34, LHCMA; 'Programme of Training at Signal Schools and Classes, December 1917', RG9-III-C-5/4443/8/5, LAC; 'Australian Corps General Staff Circular No. 1. Training – Communication Personnel', 4 January 1918, AWM25/425/26, AWM. For additional context on the BEF's training schools, see Robbins, *British Generalship*, 83–97.

[162] Williams, *Raising and Training*, 77.   [163] Ogilvie, *Umty-Iddy-Umty*, 10.

[164] Harris, *Signal Venture*, 43.

[165] 'A.D. Signals, Canadian Corps', 5 February 1918, RG9-III-C-5/4440/1/12, LAC.

[166] Hay, *Carrying On*, 134.   [167] Austin, *Schonland*, 30.

[168] MacGregor and Welti (ed.), *Experiences of a Signals Officer*, 32.

[169] *SS. 148. Forward Inter-Communication in Battle*. On the BEF's training manuals, see Griffith, *Battle Tactics*, 179–91; and, Beach, 'Issued by the General Staff'.

Plate 2.2 Cable testing station, France, 1917 (Canada. Dept. of National Defence/Library and Archives Canada/RCSigs.ca, MIKAN no. 3380989)

'authoritative manual' devoted entirely to the issue of communications. Produced in a mere eight days (a four day staff–Signal Service conference and a four day writing-up period),[170] SS. 148 not only helped cement the Signal Service's position within the army, and in the process improve staff and Signal Service relations, but it also laid down a concrete set of principles to which all units of the BEF were to conform, since, up until its publication, the communication training, practices and organisation within a particular unit had depended very largely upon its own individual experience.[171] Dealing primarily with communications forward of divisional headquarters, SS. 148 was, according to the history of the Royal Corps of Signals, 'a milestone in the history of army intercommunication in that it established a code as between the users of communications and the Signal Service, which clarified the parts to be played jointly in order to obtain the best results'.[172]

[170] Priestley, *Work of the Royal Engineers*, 180–1.
[171] 'Second Army. O.A. 766. N.M.D. 1217/G', 22 March 1915, III Corps Intelligence Summaries, March 1915, WO157/303, TNA; '[Second Army] Summary of Instructions', 8 October 1916, AWM25/311/65, AWM.
[172] Nalder, *Royal Corps of Signals*, 127.

Consisting of nine separate sections, *SS. 148* described in considerable detail issues pertaining to communications within a brigade and a battalion during an attack, communication involving tanks and aircraft, the means of obtaining information, the means of transmission and the moves of headquarters in an advance. The overall objective was to ensure that an efficient 'system of forward communication' existed so as 'to get information back and disseminate it; to get orders forward; [and] to ensure the co-operation of all arms and units, especially between the Artillery and the Infantry'.[173] Although it acknowledged that 'no one means of communication is infallible', the manual also warned that the breakdown of 'mechanical means of communication' in battle would 'not excuse a Commander remaining in ignorance of the course of events, or neglecting to keep his immediate superior and neighbouring formations constantly informed of what is occurring on his front'. To this end, *SS. 148* was not a radical departure from *FSR I (1909)*, in that it strongly emphasised the use of non-technical means of obtaining and transmitting information, such as orderlies and liaison officers.[174]

However, despite its importance, *SS. 148* had three major flaws. First, while it contained a section devoted entirely to the issue of communications in open warfare, it made no reference to communications during a retreat. This was to prove a fundamental omission given the situation that the BEF was to find itself in during the spring of 1918. Second, despite its being more than 50 pages in length, it was soon realised that *SS. 148* did not cater to the communication needs of everybody. Army and corps aside, it did not take into account the system of communication for the Heavy Artillery.[175] Third, and finally, as the battles of 1917 were to demonstrate, some of the principles laid down in *SS. 148* were simply too rigid to be applied ubiquitously. A certain degree of modification and initiative on the part of the individual signal officer concerned was required in order to suit local circumstances. Some of these modifications were included in the revised and much-improved version of the manual, *SS. 191. Intercommunication in the Field*, published in November 1917. However, as with its predecessor, *SS. 191* ignored the possibility of communications in a retreat.[176]

In spite of its limitations, over the course of 1917 *SS. 148* was largely welcomed by commanders, staff and signal officers alike. A report by

---

[173] *SS. 148. Forward Inter-Communication in Battle*, 3.
[174] Ibid., 7, 3, 38–9; *Field Service Regulations, Part 1 (1909)*, 22–6, 119–39.
[175] 'Xth Corps "G". R.A. X Corps No. 9/6/492', 5 July 1917, X Corps War Diary, WO95/852, TNA.
[176] *SS. 191. Intercommunication in the Field* (November 1917).

Robert Willan (AD Signals IX Corps) following the Battle of Messines observed that 'the principles laid down in SS. 148 are sound and should be closely adhered to. Units which had paid most attention to the instructions contained in SS. 148 being the most successful with their forward communications'.[177] Likewise, after spending two months observing communications in VIII Corps, Colonel William McCornack, the Commandant of the AEF Signal School, noted in May 1918 that *SS. 148* had 'proved to be a good basis for communications'.[178] Overall, encapsulating the lessons learnt from the experiences of 1916, *SS. 148* was a major step in the right direction, proving that British commanders clearly recognised the importance of communications and were prepared to advocate a universal set of principles in order to improve both signal training and, ultimately, communications in battle.

In summary, the personnel who made up the BEF's communications system can be divided into three main groups – the directors, the signal officers and the other ranks. The directors, though they composed a relatively small clique of pre-war Regular and Territorial officers, were nonetheless experienced, pragmatic and willing to exploit their personal and professional connections with the civilian and commercial sectors in order to furnish the army with the tools, in terms of both material and manpower, needed to construct and maintain an efficient, modern military communications system. Indeed, the signal officers below them were drawn largely from these sectors, the majority being employed in engineering-related occupations, providing a unique set of technical skills and leadership qualities that made them eminently suitable to their new positions. Likewise, the other ranks were recruited mainly from the civilian communications sector, nearly half of whom were employees of the GPO. It would not be going too far to suggest that without the relationship between the Signal Service and the GPO, the successful expansion of the Signal Service and the improvement of the BEF's communications system on the Western Front would not have been possible.

Collectively, the signallers were the 'nerves' of the BEF,[179] 'letting the right hand of the army know what the left hand is doing, and letting the world know what both are accomplishing at the same time'.[180] The technical nature of their work largely preserved them from outside

---

[177] 'Report on Signal Communications during Recent Offensive Operations on IX Corps Front', June 1917, IX Corps Signal Company War Diary, WO95/845, TNA.

[178] 'Lecture No. 16. The British Signal Service', May 1918, AEF Army Signal School, Miscellaneous Files, RG120/407/1796, NARA.

[179] Captain S. H. Watson, Typescript Memoirs, 'Signaller' (1974), 2, ANZAC (Aust.), LCL.

[180] Corcoran, *Daredevil*, 61.

interference and gave them certain privileges which made them the envy of many infantrymen. Highly skilled, unperturbed and indispensable, they were ubiquitous and yet at the same time obscure. The establishment of an official Signal Service Training Centre and the codifying of 'best practice' in the form of the training manuals *SS. 148* and *SS. 191* further demonstrates that British commanders clearly recognised the importance of good communications for conducting successful operations. They subsequently proved themselves talented in adapting to the demands of modern, industrialised warfare. While much of this success came about as a result of the pragmatic nature of the British officer corps, it also hinged upon the BEF's readiness to take advice from the civil professions and to utilise civilian equipment and technical expertise. The case of communications therefore provides another illuminating example of the way in which the BEF sought to harness the skills of its citizen soldiers in a modern, 'total war'.

3   Means of Communication

The means of communication available to British commanders through-out the First World War constituted an integral part of the army's command and control system. As one signal officer stressed after the war: 'Striking power, to-day, is out-distancing the means of control and the problem of signal communications is how to restore the balance'.[1] According to *Field Service Regulations Part I: Operations (1909)*, it was of the utmost importance that there existed 'a constant maintenance of communication between the various parts of an army'. To this end, the efficiency of the BEF's communications system depended upon the 'careful coordination and economical employment of the several means of intercommunication available'.[2] In attempting to find a solution to the intractable problem of maintaining 'real-time' communications during the heat of battle, the BEF was forced to utilise a diverse, and sometimes innovative, array of communication methods ranging from the most modern, such as telegraphy, telephony and wireless, to the more antiquated, such as visual signalling, carrier pigeons and runners. An understanding of the chief characteristics of these methods, as well as their relative strengths and weaknesses, is crucial if one is to assess the influence of communications upon British military operations on the Western Front.

Telegraph

Upon the outbreak of the First World War, the telegraph had firmly established itself as a standard method of communication within the British Army.[3] At the strategic level, since the first successful trans-Atlantic

---

[1] Major R. Chenevix-Trench, 'Signal Communications in War', *Journal of the Royal United Service Institution*, 72 (1927), 295.
[2] *Field Service Regulations Part I*, 22, 39.
[3] On the history and development of the electric telegraph, see: Irving Fang, *A History of Mass Communication: Six Information Revolutions* (Oxford: Focal Press, 1997), 77–82; Tom Standage, *The Victorian Internet* (London: Weidenfeld and Nicolson, 1998); and,

submarine cable was laid in 1866,[4] Britain had been able to establish
a comprehensive global telegraph service which interconnected the British Empire and served as 'a vital part of the network of imperial
defence'.[5] Operationally, during the Second South African, or Boer,
War (1899–1902), the telegraph had proven a rapid and efficient means
of transmitting orders, reports and other important information, particularly between the series of blockhouses that were built during the
latter stages of the conflict to divide the country and pacify the Boer
resistance.[6] However, although Sir John French was correct when he
observed in 1904 that 'telegraph communication will play a great role in
future wars',[7] there were profound limitations to its use at the tactical
level: first, its wires were susceptible to damage from shellfire and
cavalry, and vulnerable to enemy interception; second, it was an unsuit-
able method of communication for mobile operations; and, third, it
required highly trained staff to operate and maintain.[8] These weaknesses
were to be ruthlessly exposed by the conditions which prevailed on the
Western Front.[9]

Throughout the war, the BEF employed an intricate and diverse
system of telegraphy. The strategic telegraph network, from the War
Office and the Central Telegraph Office in London to the headquarters
of the lines of communication on the Channel ports, consisted of two
double-current duplex circuits. A high-speed Wheatstone automatic
system, consisting of double-current simplex circuits, operated along
the lines of communication to GHQ and army headquarters. Double-
current simplex circuits connected army and corps headquarters, while

---

Laszlo Solymar, *Getting the Message: A History of Communications* (Oxford: Oxford
University Press, 1999), 51–88.

[4] Daniel R. Headrick, *The Invisible Weapon: Telecommunications and International Politics
1851–1945* (Oxford: Oxford University Press, 1991), 17–18.

[5] P. M. Kennedy, 'Imperial Cable Communications and Strategy, 1870–1914', *English
Historical Review*, 86 (1971), 729. See also Armand Mattelart, *Mapping World
Communication: War, Progress, Culture* (Minneapolis: University of Minnesota Press,
1994), 14.

[6] 'History of the Telegraph Operations during the War in South Africa, 1899–1902, by
Lieutenant-Colonel R. L. Hippisley, C.B., R.E.', 31 May 1902, WO108/376, TNA;
Godfrey-Faussett, 'Studies on the Use of Field Telegraphs', 289–92; Captain F. S.
Morgan, 'The Development of Communication and Command', *Journal of the Royal
United Service Institution*, 76 (1931), 132.

[7] 'Report of Sir John French', 1904, Report of the Wood Committee on Army Telegraphs,
1904–5, WO32/6799, TNA.

[8] Most of these problems had been identified before the First World War. See Colonel F. J.
Davies, C.B., 'The Communications of a Division in the Field', *Journal of the Royal
United Service Institution*, 53 (1909), 885–7.

[9] See 'Report of the Committee on the Lessons of the Great War (The Kirke Report)',
October 1932, WO32/3116, TNA.

single-current simplex and buzzer circuits were the standard methods of telegraphy from corps to divisions and divisions to brigades.[10] Although this system remained largely unaltered during the course of the war, a number of improvements were made. Chief amongst these was the introduction of a 'concentrator' along the lines of communication in late 1916 and at GHQ in 1918, which enabled multiple address messages to be sent simultaneously by one operator.[11] According to one GHQ signal officer, the installation of the concentrator apparatus 'resulted in much quicker operating and a big reduction in the average delay in completing connections', as well as easing the burden of the operators at GHQ.[12]

There were two types of lines utilised by the BEF: 'Airline' and 'Cable'. The former referred to bare wire fixed to poles, buildings or trees,[13] while the latter consisted of gutta-percha or rubber insulated wire laid along the ground.[14] Airline was the prominent feature of the telegraph and telephone system to the rear of divisional headquarters, beyond the range of enemy artillery fire. Whereas the routes up to corps headquarters were of heavy permanent construction, those between corps and divisions comprised lighter, semi-permanent trestle routes, known as 'Comic Airline'.[15] The average time taken by one cable detachment – consisting of one officer, 11 men, eight horses and a wagon – to run, pull up and regulate eight wires for eight telegraph poles was between 45 and 55 minutes. This did not include the time taken to dig one pot hole (30 minutes), to arm the pole with five arms (60 minutes) and finally to erect the pole (10–15 minutes).[16] Not surprisingly, the work was exhausting, 'methodically mechanical',[17] and, as one sapper commented in early 1916, 'the rate of

---

[10] A simplex circuit was one in which telegraphic messages could flow in only one direction at a time, whereas duplex allowed communication in both directions simultaneously. The high-speed Wheatstone automatic apparatus, named after its inventor, Sir Charles Wheatstone, allowed for a much faster and intensive system of telegraphy than by simple manual operation. See Major W. A. J. O'Meara, 'The Various Systems of Multiplex Telegraphy', *Royal Engineers Journal*, 14 (1911), 353–64; Nalder, *Royal Corps of Signals*, 94.

[11] Priestley, *Work of the Royal Engineers*, 292.

[12] Captain A. Speight, R.E., 'GHQ Signal Office, France', *Post Office Electrical Engineers' Journal*, 13 (1920–1), 52–5.

[13] 'No object lying in the cross-country course of the detachment that is high enough to replace a pole, is ever spared. Whether it be a permanent telegraph pole already erected in the country, or a tall tree or a house-top – one and all they come in handy'. Corcoran, *Daredevil of the Army*, 108.

[14] Hammond, 'Communication in the Field', 140.

[15] Nalder, *Royal Corps of Signals*, 102.

[16] 'Organisation of an Airline Section When Building a Main Route, by Lieutenant J. C. Dalton, R.E.', 3 March 1918, Organisation and Work of Signals in WW1 – Papers on Various Subjects, M1599, REMA; Corcoran, *Daredevil*, 64–5.

[17] 'Signaller in France 1914–1918', 51, Craven Papers, REMA.

pole erection does not always satisfy carping critics, who perhaps do not appreciate the difficulties encountered'.[18]

Telegraphic and telephonic cable routes forward of divisional head-quarters were laid on short poles or stakes, along the sides or the bottom of trenches or simply along the ground.[19] This was certainly no easy task, as one signal officer related after the war:

It sounds so easy, laying a wire. But I swear it is the most wearying business in the world... [On] the rainy day I paid out, I was never more miserable in my life than I was after two miles... Have a thought for the wretched fellows who are getting out a wire on a dark and snowy night, troubled perhaps by persistent snipers and frequent shells![20]

Although it could be laid at a much faster rate than airline, cable was highly susceptible to faults, breakages and enemy interception.[21] Throughout the war, the BEF implemented numerous measures to combat these problems, including twisting the cable to reduce 'leakage', utilising a variety of armoured cables with steel, brass and lead covers and burying them to ever-greater depths.[22] Faults and breakages were also the result of poor cable-laying practice, with artillery signallers frequently cited as being the chief culprits.[23] Signallers had to be constantly on the prowl to repair cable blown away by shellfire, or cut accidentally by friendly troops, cavalry and tanks. Although 'difficult to access', buried cables were 'led through wooden boxes inserted into the run of the bury at intervals to permit testing'. These 'test centres' enabled linemen to 'tap into the circuits at intervals to confirm that they were in working order'. If a fault developed, the linemen had to 'venture out and trace the break in the cable and mend it accordingly'.[24] According to William Ogilvie, a signaller in the 21st Battery, CFA: 'Groping through or around the shell holes, letting the foul, slime covered wire slip through

---

[18] Anon., 'With a Signal Company on Service: A Short Account of the Doings of the 5th Signal Company, R.E., since Leaving Carlow for the War', *Sapper*, 21 (February 1916), 174.

[19] Richards, *Old Soldiers Never Die*, 109; Corcoran, *Daredevil*, 66; 'Blue Chevrons: An Infantry Private's Great War Diary' (c. 1962), 37, Surfleet Papers, IWM.

[20] Watson, *Adventures of a Motorcycle Despatch Rider*, 105–6.

[21] Mr Lambert, Interview (1985), Department of Sound Records, 009221/5, IWM.

[22] 'Lecture No. 30. Observations at the British Front', Officers' School – First Course, Monday 7 January 1918 to Saturday, 2 February 1918, RG120/404/2, NARA. On the interception of cable traffic for intelligence purposes, see Beach, *Haig's Intelligence*, 157–9.

[23] 'that single wire running, in defiance of all regulations, across the top of the trench, which neatly tipped your cap off just now, was laid by those playful humorists, the Royal Artillery'. Hay, *Carrying On*, 141. See also: Scrivenor, *Brigade Signals*, 76; Corcoron, *Daredevil*, 63–4.

[24] 'Signaller in France 1914–1918', 88–9, Craven Papers, REMA.

your hand, trying not to lose your footing in the dark was a nightmare and you swore that this was a job not fit for humans'.[25] Nevertheless, despite these notable drawbacks, the telegraph remained an important means of communication throughout the war.

Telephone

While the telegraph formed an important part of the British Army's communications system in 1914, the potential of telephony had yet to be fully appreciated.[26] The first operational use of the telephone by the army occurred during the Egyptian War of 1882, though the instruments used were part of the civil network and were not employed to convey important tactical information.[27] Although much greater use was made of the telephone in South Africa, British officers preferred to use telegraph along the lines of communication, while visual signalling and mounted orderlies were the most prominent means of communication at the tactical level.[28] Despite having been invented nearly 40 years prior to the First World War, technical limitations, considerations of mobility and secrecy and a desire to maintain a more personalised style of command and control ensured that the BEF went to war with a rather limited supply of telephones.[29] It was not until the advent of trench warfare in the winter of 1914–15 that British commanders began to realise the necessity of telephonic communication, especially at the tactical level.[30]

---

[25] Ogilvie, *Umty-Iddy-Umty*, 32. For a detailed explanation of how a signaller would repair broken cable, see E. P. F. Lynch, *Somme Mud: The Experiences of an Infantryman in France, 1916–1919* (London: Bantam Books, 2008), 302.

[26] The telephone received rather lukewarm reception from British business leaders and society in general before the war. See: Charles R. Perry, 'The British Experience 1876–1912: The Impact of the Telephone during the Years of Delay', in Ithiel de Sola Pool (ed.), *The Social Impact of the Telephone* (Cambridge, MA: MIT Press, 1977), 68–96; Paul Thompson, *The Edwardians: The Remaking of British Society* (London: Routledge, 1992), 155; Graeme J. Milne, 'British Business and the Telephone, 1878–1911', *Business History*, 49 (2007), 163–85; and, Campbell-Smith, *Masters of the Post*, 194.

[27] Nalder, *Royal Corps of Signals*, 25–6; Major C. F. C. Beresford R.E., 'The Telephone at Home and in the Field', *Journal of the Royal United Service Institution*, 36 (1892), 347–68.

[28] 'Signalling Equipment', undated, Extracts from Reports by Officers Commanding Units in South Africa during 1899–1901, WO108/278, TNA.

[29] These points are developed further in Brian N. Hall, 'The "Life-Blood" of Command? The British Army, Communications and the Telephone, 1877–1914', *War & Society*, 27 (October 2008), 43–65.

[30] 'Our experiences in this war have taught us that communication *by means of wire* is more suitable than visual in nine cases out of ten'. See 'Notes on Signal Communications', 7 January 1915, 1 Division War Diary, WO95/1228, TNA.

With the onset of trench warfare, the telephone became an indispensable tool for command and control. As Captain Wyn Griffith, staff captain of the 115th Infantry Brigade in 1916, wrote after the war, 'A telephone wire was not only the outward sign of command, but the lifeblood of its existence. A general without a telephone was to all practical purposes impotent – a lay figure dressed in uniform, deprived of eyes, arms and ears'.[31] Originally, the BEF took with it in 1914 only a limited supply of portable 'buzzer' telephones, most of which were exclusively reserved for use within the artillery.[32] Neither the D. Mk. I, nor the D. Mk. II portable buzzer telephones, however, were particularly popular instruments. Although they could be used for speaking and sending messages by Morse code,[33] according to Colonel R. M. Powell, who commanded 2 Division Signal Company in 1914:

> The hand telephone attachments were quite useless for any but short distances, and the only conversations between Division and Brigade consisted of 'speaking over the key', i.e., the Staff Officer dictated his conversation to the telegraph operator, who sent it by vibrator in Morse – the receiving operator 'translating' it to the Staff Officer at the other end; a very slow and unsatisfactory process.[34]

The design of these portable telephones rendered it 'necessary to make a fairly large sacrifice of signalling and speaking efficiency in order that the size and weight of the instruments [could] be reduced to a minimum'.[35] Thus, in late September 1914 GHQ informed the War Office that the army 'urgently required' the supply of the new, more reliable and efficient D. Mk. III telephone, which was a lot simpler to use and produced a better sound quality over a longer distance.[36] The D. Mk. III subsequently became the standard portable buzzing telephone set in service during the war.[37]

As the demand for telephonic equipment at all levels increased throughout 1915, it soon became clear that the limited number of civil telephones and switchboards commandeered and adapted for use by the Signal Service were ill suited to meet the growing telephonic requirements

---

[31] Griffith, *Up to Mametz*, 185.   [32] *Field Service Pocket Book. 1914*, 63.
[33] For which purpose a key was provided. See *Instruction in Army Telegraphy and Telephony:* Vol. 1, *Instruments* (London: HMSO, 1914), 166–8; and, Lieutenant E. J. Stevens, *Field Telephones for Army Use: Including an Elementary Course in Electricity and Magnetism* (London: Crosby Lockwood & Son, 1908), 78–98.
[34] Colonel R. M. Powell, 'Divisional Signals in 1914', *Royal Signals Quarterly Journal*, 7 (1940), 340.
[35] T. F. Purves, 'Trench Telephones', *Post Office Electrical Engineers' Journal*, 8 (1915–16), 95.
[36] GHQ to War Office, 30 September 1914, Secret Telegrams, WO33/713, TNA.
[37] Priestley, *Work of the Royal Engineers*, 13–14.

of the army. Fortunately, the Signal Service's close affiliation with the GPO ensured the supply of specially designed magneto telephones and switchboards.[38] These magneto telephones were of two types: those of 'a semi-portable nature, providing first grade speaking and ringing facilities, and, at the same time, capable of ready transportation from point to point'; and those 'designed for longer and more permanent connections established between the various headquarters, as well as for the scattered offices of the staff and administration officers'.[39] Although the majority of these magneto telephones and switchboards were of a simpler design than those utilised by the GPO in Great Britain,[40] it was not until 5 January 1916 that the establishment of 20 magneto telephones and one 20-line and one 10-line switchboard per division was authorised.[41] The adoption of this new equipment 'brought a general improvement in all army phone communication',[42] though it is clear that it took some commanders and staff officers quite a while to become proficient in its use.[43]

While the telephone became the BEF's most indispensable method of communication, its use was not without its drawbacks. Like the telegraph's, its wires were extremely vulnerable to shellfire and to enemy interception. It was also ill suited to the conditions of mobility and manoeuvre which characterised the operations of 1914 and 1918.[44] Moreover, while there was practically no limit to the operational range of the telegraph, telephones in the early twentieth century suffered from the problem of attenuation.[45] As part of Lieutenant-General Sir Henry

---

[38] Magneto telephones incorporated a small hand generator to supply the current used to contact the switchboard operator. Upon answering the call, the operator would ask the caller whom he wished to be put through to and then make the necessary connection. John William Henry Boon, Interview (1986), Department of Sound Records, 009476/7, IWM.

[39] Purves, 'Trench Telephones', 95.

[40] Lieutenant-Colonel Arthur Hemsley, Interview (1987), Department of Sound Records, 009927/7, IWM.

[41] Infantry and artillery brigades were not officially issued with magneto telephones until December 1916. See Priestley, *Work of the Royal Engineers*, 64. A new R. E. trade designated 'Telephone Switchboard Operator' took effect in early 1917. See '30/Engineers/3272 (A.G.7)', 2 February 1917, POST30/4061B/23/5, BTA.

[42] Lieutenant J. A. MacDonald, *Gun-Fire: An Historical Narrative of the 4th Brigade C.F.A. 1914–1918* (first published 1929; new ed., Uckfield: Naval and Military Press, 2004), 70.

[43] Captain Norman Davey, R.E., 'The Telephone at the Front', *Journal of the Royal Signals Institution*, 24 (2010), 11 [reprinted from *Punch*, 17 November 1915]; 'General Staff Circular Memorandum No. 45. Telephone Exchange Working', 20 November 1917, AWM25/425/41, AWM.

[44] See Chapter 4 and Chapter 7 respectively.

[45] That is, the decline in the clarity of speech as the distance of the telephone call increased. See John Bray, *The Communications Miracle: The Telecommunication Pioneers from Morse to the Information Superhighway* (London: Plenum Press, 1995), 5.

Rawlinson's staff in 1914, for example, Leopold Amery recorded in his diary on 12 October the telephone conversation he had had with Major-General Henry Wilson (MGGS, GHQ). Telephoning from the General Post Office in Ostend to GHQ, Amery noted that 'the telephone was almost inaudible and it took the best part of an hour in the early hours of the morning to get half a dozen lines from Henry'.[46] According to one signal officer after the war, 'long distance telephony with the circuits then available was extremely capricious and in any case not suitable when secrecy was necessary'.[47] The problem of inaudibility was also a feature of telephonic communication during the heat of battle. During the Battle of Loos in September 1915, one artillery signaller wrote, 'Our ears are ringing and we can only shout at one another and Morse down the telephone; voices can't be heard'.[48] Similarly, while working in the signal office of 40 Division near Hazebrouk in late August 1918, Second-Lieutenant H. A. J. Lamb noted that the 'most deafening noise of our artillery barrage' made it 'absolutely impossible to hear on [the] phone'.[49] Nevertheless, despite these issues, the telephone developed rapidly from a subsidiary means of communication in 1914 to become the BEF's primary medium during the war. As one officer noted in 1917: 'Practically all the business of an Army in the field is transacted by telephone. If the telephone breaks down, whether by an Act of God or the King's Enemies, that business is at a standstill until the telephone is put right again'.[50]

Wireless

As with the telephone, wireless was slow to win a place within the British Army's communications system prior to the war. Although the army did show a readiness to conduct wireless tests during the war in South Africa, and despite the establishment of a small experimental staff at the Army Signal School in Aldershot in 1903 and the creation of an Army Wireless Section in 1905, doubt, suspicion and scepticism hampered wireless development within the army during the pre-war period.[51] Part of the

---

[46] Typescript Diary, 12 October 1914, Leopold Amery Papers, AMEL7/12, Churchill Archives Centre, Cambridge (CAC).
[47] 'Signaller in France 1914–1918', 27, Craven Papers, REMA.
[48] Cecil Longley, *Battery Flashes* (New York: E. P. Dutton, 1916), 149.
[49] 'First World War Diary', 27 August 1918, Lamb Papers, IWM.
[50] Hay, *Carrying On*, 129.
[51] Nalder, *Royal Corps of Signals*, 37–49; Hammond, 'Communication in the Field', 141; Baker, *History of the Marconi Company*, 50–1, 161; Cusins, 'Development of Army Wireless', 763, 766, Norman Papers, IWM.

reason for this was a general lack of enthusiasm, caused predominantly by an overwhelming fear of wireless insecurity.[52] As a report written shortly after the army's 1913 autumn manoeuvres made clear:

> Wireless is one of the last methods by which important messages should be sent on service, because (i) All messages must be sent in cipher, (ii) Foreign fortresses have instruments which can locate, both in direction and range, any stations working, (iii) There is always a danger of the cipher being read... Messages going by wireless should be usually, and if possible, of transient importance, so that if read within say 12–18 hours not much harm is done.[53]

This conclusion supported the findings of a committee chaired by Sir Henry Norman MP,[54] set up in 1912 to review the state of army wireless,[55] which noted that 'grave doubts are generally felt by senior officers as to the reliability of army wireless. They would not feel safe in time of war unless an alternative means of communication were provided'. The committee subsequently recommended that 'the efficiency of our forces in time of war would be better promoted by the abandonment of wireless communication altogether... as an inefficient wireless service in war would be a constant source of doubt and danger.[56]

However, the committee's final report also stressed that 'the inefficiency of the [army's] wireless service... is to a great extent due to the present type of apparatus employed'.[57] Indeed, wireless technology was very much in its infancy in 1914. Like the early versions of computers and mobile telephones, wireless sets in the early twentieth century were large, heavy and unreliable.[58] No portable, man-carried set for army purposes yet existed. Furthermore, wireless sets in 1914 were 'almost exclusively Morse-operated with crystals or magnetised tape-detection for receivers, and arc or spark-gap radiation

---

[52] For additional context on wireless security measures and procedures, see John Ferris (ed.), *The British Army and Signals Intelligence during the First World War* (Stroud: Alan Sutton, 1992), 6–9.

[53] Captain Rupert Ommanney, 'Notes on Work at General Headquarters', 22 October 1913, WO106/51, TNA.

[54] Sir Henry Norman (1858–1939) was a Liberal MP for Wolverhampton South (1900–10) and for Blackburn (1910–23). Between 1915 and 1919 he served as a liaison officer between the British Ministry of Munitions and the French Ministry of Inventions in Paris. In 1920 he was appointed chairman of the Imperial Wireless Telegraphy Committee, which helped draw up a complete wireless scheme to connect the British Empire.

[55] 'Appointment of Committee to Consider Application of Wireless Telegraphy to the Military Service', 31 July 1912, WO32/8877, TNA.

[56] 'Final Report of the Committee on Wireless Telegraphy', 3 September 1913, WO32/8879, TNA.

[57] Ibid.

[58] Ian Poole, *Newnes Guide to Radio and Communications Technology* (Oxford: Newnes, 2003); Bray, *Communications Miracle*, 67; Solymar, *Getting the Message*, 130.

for transmission'.[59] This meant that their operational range was limited, channel selectivity was poor and very few sets could be employed on a given frontage without risk of mutual interference. Wireless telephony – the transmission of human speech by radio waves – required the use of the thermionic valve (also known as the vacuum tube amplifier), the development of which was still at an experimental stage at this time.[60]

The BEF went to war in 1914 with three principal wireless sets: the motor lorry set, wagon set and pack set.[61] Powered by a 1.5-kilowatt petrol engine and comprising two 70-foot masts, the motor lorry set was the largest and most powerful wireless apparatus in army service, and had a range of approximately 100 miles.[62] As the name suggests, this was a complete wireless telegraphy station carried within the confines of a lorry. Two operators would work within the lorry – a 'small space of twelve feet by six' – one of whom would receive and transmit messages, while the other would log and file them, usually handing them to orderlies who waited outside on bicycles for distribution.[63] According to Edward Appleton, the set made such 'a terrible noise' that 'you could often read the signals better with the head-phones off, standing outside the lorry'.[64] Wagon sets were similarly powered, weighed more than a ton and were equipped with an 80-foot, 'umbrella-like' aerial mast, transmitter and receiver, all drawn by four horses. Pack sets were lighter and thus more mobile, though four horses were still required to carry the transmitter, receiver, 0.5-kilowatt engine and two 30-foot masts. It took between 15 and 20 minutes to set up and had a range of approximately 30 miles.[65]

---

[59] Dean Juniper, 'The First World War and Radio Development', *Journal of the Royal United Services Institute*, 148 (2003), 84.

[60] Three valves/vacuum tubes in particular had been developed before the war: John Ambrose Fleming's 'diode' (1904), Lee DeForest's 'audion' (1906) and Henry Round's (Marconi Company) 'soft' triode valves (1913). All were hand-built, difficult to manufacture and not yet suitable for battlefield use. See: Anon., 'Wireless Telegraphy and Telephony', *Journal of the Royal United Services Institution*, 56 (1912), 1004–5; Bray, *Communications Miracle*, 67; Peter J. Hugill, *Global Communications since 1844: Geopolitics and Technology* (Baltimore and London: John Hopkins University Press, 1999), 141–54; and, Sungook Hong, *Wireless: From Marconi's Black-Box to the Audion* (Cambridge, MA: MIT Press, 2001), 155–6.

[61] Cusins, 'Development of Army Wireless', 763–4.

[62] 'Wireless Memories round about the First World War' (1958), 6, Raymond Priestley Papers, GS1303, LCL.

[63] Corcoran, *Daredevil*, 82.

[64] Ronald Clark, *Sir Edward Appleton G.B.E., K.C.B., F.R.S.* (Oxford: Pergamon Press, 1971), 16. Appleton was the senior wireless instructor at the Signal Service Training Centre during the war. He went on to have a distinguished academic career, receiving the Nobel Prize for physics in 1947.

[65] 'Wireless Memories', 6, Priestley Papers, 'Forty Thousand Hours of War' (Typescript Memoirs, 1971–2), 15, W. George Mead Papers, GALL194/1, LCL.

None of these sets had performed particularly well when demonstrated in front of the Norman committee in 1912.[66] Consequently, although it acknowledged that 'wireless communication between the different parts of an army in the field may be of the utmost value, rendering services with which no other method of communication can compare', the committee's final report concluded that unless the army could acquire the services of highly trained officers and men, and could obtain equipment 'of the most scientific construction', simple in operation and 'rapid in movement, erection and dismantling', then wireless communication would remain 'so inefficient as to be unreliable, and therefore practically valueless, in time of war'.[67] Given its intrinsic limitations in the early twentieth century, it is easy to understand why so many British officers had such little faith in wireless communication.[68]

Thus, as a result of the overwhelming fear of insecurity that it generated and its general technical shortcomings, in 1914 the use of wireless in the BEF was confined to the fixed and relatively stationary position of GHQ.[69] Wireless was also provided to the cavalry, since it was recognised that 'a Cavalry Division cannot usefully communicate by any means of communication employing wire or cable'.[70] GHQ was equipped with one motor wireless set and three portable wagon sets, while a further three wagon sets were allocated to the Cavalry Division headquarters and each cavalry brigade equipped with a standard pack set.[71] However, these sets proved ill suited both to the mobile operations which characterised the fighting in 1914 and to the trench conditions that prevailed from the winter of 1914–15 onwards.[72] In mid-1915, therefore, GHQ began looking at the possibility of developing lighter, portable wireless sets for use in the field.[73] Although wireless technology did not come of

[66] See, for example, 'Minutes of the Wireless Telegraph Committee, Second Meeting', 7 November 1912, WO32/9153, TNA.

[67] 'Final Report of the Committee on Wireless Telegraphy', 3 September 1913, WO32/8879, TNA. Experiments with wireless communication between aircraft and the ground also produced mixed results before 1914. See: 'W/T Experiments in Aeroplanes', January–February 1913, AIR1/626/17/63, 'Various Papers of W/T use in Aircraft, 1912–18', AIR20/699, TNA; and, Andrew Whitmarsh, 'British Army Manoeuvres and the Development of Military Aviation, 1910–1913', War in History, 14 (2007), 344.

[68] Brigadier Harry Hopthrow, Interview (1990), Department of Sound Records, 011581/7, IWM.

[69] Curtis, 'Work of Signal Units in War', 273–4.

[70] 'Committee on Co-Ordination of Methods of Communication and Schools of Telegraphy and Signalling', April 1909, WO33/3003, TNA.

[71] 'Report of Conference on Personnel and Training of Wireless Units. 1914', 15 June 1914, 3, WO33/3076, TNA.

[72] See Chapter 4.

[73] Brian N. Hall, 'The British Army and Wireless Communication, 1896–1918', War in History, 19 (2012), 298.

age during the First World War, it did undergo a sudden and rapid transition from infancy into late adolescence.[74] By the spring of 1917 the BEF was employing three main types of wireless apparatus in the field: the British Field (BF) Trench Set, the Loop Set and the Wilson Set.[75] All three had spark transmitters, which meant that they were very unselective and were highly prone to mutual interference and jamming.[76]

Theoretically, the 0.5-kilowatt BF Trench Set, introduced in 1916, could be carried by three men. In reality, it required a further six to help move it and its spare accumulators under battle conditions. Its range of communication was approximately 4,000 yards and its conspicuous 12-foot aerial made it liable to attract unwanted enemy attention.[77] As one wireless operator later remarked, it was 'the simplest instrument you could imagine but it was big, heavy and very awkward to carry... They didn't hold the tuning and the thump of a shell outside the dugout... would knock the adjustment off course'.[78] The Loop Set, which entered service in 1917, was an improvement on the BF Trench Set, but only just.[79] It was lighter, more compact and its aerial – 'a tubular loop one square yard supported on a bayonet fixed in the ground' – was much less conspicuous.[80] Although it was more suitable for operations beyond brigade headquarters, and simpler to use for the inexperienced operator, its operational range was limited to 2,000 yards, and it still required broad tuning, which 'forced a large number of stations to operate on the same narrow band, where they so interfered with one another as to be ineffective'.[81] Finally, the Wilson Set,[82] first trialled in the summer of 1915, was issued to corps to act as directing stations. With a range

---

[74] Juniper, 'First World War', 89.
[75] Different variations of these sets were tried and tested by the army during the course of the war. For comprehensive technical details of these sets, see Louis Meulstee, *Wireless for the Warrior: Compendium 1. Spark to Larkspur (Wireless Sets 1910–1948)* (Groenlo: Emaus Uitgeverij, 2009), 15–102.
[76] Cusins, 'Development of Army Wireless', 765; Captain B. F. J. Schonland, 'W/T. R.E.: An Account of the Work and Development of Field Wireless Sets with the Armies in France', *Wireless World*, 7 (1919), 178.
[77] *SS. 148. Forward Inter-Communication in Battle*, 22; Brigadier H. E. Hopthrow, 'The Use of Wireless Telegraphy by the Royal Engineers in the 1914–18 War', *The Royal Engineers Historical Society, Occasional Paper No. 2* (May 1983), 10.
[78] Bertram Neyland, Typescript of Interview (1974), 15–16, Department of Sound Records, 000318/3, IWM.
[79] *Signal Service (France). Technical Instructions No. 1. W/T Sets, Forward, Spark, 20 Watts, B., Front and Rear ('Loop' Set)* (May 1917).
[80] Nalder, *Royal Corps of Signals*, 122.
[81] Rawling, 'Communications in the Canadian Corps', 13.
[82] Which worked in conjunction with the Mark III short wave receiver. See Hall, 'British Army', 299.

between 4 and 10 miles, this set helped monitor divisional and brigade wireless traffic. It ensured that official procedure and protocol were observed by all wireless operators and in cases of emergency, or when wireless traffic was particularly heavy, the set helped facilitate the transmission of messages between brigades and divisions.[83]

The most significant development concerning British wireless technology during the war, however, was the introduction of Continuous Wave (CW) Sets in 1917.[84] In technical terms, CW 'changed the whole concept from one where a spark discharge set up a damped oscillation in a tuned, or resonant, circuit every time the Morse key was pressed to that of a continuous, almost pure, sinusoidal waveform that was produced by keying an oscillating valve'.[85] According to one wireless operator after the war, 'the valve was a sweet, tuneful sort of note... and was a joy to the receiving operator to listen to because it was so clear'.[86] Compared to the spark sets, CW offered greater range (6,000 yards) and enhanced channel selectivity for much less power expenditure. Being smaller, lighter and requiring aerials only two to three feet high, the sets were certainly more portable and less conspicuous than their predecessors.[87] However, despite these favourable characteristics and the fact that the German Army never developed CW during the course of the war,[88] the shortage of available sets in the BEF during the last 12 months of the war meant that its use was restricted mainly to counterbattery communications,

---

[83] Wireless directing stations were also in operation at the army level, dealing with wireless traffic between corps and divisions. See 'Control of Wireless Communication', 27 December 1917, Military Histories (General), 914.2, RSMA. Wilson sets were also employed by the RFC/RAF for ground station work. See Cousins, 'Development of Army Wireless', 765.

[84] As with the spark sets, these CW sets had variations (Mk. I, Mk. II and Mk. III). See Cousins, 'Development of Army Wireless', 766.

[85] Austin, *Schonland*, 49.

[86] Bertram Neyland, Typescript of Interview (1974), 16, Department of Sound Records, 000318/3, IWM.

[87] Schonland, 'W/T. R.E.', 226.

[88] Major W. Arthur Steel, 'Wireless Telegraphy in the Canadian Corps in France', *Canadian Defence Quarterly*, 11 (1930), 369. A Canadian Corps intelligence report in August 1918 put the state of the BEF's wireless technology a year ahead of the German Army's. However, largely as a result of the shortages of materials needed to mass produce telephone and telegraph cables, the Germans had made greater use of wireless for communication purposes a lot earlier in the war than either the BEF or the French Army. See: 'Wireless Intelligence Summary, German Field Stations, August 10th to August 16th (inclusive)', August 1918, RG9-III-D-3/5004/687, LAC; *SS. 537. Summary of Recent Information Regarding the German Army and Its Methods* (January 1917), 25; *SS. 713. The German Wireless System* (March 1917); 'Alternative Methods of Communication to Replace the Telephone', 25 June 1917, AWM25/425/47, AWM; and, 'Lecture No. 49. Liaison Service in the German Army', Officers' School – Fourth Course, Monday, May 27th, 1918 to Saturday, July 6th, 1918, RG120/404/4, NARA.

though it was also utilised for anti-aircraft, tank and RAF ground station signals during the Hundred Days.[89] Moreover, CW allowed the British to experiment with wireless telephony for RAF and Tank Corps signals during the last months of the war,[90] though it was never employed in actual combat.[91]

Arguably the most intriguing means of wireless communication developed during the war was the Earth Induction Set, also known as the Power Buzzer and Amplifier, and referred to by many signallers as 'ground wireless'.[92] The power buzzer used a 150- to 200-yard base line for the transmission of electrical impulses through the ground, which were picked up by a receiving amplifier over distances between 2,000 and 5,000 yards away, depending upon the nature of the soil.[93] Although the principles of earth induction telegraphy were already well known to the British before the war, it was the French, under the direction of Colonel Gustave-August Ferrié, the head of the *Radiotélé-graphie Militaire*, who led the way in research and design during the war.[94] The first instrument, known as the Parleur, was tried and tested in 1916. Sir Henry Norman, working as a liaison officer with the French Ministry of Inventions, informed the British Munitions Invention Department (MID) in June 1916 that the French had 'perfected' the sets and that the BEF required them 'with the utmost urgency', since 'we have lost thousands of men and our chief offensives have largely failed for want of them'.[95]

[89] Schonland, 'W/T. R.E.', 396–7; 'Instructions No. 10. Signal Arrangements', 4 August 1918, 2 Australian Division War Diary, WO95/3259, TNA; 'Operations. Amiens (Report on Wireless Communications) 8-8-18 to 22–8-18. Cdn. Corps Heavy Arty.', 29 August 1918, RG9-III-C-1/3923/10/6, LAC.

[90] Experiments with wireless telephony had been underway at the Brooklands testing park since 1915. In early 1916, Major Charles Prince had developed a wireless telephony set for potential use within the RFC, though the technology was not yet robust enough for use in combat. See Major C. E. Prince, 'Wireless Telephony on Aeroplanes', *Journal of the Institution of Electrical Engineers*, 58 (1920), 377–84.

[91] 'Minutes of a Meeting to Discuss the Tactical use of Wireless Telephony in the R.A.F., Held at H.Q., R.A.F.', 18 July 1918, AIR1/32/15/1/169, TNA; 'Experimental Work on Radio-Telephony', undated [summer 1918], 1st Tank Brigade Signal Company War Diary, WO95/100, TNA.

[92] Diary Entry, 20 November 1917, Brigadier Harry Ewart Hopthrow Papers 2/2, LHCMA.

[93] Bidwell and Graham, *Fire-Power*, 141; Harris, *Signal Venture*, 42; Cousins, 'Development of Army Wireless', 765; Typescript of Interview with Peter Liddle (November 1977), 7, Brigadier H. E. Hopthrow Papers, GS0795, LCL.

[94] 'Signalling from the Advanced Front by Means of Earth-Currents', 25 April 1916, Reports and Other Papers of Captain Sir Henry Norman, M.P., MUN7/320, TNA; Captain L. C. Carus-Wilson, 'Earth-Current Telegraphy', *Royal Engineers Journal*, 31 (1920), 1–12.

[95] Sir Henry Norman to MID, 9 June 1916, MUN7/320, TNA.

However, power buzzers suffered from a number of inherent flaws: first, as the Director of Army Signals noted in June 1916, not only could the sets be jammed by telephone buzzers operating within the vicinity, but their signals were also extremely prone to enemy interception.[96] SS. 148 acknowledged this latter imperfection and insisted that all messages had to be sent in code and be as short and as concise as possible;[97] second, the power buzzer worked on a one-way process only. If two-way communication was required, an additional power buzzer and amplifier had to be in use at each end.[98] The drawback, however, was that both power buzzers could not operate at the same time because of the risk of mutual interference.[99] Subsequently, once he had sent his message, the operator had no idea as to whether or not it had been successfully received and understood at the opposite end;[100] third, and finally, as many signallers after the war observed, the major disadvantage of the power buzzer was its size and weight. According to Sergeant T. E. Pennington, 'The idea was alright but the gear was cumbersome, and meant a lot of extra weight to the already loaded Signaller'.[101] The power buzzer and its accumulator weighed 7 pounds and 26 pounds, respectively, while the amplifier (consisting of an instrument box, heavy battery box, heavy accumulator, small accumulator, two reels of cable and 12 earth pins) weighed a total of 108 pounds.[102] All this meant that while the power buzzer worked relatively well in position warfare, it was less suited to the conditions of mobility that were to characterise the battles of 1918. As a result, the last four months of the war witnessed a marked decline in the use of power buzzers within the BEF.[103]

---

[96] Brigadier-General John Sharman Fowler to GHQ, 19 June 1916, MUN7/320, TNA.

[97] SS. 148. Forward Inter-Communication in Battle, 25.

[98] 'Communication by Wireless', 27 May 1917, RG9-III-C-5/4440/1/9, LAC.

[99] However, using precise compass bearings, two power buzzers could communicate with the same amplifier provided that the amplifier's receiving bases were positioned accordingly and their exact positions known to the power buzzer operators. See SS. 148. Forward Inter-Communication in Battle, 24.

[100] In seeking to resolve this issue, a memorandum issued by 2 Division Signal Company in February 1917 stipulated that when power buzzers moved forward in an advance, 'some visual signal should be sent from the receiving station to show that it is receiving signals correctly from the newly established power buzzer'. See 'Proposed Draft of Appendix on Signalling for Operation Orders', 12 February 1917, Correspondence and Papers of 2 Division Signal Company in WW1, 1915–18, A231.52, REMA.

[101] 'The Signal Section of the 16th Manchesters: A Record of Its Activities, 1914–1918. Compiled and Written by Ex-Sgt. T. E. Pennington' (1937), 38, MR 1/3/1/50, Manchester Regiment Archive, Tameside (MRA). See also: 'With the Wireless Section of the Signal Company, Royal Engineers, 1914–1918', Sergeant W. M. Rumsey Papers, GS1401, LCL; and, Steel, 'Wireless Telegraphy in the Canadian Corps', 45.

[102] SS. 148. Forward Inter-Communication in Battle, 23.   [103] See Chapter 7.

Visual and Aerial Signalling

One of the most prominent means of communication at the tactical level in 1914 was visual signalling.[104] Battalion signallers were issued with 16 blue and 16 white striped flags, roughly two feet square in size, for semaphore messaging during daylight hours.[105] Semaphore was a method of signalling in which the letters of the alphabet were spelt out according to the position of the signaller's arms in relation to his body. Although a quick and easy method, it exposed the sending operator to the enemy and was limited to a distance of approximately 1,000 yards. Flag signalling could also be achieved via Morse code, ranging from three to four miles with a small flag and five to seven miles with a large flag. Although the sending operator employing Morse was less exposed than his counterpart utilising semaphore, since he could transmit messages whilst lying flat on his back,[106] it was a slower method of visual communication than semaphore and the message was still liable to interception by the enemy.[107]

Battalion signallers were also equipped with eight heliographs and, for night time signalling, eight Begbie signalling lamps.[108] The heliograph, an instrument which utilised an oscillating mirror to direct beams of sunlight onto distant visual stations, was first adopted by the British Army in India in 1875.[109] Its standard operational range was roughly 15 miles, but the successful transmission of messages over distances nearing 100 miles was recorded during the Second South African War.[110] Although messages sent by heliograph could not be easily intercepted owing to the small angle of the flash, the process was entirely dependent upon sunshine.[111] A report written in 1908, for example, clearly anticipated the difficulties that would eventually hamper the use of heliographs on the Western Front: 'The heliograph cannot very well be worked within reach of bullets, and is liable in a European country to fail through the sun becoming obscured by mist or clouds, or before sunrise

---

[104] Frank Richards, *Old Soldier Sahib* (first published 1936; new ed., Uckfield: Naval and Military Press Ltd., 2003), 95–6; Scrivenor, *Brigade Signals*, 24.
[105] *Field Service Manual, 1914*, 55; *Training Manual – Signalling: Part II*, 6–21.
[106] Capper, 'Information on the Battlefield', 42.
[107] Davies, 'Communications of a Division', 887; Typescript Recollections, undated, 14, Dart Papers, LCL.
[108] *Training Manual – Signalling. Part II*, 6–21.
[109] Dr Frederic Wächter, Communicated by Major A. H. Bagnold, R.E., 'Visual Signalling', *Journal of the Royal United Services Institution*, 40 (1896), 149–64.
[110] 'Signalling Communication. Ninety Two Miles with a Five Inch Helio', 15 June 1902, History of Military Signalling, 908.2, RSMA.
[111] Capper, 'Information on the Battlefield', 29.

and near sunset'.[112] The standard night time signalling apparatus in the British Army at the beginning of the war was the Begbie Lamp. This device – 'a heavy metal box mounted on tripod legs consisting of an oil lamp and a mechanical shutter' – produced a flame that lasted approximately 10 hours and could be used to transmit messages up to a distance of 8 miles.[113] However, not only were they heavy and cumbersome, but they were also very noisy and transmitted a beam of light that had a wide cone of dispersion, rendering the signaller highly conspicuous.[114]

Given the nature of the fighting and the climatic and topographic conditions that generally prevailed on the Western Front, visual signalling was a precarious form of communication.[115] Besides flags, heliographs, discs, flares and rockets, a variety of signalling lamps were employed. Although the Signal Service managed to procure the use of the French Projector Lamp No. 24 to replace the Begbie Lamp in 1915, it was not until 1916 that the BEF found its own solution in the form of the Lucas Lamp. Powered by accumulators, the Lucas Lamp could be used both at night and during the day, flashing messages in Morse code up to a distance of 4,000 yards. Its cone of dispersion was markedly less than those of the Begbie and French Projector lamps, and it was much lighter and thus more portable than the Aldis and Hucks Lamps, which were used chiefly for signalling to and from aeroplanes.[116] Combined with the development and proliferation of more efficient instruments, such as discs, shutters and trench periscopes, the Lucas Lamp became the standard electric signalling lamp in the BEF from January 1917.[117]

Although the introduction of the Lucas Lamp 'revived' the BEF's interest in visual forms of communication,[118] visual signalling on the Western Front remained a very hazardous, slow and unreliable means of

---

[112] 'Memorandum on Signalling by Means of Discs', January 1908, History of Military Signalling, 908.2, RSMA.

[113] Anon., 'Recollections of a R. E. Sapper-Signaller, 1914–1918', *Mercury: Journal of the Royal Signals Amateur Radio Society*, 32 (1970), 5; Curtis, 'Work of Signal Units in War', 274.

[114] Scrivenor, *Brigade Signals*, 23; 'Divisional Signal Service Headquarters', 24 September 1914, 2 Division Signal Company War Diary, WO95/1333, TNA.

[115] Wheeler, *50th Battalion*, 15.

[116] Priestley, *Work of the Royal Engineers*, 144. Aldis Lamps would also be employed later by tanks for communication between tanks and rearward transmitting stations. See 'Detailed Operation Order No. 11 Coy. by Lieut. Col. J. Hardress-Lloyd. D.S.O. Cmmdg. "D" Bn.', 8 April 1917; 'Preliminary Instructions No. 2', 19 March 1917, Tank Corps War Diary, WO95/91, TNA.

[117] 'Signal Notes No. 1', 26 January 1917, Director of Army Signals War Diary, WO95/57, TNA.

[118] 'Lecture No. 1. Visual Signalling, Officers School – First Course, Monday, January 7th, 1918 to Saturday, February 2nd, 1918', RG120/404/91/2, NARA.

communication. As well as topographical constraints, fog, rain, dust and smoke obscured flag and lamp signals, while the lack of sunlight in winter rendered heliographs impotent. Moreover, as one signaller observed after the war, although each division established a comprehensive system of visual stations in its forward area, 'they had necessarily to be one way working, that is from front to the rear, since signals from a station facing the enemy might be observed by him'. Subsequently, each message from a forward visual station to a rear visual station had to be signalled through at least twice in what became known as the D.D.D.D. procedure, and written confirmation of it sent by runner.[119]

Aerial observation via kite balloons and aeroplanes also provided a rich source of information.[120] This was particularly so with regards to their use for counterbattery work with the artillery. Comparing the utility of the two means, a report written prior to the Battle of the Somme noted:

The balloon appears to have been the better for the purpose of reporting the general situation and the general artillery activity. Both by day and night the observer was able to keep the Artillery Group Commander informed as to the situation... As regards ranging, the aeroplanes were the more successful, and conducted shoots under weather conditions which rendered observation for the balloon impossible. Aeroplanes located many more flashes than the balloon during daylight, but none at night. The balloon was able to report the direction of flashes at night, and in some cases to identify the battery owing to the observer's intimate knowledge of the ground. The advantage of the telephonic communication of the balloon over the wireless of the aeroplane was very apparent.[121]

In spite of the advantage telephones afforded to balloons, however, aeroplanes proved much more versatile than balloons for locating German batteries. Once a target had been agreed between the airman and the artillery commander, and the time to carry out the 'shoot' arranged:

the machine would be in the air over the battery. The observer would then let out his aerial – a long piece of copper wire with a lead plummet at the end – which unwound from a drum in the cockpit, switch on the transmitter, and call up the battery in Morse. In the dugout by the battery the wireless operator would report that all was ready. The machine would call upon the battery to fire, and then

---

[119] 'A Signaller in France 1914–1918', 186, Craven Papers, REMA.

[120] On air–land cooperation in general, see: David Jordan, 'The Army Co-Operation Missions of the Royal Flying Corps/Royal Air Force 1914–1918' (PhD Thesis, University of Birmingham, 1997); Jonathan Boff, 'Air/Land Integration in the Hundred Days: The Case of Third Army', *Air Power Review*, 12 (2009), 77–88.

[121] H. A. Jones, *The War in the Air: Being the Story of the Part Played in the Great War by the Royal Air Force*, Vol. 2 (Oxford: Clarendon Press, 1928), 194.

Plate 3.1 Soldiers watching for Germans at a New Zealand signalling post on the Somme, April 1918 (Henry Armytage Sanders: Alexander Turnbull Library, Wellington, 1/2-013721-G)

watch carefully to see where the shot fell. A code was used to give the exact position of the burst in relation to the objective aimed at: 'Over', 'Short', 'Left', 'Right'. After a pause to correct his sights, the battery, on being signalled, would fire again. By this means, in three or four rounds it was usually possible to get a direct hit on the target, and the airman would send down the triumphant 'O.K'.[122]

Combined with the introduction of the Counter Battery Staff Office in early 1917 and the development of 'flash spotting' and 'sound ranging' techniques, artillery observation work undertaken by aeroplanes employing wireless communication made a very strong contribution to the BEF's successes during the last two years of the war.[123]

---

[122] Cecil Lewis, *Sagittarius Rising* (first published 1936; new ed., London: Frontline Books, 2013), 83. The method used for correcting the fall of shot was the 'clock code', introduced at Neuve Chapelle in 1915. For a detailed explanation, see Jordan, 'Army Co-Operation Missions', 151.

[123] Albert P. Palazzo, 'The British Army's Counter-Battery Staff Office and Control of the Enemy in World War 1', *Journal of Military History*, 63 (1999), 55–74; Marble, 'Infantry Cannot Do with a Gun Less', Ch. 5.

The other notable contribution of aeroplanes was contact patrol. Contact aeroplanes were introduced in 1915 and used extensively during the Battle of the Somme the following year, providing a supplementary means of communication between the frontline troops and the commanders in the rear. Their main purposes were to 'keep Headquarters of formations informed as to the progress of their troops during an attack', to 'report on the positions of the enemy' and to 'transmit messages from the troops engaged to the Headquarters of their formation'.[124] Each aeroplane had a distinctive set of markings, which were known to all ranks of the infantry. Flying over the frontline at prearranged times, contact aeroplanes would communicate with the infantry on the ground by means of sounding Klaxon horns or flashing Aldis and Hucks Lamps.[125] Ground sheets, signal panels, coloured flares, flashing mirrors and flags were utilised by the infantry to indicate their progress and other information to the aeroplane.[126] Then, as Lieutenant-General Sir John Monash explained after the war:

the observer would mark down by conventional signs on a map the actual positions of our Infantry, of enemy Infantry or other facts of prime importance, and he often had time to scribble a few informative notes also. The 'plane' then flew back at top speed to Corps H.Q., and the map, with or without an added report, was dropped in the middle of an adjacent field, wrapped in a weighted streamer of many colours. It was then brought by cyclist into the Staff Office.

According to the Australian Corps commander, this was 'a vastly superior method' of maintaining 'actual battle control', since '[t]he total time which elapsed between the making of the observation at the front line and the arrival of the information in the hands of the Corps Staff was seldom more than ten minutes'.[127]

However, there were significant drawbacks to this process: first, the absence of clear visibility rendered aerial observation extremely difficult, if not impossible; second, no information at all could be obtained if the infantry either forgot or were too preoccupied to signal to the contact aeroplane at the designated time. As one RFC officer noted after the war,

---

[124] *SS. 148. Forward Inter-Communication in Battle*, 29. Contact aeroplanes were also employed to facilitate communication between tanks and rear headquarters in 1917–18. See 'History of Tank and Aeroplane Cooperation', 31 January 1919, AIR1/1671/204/109/26, TNA.

[125] Priestley, *Work of the Royal Engineers*, 144, 247.

[126] MacGregor and Welti (ed.), *Signals from the Great War*, 83. A signalling ground sheet 'consisted of a black-and-white venetian blind – this, on an elastic return spring, opened white and closed black, and enabled the ground to send Morse messages to the machines above'. See Lewis, *Sagittarius Rising*, 85.

[127] Monash, *The Australian Victories*, 124–5.

during an attack 'men in the front line (not un-naturally) shrank from lighting fireworks which would give away their position to any German machine gun or battery for miles around. Besides, they had other things to think of... and so, during the first phase of the attack contact patrol was pretty useless';[128] and third, although contact aeroplanes delivered their messages straight to corps and sometimes division headquarters, more often than not the information was of greater value to the brigade or battalion commander. Thus, as the message was forwarded down the chain of command, the information contained within it was often rendered valueless by the time it reached the frontline commander.[129] As one signal officer after the war neatly put it: 'If the human brain had to send a written message to the shoulder, for transmission to the elbow, for re-transmission via the wrist to the hand, then the delay in letting go of a hot potato would undoubtedly result in serious burns'.[130]

Message Carriers

In every battle that the BEF fought during the First World War, message carriers provided the backbone of the communication system, particularly at the tactical level. Although *FSR I (1909)* acknowledged that 'communications in the field may be verbal or written', it specified that the written form was more suitable because 'in war, verbal messages are often incorrectly delivered or misunderstood, especially in the excitement of an engagement'.[131] As a result, a variety of methods were employed by the BEF to ensure the conveyance of written forms of communication, ranging from runners, despatch riders and liaison officers, to carrier pigeons and messenger dogs. All too often, these rather antiquated means were the only options available to British commanders as they struggled to maintain a degree of command and control in the field.

According to *SS. 135. Instructions for the Training of Divisions for Offensive Action* (December 1916), runners were 'the one means of communication which can be relied on when all other means fail'.[132] Runners were generally equipped as regular privates 'but permitted to

---

[128] Lewis, *Sagittarius Rising*, 86.
[129] See, for example, 'IX Corps Notes on Information Collected from Various Sources, Including Troops Who Have Been Engaged in the Recent Fighting', 31 July 1916, Montgomery-Massingberd Papers 7/3, LHCMA.
[130] F. S. M. [Frank Stanley Morgan], 'Signals and Mechanization', *Army Quarterly*, 16 (1928), 386.
[131] *Field Service Regulations, Part I*, 23.
[132] *SS. 135. Instructions for the Training of Divisions for Offensive Action* (December 1916), 34.

remove their equipment where necessity arises'. Most were young, aged between 18 and 20, 'marked with a distinctive badge, such as a piece of red tape fastened to the left shoulder-strap' and had to 'be familiar with all the routes to all the principal centres'.[133] Typically, runners operated forward of brigade headquarters and worked in pairs as part of a relay system if the distances involved were greater than 500 yards.[134] In terms of numbers, in mid-1916, for example, 4 Australian Division recommended two runners per company, eight per battalion (two from each company), and eight per brigade (two from each battalion).[135] Despite their bravery and tenacity, however, runners were an extremely vulnerable means of communication, for very obvious reasons. More often than not, they either were incapacitated before they arrived at their destination or carried messages containing information that was out of date and of little use by the time it reached its intended recipient.

To the rear of brigade headquarters, despatch riders served as an important means of facilitating communication throughout the war.[136] Traditionally, the quickest method of delivering written and verbal information in person had been via a messenger on a horse.[137] However, besides the provision of mounted orderlies, bicyclists and runners, the army advocated the extensive use of motorcycles for the rapid conveyance of orders, reports and other information.[138] The addition of motorcycle despatch riders to the army's signal units occurred in 1911. It was estimated that upon mobilisation the BEF would require roughly 2,500 motorcyclists, most of whom would be employed for despatching written messages between the headquarters to which they were attached.[139]

---

[133] 'Memorandum on Trench to Trench Attack by a Battalion Commander in the Fifth Army', 31 October 1916, Fifth Army Notes and Lessons on 1916 Operations, WO158/344, TNA.

[134] Scrivenor, *Brigade Signals*, 87; 'Memorandum on Trench to Trench Attack by a Battalion Commander in the Fifth Army', 31 October 1916, Fifth Army Notes and Lessons on 1916 Operations, WO158/344, TNA; 'Notes on Experience Gained during the Recent Operations, Compiled from a Conference Held on 15 August 1916 and from Reports from Brigadiers, 2nd Division, X Corps', undated, Montgomery-Massingberd Papers 7/3, LHCMA.

[135] '4th Australian Division. Circular No. 35. Communication in the Field', 16 July 1916, AWM25/425/41, AWM.

[136] The 1914 *Field Service Pocket Book* included horses, bicycles, motorcycles and motor cars within its definition of despatch riding. See *Field Service Pocket Book*, 64.

[137] In 1917, mounted orderlies were employed chiefly between advanced division and brigade headquarters. See SS. *148. Forward Inter-Communication in Battle*, 27.

[138] Michael Carragher, '"Amateurs at a Professional Game": The Despatch Rider Corps in 1914', in Spencer Jones (ed.), *Stemming the Tide: Officers and Leadership in the British Expeditionary Force 1914* (Solihull: Helion, 2013), 332–49.

[139] 'Report of the Advisory Committee on Motor Cyclists', 5 December 1911, WO33/3026, TNA; *Training Manual – Signalling. Part II*, 84.

However, apart from the initial period of mobility in 1914 and the semi-mobile operations of 1918, the majority of motorcycle despatch riders spent the war working principally along the lines of communication. As one despatch rider noted in early 1917, 'Nowadays the DR's job is one of muddied ease and his chief preoccupation is keeping from falling under the wheels of the lorries and wagons, rather than running the gauntlet of shot and shell'.[140] The establishment of the Despatch Rider Letter Service (DRLS) at the end of October 1914 'was the direct outcome of the shortage of transport at the disposal of the Postal Services'.[141] The DRLS worked initially along the lines of communication, delivering official correspondence, known in Signal Service parlance as 'packets',[142] according to a fixed timetable among GHQ, Boulogne, Abbeville, Rouen and Havre.[143] On account of its speed and efficiency, however, the service was soon extended down to corps headquarters. By early 1918, the DRLS was performing two runs between GHQ and each of the army headquarters per day and three runs between army and corps headquarters.[144]

In addition to motorcycle despatch riders, in 1914 the BEF employed a pool of specially trained volunteer drivers from the Royal Automobile Club who were to act as chauffeurs to senior commanders and staff officers. As the opening months of the war on the Western Front saw the first use of the motor car in a European conflict, even the volunteer drivers themselves were unsure in which capacity they were to be employed. According to one driver, upon mobilisation

the wildest conjectures as to our future employment were being put forward. Some visualised themselves dashing wildly at eighty miles an hour through the German lines, the bearers of messages on which the fate of armies depended; others pessimistically were convinced that we should be employed as taxi-drivers on lines of communication.[145]

---

[140] Venner (ed.), *Despatch Rider on the Western Front*, 96–7.

[141] 'History of the Organisation and Development of the Army Postal Service during the War', undated, WO161/114, TNA; 'Historical Memoranda of the Army Postal Services in World War I, 1914–19', undated, A.232.2, REMA.

[142] Scrivenor, *Brigade Signals*, 86.

[143] 'Director of Army Signals. Circular Memorandum No. 29, December 1914', Director of Army Signals War Diary, WO95/57, TNA.

[144] 'D.R.L.S., by 2/Lieuts. B. S. Taylor, R.E., and A. F. Selby, R.E.', 3 March 1918, Organisation and Work of Signals in WW1 – Papers on Various Subjects, M1599, REMA.

[145] Brigadier-General C. D. Baker-Carr, *From Chauffeur to Brigadier* (London: Ernest Benn, 1930), 14. For other accounts written by volunteer drivers, see: Frederic Coleman, *From Mons to Ypres with French* (London: Marston and Co. Limited, 1916); and, A. Rawlinson, *Adventures on the Western Front, August 1914 to June 1915* (London: Andrew Melrose, 1925).

Plate 3.2 Pigeon service despatch rider with birds, November 1917 (William Rider-Rider, Canada. Dept. of National Defence/Library and Archives Canada/RCSigs.ca, MIKAN no. 3381001)

Ultimately, as *FSR I (1909)* had prescribed, motor cars enabled commanders and their staff to 'reconnoitre rapidly an extended front' and to deliver important information by word of mouth.[146] This was important because, although they could be duplicated and disseminated widely, relay complex and lengthy ideas and provide a record of the information sent, written forms of communication were open to problems of interpretation. While *FSR I (1909)* stipulated that 'every precaution should be taken to assist the recipient of an order or report in grasping its intention with a minimum of trouble and delay',[147] the British Army realised before the war that 'no telegraphic message, however lucidly expressed, can do more than convey the bare information or order. Much that is in the mind of the sender may be unknown to the officer to whom the telegram is sent'.[148] This explains, to a large extent, why British

---

[146] *Field Service Regulations, Part 1*, 125. [147] Ibid., 25.
[148] 'Report of a Conference of Staff Officers at the Royal Military College, 12th to 15th January, 1914. Held under the Orders and Direction of the Chief of the Imperial General Staff', 38, WO107/64, TNA.

officers in 1914 were keen to convey orders to their subordinates face to face, or at the very least via a trusted staff or liaison officer. It was the task of such officers not only to act as a channel of communication, but to ensure mutual understanding and unity of purpose and action between one commander and another.[149]

A verbal account of the situation from a liaison officer often proved invaluable, as one liaison officer noted: 'Battles could not be won without it. The general who was kept without news had his hands tied behind him'.[150] However, as Edward Spears observed, when 'interpreting commanders to each other... to one side he is always a foreigner. To his own people he seems to be forever taking the side of the foreigner'.[151] This was as true for liaison between commanders belonging to the same army as it was for liaison between commanders of Allied armies who spoke different languages. As Spears related in his memoirs, British officers did not take kindly to liaison, and 'resented an officer from a higher formation interviewing their own juniors'.[152] Similarly, according to General Sir Charles Bonham-Carter, BGGS (Training) GHQ, 1917–18, liaison officers during the first two years of the war were often resented for being 'the Army Commanders' private snoopers'. As it was, 'the best use was not made' of liaison officers 'as they were not sent far enough forward'.[153]

According to Sir Henry Wilson, GOC IV Corps in 1916, one of the chief reasons for the BEF's failure on the Somme was the fact that Haig ignored 'the importance of getting in touch between GHQ and Corps by means of first class liaison officers'.[154] One possible reason for this, as suggested by Major-General Sir Ernest Swinton, was that since the commencement of trench warfare, the BEF had become too reliant upon telephonic communication, and, as such, liaison officers lost their 'special usefulness'.[155] In light of the experiences of 1916, the policy of adopting liaison officers at every level of command was pursued much more vigorously by the BEF during the last two years of the war.[156] Acting as 'the eyes and ears' of the commander,[157] liaison officers at

---

[149] 'Officers de Liaison', 16 October 1913, WO32/4731, TNA.
[150] Captain Cyril Falls Diary, 8 August 1918, CAB45/203, TNA.
[151] Spears, *Liaison 1914*, 340.   [152] Ibid., 51.
[153] Autobiography, undated, 15–17, General Sir Charles Bonham-Carter Papers, BHCT9/1, CAC.
[154] Diary, 1 September 1916, Field Marshal Sir Henry Wilson Papers, DS/MISC/80, IWM.
[155] Major-General Sir Ernest D. Swinton, *Eyewitness* (London: Hodder and Stoughton, 1932), 74.
[156] Robbins, *British Generalship*, 47–8.
[157] 'Notes on Liaison Work', 26 May 1917, X Corps War Diary, WO95/852, TNA.

corps, division, brigade and battalion levels had to be 'thoroughly acquainted with the orders and intentions of their Commanders and everything connected with the unit to which they belong'. Ultimately, they were 'responsible for keeping their own Commander informed of the dispositions of the unit to which they are attached',[158] and proved of great value as a means of keeping superior officers informed about the situation in the frontline.[159]

Not all the bearers of information were human, though.[160] Carrier pigeons, for example, had been considered by the army as an alternative message carrying service prior to the war.[161] However, it was noted in a report written shortly after their poor performance during the 1913 autumn manoeuvres that

the value of any Pigeon Service from an army point of view must depend on whether a pigeon can be relied upon to 'home' to any place where it has been housed for a short time only... I can find no evidence whatsoever that we could expect pigeons housed and trained in England to 'home' to the General Headquarters if the Expeditionary Force is abroad.[162]

Consequently, it was not until late 1914 that the army began to contemplate the value of carrier pigeons seriously. Although the French Army had provided the BEF with 15 pigeons for intelligence purposes in September that year, their use for the conveyance of tactical information was soon recognised. Pigeons were much less susceptible to shell fire and the effects of poison gas than human despatch riders and runners, and in good weather could travel at speeds of 40–60 miles per hour.[163] At the beginning of June 1915, following the successful employment of carrier pigeons during the Second Battle of Ypres, the Carrier Pigeon Service became a recognised branch of the Signal Service, rapidly growing in size to incorporate 20,000 pigeons and some 380 handlers by 1918.[164]

---

[158] SS. 148. Forward Inter-Communication in Battle, 38–9.
[159] See, for example: '19th Divisional Artillery. No. B.M. 174/6. Lessons Learned from the Recent Operations', 15 June 1917, Report on Operations for the Capture of the Messines-Wytschaete Ridge by IX Corps, WO158/415, 'Xth Corps. 41st Div. G. 55165/23', 20 June 1917, X Corps War Diary, WO95/852, TNA; 'General Staff Circular No. 36. Liaison during Operations', 14 September 1918, AWM25/425/26, AWM.
[160] For additional context on the use of animals in war, see Juliet Gardiner, The Animals' War: Animals in Wartime from the First World War to the Present Day (London: Portrait, 2006).
[161] Capper, 'Information on the Battlefield', 31.
[162] Captain Rupert Ommanney 'Notes on Work at General Headquarters', 22 October 1913, WO106/51, TNA.
[163] 'Lecture No. 35. Military Use of Pigeons, Officers School – First Course, Monday, January 7th, 1918 to Saturday, February 2nd, 1918', RG120/404/91/2, NARA.
[164] Gwilliam, 'Transmission of Messages' 203–6; Lieutenant-Colonel A. H. Osman, Pigeons in the Great War: A Complete History of the Carrier Pigeon Service during the Great War, 1914 to 1918 (London: Racing Pigeon Publishing Co., 1928), 6.

Typically, a motorcyclist would take six pigeons from the corps lofts to brigade headquarters every morning. 'Pigeoneers' would then take two birds to each battalion, who then either sent them on to their companies or kept them at battalion headquarters.[165] All messages were written on thin paper and rolled up inside a small aluminium cylinder which was clipped onto the pigeon's leg. In addition, the birds carried a small metal ring on one leg which was 'engraved with the year of birth and the regimental number of the pigeon' for identification purposes.[166] It was also imperative that when more than one bird was sent, they were of the same sex.[167] The lofts were arranged so that when a bird entered 'an electric bell is rung; the soldier on duty then goes up, removes the carrier, and either sends it complete to the nearest Signal Office, or, if a buzzer is installed in the loft, has the message transmitted at once to its destination'.[168] Given the acute problems of communication on the Western Front, pigeons often provided commanders with a useful alternative when all other options had failed them.[169] However, pigeons were of limited value in more mobile operations because once the pigeon lofts were moved, the birds had to be re-trained in order to become accustomed to their new route.[170] In addition, as a result of the inability to utilise the birds at night, the limited amount of word space on a carrier pigeon message and the fact that many soldiers were 'inclined to make pets of the birds and feed them, so that the pigeons did not always fly directly back to their lofts',[171] the carrier pigeon system was not necessarily the safest and surest method of communication.[172]

Finally, messenger dogs were another method of communication introduced to meet the requirements of trench warfare.[173] A War Dog School was officially established in mid-1917 to train dogs for message

[165] Scrivenor, *Brigade Signals*, 69.   [166] Gwilliam, 'Transmission of Messages', 205–6.

[167] Lieutenant-Colonel Arthur Hemsley, Interview (1987), Department of Sound Records, 009927/7, IWM.

[168] 'Organisation of a Carrier Pigeon Service for the Armies in France', 28 August 1915, R.E. Carrier Pigeon Service War Diary, WO95/123, TNA.

[169] Such was their usefulness, on 23 May 1918, the BEF gave the American Expeditionary Force (AEF) a gift of 600 carrier pigeons and 18 mobile lofts. See 'Letter from Officer in Charge, AEF Homing Pigeon Service to Chief Signal Officer, AEF Headquarters Services of Supply', 1 June 1918, AEF Army Signal School, RG120/406/1795, NARA.

[170] It took approximately six weeks to train a carrier pigeon before it could be used under battle conditions. See *SS. 123. Notes on the Use of Carrier Pigeons* (August 1916), 4.

[171] F. W. Dopson, *The 48th Divisional Signal Company in the Great War* (Bristol: J. W. Arrowsmith, 1938), 32.

[172] One signal officer noted after the war that carrier pigeons 'gave a great deal more trouble than they were worth... It is a matter of regret now that we did not eat the birds while we had the chance'. Scrivenor, *Brigade Signals*, 69, 71.

[173] Lieutenant-Colonel E. H. Richardson, *British War Dogs: Their Training and Psychology* (London: Skeffington and Son, 1920), Ch. 2.

carrying purposes.[174] It was found that large breeds such as German Shepherds and Golden Retrievers made the best messenger dogs.[175] They were taken into the line to work for a week at a time and were not to operate over stretches of more than four miles.[176] However, reports as to their effectiveness varied considerably. Although they were relatively quicker and less conspicuous than runners, they could only work in one direction when delivering messages to their handler. A report by XVII Corps in early October 1917 also noted that many of its brigade commanders did not entrust dogs with important messages in battle, preferring instead to use them to carry morning and afternoon situation reports from support and reserve battalion headquarters.[177] One of the major problems with utilising messenger dogs, however, was the attention they received from soldiers, whose affection for the animals inevitably delayed their journeys. Although they wore blue and white collars to identify them as messenger dogs, many soldiers, contrary to orders, found it difficult to resist the temptation of treating them as pets, thus much decreasing their value as a speedy and reliable means of communication.[178]

In summary, this chapter has endeavoured to outline the various means of communication employed by the BEF during the First World War, highlighting their chief characteristics and analysing their relative strengths and limitations. Such an understanding is crucial if one is to assess how, and to what extent, communications affected British military operations on the Western Front. When war broke out in August 1914, the British Army was caught in a period of transition as it sought to integrate the newer and more elaborate means of communication with the older, more traditional methods. Despite the addition of telephones and wireless, however, the more established means of communication, such as visual signalling and message carriers, were favoured. This can partly be attributed to the technical deficiencies of telephonic and wireless communication at the time, particularly their limitations for mobile warfare, which it was widely believed would characterise the next European conflagration.[179] However, it also owed much to the desire

---

[174] Priestley, *Work of the Royal Engineers*, 222–3.

[175] Hemsley, Interview (1987), Department of Sound Records, 009927/7, IWM.

[176] 'Signal Instructions No. 8. Messenger Dogs', 30 April 1918, AWM25/425/25, AWM.

[177] 'Précis of Reports on War Dogs', 3 October 1917, Third Army War Diary, WO95/367, TNA.

[178] 'R. A. Stanley (O.C. 5 Aust. Div. Signal Co.) to A. D. Signals, Australian Corps', 1 July 1918, 5 Australian Division Signal Company War Diary, WO95/3596, TNA.

[179] For the origins and debate on the 'Cult of the Offensive', see: Tim Travers, 'The Offensive and the Problem of Innovation in British Military Thought, 1870–1915', *Journal of Contemporary History*, 13 (1978), 531–53; Tim Travers, 'Technology,

amongst British officers to maintain a personalised style of command and control. While this approach would prove somewhat advantageous during the opening weeks of the war, it was totally unsuited to the conditions of trench warfare which prevailed over the Western Front for the following three and a half years.

It is important to stress, however, that the lack of suitable mobile, 'real-time' communications was not only 'the supreme technological deficiency in all armies of the 1914–18 era', but 'a fact of life, based not just on technological shortcomings but on the deficiencies of pure science at the time'.[180] None of the means of communication examined in this chapter was infallible. Thus, in attempting to ensure the safe, accurate and speedy conveyance of information during the heat of battle, the BEF was forced to develop a communications system with 'built-in redundancy', whereby if one method of communication broke down, there were alternatives in place to carry the message.[181] As Hunter-Weston informed his divisional commanders at a conference prior to the Battle of the Somme, 'it is impossible to have too many alternative measures for passing information'.[182] Indeed, according to the future signal officer in chief of the BEF upon the outbreak of the Second World War, one of the key lessons to be drawn from studying the means of communication employed during the First World War was that 'none of these can stand alone; they must be co-ordinated so that each by its special capabilities makes good the weak points in the others'.[183]

Tactics, and Morale: Jean de Bloch, the Boer War, and British Military Theory, 1900–1914', *Journal of Modern History*, 51 (June 1979), 264–86; Michael Howard, 'Men against Fire: The Doctrine of the Offensive in 1914', in Peter Paret (ed.), *Makers of Modern Strategy from Machiavelli to the Nuclear Age* (Princeton, NJ: Princeton University Press, 1986), 510–26; Steven E. Miller, Sean M. Lynn-Jones and Stephen Van Evera (eds.), *Military Strategy and the Origins of the First World War: An International Security Reader* (Princeton, NJ: Princeton University Press, 1991); and, A. J. Echevarria II, 'The "Cult of the Offensive" Revisited: Confronting Technological Change Before the Great War', *Journal of Strategic Studies*, 25 (2002), 199–214.

[180] Michael Crawshaw, 'The Impact of Technology on the BEF and Its Commander', in Brian Bond and Nigel Cave (eds.), *Haig: A Reappraisal 70 Years On* (Barnsley: Leo Cooper, 1999), 167.

[181] John Downer, 'When Failure Is an Option: Redundancy, Reliability and Regulation in Complex Technical Systems', *Discussion Paper No. 53, Centre for Analysis of Risk and Regulation at the London School of Economics and Political Science* (London: Kube, 2009), 1–24.

[182] 'Notes on a Conference Held at Corps Headquarters on May 23rd', 23 May 1916, Lieutenant-General Sir Aylmer Hunter-Weston Papers, Add.48357, British Library, London (BL).

[183] Chenevix-Trench, 'Signal Communications in War', 296.

Although inroads were clearly made, particularly with regards to the development and employment of wireless, most notably CW wireless and the experiments conducted in wireless telephony during the final year of the war, the technology had yet to reach a level of maturity that would enable British commanders to exercise more effective command and control.

4   1914–1915

The nature of the war on the Western Front in 1914 conformed strongly with pre-war expectations. From its opening encounter with the German Army at the Battle of Mons on 23 August until the conclusion of the First Battle of Ypres in mid-November, the BEF's operations were characterised by mobility and manoeuvre. The exception to this was the brief period of stalemate that prevailed along the River Aisne during the second half of September, which provided British commanders with their first taste of modern, entrenched warfare.[1] While popular accounts of the opening months of the war have generally emphasised the heroics of Britain's 'contemptible little army' in helping prevent a German victory in western Europe,[2] recent scholarship has begun to provide a much more balanced and nuanced assessment of the BEF's exploits.[3] However, although certain features of the BEF's communication system are discussed within some of these studies, that system is not the main focus of their analysis.[4] This is significant, because the scale and intensity of the 1914 campaign put the BEF's communications system under enormous strain, which in turn severely handicapped the ability of British commanders to exercise efficient command and control. Moreover, the lessons learnt by the BEF in 1914, particularly during the periods of trench

---

[1] For the British official history, see J. E. Edmonds, *Military Operations: France and Belgium, 1914*, 2 Vols. (London: HMSO, 1922 and 1925).

[2] Terraine, *Mons: The Retreat to Victory*; Anthony Farrar-Hockley, *Death of an Army* (London: Arthur Baker, 1967); David Ascoli, *The Mons Star* (London: George Harrap, 1981); Lyn Macdonald, *1914* (London: Hodder and Stoughton, 1987); Richard Holmes, *Riding the Retreat: Mons to the Marne 1914 Revisited* (London: Cape, 1995); and, Malcolm Brown, *The Imperial War Museum Book of 1914* (London: Sidgwick and Jackson, 2004).

[3] Gardner, *Trial by Fire*; Ian F. W. Beckett, *Ypres: The British Army and the Battle for Flanders, 1914* (London: Longman, 2004); Holger H. Herwig, *The Marne, 1914: The Opening of World War I and the Battle That Changed the World* (New York: Random House, 2009); and, Spencer Jones (ed.), *Stemming the Tide: Officers and Leadership in the British Expeditionary Force 1914* (Solihull: Helion, 2013).

[4] See, for example, Barr, 'Command in the Transition from Mobile to Static Warfare', 13–38; and, Carragher, '"Amateurs at a Professional Game"'.

stalemate on the Aisne in September and around Ypres in November and December, had an important bearing upon future British communications policy and practice.

These lessons were further reinforced by the experiences of 1915, as the BEF attempted to overcome the challenges posed by the unprecedented scale of trench warfare. The BEF embarked upon four offensives during the year: the Battle of Neuve Chapelle (10–12 March), the Battle of Aubers Ridge (9 May), the Battle of Festubert (15–27 May) and the Battle of Loos (25 September–13 October). In conjunction with the major offensives undertaken by the French Army, none of these battles came close to achieving a decisive breakthrough.[5] However, the BEF learnt a number of invaluable lessons from its experiences,[6] not least of which were those concerning communications. Although conspicuously overlooked by historians, ultimately these lessons would shape the BEF's attitude towards communications as it prepared for the Somme campaign the following year. The primary aim of this chapter, therefore, is to provide a much more thorough examination of the influence of communications upon the BEF's operations in 1914 and 1915 than has so far been presented within the historiography.

Mons and Le Cateau

Commanded by Field Marshal Sir John French, the BEF in August 1914 numbered approximately 120,000 men and was initially composed of two corps: I Corps, commanded by Lieutenant-General Sir Douglas Haig, consisted of 1 and 2 Divisions; and II Corps, commanded by General Sir Horace Smith-Dorrien,[7] comprised 3 and 5 Divisions. In

---

[5] For the British official history, see J. E. Edmonds and G. C. Wynne, *Military Operations: France and Belgium, 1915*, Vol. 1 (London: HMSO, 1927) and J. E. Edmonds, *Military Operations: France and Belgium, 1915*, Vol. 2 (London: HMSO, 1928). See also: Prior and Wilson, *Command on the Western Front*, 17–134; Lloyd, *Loos 1915*; Nick Lloyd, '"With Faith and without Fear": Sir Douglas Haig's Command of First Army During 1915', *Journal of Military History*, 71 (2007), 1051–76; and, Spencer Jones (ed.), *Courage without Glory: The British Army on the Western Front 1915* (Solihull: Helion, 2015). For the French Army's experiences, see Jonathan Krause, *Early Trench Tactics in the French Army: The Second Battle of Artois, May–June 1915* (Farnham: Ashgate, 2013).

[6] For an overview of the tactical and operational development of the BEF throughout 1915, see: Griffith, *Battle Tactics*, 47–64; Sheffield, *Forgotten Victory*, 124–33; and, J. P. Harris and Sanders Marble, 'The "Step-by-Step" Approach: British Military Thought and Operational Method on the Western Front 1915–17', *War in History*, 15 (2008), 19–28.

[7] The original commander of II Corps, Lieutenant-General Sir James Grierson, had died of a heart attack on 17 August.

addition, Secretary of State for War Lord Kitchener dispatched four brigades of cavalry, forming the Cavalry Division under the command of Major-General Edmund Allenby, and one further cavalry brigade, which was attached to I Corps.[8] By 20 August, the landing and concentration of the BEF in France had been completed and units of I and II Corps began arriving in the vicinity of the Belgian industrial town of Mons two days later. Having marched approximately 10 miles in relative comfort, the BEF experienced very little communication difficulty on its journey from Maubeuge and Le Cateau into Belgium.[9] Motorcycle despatch riders provided the main means of communication during the day, while the French civil telegraph system was used to connect headquarters with each other at night.[10]

The BEF's position at Mons on 23 August was, as Smith-Dorrien later wrote, 'almost impossible to defend'.[11] Nevertheless, every effort was made by the Signal Service to establish an efficient system of communications. While as much use as possible was made of the permanent civilian telephone and telegraph lines, particularly amongst the brigades, the divisional signal companies also laid a great deal of cable in the rear areas, thus connecting corps and divisional headquarters.[12] The problem, however, was that once the Germans began to overwhelm the British position in the early afternoon of 23 August, virtually all of this cable had to be abandoned.[13] Given that the Signal Service, like the rest of the BEF, was expecting a short, sharp war of mobility, it had been provided with only a bare minimum supply of cable. According to the OC 2 Division Signal Company, the total amount of spare cable carried by the division in 1914 was two miles, which was 'supposed to last for the campaign!'[14] The Signal Service could therefore ill afford to lose what little precious cable it had. Yet, writing in his diary on 24 August, Arthur Hildebrand, OC II Corps Signal Company, noted that 'one estimate puts the amount of cable lost by the whole Army at nearly 50 miles in length'.[15]

Despite being in short supply, the provision of line-based communications served the BEF relatively well during the Battle of Mons.

[8] Terraine, *Mons*, 200–2.
[9] Edmonds, *Military Operations, 1914*, Vol. 1, 49; Gardner, *Trial by Fire*, 34.
[10] Priestley, *Work of the Royal Engineers*, 17.
[11] General Sir Horace Smith-Dorrien to Major Archibald F. Becke, 31 March 1920, General Sir Horace Smith-Dorrien Papers, CAB45/206, TNA.
[12] Anon., 'With a Signal Company on Service: A Short Account of the Doings of the 5th Signal Company, R.E., since Leaving Carlow for the War', *Sapper*, 21 (December 1914), 104.
[13] Nalder, *Royal Corps of Signals*, 91.   [14] Powell, 'Divisional Signals in 1914', 340.
[15] Hildebrand, 'Second Army Signals, 1914', 134.

According to one witness, 'telegraph staff [were] kept very busy with messages'.[16] This was just as well because the enclosed nature of the Mons position presented little opportunity for visual signalling, except over very short distances.[17] Extensive use was made of despatch riders to expedite the transfer of vital information; such was the case during the mid-afternoon of 23 August when Smith-Dorrien gave the order for 3 and 5 Divisions to pull back to a second defensive position two to three miles south of the Mons-Condé Canal.[18] The difficulty in locating the headquarters of individual units and conveying this information to them, however, is illustrated by the experience of William Watson, a motor-cycle despatch rider with 5 Division. According to Watson, both he and four despatch riders before him had been sent with a message to the commander of the 15th Infantry Brigade, Brigadier-General Count Edward Gleichen, yet none of them could locate the whereabouts of his headquarters. Eventually, Watson returned to 5 Division's signal office at Dour with information from Brigadier-General Gerald Cuthbert, commanding 13th Infantry Brigade, and a verbal message from his signal officer that the 15th appeared to be cut off and the right flank of the 13th had been badly turned. In light of this news, 5 Division began its withdrawal: 'We viciously smashed all the telegraph instruments in the office and cut all the wires'.[19] The difficulties encountered by some despatch riders during the Battle of Mons were called to the attention of the Director of Army Signals, who, on the very same day of the battle, issued the following instructions:

Signal officers must continually bear in mind the necessity of keeping the Signal Offices in which they are in communication constantly informed of any proposed or actual change of their Headquarters. Neglect to do so may have most disastrous results, and has already resulted in serious delay to most important orders.[20]

Nevertheless, despite the problems that Watson and other despatch riders experienced, a major catastrophe at Mons was prevented. The vast majority of the units of II Corps had received the order to retire and had done so successfully by the early evening.[21]

---

[16] Anon., 'With a Signal Company on Service', 104.
[17] 'Southampton to the Marne, 1914', undated, M. J. Millie Papers, Western Front, Recollections M-Y, LCL.
[18] 3 Division War Diary, 23 August 1914, WO95/1375, 5 Division War Diary, 23 August 1914, WO95/1510, TNA.
[19] Watson, *Adventures of a Motorcycle Despatch Rider*, 21–2.
[20] 'Director of Army Signals. Circular Memorandum No. 12, 23 August 1914', Director of Army Signals War Diary, WO95/57, TNA.
[21] Edmonds, *Military Operations, 1914*, Vol. 1, 83; Gardner, *Trial by Fire*, 44–5.

The practical problems involved in extricating the BEF from Mons were compounded by the fragile and varied means of communication commanders had at their disposal. During the night of 23–4 August, for example, the chiefs of staff of both corps and the Cavalry Division were summoned to GHQ, unsuitably located 35 miles away at Le Cateau, to receive further orders. As the war diaries of I and II Corps testify, direct communication with GHQ throughout 23 August had been virtually non-existent. Even when communication was attempted, such as the message sent by II Corps shortly after 3 p.m. informing GHQ of the gap between 3 and 5 Divisions during the planned withdrawal, there is no indication that GHQ actually replied to it.[22] Similarly, the war diary of 1st Signal Section on 24 August reveals that the Cavalry Division also had difficulty in communicating with GHQ. On three separate occasions a wireless report of the division's situation had been sent to GHQ, but no reply was received.[23] Thus, all three chiefs of staff had to make very time-consuming motor car journeys on the night of 23–4 August. Brigadier-General John Gough, BGGS I Corps, was the first to arrive at GHQ. Upon receiving the order to 'retreat at once on Bavai', Gough was able to telegraph the information to I Corps headquarters shortly after 1 a.m.[24] Haig was informed of the withdrawal at 2 a.m. and subsequently began to make the necessary arrangements.[25] The result was that by 4:45 a.m., both Major-General Samuel Lomax's 1 Division and Major-General Charles Monro's 2 Division had begun their retirement.[26]

Undoubtedly, the smooth and speedy withdrawal of I Corps would not have been made possible without the telegraph link between GHQ and I Corps headquarters. Unfortunately for Brigadier-General George Forestier-Walker and Colonel John Vaughan, chiefs of staff of II Corps and the Cavalry Division, respectively, such a 'real-time' link was not available. After receiving their orders shortly after 1 a.m., both men had to climb back into their cars and travel back to their respective headquarters. As Smith-Dorrien related in his memoirs, because II Corps headquarters at Sars-la-Bruyére was not in telegraphic communication with

---

[22] I Corps War Diary, 23 August 1914, WO95/588, II Corps War Diary, 23 August 1914, WO95/630, Smith-Dorrien War Diary, 23 August 1914, CAB45/206, TNA.

[23] 1 Cavalry Division Signal Section War Diary, 24 August 1914, WO95/1103, TNA.

[24] Ian F. W. Beckett, *Johnnie Gough, V.C.* (London: Tom Donovan, 1989), 181.

[25] 'Johnnie Gough to I Corps', 24 August 1914, General Sir Horace Smith-Dorrien Papers, 87/47/10, IWM; Field Marshal Sir Douglas Haig Diary, 24 August 1914, WO256/1, TNA; Sheffield and Bourne (eds.), *Douglas Haig: War Diaries and Letters*, 62–4.

[26] 1 Division War Diary, 24 August 1914, WO95/1227, 2 Division War Diary, 24 August 1914, WO95/1283, TNA.

GHQ, 'it was past 3 a.m. on the 24th when Forestier-Walker returned to my headquarters to say that the C-in-C had, in view of fresh information, decided that instead of standing to fight, the whole BEF was to retire'.[27] Subsequently, in contrast to the 'very active and pushing' retreat of I Corps, II Corps was unable to withdraw quickly enough and in good order and, as a consequence, bore the brunt of a severe German bombardment just before dawn on 24 August.[28] As a post-war Staff College report concluded, 'The lateness of the receipt of information, and lack of speedy inter-communication... seriously prejudiced the conduct of operations'.[29] Indeed, II Corps fought continuous rearguard actions throughout 24 August, suffering more than 2,500 casualties in the process.[30] Many of these rearguards fought to near-extinction as a result of the inability of the retiring main body to keep them adequately informed of the situation.[31]

On the morning of 25 August, the two corps of the BEF separated to bypass the Forest of Mormal.[32] Both Haig and Smith-Dorrien had been instructed by GHQ to begin moving 'to a position in the neighbourhood of Le Cateau'.[33] With I Corps having been allocated the road to the east of the forest and II Corps the Roman Road to the west, the Forest of Mormal proved to be an 'impenetrable wall' for communications. As Smith-Dorrien later observed, maintaining communications with I Corps became 'a matter of supreme difficulty. As a matter of fact, I heard nothing of the I Corps throughout the day. No information was sent me by GHQ concerning it, and I imagined that all was going well and we should join upon the Le Cateau position in the evening'.[34] With a gap of some 10 miles between them, however, the two corps did not meet at Le Cateau that evening as instructed.[35] Haig, realising he could not get

---

[27] Smith-Dorrien, *Memories*, 387.

[28] Field Marshal Sir John French Diary, 24 August 1914, PP/MCR/C32, IWM.

[29] 'Senior Division, Staff College, Camberley Report: The Retreat from Mons', April 1925, Captain Sir Basil Liddell Hart Papers, 15/2/49/1, LHCMA.

[30] Edmonds, *Military Operations, 1914*, Vol. 1, 112.

[31] Such was the case at Elouges, where the 1/Cheshire Regiment never received the order to retire, since the adjutant bearing the message was killed on route and neither a bicycle orderly nor a runner was able to reach them in time. On the morning of 24 August, the strength of the 1/Cheshire Regiment had been recorded as 28 officers and 933 men. At roll call at the end of the day, just 7 officers and 199 men answered. See: ibid., 99–105; Terraine, *Mons*, 104–10; and, Holmes, *Riding the Retreat*, 135–46.

[32] Edmonds, *Military Operations, 1914*, Vol. 1, 112. See also, Nikolas Gardner, 'Command in Crisis: The British Expeditionary Force and the Forest of Mormal, August 1914', *War & Society*, 16 (1998), 13–32.

[33] 'GHQ Operation Order No. 7', 24 August 1914, GHQ War Diary, WO95/1, TNA.

[34] Smith-Dorrien, *Memories*, 393.

[35] Smith-Dorrien Diary, 25 August 1914, Smith-Dorrien Papers, IWM.

to Le Cateau in time, contravened Operation Order No. 7 and halted I Corps in the vicinity of Landrecies, seven miles north-east of its intended destination.[36] While elements of I Corps were involved in fierce skirmishes with the advanced guard of the German Army that night, Smith-Dorrien had decided to stand fast on the Le Cateau position and prepare a defensive counterattack.[37]

According to Smith-Dorrien's memoir, having been informed of II Corps' decision to stand, Sir John French responded swiftly: 'If you can hold your ground the situation appears likely to improve... Although you are given a free hand as to method this telegram is not intended to convey the impression that I am not as anxious for you to carry out the retirement, and, you must make every endeavour to do so'. GHQ confirmed this written instruction with perhaps the most important telephone conversation of the war thus far. As Smith-Dorrien recalled, at about 6:45 a.m. on 26 August, 'a cyclist brought me a message from Bertry Station, distant about half a mile, saying Sir John French wished to speak to me on the railway telephone'.[38] When he arrived at the station, however, Smith-Dorrien found that it was Sir Henry Wilson, the MGGS, not the commander-in-chief, on the end of the line. Although Wilson urged Smith-Dorrien to continue with the retreat as originally intended, the II Corps commander stated that he was confident of delivering the enemy a 'stopping blow'.[39] Informing GHQ of his decision to stand and fight at Le Cateau was made all the more easier for Smith-Dorrien by the French railway telephone system. Communicating that same message to the rest of II Corps, however, proved much more problematic. 'Communication was most difficult', Smith-Dorrien later remarked, 'and it was impossible to find out the positions of units until hours after they had reached them'.[40] According to the official history, many units in

---

[36] Adding to his original diary entry for 26 August after the war, Haig noted that 'direct communication with II Corps was cut off, and touch was not regained until the I Corps reached Villers-Cotterets on the 1st September'. See Haig Diary, 26 August 1914, WO256/1, TNA; Sheffield and Bourne (eds.), *Douglas Haig War Diaries and Letters*, 66.

[37] Haig Diary, 25 August 1914, WO256/1, TNA; Smith-Dorrien Diary, 26 August 1914, IWM.

[38] Smith-Dorrien, *Memories*, 403, 405.

[39] Smith-Dorrien Diary, 26 August 1914, CAB45/206, TNA; Field Marshal Sir Henry Wilson Diary, 26 August 1914, Field Marshal Sir Henry Wilson Papers, DS/MISC/80, IWM; Major-General Sir C. E. Callwell, *Field-Marshal Sir Henry Wilson: His Life and Diaries, Vol. I* (London: Cassell, 1927), 169; Brigadier-General A. Hildebrand, 'Recollections of Sir Horace Smith-Dorrien at Le Cateau, August 1914', *Army Quarterly*, 21 (October 1930), 17; and, Peter T. Scott (ed.), 'The View From GHQ: The Second and Third Parts of the War Diary of General Sir Charles Deedes, KCB, CMG, DSO', *Stand To! Journal of the Western Front Association*, 11 (1984), 10.

[40] Smith-Dorrien, *Memories*, 398.

5 Division did not receive news of the decision to engage the Germans until it was too late. Consequently, the German attack that began on the morning of 26 August came as a surprise to many frontline commanders, who were unprepared as a result.[41]

The exploits of II Corps at the Battle of Le Cateau have been recounted elsewhere.[42] It is sufficient to note that Le Cateau was a much more impromptu engagement than Mons and thus the Signal Service had very little time to prepare an elaborate system of communications. Added to this time constraint was the fact that, unlike Mons, Le Cateau was an open, rural district and as such, local telegraph and telephone lines were few and far between. While II Corps headquarters could rely upon the French railway telephone system for speedy intercommunication with GHQ, those formations below division had to make use of their already diminishing stores of cable.[43] Although cable was laid to link up division, brigade and battalion headquarters, the full weight of the German artillery bombardment cut the majority of these lines.[44] Colonel Rory Macleod of the 80th Battery, RFA, noted that 'the telephone line running from the Battery to the O.P. was broken by the hostile fire, and communication was established by flag until every signaller in the Battery became a casualty'.[45] Indeed, the sheltered position of the surrounding countryside meant that visual signalling was used to a much greater extent than at Mons. However, although it proved to be of some use, the waving of semaphore flags, often within distances as close as 1,200 yards of the enemy, resulted in a high proportion of casualties for the signallers involved.[46]

As at Mons, the inadequacies of the BEF's communications system were made terribly apparent once the order for II Corps to retire was issued in the early afternoon. Smith-Dorrien later complained that 'there was the greatest difficulty in getting the orders round – in fact some few units never got them, but conformed to the movements of the troops which had'.[47] This was particularly the case with regards to 4 Division, which had arrived on 25 August and acted as a covering force for II Corps and the Cavalry Division that day.[48] Commanded by

---

[41] Edmonds, *Military Operations, 1914*, Vol. 1, 143–4.
[42] Ibid., 141–202; Terraine, *Mons*, 120–42; Richard Holmes, *The Little Field Marshal: A Life of Sir John French* (London: Weidenfeld and Nicolson, 2004), 221–4; and, Gardner, *Trial by Fire*, 54–7.
[43] Priestley, *Work of the Royal Engineers*, 19.
[44] Anon., 'With a Signal Company on Service', 106.
[45] Colonel R. Macleod, 'An Artillery Officer in the First World War', 26 August 1914, Liddell Hart Papers 15/14/1, LHCMA.
[46] Priestley, *Work of the Royal Engineers*, 20.   [47] Smith-Dorrien, *Memories*, 405.
[48] Gardner, *Trial by Fire*, 54.

Major-General Thomas Snow, 4 Division was at a considerable disadvantage in relation to 3 and 5 Divisions, since it was without a signal company. Thus, Snow had to rely entirely upon mounted officers and runners for the maintenance of communication along the five-mile front that 4 Division occupied.[49] Given that these were rather time-consuming methods, the absence of a signal company had a significant impact on the nature of 4 Division's retreat from Le Cateau on the afternoon of 26 August. As Snow recollected after the war:

It is always difficult to get orders to everyone in the frontline but ten times more so when you have no machinery to help you as was the case in this instance... I was heavily handicapped by the absence of my signal company, as I was unable to get messages to the Brigadiers, except by sending off my staff to carry such messages. The Brigadiers were even worse off than I was as, having a smaller staff, it was as much as they could do to get their orders to the troops without worrying about sending back information, the consequence being that I was very much in the dark as to what was going on in the front line.[50]

The retirement of 4 Division from Le Cateau was 'much mixed up' as a result of the *ad hoc* system of communications.[51] The 10th Infantry Brigade, for instance, did not receive the order to withdraw until 5 p.m., some two and a half hours after it had been issued.[52] Subsequently, during the rearguard action at Ligny-Harcourt on the left flank of the British position, tenuous communications 'rendered the control of subordinate units on a front of some five miles, a great deal of which was under heavy shell and rifle fire, a most difficult and arduous task... It was impossible for them (Staff Officers) to go to direct units on the right road of retirement'.[53]

Despite suffering 7,812 casualties and losing 38 guns, Smith-Dorrien's decision to stand and fight on 26 August is now widely accepted amongst historians as having saved the BEF.[54] Forestier-Walker wrote after

[49] Edmonds, *Military Operations, 1914*, Vol. 1, 139.

[50] General T. D'O. Snow, 'Account of the Retreat of 1914', undated, Correspondence Regarding the Retreat from Mons, CAB45/129, TNA; 'The Story of the 4th Div. B.E.F., August and September 1914', Lieutenant-General Sir Thomas D'Oyly Snow Papers 76/79/1, IWM, 19.

[51] Dan Snow and Mark Pottle (eds.), *The Confusion of Command: The War Memoirs of Lieutenant General Sir Thomas D'Oyly Snow, 1914–1915* (London: Frontline Books, 2011), 26.

[52] 'General Report on the Battle of Le Cateau', 26 August 1914, Smith-Dorrien Papers, CAB45/206, TNA.

[53] 'Action of Ligny-Harcourt, 26 August 1914', Montgomery-Massingberd Papers 5/1, LHCMA.

[54] Terraine, *Mons*, 143; Holmes, *Little Field Marshal*, 224; Andy Simpson, *The Evolution of Victory: British Battles on the Western Front 1914–1918* (London: Tom Donovan, 1995), 8–11.

the war: 'Had there been no Le Cateau, there would almost certainly have been no Marne, and even the man in the street realises that the battle of the Marne was the turning point of the war'.[55] Even Sir John French, who had initially disapproved of Smith-Dorrien's decision, acknowledged to Lord Kitchener that 'the troops under Smith-Dorrien made a magnificent stand'.[56] The BEF's communications system, however, had been found wanting on numerous occasions. The technical proficiency of the Signal Service had been negated by the chaotic nature of the retreat and the profound difficulties that the war of movement had so far produced. Unfortunately for British commanders, many of these difficulties were to re-surface throughout the duration of the subsequent retreat.

The 'Great Retreat' and the Battle of the Marne

As early as 7 August, the Director of Army Signals had been working closely with the French Department of Posts, Telegraphs and Telephones. In his first circular memorandum, Fowler explained that such cooperation had provided diagrams and information regarding the French civilian telegraph and telephone lines and that arrangements had been made 'to place such circuits as are required at the disposal of the British Signal Service'. In light of the Signal Service's limited supplies, all cable was to be 'economised as far as possible by making use of the permanent lines of the country'.[57] In a speech given at Aldershot two years earlier on the military geography of western Europe, Sir William Robertson, then Commandant of the British Staff College at Camberley, had observed that communications throughout Belgium and France were 'abundant and for the most part very good'.[58] Nevertheless, prior to the Battle of Mons, Fowler oversaw the installation of a military telephone exchange at Amiens, which established line communications

---

[55] 'Extracts from a Letter Dated 27 February 1934', Smith-Dorrien Papers, CAB45/ 206, TNA.

[56] French to Kitchener, 27 August 1914, Field Marshal Lord Kitchener Papers, PRO30/ 57/49, TNA. Privately, however, Sir John always resented Smith-Dorrien for disobeying his orders, a reflection of the personal rivalry that had existed between the two men long before the war began. See: Holmes, *Little Field Marshal*, 222–5; and, Ian F. W. Beckett (ed.), *The Judgement of History: Sir Horace Smith-Dorrien, Lord French and 1914* (London: Tom Donovan, 1993).

[57] 'Director of Army Signals. Circular Memorandum No. 1, 7 August 1914', 'Director of Army Signals. Circular Memorandum No. 5, 17 August 1914', Director of Army Signals War Diary, WO95/57, TNA.

[58] 'Speech at Aldershot on the Military Geography of Western Europe, 1912', Field Marshal Sir William Robertson Papers 1/3/2, LHCMA.

to Le Cateau, Havre, Wassigny, Landrecies and Busigny. A Signal Park, where all signal stores were to be kept, was also established at the Advanced Base at Amiens.[59] Thus, at the outset of the campaign, the BEF had access to an extensive telecommunications network. As the liaison officer, Edward Spears, recalled in an article in the *Daily Telegraph* after the war: 'There could be nothing wrong with the system of communications, it was perfect and undisturbed... Civil inter-communication had been suspended so that nothing should interfere with military messages'.[60]

While some units did find the French civilian network to be a 'most useful communication tool',[61] once the retreat from Mons began, 'such attempts as were made to use the permanent lines were futile', since 'formations were moving much too rapidly and personnel were too used up on D[espatch].R[ider]. work'.[62] In the conditions which prevailed in late August and early September, having to rely upon the fixed network of telegraph and telephone lines would have seriously restricted the freedom and mobility of a commander. Furthermore, the laying of cable was totally impractical because most formations seldom remained in the vicinity to make effective use of it. Almost as quickly as it was laid, the cable had to be recovered. Yet, as the *Training Manual – Signalling, Part II (1914)* made clear: 'Reeling up the cable is far the most arduous work that the [signal] section will have to perform'.[63] Thus, 'the difficulty, if not impossibility, of laying line telegraphy in so rapidly moving a retreat'[64] meant that it was considered much easier and more practical to use despatch riders by day and establish communication by cable at night when units halted.[65] Although the Signal Service improvised and used the French civilian network to connect GHQ with I and II Corps by night, the hectic nature of the retreat and the lack of adequate stores meant that telegraphic communication was rarely extended to lower formations.[66] However, as the war diary of the Director of Army

---

[59] 'Director of Army Signals. Circular Memorandum No. 10, 19 August 1914', Director of Army Signals War Diary, WO95/57, TNA.

[60] E. L. Spears, 'The Great Retreat of 1914', *Daily Telegraph*, 24 February 1930, Liddell Hart Papers 15/2/48, LHCMA.

[61] 1 Cavalry Division Signal Section War Diary, 22 August 1914, WO95/1103, TNA.

[62] Powell, 'Divisional Signals in 1914', 346.

[63] *Training Manual – Signalling, Part II*, 122.

[64] 'Senior Division, Staff College, Camberley Report: The Retreat from Mons', April 1925, Liddell Hart Papers 15/2/49/1, LHCMA.

[65] Lieutenant J. R. Pinsent, R.E., 'The Diary of a Cable Section Officer from August to November, 1914', *The Royal Signals Quarterly Journal*, 3 (1935), 16.

[66] 'Extract from a Letter Received from an Officer of the Headquarters Staff of a Division at the Front', 24 November 1914, Hunter-Weston Papers, Add. 48355, BL.

Signals makes clear, even the telegraphic link established between GHQ and each of the corps was frequently cut during the retreat.[67] Finally, many British officers felt that it was much safer and simpler to send information via traditional message carrying services than by telegraph and telephone because of the unreliability of the latter. As Edward Spears noted:

There was the problem of transmitting information; exasperating delays at the telephone, when every moment was of value; the connection obtained at last through a dozen exchanges, sometimes after several hours' delay, only to find it impossible to hear; or to be suddenly cut off. It was amusing, but a poor consolation, to get through to the Germans by mistake, as I did upon a number of occasions during the retreat, and it showed the danger of the telephone.[68]

Telegraph and telephone undoubtedly had their limitations during the opening weeks of the war. Nevertheless, they were much more convenient and secure methods of communication than wireless. Although its importance grew during the First World War, wireless was 'a somewhat doubtful proposition' in 1914.[69] Its use was exclusively reserved for GHQ and the Cavalry Division.[70] However, the wagon and pack sets then available were seemingly unreliable. On 30 August, for example, the Cavalry Division had to destroy and abandon one of its pack sets as a result of wear and tear.[71] Overall, apart from its application in intercepting German wireless traffic,[72] the BEF made little use of wireless as a means of conveying information during the opening weeks of the war.[73]

By far the most widely utilised means of communication in the BEF during the 1914 campaign were motorcycle despatch riders.[74] According to Captain Powell, from Mons to the Aisne 'practically the whole of the signal work was done by motor cyclist D.R.s'.[75] Indeed, motorcycle despatch riders formed the backbone of the army's communications

---

[67] Director of Army Signals War Diary, 28 August 1914, WO95/57, TNA.

[68] Spears, *Liaison 1914*, 118.

[69] 'With the Wireless Section of the Signal Company, Royal Engineers, 1914–1918', Rumsey Papers, LCL.

[70] 'ZCO 1914–1919. Narrative by J. H. S. Christian, M.C.' (October 1959), 11, Captain J. H. Christian Papers, 90/28/1, IWM.

[71] 1 Cavalry Division Signal Section War Diary, 30 August 1914, WO95/1103, TNA.

[72] 'History of Wireless Telegraphy in the Royal Naval Air Service, Royal Flying Corps and Royal Air Force, from August 1914 to November 1918', undated, AIR1/2217/209/33/6, TNA.

[73] For additional context, see Hall, 'British Army and Wireless Communication'. For wireless intelligence, see: John Ferris, 'The British Army and Signals Intelligence in the Field during the First World War', *Intelligence and National Security*, 3 (1988), 25–6; Ferris (ed.), *The British Army and Signals Intelligence*, 5; and, Beach, *Haig's Intelligence*, 159.

[74] Carragher, '"Amateurs at a Professional Game"', 332–49.

[75] Powell, 'Divisional Signals in 1914', 346.

system. Working day and night, and sleeping whenever and wherever they could, motorcycle despatch riders ensured the rapid and efficient conveyance of orders and reports throughout the BEF that telegraph, telephone and wireless were unable to offer consistently during the hurried and prolonged retreat of 1914. The war diary of 2 Division Signal Company, for example, noted that the work done by despatch riders was 'invaluable, as without them all communication would have failed'.[76] Similarly, the Cavalry Division Signal Section acknowledged on 12 September that 'communication became impossible without a good service of despatch riders. [They are] practically the only means between brigade and division headquarters'.[77] Praise for the work carried out by despatch riders also came from the highest levels of the BEF's command. While Smith-Dorrien recorded in his diary, 'We have... a most undaunted lot of motorcyclists, from Universities and Public Schools, who know no fear and never seem to be tired',[78] Sir John French paid a glowing, personal tribute in his Official Despatch of 20 November 1914:

I am anxious in this despatch to bring to Your Lordship's special notice the splendid work which has been done throughout the campaign by the Cyclists of the Signal Corps. Carrying despatches and messages at all hours of the day and night in every kind of weather, and often traversing bad roads blocked with transport, they have been conspicuously successful in maintaining an extraordinary degree of efficiency in the service of communications. Many casualties have occurred in their ranks, but no amount of difficulty or danger has ever checked the energy and ardour which has distinguished their Corps throughout operations.[79]

However, as important as they were to the exercise of command and control, despatch riders also had to contend with a host of challenges. One of the most common inconveniences experienced was the difficulty in locating the continuously shifting headquarters of units they had been sent to find, whilst navigating through unfamiliar territory, without adequate maps and along roads that were blocked by marching columns, supply vehicles and hordes of refugees. According to one motorcycle despatch rider: 'The British soldier never knows where he is, much less the names of the neighbouring towns or villages'.[80] Another noted after

[76] 2 Division Signal Company War Diary, 24 August 1914, WO95/1333, TNA.
[77] 1 Cavalry Division Signal Section War Diary, 12 September 1914, WO95/1103, TNA.
[78] Smith-Dorrien War Diary, 10 September 1914, CAB45/206, TNA. Officers of the Intelligence Corps were also utilised as motorcycle despatch riders in 1914. See Beach, '"Intelligent Civilians in Uniform"', 5–7.
[79] French, *Despatches of Lord French*, 122.
[80] W. H. Foster, Typescript Memoirs, undated, 10, Lieutenant W. H. Foster Papers, 99/36/1, IWM.

the war: 'At one in the morning (30 August) I was sent off to a Chateau in the Forest of Compiègne. I had no map, and it was a pure accident that I found my way there and back'.[81] It was therefore of vital importance that every unit was kept up to date with the movements of both its subordinate and superior formation's headquarters. Without this information it became impossible to deliver messages on time or to redirect despatch riders accordingly.[82]

In addition to the difficulties experienced in locating headquarters during the retreat, travelling in close proximity of the enemy exposed motorcycle despatch riders to fire from both friend and foe alike. Prior to the Battle of Mons, Fowler had issued a circular memorandum warning all despatch riders that they were 'liable to be stopped by Guards placed on the roads by the French Authorities'.[83] Indeed, it was not unusual for a despatch rider to be stopped every three-quarters of a mile or so as he made his way to and from his intended destination. Not only was this 'an extraordinarily tiring method of getting along', it was also fraught with danger because most sentries 'fired almost as quickly as they challenged'.[84] Working continuously around the clock to preserve the integrity of the BEF's communications system took a heavy toll on both men and machines throughout the gruelling 13-day, 170-mile retreat. By 6 September many signal companies were reporting a severe shortage of motorcyclists due to a combination of 'trigger-happy' sentries and ill health as a result of overwork.[85] A report by I Corps even recorded 'cases of men meeting with accidents owing to falling asleep while actually riding'.[86] Reflecting on the lessons learnt during the retreat, Captain Powell felt that 'the establishment of despatch riders proved quite inadequate for the task, nor do I think it was ever based on the assumption that communication to so many destinations would be required'.[87] Combined with a grave lack of spare parts for motorcycle maintenance, the end of the BEF's retreat on 5 September was some relief, since this provided despatch riders with the opportunity to obtain badly needed

---

[81] Watson, *Adventures of a Motorcycle Despatch Rider*, 38.
[82] 1 Cavalry Division Signal Section War Diary, 12 September 1914, WO95/1103, TNA.
[83] 'Director of Army Signals. Circular Memorandum No. 4, 17 August 1914', Director of Army Signals War Diary, WO95/57, TNA.
[84] Watson, *Adventures of a Motorcycle Despatch Rider*, 18; Typescript Memoirs, 10, Foster Papers, IWM.
[85] 1 Division Signal Company War Diary, 5 September 1914, WO95/1255, 3 Division Signal Company War Diary, 6 September 1914, WO95/1404, TNA.
[86] 'Motor Cyclists Divisional Signal Companies', 28 September 1914, I Corps War Diary, WO95/588, TNA.
[87] 'Divisional Signal Service Headquarters', 24 September 1914, 2 Division Signal Company War Diary, WO95/1333, TNA.

spare parts and petrol. A slow wave of reinforcements was also introduced to bolster the much-depleted ranks of the Despatch Rider Service.[88]

Despite these difficulties, a certain degree of routine and familiarity had been established by the latter stages of the retreat, which enabled the Motor Cycle Despatch Rider Service to provide the mainstay of the BEF's communications system. Each division allotted two despatch riders to its flank guard, two to the rear guard and two to division headquarters. In addition, two despatch riders were permanently assigned to each brigade.[89] As a precaution, when travelling close to enemy lines, despatch riders were sent out in twos or threes at 300-yard intervals. According to William Foster: 'The first rider carried the despatch in a marked pocket and the next rider was instructed to take the despatch and continue with the assignment if the first rider was shot'. Some despatch riders were even told to eat the despatch they were carrying should they fall into enemy hands.[90] Given the limitations of telephone, telegraph and wireless during the retreat, motorcycle despatch riders held the BEF's communications system together, providing commanders with an essential tool for command and control.

In addition to motorcycle despatch riders, the BEF employed a group of specially trained volunteer drivers from the Royal Automobile Club who were to act as chauffeurs to commanders, staff and liaison officers. Often, these chauffeurs and their motor cars were the only means commanders had to expedite the transfer of information. As Haig noted in his diary on 24 August:

Thanks to the motor I was able to give personal orders to all the chief commanders concerned in the operation in the space of an hour and enable them to cancel the orders which their troops were on the point of carrying out for a forward movement. Written orders reached them later, but the movement in retreat was started on certain definite lines in a way which would have been impossible by written orders and without the help of a motor.[91]

Major-General Snow also noted that throughout the retreat, 'the difficulty was to find out what was going on... We had no way of getting information ourselves, except by sending out staff officers in motor cars'.[92] In light of the inadequacies of the more elaborate means of communication during this period, British commanders came to rely

---

[88] 1 Cavalry Division Signal Section War Diary, 3 September 1914, WO95/1103, TNA.

[89] Priestley, *Work of the Royal Engineers*, 24.

[90] Typescript Memoirs, 12, Foster Papers, IWM; Corcoran, *Daredevil of the Army*, 20.

[91] Haig Diary, 24 August 1914, WO256/1, TNA; Sheffield and Bourne (eds.), *Douglas Haig War Diaries and Letters*, 64.

[92] 'The Story of the 4th Div. B.E.F., August and September 1914', 21, Snow Papers, IWM; Snow and Pottle (eds.), *Confusion*, 18.

heavily upon motor car chauffeurs. As one driver later recalled, 'As soon as I had brought one passenger back to GHQ, I found another waiting impatiently for a car to proceed in haste on business, urgent and pressing'.[93] Likewise, Smith-Dorrien informed Frederic Coleman, an American volunteer chauffeur, 'You gentlemen with your cars are certainly of use, of great use – of that you may be sure'.[94] Motor cars were of particular use to liaison officers, who were themselves employed by the BEF to facilitate communication among the various formations of the army. Major-General Hubert Hamilton, GOC 3 Division, informed GHQ that 'despite every intention of keeping the Corps fully informed, it has been found in practice that the latter does not as a rule get as much information as is desirable unless these liaison officers are provided'. As telegraph and telephone were frequently not an option and motorcycles constantly breaking down, 'a liaison officer is usually the most effective channel of communication during operations'.[95]

However, like motorcycle despatch riders, motor car drivers encountered numerous problems. Not only did they frequently get too close to the enemy,[96] they also had regular contact with nervous sentries and 'lunatic armed civilians' who guarded the main roads. As Edward Spears informed Sir John French after the war: 'These posts had no idea of what they were expected to do, but very often, at night especially, they used to just fire and as they were often armed with shot guns, the chance of their doing damage was very great indeed'.[97] Difficulties with car maintenance were also a significant cause for concern during the retreat. This owed as much to the rough and slippery condition of the French roads as it did to the unreliability of early twentieth-century motor cars. 'Bought straight out of shop windows', Spears later recalled, 'many of them had never been tuned up or run in, and broke down constantly. Several cars I had were equipped with lighting sets that worked for about ten minutes and then had to be refilled with carbide'. Finally, motor car drivers experienced the constant difficulty in locating the whereabouts of individual

---

[93] Baker-Carr, *From Chauffeur to Brigadier*, 16–17.

[94] Coleman, *From Mons to Ypres with French*, 36. General Sir Beauvoir De Lisle, commanding 2nd Cavalry Brigade in 1914, also praised the work done by these drivers during the retreat. See 'My Narrative of the Great German War, Vol. 1', 27–8, General Sir Beauvoir De Lisle Papers 3/1, LHCMA.

[95] 'Notes, Based on the Experience Gained by the Second Corps during the Campaign', October 1914, II Corps War Diary, WO95/629, TNA.

[96] Smith-Dorrien, for example, noted in his diary on 23 August that a German shell 'just missed the car' as he was travelling to the frontline. See Smith-Dorrien Diary, 23 August 1914, CAB45/206, TNA.

[97] Spears to Field Marshal Lord French, 16 May 1919, Major-General Sir Edward Spears Papers 2/3/21, LHCMA.

headquarters and simultaneously navigating through overcrowded roads and slow moving traffic. Spears complained that he often found himself 'seeking commanders at places they had never been at, or endeavouring to locate troops that seemed to have disappeared into thin air, and almost invariably finding the situation I had been sent to deal with completely changed by the time I arrived on the scene'.[98] Similarly, in attempting to reach Smith-Dorrien at Le Cateau on 26 August, Sir John French's motor car journey had to be abandoned 'as [the] roads were blocked with transport and refugees'.[99]

The retreat from Mons eventually came to an end on 5 September. The following day, the BEF joined the French Army in a counteroffensive, known as the Battle of the Marne, which, by 12 September, pushed the German Army back to the River Aisne.[100] Communications during this period remained much the same as they had been during the preceding two weeks, with the notable distinction that the Signal Service was now providing communications for an army on the advance and without constant enemy harassment. Subsequently, even when cable could not be recovered in time, the BEF's signal companies were at least safe in the knowledge that their diminishing supplies were no longer falling into enemy hands. Despite these seemingly favourable circumstances, however, the BEF's communications system remained far from ideal. Maintaining telephonic and telegraphic communication, for example, became an arduous task since the German Army systematically destroyed the French civilian network as they retreated.[101] Desperately short of cable, the Signal Service improvised by allocating a cable detachment to each of the forward divisions to repair the permanent civil line routes ahead of the main body of the army. These lines were subsequently strengthened as each successive formation occupied them, thus establishing a permanent main 'artery'.[102] However, despite the best efforts of the Signal Service, Fowler noted on 11 September that all these new lines were faulty. Although every effort was made to repair these faults as quickly as possible, both a 'lack of cable' and 'training for this work in peace[time]' meant that it was not until 23 September, when the fighting had become static, that the Director of Army Signals could report, 'All lines working well'.[103] The inefficiency of the permanent civilian system particularly

[98] Spears, *Liaison 1914*, 118, 452.
[99] GHQ War Diary, 26 August 1914, WO95/1, TNA; Field Marshal Viscount French, *1914* (London: Constable, 1919), 69.
[100] Edmonds, *Military Operations, 1914*, Vol. 1, 271–322; Strachan, *First World War*, 242–62; Gardner, *Trial by Fire*, 73–86; Herwig, *Marne, 1914*, 191–319.
[101] Powell, 'Divisional Signals in 1914', 347.   [102] Nalder, *Royal Corps of Signals*, 93.
[103] Director of Army Signals War Diary, 11–23 September 1914, WO95/57, TNA.

affected formations from divisional level down.[104] Corps and GHQ were more fortunate, as Smith-Dorrien observed in his diary: 'Our Signal Service, under Major Hildebrand and Captain Ganly, have never failed us for an instant... Up to the present time they have always kept us in telephonic or telegraphic communication both with the troops in the field and with the Commander-in-Chief's headquarters'.[105]

The unreliability of the permanent telecommunications network meant that it fell on the shoulders of despatch riders once again to provide the primary means of communication. As the war diary of III Corps Signal Company noted, despatch riders were 'much preferred', for when corps headquarters was constantly on the move, 'cable as soon as [it was] laid became useless in consequence'.[106] Despite despatch riders' general success, however, their casualties continued to mount during the advance, particularly in light of heavy rain, which made the French roads extremely slippery and dangerous for motorcyclists.[107] Overall, the lessons learnt concerning communications during the advance to the Aisne were much the same as those during the retreat. Mobile warfare necessitated the use of despatch riders, while telephonic and telegraphic communication could only be utilised at night when formations rested.

Trench Warfare on the Aisne and the First Battle of Ypres

The advance of the British and French Armies continued until 13 September when, upon reaching the River Aisne, they were checked by German forces dug into strong defensive positions. Despite repeated attempts to remove them, it soon became evident that the Germans, supported by an overwhelming superiority in artillery, were not to be shifted. Subsequently, the BEF consolidated and strengthened its own position, and a defensive stand-off descended with both sides settling into a primitive form of trench warfare.[108] Although the static conditions on the Aisne provided the Signal Service with the opportunity to lay a comprehensive telegraph system to connect GHQ, corps and divisional headquarters, the onset of trench warfare also entailed a whole host of communication difficulties. However, British commanders responded to the challenges posed by this new and unfamiliar style of warfare by

---

[104] 4 Division Signal Company War Diary, 11 September 1914, WO95/1471, TNA.
[105] Smith-Dorrien Diary, 10 September 1914, CAB45/206, TNA.
[106] III Corps Signal Company War Diary, 8 September 1914, WO95/701, TNA.
[107] 1 Division Signal Company War Diary, 10 September 1914, WO95/1255, III Corps Signal Company War Diary, 12 September 1914, WO95/701, TNA.
[108] Edmonds, *Military Operations, 1914*, Vol. 1, 324–410; Gardner, *Trial by Fire*, 86–95.

modifying existing practice and implementing new technology to improve the overall effectiveness of the communications system. The lessons learnt by British commanders during this period are significant because they provided the framework for the development of the BEF's communications system for the remainder of the war.

In late September and early October, each of the three corps of the BEF submitted a detailed report to GHQ,[109] based on its experiences of the opening stages of the war and, in particular, the lessons observed during the recent period of stalemate on the Aisne.[110] Each corps highlighted the increasing difficulties experienced in exercising command and control, emphasising in particular the need for improved methods of communication. All were in agreement as to the significant factor that necessitated such improvements, as the report by II Corps noted: 'Perhaps the most unexpected feature of the present war has been the arresting power of modern artillery, and of howitzers and heavy artillery, both as regards their material and moral effect'.[111] The German Army enjoyed an overwhelming superiority over the BEF in terms of the number of guns and the quantity of ammunition. British ammunition supplies were very much depleted.[112] As Frederic Coleman observed after the war: 'In spite of the arrival from England of half a dozen batteries of 60-pounders, the Germans were able to fire thirty shells to our one'.[113]

The 'arresting power' of the German artillery had a devastating effect upon the BEF's communications. The war diaries of British units throughout September record that heavy enemy shelling destroyed telephonic and telegraphic cables and rendered cable laying virtually impossible.[114] Linemen worked extremely hard to locate and repair breakages in telegraph and telephone cables, though casualties were very high. Smith-Dorrien noted in his diary, for instance, the unfortunate case of Lieutenant George Hutton, a signal officer in 3 Division, who 'was drowned on the night of the 19th/20th swimming across the Aisne with a wire to get communication between the 3rd Divisional Headquarters

---

[109] III Corps had been formed on 30 August under the command of Lieutenant-General William Pulteney.

[110] 'Memorandum', 24 September 1914, I Corps War Diary, WO95/588, 'Notes, Based on the Experience Gained by the Second Corps during the Campaign', October 1914, II Corps War Diary, WO95/629, 'Report of III Corps', October 1914, III Corps War Diary, WO95/668, TNA.

[111] 'Notes, Based on the Experience Gained by the Second Corps during the Campaign', October 1914, II Corps War Diary, WO95/629, TNA.

[112] Brown, *British Logistics*, 62.   [113] Coleman, *From Mons to Ypres with French*, 162.

[114] 1 Cavalry Division Signal Section War Diary, 17 September 1914, WO95/1103, I Corps War Diary, 26 September 1914, WO95/588, TNA.

and one of the Brigades on the north bank'.[115] Compounding the work of the linemen were 'the continuous wet weather and very heavy mud [which] caused much trouble in [the] maintenance of lines'.[116]

In spite of these difficulties, the BEF was quick to introduce a range of new measures designed to strengthen and improve the system of cable communication at the frontline. One such development was the duplication of all lines forward of division headquarters. Alternative routes were also provided so that units were not solely dependant upon one line for intercommunication. This measure involved connecting units laterally as well as vertically, so that, for example, a battalion headquarters that had had its direct line with its brigade cut would still be able to communicate with it by utilising the lateral line between itself and a neighbouring battalion.[117] The value of lateral communication was quickly appreciated by British commanders.[118] As a report submitted by 4 Division on 27 September observed:

There has been great difficulty up to date in keeping up proper communication between units and the duty of maintaining touch should be impressed on everyone. This applies of course to communication between neighbouring units as well as to the usual communications upwards and downwards between subordinate and higher formations.[119]

In addition, to help preserve the fragile and vulnerable network of cable communications in the forward area, all units were ordered to lift their cables off the ground and mount them onto poles in the last week of September. This helped reduce the number of faults and breaks in the cable, thus making it easier for linemen 'to cope with the maintenance of their circuits'.[120] The creation of an elaborate maze of cable communications during the period spent along the River Aisne provided the template for the communications system that the BEF would come to rely upon for the rest of the war.

As well as taking steps to improve and protect the army's forward communications system from the effects of German artillery, British

[115] Smith-Dorrien Diary, 21 September 1914, CAB45/206, TNA. Hutton had joined the Royal Engineers in 1910 and was 23 years old when he died. Colonel C. A. Clutterbuck (ed.), *The Bond of Sacrifice: A Biographical Record of All British Officers Who Fell in the Great War*, Vol. 1: *Aug.–Dec. 1914* (London: Cranford Press, 1917), 201.

[116] 2 Division Signal Company War Diary, 22 September 1914, WO95/1333, TNA.

[117] Priestley, *Work of the Royal Engineers*, 33.

[118] II Corps War Diary, 'Notes, Based on the Experience Gained by the Second Corps during the Campaign', October 1914, WO95/629, TNA.

[119] 'Suggestions for Short Instructions for Benefit of Formations and Individuals Arriving in the Theatre of War, Based on the Experience Gained in the Campaign', 27 September 1914, Montgomery-Massingberd Papers 5/1, LHCMA.

[120] Priestley, *Work of the Royal Engineers*, 35.

commanders implemented new measures and techniques to increase the effectiveness of their own artillery and enhance coordination between the infantry and artillery. Central to improving the tactical ability of the BEF, therefore, was the need for more efficient and effective methods of communication. The onset of trench warfare and the dominance of German artillery on the Aisne had forced the BEF's artillery 'to seek positions on the reverse slopes of hills or folds in the ground'.[121] Without a direct line of sight, British gunners now had to rely upon a comprehensive network of communications to help them locate targets and keep in contact with the infantry in the frontline. One such method was allocating Forward Observation Officers (FOOs) to the frontline and connecting them by telephone to their battery. These forward observers would provide the eyes for their gunners in the rear who could no longer see the battle they supported.[122] In adjusting to this process of indirect fire, many artillery commanders began to recognise the inherent value of the telephone. As Captain Powell observed after the war, 'the possibility of long telephone communication to O.P.s had never been envisaged'.[123] The report by II Corps stressed:

The telephone equipment is extremely valuable... Observation posts have frequently to be at abnormal distances from the battery, and without telephones the service of the guns is unsatisfactory and slow. The equipment should, therefore, be treated as if it were made of glass, and as if it were as valuable as diamonds.[124]

Similarly, Lieutenant-Colonel Dalrymple Arbuthnot, commanding 44th Brigade, RFA, spoke for many artillery commanders when he stated: 'Telephone work is of the utmost importance – in fact I may say that one never shoots without it... Every section ought to have complete telephone equipment'.[125] In late September, GHQ informed the War Office that the army 'urgently required' the supply of the new and more efficient D. Mark III telephone.[126] However, while there was widespread recognition throughout all levels and all arms of the value of telephones for command and control, supply could not meet demand.[127] As a result,

---

[121] Bidwell and Graham, *Fire-Power*, 67.
[122] 'Notes, Based on the Experience Gained by the Second Corps during the Campaign', October 1914, II Corps War Diary, WO95/629, TNA.
[123] Powell, 'Divisional Signals in 1914', 340.
[124] 'Notes, Based on the Experience Gained by the Second Corps during the Campaign', October 1914, II Corps War Diary, WO95/629, TNA.
[125] 'Notes by Lt. Colonel D. Arbuthnot, Commanding 44th. Bde. (Howr.) R.F.A.', November 1914, 2 Division Artillery War Diary, WO95/1313, TNA.
[126] GHQ to War Office, 30 September 1914, WO33/713, TNA.
[127] 'Extract from a Letter Received from an Officer of the Headquarters Staff of a Division at the Front', 24 November 1914, Hunter-Weston Papers, Add.48355, BL.

the BEF was left chronically short of telephonic equipment in the winter of 1914–15 and, as such, British commanders were forced to beg, borrow or steal instruments and 'every scrap of spare wire' they could.[128]

The vulnerability of telephone lines and the lack of adequate telephonic equipment meant that many observation officers and battalion commanders on the Aisne had to rely upon despatch riders and visual signalling for intercommunication.[129] A report by I Corps noted that 'a simple visual signal such as a flare, coloured lamp, or similar device has provided a rapid means of calling from the trenches for the support of guns'.[130] However, given the close proximity of the enemy, visual signalling fell into serious disrepute on the Aisne.[131] Fog, rain, dust and smoke obscured flag signals, while the lack of sunlight rendered heliographs impotent.[132] Furthermore, as Captain Powell remarked, 'all are agreed as to the futility of attempting to use the Begbie lamp by night when in contact with the enemy, owing to the noise and the want of secrecy'.[133] Despite the difficulties of providing an efficient communications system, it was noted by I Corps that

the system of transmission of information has improved and towards the end of the month communication from observer to battery became quite satisfactory, with the result that a number of direct hits have been reported, and the hostile batteries have been compelled to change their position very frequently.[134]

However, another report also stressed that there was still 'room for improvement' in the army's ability to observe and control its artillery fire, adding: 'The Germans appear to be superior to us both in ingenuity and science. We must learn from their methods'.[135]

One such method was the use of aerial observation to improve the effectiveness of the artillery. As Haig noted in his diary on 18 September, 'much use had been made of observers in aeroplanes to locate the

[128] Priestley, *Work of the Royal Engineers*, 59; MacDonald, *Gun-Fire*, 69.
[129] 'Report by Major H. Newcome, 475th Battery (RFA)', 15 September 1914, 2 Division Artillery War Diary, WO95/1313, TNA.
[130] 'Operations of the 1st Corps on the River Aisne, 13–30 September 1914', undated, I Corps War Diary, WO95/588, TNA.
[131] 'Suggestions for Short Instructions for Benefit of Formations and Individuals Arriving in the Theatre of War, Based on the Experience Gained in the Campaign', 27 September 1914, Montgomery-Massingberd Papers 5/1, LHCMA.
[132] 'Extract from a Letter Received from an Officer of the Headquarters Staff of a Division at the Front', 24 November 1914, Hunter-Weston Papers, Add.48355, BL.
[133] 'Divisional Signal Service Headquarters', 24 September 1914, 2 Division Signal Company War Diary, WO95/1333, TNA.
[134] 'Operations of the 1st Corps on the River Aisne, 13–30 September 1914', undated, I Corps War Diary, WO95/588, TNA.
[135] 'Memorandum on British and German Tactics', 27 September 1914, I Corps War Diary, WO95/588, TNA.

enemy's guns and trenches, as well as to direct the fire of our own artillery'.[136] The first experiments with this innovative measure involved visual signalling from air to ground. However, it was found that 'unless wireless is available this procedure becomes so slow as to be practically ineffective'.[137] After the aerial observer had provided the location of the German batteries to be targeted, 'an hour at which fire is to be opened is fixed. At that hour the aeroplane again goes up, observes the fire, and signals any necessary corrections by wireless'.[138] The results of this revolutionary procedure were so impressive that 'almost every Field Battery Commander applied for a wireless mechanic and a ground station to be detailed for their guidance, and to effect improvement in their gunnery'.[139] Although there were obvious limitations to the procedure, such as the inability to carry it out during periods of bad weather and, particularly during the first few months of the war, the limited number of aeroplanes available,[140] the technique improved the effectiveness of the BEF and helped raise the profile of wireless in the process.

The BEF remained on the Aisne until the first week of October, when General Joseph Joffre, commander of the French Army, agreed to Sir John French's request for the transfer of the BEF to Flanders. This redeployment would be beneficial to the BEF as it would shorten its lines of communication with the Channel ports.[141] During its advance north, the BEF, alongside the French Army, collided with German forces as each side attempted to turn the other's flank. The 'Race to the Sea', as it has since become known, ended for the BEF when it reached the vicinity of the small Belgian town of Ypres and GHQ was established at St Omer on 13 October. From 20 October to 24 November the Germans mounted a series of offensives in the hope of bringing the war to an end before the onset of winter. These engagements, known collectively as the First Battle of Ypres, came perilously close to breaking the Allied lines.[142] Although it succeeded in repelling the German attacks and inflicted heavy casualties in the process, the BEF paid a significant

---

[136] Haig Diary, 18 September 1914, WO256/1, TNA.

[137] 'Artillery-RFC Observation', September 1914, I Corps War Diary, WO95/588, TNA.

[138] 'Operations of the 1st Corps on the River Aisne, 13–30 September 1914', undated, I Corps War Diary, WO95/588, TNA.

[139] 'History of Wireless Telegraphy in the Royal Naval Air Service, Royal Flying Corps and Royal Air Force, from August 1914 to November 1918', undated, AIR1/2217/209/33/6, TNA.

[140] 'Notes by Lt. Colonel D. Arbuthnot, Commanding 44th. Bde. (Howr.) R.F.A.', November 1914, 2 Division Artillery War Diary, WO95/1313, TNA.

[141] GHQ War Diary, 2–3 October 1914, WO95/1, TNA.

[142] Beckett, *Ypres: The First Battle, 1914*, 5–6.

price. As Lieutenant-General George Macdonogh, the head of GHQ's Intelligence Section in 1914, informed Sir James Edmonds after the war, 'The old British Army was destroyed at 1st Ypres'.[143] Ultimately, the battle marked the culmination of the 1914 campaign for the BEF and ushered in the trench deadlock that was to characterise the Western Front for the next three and a half years.

During the BEF's transition to Flanders, communications remained much as they had been during the advance to the Aisne in early September. Despatch riders were used throughout the day, while the Signal Service worked hard to connect headquarters to the permanent civilian lines at night. However, it was the former, rather than the latter, which was of more value during this final mobile phase of the campaign. I Corps, for example, issued an order in early October reminding all sentries on roads and bridges that 'officers and despatch riders must not be unnecessarily delayed'.[144] The journeys made by despatch riders during this period also entailed significant risk, given the close proximity of the enemy. On 9 October, the motor car chauffeur Toby Rawlinson was despatched by Sir John French with orders for his older brother, Lieutenant-General Sir Henry Rawlinson, who commanded the newly formed IV Corps. As the younger Rawlinson related after the war, 'He [Sir John French] was not prepared to entrust me with any written communication at all, for such a document might afford valuable information to the enemy in the extremely probable event of it falling into their hands'.[145] The danger of sending information via despatch riders was one that British commanders were apparently still willing to risk, given their value thus far in the war and the lack of alternative means available to them.

When the BEF arrived in Ypres, much of the civilian telephone system in the town had been thoroughly destroyed by the Germans.[146] As on the Aisne, therefore, cable had to be laid both vertically and laterally between divisions, brigades and, where possible, battalions. Yet before this system could be completed, the Germans launched a major offensive on 20 October, characterised by an unprecedented concentration of artillery, which severely disrupted the BEF's cable communications. Telegraph and telephone lines were continuously cut, costing the lives of many

---

[143] Lieutenant-General Sir George Macdonogh to Sir James Edmonds, 19 July 1938, CAB45/136, TNA.

[144] 'Orders to Sentries on Roads and Bridges', 9 October 1914, I Corps War Diary, WO95/588, TNA.

[145] Rawlinson, *Adventures on the Western Front*, 160–1.

[146] Diary Entry, 15 October 1914, Lieutenant-Colonel F. S. Garwood Papers, 91/23/1, IWM.

linemen attempting to repair them.[147] Although the process of laying lines was speeded up by the replacement of some horsed cable wagons with cable motor lorries, the difficult conditions meant that it fell on the shoulders of linemen to lay and repair the lines by hand.[148]

In light of the difficulties involved in establishing cable communication, the unpopularity of visual signalling and the growing number of regimental signallers being forced into the firing line, communications forward of brigade headquarters began to fall into a state of near-disrepair.[149] By the end of October, the BEF had not yet developed an elaborate network of interconnecting trenches. This, combined with the unprecedented scale and intensity of German firepower, meant that communication between neighbouring battalions could not be successfully maintained. As noted by Major F. S. Garwood, OC 7 Division Signal Company, 'the system of communication [had been] reduced to the sending of messages by hand'.[150] A very time-consuming process was established whereby communication between two neighbouring battalions could only be achieved through sending messages back to brigade and even division headquarters and then having them distributed forward from there.[151] This lengthy procedure only added to the difficulties of command and control throughout the period (Figure 4.1).

Compounding these dilemmas was the issue of supply. Throughout the First Battle of Ypres and well into 1915, the Signal Service struggled with extremely slender resources. Although GHQ insisted in early November that every artillery commander have 'a highly developed telephone system connecting him directly to the commander, the various artillery commanders under his orders, the observation posts and batteries', there was simply not enough telephonic equipment to make this a reality.[152] In spite of measures taken by the Director of Army Signals to establish a more efficient system of supply 'so that losses might be quickly replaced',[153] at the end of October the Cavalry Division complained that its Signal Section was 'still a skeleton one, and has little or no transport and equipment'.[154] Similarly, Major Garwood noted on 8 November

---

[147] 2 Division Signal Company War Diary, 21–2 October 1914, WO95/1333, TNA.
[148] A cable lorry could lay cable at a speed of eight miles per hour. See 'Report on Working of Cable Lorry', 28 October 1914, Cavalry Corps Signal Company War Diary, WO95/584, 4 Division Signal Company War Diary, 10 November 1914, WO95/1471, TNA.
[149] Priestley, *Work of the Royal Engineers*, 45.
[150] Diary Entry, 31 October and 1 November 1914, Garwood Papers, IWM.
[151] Edmonds, *Military Operations, 1914*, Vol. 2, 286.
[152] 'Instructions Regarding the Employment of Artillery', 9 November 1914, French Papers, JDPF 7/2(I), IWM.
[153] Director of Army Signals War Diary, 26 October 1914, WO95/57, TNA.
[154] 1 Cavalry Division Signal Section War Diary, 25 October 1914, WO95/1103, TNA.

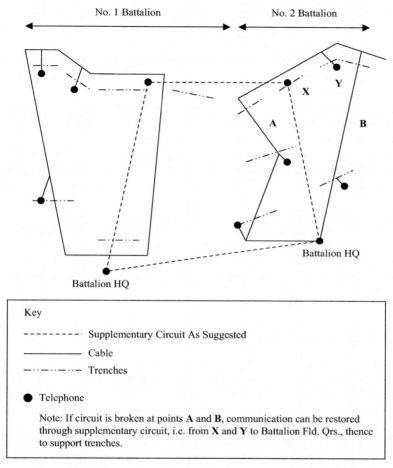

Figure 4.1 Battalion trench communications, December 1914

that 'the depots had been depleted of trained personnel and the Ord-
nance Stores of technical vehicles, there was nothing left'.[155] The lack of
trained personnel and the inadequate provision of telephones and cable
led to many units' having to forage for what they could.[156] In one
incident, Captain Lionel Sadleir-Jackson, commanding Cavalry Corps
Signal Company, 'endeavoured to utilise a quantity of fine German field

[155] Diary Entry, 8 November 1914, Garwood Papers, IWM.
[156] Indian Corps Signal Company War Diary, 30 November 1914, WO95/1094, Lahore
Division Signal Company War Diary, 12 December 1914, WO95/3919, TNA.

telegraph wire' on 26 October to establish communications at Messines. However, according to Frederic Coleman, who witnessed the event, 'four times that morning zealous individuals had cut it, thinking it an enemy line. He had it put up for a last time, but had no better luck. In an hour a passing trooper had severed it at some point, and Jackson gave it up as a bad job'.[157]

Close scrutiny of the Signal Service's stores was maintained throughout the winter of 1914–15 and any large requests for equipment required the approval and signature of the Director of Army Signals himself. As Fowler instructed: 'Officers commanding Signal Units must personally see that all demands are reasonable, and that, when necessary, explanations are forwarded'.[158] While reserves of cable and other stores were gradually built up for a possible future emergency, the signal depot was moved to Abbeville in December and a signal training school established as well.[159] Thus, at the end of 1914, in light of the depletion of cable and other equipment, and the loss of many highly trained officers and men, the Signal Service had begun introducing measures designed to secure both its long-term future and that of the BEF's communications system as a whole.

Trench Warfare, 1915

The development of the BEF's communications system in 1915 was shaped by two significant factors: the expansion of the British Army and the growth of artillery. With regards to the former, the BEF grew exponentially in terms of both size and complexity throughout 1915 as it began to absorb the Territorial forces and the volunteers of the New Armies.[160] In March 1915 the BEF constituted two armies, which comprised five infantry corps and two cavalry corps and was further subdivided into 10 infantry divisions.[161] By 1 July 1916, the BEF had expanded to a force of more than 1.5 million men, consisting of five armies containing 18 infantry corps and 57 divisions.[162] This huge

---

[157] Coleman, *From Mons to Ypres with French*, 222.

[158] 'Director of Army Signals. Circular Memorandum No. 24, 12 December 1914', Director of Army Signals War Diary, WO95/57, TNA.

[159] Priestley, *Work of the Royal Engineers*, 50.

[160] For the Territorials, see Beckett, 'The Territorial Force', 127–63. For the New Armies, see Simkins, *Kitchener's Army*.

[161] These figures include the Indian Corps. See Edmonds and Wynne, *Military Operations, 1915*, Vol. 1, 363–5.

[162] These figures include the Canadian and ANZAC Corps. See J. E. Edmonds, *Military Operations, France and Belgium, 1916*, Vol. 1 (London: HMSO, 1932), 18–24.

growth necessitated the enlargement of the BEF's communications system in order to accommodate the needs of the expanding force. However, in arguing the case against the introduction of the army level of command between GHQ and corps, Sir John French had informed Lord Kitchener in December 1914:

As the formation of Armies will add largely to the demand for Staff Officers and signalling establishment, some appreciable gain must present itself. Another channel of inter-communication interposed between Corps and GHQ would mean more delay in the transmission of important messages, largely increased signalling establishments, and an inelastic organisation which might hamper the execution of the C-in-C's plans.[163]

Clearly, Sir John French was worried that the expansion of the BEF would impair his ability to maintain control over it. Yet he was also concerned that the introduction of an army level of command would add to the difficulties of communication.[164] Although crucial to Britain's continued involvement in the war, the organisational transformation of the BEF was to add further pressure to its already overburdened communications system.

Alongside the expansion of the BEF, the development of artillery in 1915 had profound implications for the BEF's communications system. According to many historians, artillery was *the* key weapon of the First World War.[165] However, the growth of its destructive power in 1915 meant that the means of procuring and transmitting information which had formed the backbone of the BEF's communications system in 1914, such as motorcycles and motor cars, were now simply too vulnerable and of little use forward of division headquarters. In January 1916, for example, Major R. M. Powell, AD Signals X Corps, informed an audience of senior officers from Third Army that because the Signal Service had originally been trained for mobile operations, 'much of the equipment carried is not of the most suitable form for the work now required'.[166]

The communication difficulties that were to plague British operations throughout the war were graphically illustrated at the Battle of Neuve

---

[163] French to Kitchener, 1 December 1914, Kitchener Papers, PRO30/57/49, TNA.

[164] Haig, too, initially had his reservations, though, unlike French, he did not regard armies as mere post offices. See Simpson, *Directing Operations*, 11.

[165] See, for example, Jonathan Bailey, 'British Artillery in the Great War', in Griffith (ed.), *British Fighting Methods*, 23–49; Marble, 'Infantry Cannot Do with a Gun Less'.

[166] 'Lecture Given to the Senior Officers Class. 3rd Army. On Communications (a) During Trench Warfare (b) During an Attack, Major R. M. Powell, R.E., 31 January 1916', X Corps Signal Company War Diary, WO95/875, TNA.

Chapelle in March 1915, the army's first major offensive under trench conditions. Despite the initial success of the attack undertaken by 8 Division (IV Corps) and the Meerut Division (Indian Corps) on the morning of 10 March, the attempt to convert the *break-in* into a *breakthrough* proved unsuccessful, largely as a result of the breakdown of communications. When the battle was eventually abandoned late on 12 March, the BEF had managed to penetrate to a maximum depth of just 1,200 yards on a 4,000-yard front, for the loss of 11,652 officers and men.[167] Despite the provision of an extensive communications system, which established telephonic and telegraphic communication among army, corps and divisional headquarters, and between the brigades and batteries of the Royal Artillery and their FOOs,[168] within two hours of the first waves of infantry leaving their trenches, information as to their progress became 'intermittent owing to the constant breakages of the telephone wire between forward observing officers and their batteries by hostile Artillery fire and the numerous casualties among the forward observing officers themselves'.[169] Henry Rawlinson, GOC IV Corps, had great difficulty in assessing the progress of the battle from his headquarters, since 'the news that comes back from the actual trenches is much delayed owing to the difficulties of passing messages – always the case in trench warfare and the source of constant misunderstanding'.[170] According to Haig, now GOC First Army, because of the breakdown of communications and the 'uncertainty regarding [the] position of units... Rawlinson himself went up... to see what was going on'.[171] However, he could do little to alleviate the situation. With telephonic communication down and runners taking anything between two and three hours to return messages from the frontline,[172] the confusion that arose from the lack of accurate 'real-time' information resulted in the loss of initiative and momentum.[173] Consequently, as Major-General John Du Cane, GHQ's senior artillery officer in 1915, explained in a report to Sir William Robertson:

---

[167] Edmonds and Wynne, *Military Operations, 1915*, Vol. 1, 98–157; Prior and Wilson, *Command on the Western Front*, 44–73.

[168] 'Report on Action at Neuve Chapelle', 22 March 1915, First Army, Neuve Chapelle, March 1915, WO158/258, 'Organisation of the Artillery of the 1st Army for the Operations 10th–16th March 1915', undated, First Army War Diary, WO95/154, TNA.

[169] 'Control of Fire during the Operations 10th–16th March 1915', undated, First Army War Diary, WO95/154, TNA.

[170] Rawlinson Diary, 10 March 1915, General Lord Rawlinson Papers, RWLN1/1, CAC.

[171] Haig Diary, 11 March 1915, WO256/3, TNA.

[172] Edmonds and Wynne, *Military Operations, 1915*, Vol. 1, 125.

[173] 'Report on the Operations of the IVth Army Corps from 10th to 15th March, 1915', undated, WO158/374, TNA.

'The enemy thus gained sufficient time to bring up reinforcements and to oppose us with sufficient forces as to make a further advance impossible without a pause to reorganise. Our losses and the expenditure of artillery ammunition were heavy'.[174]

Attempts to find solutions to the communication difficulties experienced at Neuve Chapelle began almost immediately after the battle had ended. For instance, combined with the scarcity of trained telegraph operators at the end of 1914, the onset of trench warfare and the growing dominance of artillery resulted in the widespread adoption of the telephone as the primary means of communication in the BEF.[175] However, this in itself resulted in a number of complications. First, as the official history notes, 'the demand... for field telephones and lines up to the trenches, and for artillery service far outran anything that had ever been contemplated, and could only gradually be satisfied'.[176] Many units complained about the shortage of telephonic and telegraphic equipment and the lack of trained operators during the first half of 1915.[177] Second, in spite of the growing appreciation of the telephone for command and control, some British officers remained sceptical.[178] As an unnamed staff officer wrote after the war:

Telephones vary; so do the people who are listening at the other end; so do the tempers of the listeners... The writer once found he was speaking to a very "big gun" whose furious voice roared at him: "If you *must* ring me up to tell me there are no mines on your front, why the – should you buzz the – thing in my ear!"... It is not so good to speak to a man over the telephone as to speak to him face to face, but it is often (not always) better than writing. In all cases, patience![179]

Similarly, Lieutenant W. J. Gwilliam recalled how, during the Battle of Neuve Chapelle, the Signal Service had connected a telephone line to an unnamed general's headquarters without his knowledge or consent. The house in which the telephone had been fixed was known as the 'Red Barn'. According to Gwilliam, 'The troops who happened to be near

---

[174] 'Tactical Lessons of the Battle of Neuve Chapelle and Their Bearing on the Strategic Problem That Confronts Us', 15 March 1915, General Staff Notes on Operations, WO158/17, TNA. For additional context, see Harris and Marble, 'The "Step-by-Step" Approach', 21–4.

[175] Priestley, *Work of the Royal Engineers*, 60.

[176] Edmonds and Wynne, *Military Operations, 1915*, Vol. 1, 6–7.

[177] See, for example: 'Notes on Some of the Duties of the Brigadier When His Troops Are in the Trenches', February 1915, Hunter-Weston Papers, Add. 48355, BL; and, MacDonald, *Gun-Fire*, 69.

[178] For the reasons why, see Hall, 'The "Life-Blood" of Command?', 43–65.

[179] An Ex-Staff Officer, 'Some Staff Duties', *Journal of the Royal United Service Institution*, 68 (1923), 607.

enough to hear the General's remarks [upon answering the telephone for the first time] re-christened it "Blue Barn"'.[180]

Third, and finally, throughout 1915 the increase in German 5.9-inch howitzer activity forced the BEF initially to raise its telephone cables off the ground and onto short poles and stakes, and then to bury its telephone lines to ever-greater depths and multiply the number of cable routes.[181] By the summer of 1915 the standardised depth of telephone lines forward of division headquarters was two feet six inches.[182] By the end of the year, this had been deepened to five feet, but it was found that this still did not provide adequate protection.[183] The safeguarding of telephone lines was further strengthened by the increase in the number of cable routes. For example, as a result of previous experience, and upon the orders of the V Corps commander, Lieutenant-General Edmund Allenby, prior to Second Army's minor operation at Bellewaarde on 16 June 'all telegraph and telephone wires were laid in triplicate by different routes; communication, in consequence, remained unbroken throughout up to brigade headquarters, and for the greater part of the time to the front trenches'.[184]

However, the deepening of cable buries and the multiplication of telephone lines also generated new concerns. As Major Powell noted in early 1916, 'Once a buried system has been prepared, it will be very difficult to alter it, owing to the considerable labour and time involved in burying lines to a safe depth'. Essentially, once a unit went on the move, 'all the present elaborate telephone system will have to go by the board' because the location of headquarters was restricted according to whether or not they could connect themselves to such a rigid telephone system. Furthermore, the burying of several cables in one trench meant that 'the effect of induction becomes very bad'.[185] In light of the breakdown

[180] Gwilliam, 'Signal Master on Active Service', 334.
[181] Dopson, 48th Divisional Signal Company, 40.
[182] 'Director of Army Signals. Circular Memorandum No. 47, 24 July 1915', Maps and Papers Relating to the Service of Signal Companies of 2nd and 20th Division during the Great War, IWM.
[183] Edmonds, Military Operations, 1916, Vol. 1, 69. For instance, one artillery signaller noted in his diary on the first day of the Battle of Loos that telephone lines required 'frequent patrolling and mending'. See Longley, Battery Flashes, 151.
[184] Edmonds, Military Operations, 1915, Vol. 2, 98–9; General Sir Archibald Wavell, Allenby: A Study in Greatness (London: George G. Harrap, 1940), 156–7.
[185] 'Lecture Given to the Senior Officers Class. 3rd Army. On Communications (a) During Trench Warfare (b) During an Attack, Major R. M. Powell, R.E., 31 January 1916', X Corps Signal Company War Diary, WO95/875, TNA. The induction Powell referred to concerned the electro-magnetic 'leakage' from poorly insulated telephone cables, which meant that a conversation taking place over one line could be picked up by another cable in close proximity, or, worse still, by enemy interception.

of communications during the Battle of Loos, Robertson warned in November 1915 that, despite the duplication and triplication of telephone lines, 'lavish expenditure [of cable] does not necessarily mean good signals'.[186]

As well as the vulnerability of telephone lines to shellfire, they were susceptible to enemy interception. Throughout the second half of 1915, British commanders became increasingly concerned about the 'leakage' of information to the Germans through the forward telephone network.[187] The BEF began to introduce a number of measures from the summer of 1915 to combat this problem, including thorough spot checks of cable insulation, the twisting of new cable for added security and the introduction of formal voice procedures for all telephone users.[188] All portable telephones were 'not to be taken out of their leather cases when used in or near the advanced trenches'.[189] Fears concerning enemy interception increased in 1916, and an Intercepting Telephone (IT) organisation was established, which 'consisted of men with a fluent knowledge of German' manning 'listening posts in saps, trenches, and underground galleries in or near No-Man's-Land', who 'not only listened to enemy conversation, but reported back to Headquarters indiscretions in telephone speech over the cables on the British side'.[190] According to one former intelligence wireless-intercept operator: 'It was possible to hear on the phones telephonic conversations carried on by the German telephonists as far away as a thousand yards'.[191] Indeed, the BEF was not alone in trying to combat the problem of enemy eavesdropping. A captured German Army document, dated March 1916, revealed that as a result of increased enemy attempts to infiltrate the German telephone system, 'all front line trench telephone stations were to be withdrawn at least as far as the second line'. This was obviously a problem that both the BEF and the German Army found particularly difficult to resolve.[192] Evidently, the difficulties that both armies had in trying to overcome enemy interception during the

---

[186] 'G.H.Q. No. O.B./618', 10 November 1915, Correspondence and Papers of 2 Division Signal Company in WW1, 1915–18, A231.52, REMA.

[187] Director of Army Signals War Diary, 27 August 1915, WO95/57, TNA.

[188] Haig Diary, 9 September 1915, WO256/5, TNA; Priestley, *Work of the Royal Engineers*, 98–114.

[189] 'Instructions to Prevent Overhearing of Telephones or Vibrator Signals by the Enemy', 12 August 1915, VI Corps Signal Company War Diary, WO95/793, TNA.

[190] Dopson, *48th Divisional Signal Company*, 41–2.

[191] Typescript Memoir, undated, Rumsey Papers, LCL.

[192] 'Listening and Overhearing on the Telephone (German)', 17 May 1917, Major-General William Dimoline Papers 1/3, LHCMA. For more information concerning British telephone interception efforts, see Beach, *Haig's Intelligence*, 157–9.

war were a reflection of the dangers associated with the large-scale expansion of the telephone system.

The exponential growth of telephony in the BEF during 1915 led to a huge increase in the volume of signal traffic generated. Over the course of three day's fighting at Neuve Chapelle, for example, First Army's signal office sent and received 1,390 and 1,010 messages, respectively. Just six months later, on the opening day of the Battle of Loos, First Army dealt with 3,400 messages.[193] The inevitable consequence was that the BEF's communications system often overloaded at peak times. After studying reports on communications during the Battle of Festubert in preparation for the Battle of Loos, for example, Lieutenant (later Major Sir) Owen Morshead, a signal officer in 7 Division, noted in his diary that 'the crush of messages along the wires' appeared to be one of the chief difficulties experienced.[194] In order to relieve some of the pressure on the telephone system, therefore, the BEF advocated a range of alternative means of communication. One particular solution was wireless. Between 15 and 17 June, experiments using four RFC Sterling spark transmitters and four short-wave receivers were carried out within V Corps, following the success of which further tests were conducted between observation posts and the headquarters of heavy artillery batteries.[195] On 9 August, the first attempt to establish communication between division and brigade head-quarters using portable wireless sets occurred during a small-scale engagement at Hooge. Given the size, weight and technical limitations of the sets, however, communication could not be established.[196] Finally, two motor-lorry sets, two pack sets and six short-range sets were issued to First Army as a means of emergency communication between division and brigade headquarters during the fighting at Loos. Although on three separate occasions during the battle important messages were sent and received by wireless, on the whole wireless remained in its infancy during 1915, and thus largely unpopular amongst commanders and staff.[197] This was reflected in *SS. 100. Notes on Wireless*, issued by GHQ in January 1916, which asserted that wireless sets were 'far more compli-cated and delicate than those of an ordinary telephone and much less able to stand rough handling in transport and exposure to wet and dirt'.

[193] 'Traffic Chart 1st Army HQRS. Signal Office, March 1915', 'Traffic Chart 1st Army HQRS. Signal Office, Sept. 1915', First Army Signal Company War Diary, WO95/199, TNA.
[194] Diary Entry, 2 September 1915, Major Sir Owen Morshead Papers 05/50/1, IWM.
[195] Hall, 'British Army and Wireless Communication', 298.
[196] Edmonds, *Military Operations, 1915*, Vol. 2, 108–9.
[197] Priestley, *Work of the Royal Engineers*, 88–9.

Consequently, it stressed, 'Wireless is not suitable to replace the normal means of communication by telegraph and telephone'.[198]

Besides wireless, the two other main alternatives to telephonic communication in 1915 were carrier pigeons and visual signalling (Figure 4.2). However, their performance throughout the year left much to be desired. While the Director of Army Signals noted in late August that 'carrier pigeons cannot be considered as an efficient substitute for telegraphic or telephonic communication', a First Army note shortly before the Battle of Loos made clear the inadequacies of flags, heliographs and electric lamps.[199] Indeed, writing in his diary on 1 May, one artillery signaller commented: 'Flags, of course, we have not used since we have been out here; to do so would both give away positions and also ask for bullets'.[200] In many respects, the use of visual signalling and carrier pigeons demonstrated, in a similar manner to wireless, that many of the methods which were relied upon in 1915 were seen as immediate stop-gap measures by an army struggling to adapt its communications to trench warfare. More often than not the mainstay of the BEF's communications system at the tactical level in 1915 was provided by the traditional runner. The chief problem with this method, as identified in a IV Corps report on the Battle of Neuve Chapelle, was that 'messages by orderlies who have to return over the difficult and fire swept ground take long to arrive even if the messengers do not become casualties'.[201]

Thus, by the end of 1915, many significant changes had occurred within the realm of communications policy and practice. The R.E. Carrier Pigeon Service had been firmly established, experiments with portable wireless telegraphy sets for conveying tactical information were well underway and burying telephone cable to ever-greater depths had become standard practice. The two driving forces behind these changes were undoubtedly the development and increasing power of artillery and the growth of the BEF as a whole. These two factors had led to the widespread adoption of the telephone, which subsequently resulted in the enormous expansion of the BEF's communications system. Despite these reforms, however, the BEF's communications system at the close of the year remained far from ideal.

---

[198] SS. 100. Notes on Wireless (January 1916), 3.

[199] 'Organisation of a Carrier Pigeon Service for the Armies in France', 28 August 1915, R.E. Carrier Pigeon Service War Diary, WO95/123, 'Communication between Cavalry and Artillery of Army Corps and Divisions in the Event of an Advance', 24 September 1915, First Army War Diary, WO95/158, TNA.

[200] Longley, Battery Flashes, 81.

[201] 'Report on the Operations of the IVth Army Corps from 10th to 15th March, 1915', undated, WO158/374, TNA.

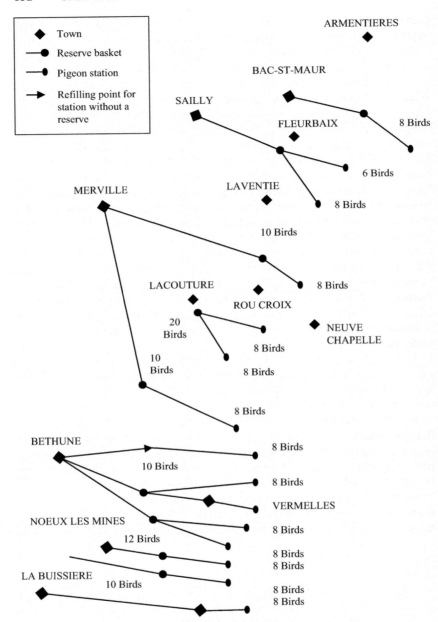

Figure 4.2 First Army Carrier Pigeon Service, December 1915
Source: '1st Army Pigeon Organisation, 1915', First Army Signal
Company War Diary, WO95/199, TNA.

As one officer later informed the official historian, during the fighting at Loos 'nobody, from the brigade commanders downwards, had any idea of the situation at any stage in the proceedings'.[202] Although several measures had been introduced throughout the year, a solution to the problems posed by inadequate communications was as yet by no means assured.

In summary, the opening months of the war proved a difficult and gruelling test for the BEF. Tenuous communications undoubtedly added to the difficulties of command and control during this period. Given the limitations of telephones, telegraph and wireless in mobile warfare in the early twentieth century, it was left to motorcycle despatch riders, motor car chauffeurs and liaison officers to provide the mainstay of the BEF's communications system during the retreat from Mons and the advance to the Aisne in late August and early September. Although these methods assisted command and control greatly, they could do little to alleviate what General Sir Hubert Gough later described as an 'atmosphere of agonising uncertainty'.[203] The transition from mobile to static warfare, first on the Aisne in mid-September and then during the First Battle of Ypres in late October and November, presented a new set of challenges for the BEF's communications system. By far the main factor responsible for creating these problems was the power of modern artillery and its devastating impact on communications at the tactical level of command. However, through the widespread recognition of the value of the telephone as a rapid means of communication, the duplication and re-routing of telegraph and telephone lines, and the use of wireless in the development of scientific gunnery, British commanders began implementing a range of new measures and techniques designed to improve both command and control. Collectively, these responses to the unprecedented challenges of waging modern, entrenched warfare were highly significant, since they laid the foundations for future British communications policy and practice.

Nevertheless, although the BEF managed to avoid a major communications breakdown during the opening months of the war, it would be fair to say that at no point did British commanders have at their disposal a communications system that was fast, integral and secure. In common with the rest of the BEF, the Signal Service was ill equipped and unprepared for the modern war of attrition that lay ahead. Indeed, the dramatic expansion of the BEF, combined with the growth and power of modern

---

[202] Major J. Buckley (9/KOYLI) to Edmonds, 1 January 1927, CAB45/121, TNA.
[203] General Sir Hubert Gough, *The Fifth Army* (London: Hodder and Stoughton, 1931), 25.

artillery, the subsequent widespread demand for telephonic communication and the dearth of reliable alternative methods all added to the difficulties of command and control in 1915, as British commanders struggled to deal with the unprecedented scale of trench warfare. The communication difficulties which were to hamper British operations for the remainder of the war were graphically illustrated at the Battle of Neuve Chapelle. As one post-action report observed, although 'the commander can ensure that the general plan of attack is sound and that the troops start the attack knowing their tasks and objectives and well provided with all essentials', once the battle has begun, 'control passes largely out of his hands except under exceptionally favourable circumstances'.[204] The breakdown of communications rendered the conveyance of accurate and timely information extremely difficult, and consequently, at Neuve Chapelle, Aubers Ridge, Festubert and Loos, 'the whole machine clogged and stopped'.[205]

However, despite the negative influence that communications had upon the BEF's operations in 1915, there were clear signs that British commanders were actively searching for solutions. The implementation of new measures and techniques, such as burying telephone lines to ever-greater depths, multiplying the number of cable routes and imposing strict security procedures, were responses designed to improve the integrity, safety and overall efficiency of the BEF's communications system. Ultimately, the lessons learnt from the experiences of 1915, and the subsequent changes that were made, were to form the basis of the BEF's communications system for the Battle of the Somme.

---

[204] 'Report on the Operations of the IVth Army Corps from 10th to 15th March, 1915', undated, WO158/374, TNA.
[205] Brigadier-General John Charteris, *At GHQ* (London: Cassell, 1931), 81.

5   1916

On 1 July 1916, the Fourth Army of the BEF, alongside the French Sixth Army, launched what was to date the largest offensive on the Western Front.[1] The Battle of the Somme was to continue until mid-November and in the process attain infamous status within the annals of British military history. The huge loss of life combined with the paltry territorial gains, particularly on the opening day of the battle, has made the Somme a byword for incompetence and futility, symbolising all that was wrong about the fighting on the Western Front. It has subsequently attracted enormous attention within the historiography.[2] In analysing the BEF's military performance in 1916, some historians have argued that the Somme 'marked the beginning of a steep learning curve in many areas', transforming the BEF 'from a largely inexperienced mass army into a largely experienced one'.[3] Although some of these studies do touch upon the issue of communications, it is not a central component of their analysis. Compared to the attention historians have given to other aspects of the campaign, such as the relationship between Haig and his subordinates, the role of artillery and the introduction of the tank, the issue of

---

[1] On the contentious issue of British strategy in 1916, see: Hew Strachan, 'The Battle of the Somme and British Strategy', *Journal of Strategic Studies*, 21 (1998), 79–95; Elizabeth Greenhalgh, 'Why the British Were on the Somme in 1916', *War in History*, 6 (1999), 147–73; William Philpott, 'Why the British Were Really on the Somme: A Reply to Elizabeth Greenhalgh', *War in History*, 9 (2002), 446–71; Elizabeth Greenhalgh, 'Flames over the Somme: A Retort to William Philpott', *War in History*, 10 (2003), 335–42; and, Elizabeth Greenhalgh, *Victory through Coalition: Britain and France during the First World War* (Cambridge: Cambridge University Press, 2006), 43–63.

[2] For the British official history, see: J. E. Edmonds, *Military Operations, France and Belgium, 1916*, Vol. 1 (London: HMSO, 1932), and W. Miles, *Military Operations, France and Belgium, 1916*, Vol. 2 (London: HMSO, 1938). The standard popular work has, for many years, been Martin Middlebrook, *The First Day on the Somme* (London: Allen Lane, 1971). For more academic studies, see: Travers, *Killing Ground*, 127–99; Prior and Wilson, *Command on the Western Front*, 137–260; Sheffield, *Somme*; Prior and Wilson, *Somme*; and, William Philpott, *Bloody Victory: The Sacrifice on the Somme and the Making of the Twentieth Century* (London: Little, Brown, 2009).

[3] Robbins, *British Generalship*, 133; Griffith, *Battle Tactics*, 65.

communications has generally received short shrift.[4] This chapter, therefore, will address three principal questions: first, how extensive were the BEF's communication preparations for the battle? Second, what influence did communications have upon the fighting? Third, and finally, to what extent did the BEF's communications system show signs of improvement over the course of the campaign?

Preparations

Historians examining the BEF's preparations for the Somme have generally focused their attention on the conflicting aims and objectives of Haig and the Fourth Army commander General Sir Henry Rawlinson.[5] It is curious, though, that the issue of communications is rarely touched on, since, in early March, while in the preliminary stages of formulating Fourth Army's plan of attack, Rawlinson observed that the question of communications was 'an important one and should be gone into in detail as early as possible'.[6] Rawlinson's words were echoed in *SS. 109. Training of Divisions for Offensive Action*, issued by GHQ in May, which stipulated that a 'thorough system of good communication... is of the first importance... All ranks must be warned of the vital importance of forwarding accurate and speedy information'.[7] Similarly, reflecting on the lessons of 1915, Fourth Army's 'Tactical Notes' demonstrated that the high command was clearly anticipating a certain degree of communication difficulties during the forthcoming offensive. For example, it acknowledged that general observation of the battle and the gaining of timely information as to the advancing infantry's progress were likely to be difficult owing to 'dust and smoke, the varying rates of the advance of the infantry, the varieties of obstacles and resistance to be overcome, the probable interruption of telephone communication between infantry and artillery and between artillery observers and their guns'.[8] It was of paramount importance, therefore, that

---

[4] The operational and tactical aspects of the Somme are covered in: Bill Rawling, *Surviving Trench Warfare: Technology and the Canadian Corps 1914–1918* (Toronto: University of Toronto Press, 1992), 70–91; Griffith, *Battle Tactics*, 65–79; Samuels, *Command or Control?* 124–57; and, Harris and Marble, 'The "Step-by-Step" Approach', 17–42.

[5] Travers, *Killing Ground*, 127–46; Prior and Wilson, *Command on the Western Front*, 137–53; Gary Sheffield, *The Chief: Douglas Haig and the British Army* (London: Aurum Press, 2011), 165–9.

[6] 'Battle of the Somme. Preparations by the Fourth Army', 6 March 1916, Fourth Army Records, Vol. 1, IWM.

[7] *SS. 109. Training of Divisions for Offensive Action* (May 1916), 3.

[8] 'Fourth Army. Tactical Notes', May 1916, 26, Montgomery-Massingberd Papers 7/33, LHCMA.

Fourth Army had in place an effective system for obtaining and transmitting information before the battle commenced.

Particular emphasis was placed upon the need for an efficient system of
communication between the infantry and artillery.[9] In order to improve
cooperation between the two arms it was suggested that the advanced
headquarters of infantry brigades and the artillery group supporting it
'should be in the same house or dug-out'. Two FOOs from each artillery
group were to follow the infantry advance and act as liaison with the two
battalions of the brigade they were supporting.[10] In many divisions prior
to the Somme, this was advocated as standard practice. As a result, 'not
only is the communication problem vastly simplified thereby, and economy effected but in the event of Infantry lines being cut information that
comes back from the O.P.'s over Artillery lines can at once be communicated to the Infantry Brigade Staff'.[11] However, as Major R. M. Powell,
AD Signals X Corps, warned in January: 'It is impossible to lay down a
hard and fast rule as to what communications are necessary for a division
in battle: much must depend on actual conditions and the requirements
of the particular staff concerned'. He concluded that 'simplicity is the key
word of Battle Communications, and the simpler the scheme the more
likely it is to prove efficient'.[12] Likewise, Lieutenant-General Sir William
Pulteney, GOC III Corps, acknowledged that 'too elaborate communications will fail for want of maintenance'.[13] How, therefore, was the BEF
to attain a simple yet thorough communications system?

The mainstay of the BEF's communications system for the battle was to
be provided by an elaborate network of deep-buried telephone lines.[14]
Forward of divisional headquarters telephone cables were to be duplicated
and triplicated wherever possible, and laid to a depth of six feet
up to battalion headquarters (Figure 5.1).[15] Lateral spurs were also constructed from the main divisional arteries 'to link subordinate headquarters,

---

[9] 'Notes on Army Conference with Corps Commanders', 17 May and 12 June 1916,
  Fourth Army Records, Vol. 1, IWM.
[10] '18 Division Artillery Operation Order No. 1', 17 June 1916, General Sir Ivor Maxse
  Papers, PP/MCR/C42, IWM.
[11] 'Battle Communications', January 1916, X Corps Signal Company War Diary, WO95/
  875, TNA.
[12] Ibid.
[13] 'Principal Points to Be Attended To in Making Preliminary Arrangements', June 1916,
  III Corps War Diary, WO95/673, TNA.
[14] 'Memorandum on Arrangements for Communications in 10th Corps during Offensive
  Operations', 12 June 1916, X Corps Signal Company War Diary, WO95/875, TNA.
[15] 'Major-General H. A. Williams to 1st ANZAC Corps', 30 April 1916, AWM25/425/26,
  AWM; '18 Division Artillery Operation Order No. 1', 17 June 1916, Maxse Papers,
  IWM; 4 Division Signal Company War Diary, 1 July 1916, WO95/1471, 18 Division
  Signal Company War Diary, 1 July 1916, WO95/2028, TNA.

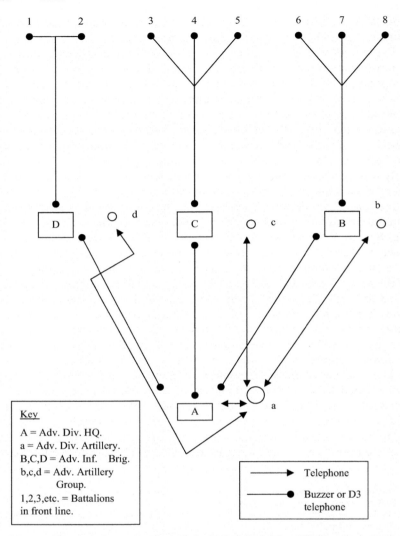

Figure 5.1 Communications in front of Division HQ, January 1916
Source: X Corps Signal Company War Diary, Appendices, January 1916, WO95/875, TNA.

artillery positions and observation posts'.[16] This was the beginning of the standardised 'grid' or 'ladder' system – a robust and practical network of

[16] Nalder, *Royal Corps of Signals*, 112.

cable communications, which could be built upon if the frontline advanced or if a division moved sideways.[17] The grid system also ensured that 'if any cable [was] cut the current [would] find an alternative path'.[18] The decision to bury the lines to a depth of six feet 'was estimated to be proof against a direct hit by 9.2" shells'. As a report by XIII Corps Signal Company made clear: 'Conversations with officers of the French Telegraph Service who have been at Verdun removed any doubt as to the necessity of such a depth'.[19] The first deep cable project had been undertaken by the Canadian Corps around Kemmel, south of the Ypres salient, between April and June 1916. In total, the Canadians managed to lay about 420 miles of cable during this period.[20] In addition to this practice's becoming standard in the BEF,[21] artillery lines were to be laid on the north and west sides of roads and trenches, while infantry lines were to run on the south and east. A system of labelling the lines was also introduced so as to ensure uniformity and help improve maintenance.[22]

The amount of cable laid during the build-up to 1 July was remarkable. In April, Robert Earle, DD Signals Fourth Army, estimated that the army required 9,000 miles of cable, 6,000 of which was for artillery communications alone. X Corps estimated its cable requirement was 1,337 miles, with its artillery necessitating 877 miles of this total.[23] To the rear of divisional headquarters, the total number of 'wire-miles' laid by the lines of communication, army and corps signal companies combined was roughly 20,000. However, as this area was well protected from the effects of German artillery, much of this cable was laid overhead on

---

[17] This was also referred to as the 'chess board' system. See: 'Intercommunications – Notes on Signal Communications, July 1916', 14 July 1916, AWM25/425/37, AWM; and, 'Theoretical Diagram of Main System of Cable Communications in Front of Divisional Headquarters', Third Army Signal Company War Diary, WO95/408, TNA.

[18] 'Lecture Given to the Senior Officers Class. 3rd Army. On Communications (a) During Trench Warfare (b) during an Attack, Major R. M. Powell, R.E., 31 January 1916', X Corps Signal Company War Diary, WO95/875, TNA.

[19] 'Reports by XIII Corps Signal Company, R.E., on Preparations for the Offensive, and Signals during the Battle of the Somme, August–September 1916', undated, XIII Corps Signal Company War Diary, WO95/906, TNA.

[20] Priestley, *Work of the Royal Engineers*, 118; Edmonds, *Military Operations, 1916*, Vol. 1, 69.

[21] The German Army buried their telephone cables to a depth of 10 feet. See *SS. 537. Summary of Recent Information*, 24.

[22] 'Lecture Given to the Senior Officers Class. 3rd Army. On Communications (a) during Trench Warfare (b) during an Attack, Major R. M. Powell, R.E., 31 January 1916', X Corps Signal Company War Diary, WO95/875, TNA.

[23] 'Letter from Deputy Director Army Signals Fourth Army to X Corps', 20 April 1916; 'Estimate of Cable Required, X Corps', 21 April 1916, X Corps War Diary, WO95/851, TNA.

airline.[24] Although much emphasis was placed upon the buried cable system to provide safe, efficient and reliable communications during the upcoming offensive, and despite the 'immense expenditure of time and labour involved in its construction',[25] the grid system was not without its drawbacks.

For instance, one of the major obstacles preventing the widespread completion of the deep-buried network immediately prior to the battle was the scarcity of labour required to dig and fill in the cable trenches. The shortage of available labour was also compounded by the lack of adequate time and by the need to 'economise cable' everywhere as supply was still quite limited.[26] In order to overcome some of these problems, upon occupying the German frontline, the infantry were warned against 'indiscriminately cutting lines found in hostile trenches' as they 'may be useful to prolong our cable lines'.[27] As Hunter-Weston noted: 'As soon as the objective has been obtained, Divisional Signal Officers will arrange for a careful reconnaissance to be made with a view of finding German cable lines, buried or otherwise, which could be used by us'.[28] Prior to 1 July, digging parties made up of ordinary infantrymen, artillerymen and pioneers were allotted the task of digging trenches and laying cable.[29] The work was often long and gruelling, and many infantrymen resented the fact that they were doing an engineer's job yet were not being paid an engineer's wage.[30] Much of the work forward of brigade headquarters also had to be carried out under the cover of darkness, as one signal officer recalled after the war: 'I was told to bury my cable up to Battalion headquarters 6 feet deep. A working party was supplied. As it was in view of the enemy we could only work at night. I was engaged on this job for nearly a month before the 1st July and had very little sleep at that time'.[31] Besides the lack of sleep and the constant threat of enemy observation, digging parties routinely came

[24] Nalder, *Royal Corps of Signals*, 112–3.   [25] Priestley, *Work of the Royal Engineers*, 123.

[26] 'Precis of Conference Held at Fourth Army Headquarters to Discuss the Question of Inter-Communication', 12 May 1916, Fourth Army Records, Vol. 6, IWM.

[27] 'Memorandum on Arrangements for Communications in 10th Corps during Offensive Operations', 12 June 1916, X Corps Signal Company War Diary, WO95/875, TNA; 'Principal Points to Be Attended To in Making Preliminary Arrangements', June 1916, III Corps War Diary, WO95/673, TNA.

[28] 'VIII Corps. Scheme for Offensive', June 1916, Hunter-Weston Papers, Add.48357, BL.

[29] 'Blue Chevrons', 37, Surfleet Papers, IWM.

[30] Sappers started on a basic wage of 1/2*d* a day, whereas an infantry private earned 1/0*d* per day. See *Field Service Pocket Book. 1914*, 179.

[31] 'Memories 1914–1919 by a Signal Officer', 16, Major E. F. Churchill Papers, 83/23/1, IWM. See also, Dopson, *The 48th Divisional Signal Company*, 45.

across the bodies of dead soldiers 'which had been buried by shells and trench mortars'.[32]

At the southernmost point of the British line, Lieutenant-General Sir Walter Congreve's XIII Corps was able to complete its deep-buried network of cable communications within the space of just five days at the end of May. The main trunk route, consisting of 20 wires, was built from XIII Corps headquarters at Corbie 'along the Bray road to Chipilly, which was to be the Corps Report Centre, thence forward via Etinehem to Divisional Report Centres etc. in the neighbourhood of Bray'.[33] The speedy and successful completion of XIII Corps' buried line system owed much to the use of mechanical excavators, which the French Sixth Army had long been making use of during the construction of their forward cable routes. These machines could dig 20 yards of trenches, six feet deep and two feet wide, in the space of one hour, which was much more effective than a working party of soldiers. Admittedly, the chalky ground of this sector of the Somme added to the ease of the excavator's work, as the machines were liable to be bogged down in the more muddy terrain of the northern portion of the line and especially around the Ypres salient.[34] Nevertheless, as an example of Anglo–French cooperation,[35] the use of these mechanical excavators and the completion of three new trenches by the 'Chef du Service Telegraphique, VI Armee... helped greatly increase the safety of [XIII] Corps lines and undoubtedly reduced the work of maintenance during the offensive'. Consequently, through-out 1 July, XIII Corps experienced 'very little trouble... with any of the circuits in the original buried system... A very reliable system... [of communication] emerged'.[36]

By contrast, as the OC 29 Division Signal Company acknowledged after the war, the buried cables that made up the grid system on VIII Corps' front, opposite Beaumont Hamel at the far north of Fourth Army's line of attack, had been laid in shallow trenches and ditches 'or whatever cover presented itself' prior to 1 July.[37] The war diary of 4 Division Signal

---

[32] 'Memoirs of His Army Service in the Great War', 27, Guy Buckeridge Papers, 04/39/1, IWM.

[33] 'Reports by XIII Corps Signal Company, R.E., on Preparations for the Offensive, and Signals during the Battle of the Somme, August–September 1916', undated, XIII Corps Signal Company War Diary, WO95/906, TNA.

[34] Priestley, *Work of the Royal Engineers*, 127–8.

[35] Greenhalgh, *Victory through Coalition*, 93–4.

[36] 'Reports by XIII Corps Signal Company, R.E., on Preparations for the Offensive, and Signals during the Battle of the Somme, August–September 1916', undated, XIII Corps Signal Company War Diary, WO95/906, TNA.

[37] Major C. M. Simpson to Brigadier-General J. E. Edmonds, 1 September 1930, CAB45/137, TNA.

Company, which occupied 29 Division's left flank, also suggests that although an 'extensive system of communication existed for the battle', it was not yet complete.[38] Accordingly, as the telephone log of 4 Division testifies, during the course of 1 July telephonic communication with its forward units was often sporadic and intermittent and ensured that 'at no time did divisional headquarters have a clear idea of the state of the battle on their section of the front'.[39]

In determining why the operations undertaken by XIII Corps in the south on 1 July were generally much more successful than those of VIII, X, III and XV Corps to the north, Robin Prior and Trevor Wilson have put forward a number of explanations, including the better artillery observation available to XIII Corps, the contribution of the neighbouring French Sixth Army and the success of its counter-battery work, and the weaker state of the German defences in the south.[40] Communications should also be added to this list. Prior to 1 July, XIII Corps had much more success than VIII Corps in establishing a safe, comprehensive and elaborate grid system of cable communications. As a post-battle report by Brigadier-General Hubert Rees, GOC 94th Infantry Brigade, noted, only one telephone line from 31 Division to his headquarters had been buried to the required six-foot depth.[41] The remaining shallow buries on VIII Corps' front were subsequently exposed to the full destructive power of the German artillery, while the six-feet buries in front of XIII Corps remained largely intact. Thus, the communication of information on 1 July was much smoother and more efficient in XIII Corps, whereas information concerning the progress of the attack on VIII Corps front remained 'vague and uncertain' throughout the day.[42]

Beside the problems involved during its construction, the other major flaw of the deep buried cable system lay in its rigidity. During an advance, formation headquarters could not simply move about at will.

---

[38] 4 Division Signal Company War Diary, 1 July 1916, WO95/1471, TNA.

[39] 'Messages Received on the Telephone 1st July 1916', 4 Division War Diary, WO95/1445, TNA; Prior and Wilson, *Somme*, 79. See also, Major-General Hon. Sir William Lambton [GOC 4 Division] to Edmonds, 29 October 1929, CAB45/189, TNA.

[40] Prior and Wilson, *Somme*, 102–11.

[41] 'Notes as to the Battle of Serre on the Morning of 1st July, 1916, by Brigadier General H. C. Rees, D.S.O., Temporarily Commanding 94th Infantry Brigade, 31st Division', undated, Hunter-Weston Papers, Add.48365, BL.

[42] 'Report on Operations of the VIII Corps on the 1st July 1916', 2 July 1916, Fourth Army Records, Vol. 1, IWM. It was a similar situation in X Corps, where the telephone lines of 32 Division's Left Artillery Group could only be buried to a depth of two feet before the battle. Consequently, communication was precarious throughout 1 July as these telephone lines were constantly cut. See Stuart Mitchell, 'An Inter-Disciplinary Study of Learning in the 32nd Division on the Western Front, 1916–1918' (PhD Thesis, University of Birmingham, 2013), 56–7.

Instead, they had to conform to the layout of the grid system and were restricted to establishing headquarters at particular locations. This only added to the relative immobility of the BEF in 1916.[43] Furthermore, as one signal officer noted, the danger of getting too accustomed to the telephone grid system was that, once on the move, officers and staff 'will not be accustomed to write orders and messages for transmission by telegraph, D.R. or orderly'.[44] The New Armies were relatively inexperienced at the start of the Somme offensive and 'only just learning the value of buried routes'.[45] The grid system was 'embryonic by later standards'[46] and would take time to perfect. As such, problems were bound to occur during the course of the battle. More importantly, however, the grid system of buried cables did not solve the most pressing communication problem for the BEF, which was the need for 'a satisfactory method of keeping up communication between troops who have captured trenches and the directing force in rear'.[47] The grid network could only assure communication up to the 'cable head'. In 1916 British commanders were still searching for a solution that would bridge the most important communications gap, namely, that between the barrage zone forward of the deep-buried 'cable head' and the troops advancing out across 'no-man's-land' and beyond.

One of the principal aims on 1 July was to 'extend the cable communication to the first and second objectives'.[48] However, until the lines were established, British commanders had to rely upon a number of alternative means of communication. In June, a memorandum issued by X Corps Signal Company noted: 'Preparation must be made to make full use of every other available means of communication... in case of a cable breakdown and during the assault and after, till communication by wire can be re-established'.[49] Visual signalling, for example, was to supplement cable communication in every division. It was agreed at a Fourth Army conference on 12 May that during the initial stages of the battle 'Central Visual Centres' or 'Stations' were to be established in each divisional area.[50] Signallers were 'to depend on their own initiative

---

[43] Priestley, *Work of the Royal Engineers*, 123.
[44] 'Lecture Given to the Senior Officers Class. 3rd Army. On Communications (a) during Trench Warfare (b) during an Attack, Major R.M. Powell, R.E., 31 January 1916', X Corps Signal Company War Diary, WO95/875, TNA.
[45] R. W. Brims to Edmonds, 23 June 1934, CAB45/132, TNA.
[46] Harris, *Signal Venture*, 29.   [47] Gwilliam, 'Signal Master on Active Service', 263.
[48] Major C. M. Simpson to Edmonds, 1 September 1930, CAB45/137, TNA.
[49] 'Memorandum on Arrangements for Communications in 10th Corps during Offensive Operations', 12 June 1916, X Corps Signal Company War Diary, WO95/875, TNA.
[50] 'Precis of Conference Held at Fourth Army Headquarters to Discuss the Question of Inter-Communication', 12 May 1916, Fourth Army Records, Vol. 6, IWM.

in selecting suitable positions in enemy lines' from which they could use visual means of communication. Visual messages were also to be kept as short and as concise as possible, because of the likely impediments of dust and smoke thrown up during the course of the battle and to the threat of enemy observation and subsequent retaliation.[51] A variety of visual signalling methods were to be employed during the Battle of the Somme. Flags, heliograph and the introduction of two new electric signalling lamps – the French projector lamp No. 24 and the 'Lucas' daylight signalling lamp – were all made available for the upcoming offensive. More than 200 electric lamps were issued to the attacking brigades and battalions of Fourth Army prior to the battle.[52] In addition to these means of communication, some units introduced their own visual methods. For example, in XIII Corps every infantryman was required to wear a 'white, yellow or bright metal disc' on his back so as to 'render the troops more conspicuous to ground stations in rear'.[53]

With regards to other alternative methods of communication, although a more plentiful supply of carrier pigeons was made available for the battle, they were primarily 'for use in the case of emergency in the event of telephonic communication to Battalion headquarters being broken'.[54] Provisions were also put in place for the use of wireless during the offensive. Wilson Sets, with a range of up to 6,000 yards, were issued to each corps to act as directing stations, while each division was provided with two BF Trench Sets with a range of between 2,000 and 4,000 yards.[55] In the case of 32 Division, for instance, it allocated to each of its brigades a Trench Set, 'packed up and ready to go forward' when they advanced on 1 July.[56] However, despite the attempts by some formations

51 'Memorandum on Arrangements for Communications in 10th Corps during Offensive Operations', 12 June 1916, X Corps Signal Company War Diary, WO95/875, 32 Division Signal Company War Diary, 1 July 1916, WO95/2384, TNA.
52 'Notes on Conference Held at Fourth Army Headquarters', 16 April 1916, 'Precis of Conference Held at Fourth Army Headquarters to Discuss the Question of Inter-Communication', 12 May 1916, Fourth Army Records, Vol. 6, IWM.
53 'XIII Corps. Plan of Operations', 15 June 1916, XIII Corps War Diary, WO95/895, TNA. This was not an entirely novel method, however, as something very similar had been used by 29 Division at the Battle of Gully Ravine (Gallipoli) on 28 June 1915. See Brian N. Hall, 'Technological Adaptation in a Global Conflict: The British Army and Communications beyond the Western Front, 1914–1918', *Journal of Military History*, 78 (2014), 51.
54 2 Division Signal Company War Diary, 23 January 1916, WO95/1333, TNA. See also, *SS. 123. Notes on the Use of Carrier Pigeons*, 8.
55 'Precis of Conference Held at Fourth Army Headquarters to Discuss the Question of Inter-Communication', 12 May 1916, Fourth Army Records, Vol. 6, TNA.
56 32 Division Signal Company War Diary, 1 July 1916, WO95/2384, TNA.

to utilise wireless communication, by and large British commanders were still reluctant to employ it on a larger scale at the tactical level, partly because of 'mistrust on the part of battalion and brigade commanders', and partly of 'a general misunderstanding of the possibilities and limitations of the wireless system'.[57] This is clearly evident in SS. 100. Notes on Wireless, issued by GHQ in January 1916, which stipulated that 'restrictions as to the use of wireless are essential' because the process of enciphering and deciphering messages was generally found to be too time-consuming and the fear of 'the risk of important information being given to the enemy' still fairly widespread.[58] Thus, as the Battle of the Somme commenced, the forward tactical use of wireless in the BEF continued to be very limited.[59]

In the absence of cable communication, and when the alternative methods indicated failed, the brunt of the communication process was to fall on the shoulders of despatch riders and runners.[60] The custom of establishing 'relay systems' or 'posts', 'by which a combination of Motor Cyclist, Mounted D.R. and runner can be obtained', was widely adopted.[61] All despatch riders were to have a thorough understanding of which roads were best to use and, along with runners, had to have intimate knowledge of the local terrain, trench systems and exact location of headquarters.[62] As Hunter-Weston informed his divisional commanders at a conference on 23 May, 'the importance of having a supply of well trained orderlies... who know their way about all the trenches on the Divisional front... cannot be overrated'.[63] Fourth Army's 'Tactical Notes' predetermined, therefore, that the route of advancing brigade and battalion headquarters 'should be well-defined and known so that runners... will know the route'.[64] As the following section will highlight, throughout the Somme campaign British commanders placed a heavy reliance upon the abilities of runners to expedite the transfer of information across the shell-swept battlefield. It was, however, a precarious

[57] Major W. Arthur Steel, 'Wireless Telegraphy in the Canadian Corps in France', Canadian Defence Quarterly, 6 (July 1929), 450. See also, Schonland, 'W/T. R.E.', 176.
[58] SS. 100. Notes on Wireless, 3.
[59] For additional context, see Hall, 'British Army and Wireless Communication'.
[60] 'Signal Traffic during Operations', 19 June 1916, X Corps Signal Company War Diary, WO95/875, TNA.
[61] 'Memorandum on Arrangements for Communications in 10th Corps during Offensive Operations', 12 June 1916, X Corps Signal Company War Diary, WO95/875, TNA.
[62] 'Precis of Conference Held at Fourth Army Headquarters to Discuss the Question of Inter-Communication', 12 May 1916, Fourth Army Records, Vol. 6, IWM.
[63] 'Notes on a Conference Held at Corps Headquarters on May 23rd', 23 May 1916, Hunter-Weston Papers, Add.48357, BL.
[64] 'Fourth Army. Tactical Notes', May 1916, 29, Montgomery-Massingberd Papers 7/33, LHCMA.

means of communication. All too often, the reason for the non-receipt of a message 'became only too apparent' to a commander, who, after searching the surrounding area, 'found a large, freshly-made shell-hole, on the edge of which reposed a charred message pad'.[65]

In sum, it is clear that British commanders spent a great deal of time and effort addressing the issue of communications when preparing for the Battle of the Somme. Although the development of an extensive deep-buried cable network was the main priority, it was appreciated that as soon as the battle began a vulnerable gap would once again emerge forward of the original frontline. The BEF made every effort therefore to ensure that the attacking divisions were equipped with a variety of alternative means of communication, including electric signalling lamps, wireless and runners, so as to ensure that the commanders to the rear could keep up to date with the progress of the battle.

Execution

The opening day of the Battle of the Somme was a costly failure for the British. By nightfall on 1 July, the BEF had suffered 57,470 casualties, with only XV and XIII Corps at the southern end of the front having made any notable territorial gains.[66] The battle, however, was far from over. Between 2 and 13 July, Fourth Army mounted a number of hastily planned and poorly executed operations, resulting in a further 25,000 casualties. Despite the initial successes of two large-scale, set-piece attacks – a 'dawn assault' carried out by XV and XIII Corps on 14 July, and the Battle of Flers-Courcelette on 15 September, which saw the first use of tanks in war – the British campaign on the Somme degenerated into a series of small, narrow-front attacks, resulting in meagre territorial gains and further loss of life. When the campaign was finally brought to a close on 18 November, the BEF had suffered 432,000 casualties, having penetrated to a maximum depth of just six miles.[67]

From the initial attack on 1 July to the final battles of mid-November, British commanders at all levels placed continuous faith in the ability of cable communications to maintain the rapid and secure conveyance of information throughout the army. Many unit war diaries and post-battle

---

[65] Dopson, *48th Divisional Signal Company*, 54.   [66] Harris, *Douglas Haig*, 230–7.

[67] Prior and Wilson, *Somme*, 300–9. Sheffield, *Chief*, 197 gives the slightly lower figure of 419,654 British casualties. The major point of disagreement between these, and other, historians concerns German casualty figures. See James McRandle and and James Quirk, 'The Blood Test Revisited: A New Look at German Casualty Counts in World War I', *Journal of Military History*, 70 (2006), 667–701.

reports acknowledged the value of the deep-buried cable system.[68] For example, Major Powell reported in mid-August that the six-foot buried cable lines of X Corps had withstood, for the most part, the terrific weight of German artillery bombardments, as most direct hits were measured at four and a half feet deep. However, direct hits from enemy eight-inch shells produced less fortunate results.[69] Similarly, Major P. R. Bald, AD Signals XIII Corps, noted that a 'very reliable system' of communication emerged over its deep-cable network throughout the opening weeks of the campaign.[70] Indeed, 30 Division, attacking on the far right of the British line on 1 July, reported that 'very few of the brigade lines were cut and any that were cut were at once transferred on to the alternative routes'. This subsequently helped ensure that 'by 11 a.m. the whole of its final objective had been gained' and at the least cost of any other attacking division that day.[71]

However, beyond the deep-buried cable head, the position of which was given in divisional operation orders, great difficulty was experienced in the maintenance of 'freshly laid' lines to the advancing infantry.[72] Although every effort was made to run cables out immediately after the assault, many units reported that 'practically every wire was cut before communication was complete' and that subsequent communication 'was infrequent and unsatisfactory'.[73] On 1 July, for example, 8 Division Signal Company managed to lay a series of new telephone lines 'in an open trench 3 feet deep at the foot of a very steep railway embankment', yet the wires were 'constantly broken by shellfire'. Similarly, on 30–1

[68] 8 Division Signal Company War Diary, 1 July 1916, WO95/1701, 18 Division Signal Company War Diary, 1 July 1916, WO95/2028, 'Notes on Attacks Carried Out by the 7th Division in July 1916', 7 Division War Diary, WO95/1631, 'Lessons Learnt from the Recent Operations', 28 November 1916, Fifth Army Notes and Lessons on 1916 Operations, WO158/344, TNA; 'XIII Corps. Lessons Deduced', 6 August 1916, Montgomery-Massingberd Papers 7/3, LHCMA.

[69] 'Notes on Communications during Recent Operations', 15 August 1916, X Corps Signal Company War Diary, WO95/875, TNA.

[70] 'Reports by XIII Corps Signal Company, R.E., on Preparations for the Offensive, and Signals during the Battle of the Somme, August–September 1916', undated, XIII Corps Signal Company War Diary, WO95/906, TNA.

[71] 30 Division Signal Company War Diary, 1 July 1916, WO95/2323, 'XIII Corps Operations on the Somme. July 1st–August 15th 1916', undated, XIII Corps War Diary, WO95/895, TNA.

[72] 'Reports by XIII Corps Signal Company, R.E., on Preparations for the Offensive, and Signals during the Battle of the Somme, August–September 1916', XIII Corps Signal Company War Diary, WO95/906, 18 Division Signal Company War Diary, 1 July 1916, WO95/2028, TNA.

[73] 'Questions Relating to an Initial Attack after Lengthy Preparation', 16 August 1916, X Corps War Diary, WO95/851, 34 Division Signal Company War Diary, 1 July 1916, WO95/2450, TNA.

Plate 5.1 Signallers running out a wire from brigade headquarters
(Henry Armytage Sanders: Alexander Turnbull Library, Wellington,
1/2-012940-G)

August communication within Delville Wood was 'extremely difficult...
since the telephone lines laid on the surface were seldom intact for an
hour at the quietest times'.[74] With regards to artillery communication
too, FOOs located in the frontline required 'very long telephone lines
which were being continually cut. This involved heavy casualties among
signalling personnel and rendered communication extremely difficult'.[75]
Second-Lieutenant Richard Talbot Kelly, a FOO with the 52nd Brigade,
RFA, noted after the war that it was 'impossible to keep a telephone line
intact for more than ten minutes... Our telephone lines were cut so many
times that we were completely useless, having no connecting link whatever with our guns behind us'.[76]

[74] 8 Division Signal Company War Diary, 1 July 1916, WO95/1701 [?] to Edmonds,
18 January 1935, CAB45/136, TNA.
[75] Colonel R. V. Turner to Edmonds, 13 June 1934, CAB45/138, TNA. See also: '42nd
Brigade, R.F.A. in Action from July 8th to 14th 1916', undated, CAB45/132, Major [?]
Cameron to Edmonds, 4 March 1936, CAB45/132, TNA.
[76] R. B. Talbot Kelly, *A Subaltern's Odyssey: A Memoir of the Great War 1915–17* (London:
William Kimber, 1980), 98.

A number of suggestions were provided as to how best to protect the vulnerable telephone lines that stretched out across 'no-man's-land' during an attack. Major Powell concluded from the experience of X Corps that it was not worth running out cables during the initial stages of an assault 'as they get cut before they can be of any practical use'. Instead, he suggested that the best method was to wait until the first objective was gained and consolidated before reeling out any cable.[77] Meanwhile, Major Bald called for the 'systematic extension of the deep cable trench as the advance progresses', yet, like other signal officers, was well aware that the success of this procedure 'boils down to the question of labour'.[78] Finally, after consulting all of its brigade commanders, Fifth Army[79] concluded in late November that 'it seems essential to look for German buried cable lines as soon as the objectives have been reached... Subsequent communication is greatly facilitated'.[80] Despite Fifth Army's optimism, however, there remained no foolproof method of maintaining secure line-based communications across 'no-man's-land'. As *SS. 135. Instructions for the Training of Divisions for Offensive Action*, issued by GHQ in December 1916, noted, although the telephone was still 'the most valuable form of communication..., the rapid establishment of good communications immediately after the assault, is one of the most important, though one of the most difficult things to be dealt with'.[81] An unnamed battalion commander remarked in late October: 'The line is only really required for use for the first ½ hour, which is the crucial period, and every minute saved in conveying information to battalion headquarters is of vital importance'.[82] Yet it was during this initial half-hour of an attack when superimposed cable was at its most vulnerable. Subsequently, in light of the difficulties of maintaining telephonic communication across 'no-man's-land', British commanders on the Somme

---

[77] 'Notes on Communications during Recent Operations', 15 August 1916, X Corps Signal Company War Diary, WO95/875, TNA.

[78] 'Reports by XIII Corps Signal Company, R.E., on Preparations for the Offensive, and Signals during the Battle of the Somme, August–September 1916', undated, XIII Corps Signal Company War Diary, WO95/906, TNA. See also, 'Notes on Operations of the 56th (London) Division on the Somme, 7/9/16 to 10/10/16', 29 October 1916, 56 Division War Diary, WO95/2932, TNA.

[79] Commanded by General Sir Hubert Gough, the Reserve Army had taken control of VIII and X Corps on 2 July and played a substantial part in the Somme campaign thereafter. It was renamed Fifth Army at the end of October.

[80] 'Lessons Learnt from the Recent Operations', 28 November 1916, Fifth Army Notes and Lessons on 1916 Operations, WO158/344, TNA.

[81] *SS. 135. Instructions for the Training of Divisions for Offensive Action* (December 1916), 34.

[82] 'Memorandum on Trench to Trench Attack by a Battalion Commander in the Fifth Army', 31 October 1916, Fifth Army Notes and Lessons on 1916 Operations, WO158/344, TNA.

were forced to utilise an array of alternative methods in order to facilitate the safe and rapid transmission of information.

One such method was visual signalling. During the initial stages of an attack, battalion visual stations often took virtually all messages from the advancing infantry until cable communications could be established. However, the success rate of visual signalling was dependant upon a number of factors and its performance varied over the course of the campaign. The nature and contour of the topography, for instance, had a very real impact on the performance of visual means of communication.[83] XIII Corps recorded very favourable results from visual signalling throughout August and September as the terrain over which it fought 'favoured the use of this method of communication'.[84] However, 4 Division, attacking formidable German defences north of Beaumont Hamel on 1 July, noted that as a result of the inability to find suitable cover to protect its signallers, only 'about 3 or 4 messages were sent back from the battalions' to the visual receiving stations all day.[85] Perhaps more significantly, visual messages were subject to numerous interruptions. Signalling via electric lamp, heliograph or flags was often impossible because of the smoke and dust created by the battle itself and adverse weather conditions, such as low cloud, mist and fog.[86] A report by XIII Corps Signal Company observed that visual messages 'often have to be repeated three times' as a result of obstructions, but even then 'several instances occurred of portions only of messages being obtained by one of the Divisional Receiving Stations during the attack on 1st July'.[87] Lieutenant-General Sir Thomas Morland, GOC X Corps, also acknowledged in August that 'owing to the dust' the employment of visual methods of communication 'is impossible during a heavy barrage'.[88] Indeed, while manning a visual station during an attack at High Wood on 20 July, Frank Richards noted: 'The ground shook and rocked and we were continually having to reset the heliograph. When receiving a message the smoke of the bursting shells and the earth and dust that was

---

[83] Ibid.
[84] 'Reports by XIII Corps Signal Company, R.E., on Preparations for the Offensive, and Signals during the Battle of the Somme, August–September 1916', undated, XIII Corps Signal Company War Diary, WO95/906, TNA. See also, 18 Division Signal Company War Diary, 1 July 1916, WO95/2028, TNA.
[85] 4 Division Signal Company War Diary, 1 July 1916, WO95/1471, TNA.
[86] 34 Division Signal Company War Diary, 1 July 1916, WO95/2450, TNA.
[87] 'Reports by XIII Corps Signal Company, R.E., on Preparations for the Offensive, and Signals during the Battle of the Somme, August–September 1916', undated, XIII Corps Signal Company War Diary, WO95/906, TNA.
[88] 'Questions Relating to an Initial Attack after Lengthy Preparation', 16 August 1916, X Corps War Diary, WO95/851, TNA.

being thrown up constantly obscured our vision, and we could only receive a word now and then'.[89] To compound matters, except on rare occasions, visual signalling was a one-way process only. It was noted at a conference held at 21 Division headquarters on 8 July that during recent operations 'heliograph were... used to the [observation] balloon but the operator could not tell if the message had been received'.[90] This one-way process, which involved the necessity that messages be repeated two or three times, could only be used from front to rear 'owing to the danger of the rear station being spotted and shelled if it signalled forward'.[91] Indeed, visual signalling entailed significant risks for the signallers themselves. To cite just one example, during the Battle of Flers-Courcelette on 15 September, visual signalling was attempted by the attacking units of 41 Division but in one recorded incident the enemy 'noticed the flashing' and 'the result was that the place... was immediately shelled'.[92] Needless to say, casualties amongst visual signallers during the Somme campaign were considerable, with some units recording losses as high as 50 per cent.[93]

Nevertheless, despite its limitations, visual signalling could on occasions produce very favourable results that ensured the quick and efficient conveyance of information from one part of the battlefield to the other. The French projector lamp No. 24 and the Lucas daylight signalling lamp proved both useful and popular tools of communication, enabling messages to be transmitted over distances between 2,500 and 4,000 yards. Overall, though, visual signalling remained hazardous and unreliable. Topographical constraints, visual interruptions and obstructions, and the constant danger of exposure to enemy observation meant that visual signalling remained far from the most reliable method of communication throughout the Battle of the Somme.[94]

[89] Richards, *Old Soldiers*, 188.
[90] 'Conference Held at Divisional Headquarters, 8 July 1916, 21 Division', Montgomery-Massingberd Papers 7/3, LHCMA.
[91] Nalder, *Royal Corps of Signals*, 103; Priestley, *Work of the Royal Engineers*, 143.
[92] 'Report on Signal Communications during Offensive Operations, 14th–17th Septr. 1916', undated, 41 Division Signal Company War Diary, WO95/2627, TNA.
[93] 'Notes on Communications during Recent Operations', 15 August 1916, X Corps Signal Company War Diary, WO95/875, 'Notes on Attacks Carried out by 7th Division in July 1916', 7 Division War Diary, WO95/1631, TNA.
[94] 'Notes on Attacks Carried out by 7th Division in July 1916', 7 Division War Diary, WO95/1631, 'Questions Relating to an Initial Attack after Lengthy Preparation', 16 August 1916, X Corps War Diary, WO95/851, 3 Division Signal Company War Diary, 14 July 1916, WO95/1404, Robert Peers [33 Division Signal Company] to Edmonds, 23 August 1934, CAB45/136, TNA; 'Notes on Recent Operations – 2nd Phase. 20th–30th July 1916, 19 Division', Montgomery-Massingberd Papers 7/3, LHCMA.

Like visual signalling, carrier pigeons were of limited utility as a means of procuring information from the frontline. On the whole, pigeons seem to have been employed very little during the campaign, partly because there was an insufficient number of trained birds and partly because they were seen as 'a last hope of communication' when all others failed.[95] It would also appear that carrier pigeons were not always the most popular means of communication amongst the troops, either. For example, Rawlinson recorded an amusing incident in his diary entry for 14 July:

We provided the attacking infantry with carrier pigeons. . . Soon after the attack was launched, a carrier pigeon was seen coming back to the loft at a corps headquarters. Great was the excitement amongst the staff as the message was carefully unwound, and this is what they read: 'I am fed up with carrying this bloody bird!'[96]

However, as with other alternative means of communication, carrier pigeons were sometimes 'the only means of obtaining information from the troops right in front'.[97] Although they were seen as a last resort, carrier pigeons could produce favourable results. On 1 July, for example, 30 Division's Signal Company war diary reveals that 'the first message received after our troops' entry into Montauban was by pigeon post, the time taken being 23 minutes'.[98] Similarly, X Corps Signal Company recorded an incident in mid-August in which 'a pigeon message enabled a barrage to be put on in 15 minutes'.[99] On the basis of these and other successes, SS. 123. Notes on the Use of Carrier Pigeons, issued by GHQ in August 1916, recognised that 'this means of communication is capable of further development'.[100] Indeed, in January 1917 the Director of Army Signals issued a memorandum which stated

[95] 'Lessons Learnt from the Recent Operations', 28 November 1916, Fifth Army Notes and Lessons on 1916 Operations, WO158/344, 'Notes on Communications during Recent Operations', 15 August 1916, X Corps Signal Company War Diary, WO95/875, TNA.

[96] Rawlinson Diary, 14 July 1916, cited in Major-General Sir Frederick Maurice (ed.), The Life of General Lord Rawlinson of Trent (London: Cassell, 1928), 167. It would appear that this was not an isolated incident. See, Baker-Carr, From Chauffeur, 201; Dopson, 48th Divisional Signal Company, 32–3; and, Field Marshal the Viscount Montgomery, The Memoirs of Field-Marshal the Viscount Montgomery of Alamein (London: Collins, 1958), 34–5.

[97] 'Reports by XIII Corps Signal Company, R.E., on Preparations for the Offensive, and Signals during the Battle of the Somme, August–September 1916', undated, XIII Corps Signal Company War Diary, WO96/906, TNA.

[98] 30 Division Signal Company War Diary, 1 July 1916, WO95/2323, TNA.

[99] 'Notes on Communications during Recent Operations', 15 August 1916, X Corps Signal Company War Diary, WO95/875, TNA.

[100] SS. 123. Notes on the Use of Carrier Pigeons, 3.

that the results obtained from the use of carrier pigeons during the Somme had 'justified an increase in the number of lofts and pigeons within the force'.[101]

Compared to the gradual development of the Carrier Pigeon Service, wireless made but little progress during the course of 1916. The experience of XIII Corps pretty much sums up the value of wireless as a means of communication on the Somme: 'The useful results obtained from the Wireless System during two months offensive operations were practically nil... The number of casualties to wireless personnel exceeded the number of useful messages for the whole period'.[102] Although a few notable successes were recorded,[103] on the whole, reports concurred that wireless was a very vulnerable method of communication and that 'sets should not be put forward of Brigade HQ'.[104] It must be stressed that wireless sets in 1916 were 'not all of good design', and a major problem 'was found to be the training of operators to get [them] going after an advance'.[105] Numerous unit war diaries and post-battle reports recalled how wireless aerials had been 'shot away' and 'repeatedly destroyed', thus putting the sets completely out of action.[106] Thus, the tactical contribution of wireless in the BEF remained 'negligible'.[107] Its primary purpose still lay within the realms of intelligence and air–ground communication between the observers of the RFC and the artillery.[108] Overall, given the technical limitations of wireless sets in 1916, the shortage of trained operators, time constraints involved in enciphering and deciphering messages, and fears over security breaches,

[101] 'Director of Army Signals. Circular Memorandum No. 182, Carrier Pigeon Service', 16 January 1917, Director of Army Signals War Diary, WO95/57, TNA.

[102] 'Reports by XIII Corps Signal Company, R.E., on Preparations for the Offensive, and Signals during the Battle of the Somme, August–September 1916', undated, XIII Corps Signal Company War Diary, WO96/906, TNA.

[103] 30 Division Signal Company's war diary, for example, reveals that during operations around Fricourt between 11 and 21 October, wireless 'was used with success. Over 100 messages were sent during operations'. See 30 Division Signal Company War Diary, 21 October 1916, WO95/2323, TNA.

[104] 'Questions Relating to an Initial Attack after Lengthy Preparation', 16 August 1916, X Corps War Diary, WO95/851, TNA.

[105] W. L. M. Carey to Edmonds, undated, CAB45/132, TNA.

[106] 'Notes on Recent Operations – 2nd Phase. 20th–30th July 1916, 19 Division', Montgomery-Massingberd Papers 7/3, LHCMA; 'Reports by XIII Corps Signal Company, R.E., on Preparations for the Offensive, and Signals during the Battle of the Somme, August–September 1916', undated, XIII Corps Signal Company War Diary, WO95/906, 29 Division Signal Company War Diary, 1 July 1916, WO95/2294, 'Communications during the Action of July 1st '16', 8 July 1916, 4 Division War Diary, WO95/1445, TNA.

[107] John S. Moir, *History of the Royal Canadian Corps of Signals 1903–1961* (Ottawa: Royal Canadian Corps of Signals, 1962), 20.

[108] Ferris, 'British Army and Signals Intelligence', 36; Beach, *Haig's Intelligence*, 159–65.

most British commanders were reluctant to employ wireless forward of brigade headquarters.[109] As such, wireless had yet to win a place within the mainstay of the BEF's communications system.

When communication via cable failed and the aforementioned alternative methods could not be utilised, the brunt of the communications system was borne by despatch riders and, in particular, runners. Recalling his experience as a signal officer around Leuze Wood in September 1916, Captain W. G. Wallace noted that 'signalling became a farce and degenerated into sending braver men than myself as runners across the shell swept inferno behind us'.[110] Certainly, a number of post-action reports testify to the skill, tenacity and reliability of runners as a means of communication.[111] However, a far greater proportion of officers were keen to stress the drawbacks. For example, Major Bald warned that 'too much reliance should not be put on the chances of a Runner getting back with a message', such were the risks involved.[112] On 1 July, after being ordered to take a message from the frontline to brigade headquarters, Lance Corporal G. Bilson, a runner with the 55th Infantry Brigade (18 Division), did not return to his battalion until the following morning because, on his way back from brigade headquarters, he had been knocked unconscious for several hours by an exploding shell.[113] Bilson was perhaps quite fortunate. Casualties amongst runners were extremely high and it was not uncommon for them to disappear, never to be seen again.[114] Furthermore, as Arthur Wrench, a battalion runner with the Seaforth Highlanders, remarked, runners had 'hardly a minute'

---

[109] 'Intercommunications – Notes on Signal Communications, July 1916', 14 July 1916, AWM25/425/37, 'G.S. Circular Memorandum No. 12. Signal Communication during Operations', 1 November 1916, AWM25/425/3, AWM; 'General Report on Wireless Telegraph Communication in the Canadian Corps, Feb. 1915–Dec. 1918', 16 April 1919, RG9-III-D-3/5058/968, LAC.

[110] 'Memoirs of 1914–1918', 49, Wallace Papers, IWM.

[111] 'Notes on Communications during Recent Operations', 15 August 1916, X Corps Signal Company War Diary, WO95/875, TNA; 'Notes as to the Battle of Serre on the Morning of 1st July, 1916, by Brigadier General H. C. Rees, D.S.O., Temporarily Commanding 94th Infantry Brigade, 31st Division', undated, Hunter-Weston Papers, Add.48365, BL.

[112] 'Reports by XIII Corps Signal Company, R.E., on Preparations for the Offensive, and Signals during the Battle of the Somme, August–September 1916', undated, XIII Corps Signal Company War Diary, WO95/906, TNA.

[113] Nichols, *18th Division*, 42.

[114] 34 Division Signal Company War Diary, 1 July 1916, WO95/2450, 'Questions Relating to an Initial Attack after Lengthy Preparation', 16 August 1916, X Corps War Diary, WO95/851, TNA; Nugent to His wife, 11 July 1916, in Nicholas Perry (ed.), *Major-General Oliver Nugent and the Ulster Division 1915–1918* (Stroud: Sutton Publishing Limited for the Army Records Society, 2007), 104–5.

to themselves: 'As soon as we return from one delivery of despatches there is another bundle ready to be sent out at once'.[115]

Although runners were 'very often the only means available' for the conveyance of orders and situation reports forward of brigade headquarters, a number of commanders found faults with the runner relay system. Most observed that it was simply too slow, because of a 'tendency among orderlies to remain at relay stations until shelling ceases'.[116] Fifth Army subsequently impressed upon all its battalion runners that 'the quicker they go the safer they are'.[117] However, this was easier said than done. Overall, no amount of personal bravery and tenacity could disguise the fact that runners were a very vulnerable means of communication. Yet the breakdown of telephonic, visual and wireless communication left British commanders on the Somme with little option other than to place their faith in the safe and speedy transfer of vital information in the hands of a runner. Sometimes it worked. In many cases, however, it failed.

New Methods and Challenges

A variety of new means of communication were tried and tested during the course of the Somme campaign. Some of these clearly reflected the growing desperation amongst commanders to bridge the communication gap at the tactical level. Major-General Charles Hull, GOC 56 Division, for example, requested the design of '[a] message thrower, capable of propelling the container of a message 500 x to 800 x... It is understood that the 6th Division use a Stokes Mortar with a specially prepared projectile for this purpose. The value of such a device cannot be overestimated'.[118] Since November 1915, the BEF had been experimenting with message-carrying rockets, and these trials were to continue throughout 1916. It was not until September 1917, however, that two types of message carrying rocket, one long-range (2,300 yards) and the other, a lighter device with a shorter range, were adopted.[119]

---

[115] 'Diary of the World War', 22 July 1916, Arthur E. Wrench Papers, 85/51/1, IWM.
[116] 'Miscellaneous Notes Gathered from Divisions Who Have Taken Part in Recent Offensive Operations', 17 August 1916, Fifth Army Notes and Lessons on 1916 Operations, WO158/344, TNA.
[117] 'Memorandum on Trench to Trench Attack by a Battalion Commander in the Fifth Army', 31 October 1916, Fifth Army Notes and Lessons on 1916 Operations, WO158/344, TNA.
[118] 'Notes on Operations of the 56th (London) Division on the Somme, 7/9/16 to 10/10/16', 29 October 1916, 56 Division War Diary, WO95/2932, TNA.
[119] Priestley, *Work of the Royal Engineers*, 152–3.

Another innovative, though far more significant, method of communication, which had been designed in response to the increasing concerns over German telephone tapping in 1915, was the Fullerphone. Named after its inventor, Captain Algernon Fuller,[120] the Fullerphone worked by transmitting a very weak Morse signal over a line which was virtually immune to enemy interception.[121] The first instruments were tested in France at the end of 1915 and approval for large-scale manufacture granted in January 1916.[122] Compared to the standard telephone, the Fullerphone was a very delicate instrument, and reaction to its performance during the Somme campaign was somewhat mixed.[123] The weight of opinion amongst brigade and battalion commanders in X Corps, for example, was that Fullerphones were 'complicated and liable to get out of order and difficult to work in forward dug outs'. A simpler and more lightweight instrument was requested and further training required for brigade and battalion signallers.[124] The major drawback to utilising the Fullerphone, however, was that, while telegraphic messages could not be intercepted, speech transmissions were liable to be overheard.[125] In April 1917, a set of instructions issued by I Corps categorically warned that the transmission of messages by speech on Fullerphones was 'absolutely forbidden' within 2,000 yards of the frontline,[126] though, as one brigade

---

[120] Captain [later Major-General] Algernon Clement Fuller (1885–1970), received his commission from Woolwich in 1904 and in 1910 joined the army's Wireless Company at Aldershot, where he developed the 'Dynaphone' (a wireless amplification technique which rivalled the thermionic valve). He invented the Fullerphone in late 1915 and after the war served in a variety of roles, including Experimental Officer, Signals Experimental Establishment, Woolwich (1916–1920); Member of Royal Engineers and Signals Board (1920–1933); Chief Inspector, Royal Engineers and Signals Equipment, Woolwich (1933–1937); Deputy Director of Mechanisation, War Office (1938–1940); Director of Engineering and Signals Equipment, Ministry of Supply (1940); and, Deputy Director General, Ministry of Supply (1941). He retired in 1941 and received a C.B.E. in recognition of his achievements. See Elizabeth Bruton and Graeme J. N. Gooday, 'Fuller, Algernon Clement (1885–1970)', *Oxford Dictionary of National Biography*, www.oxforddnb.com/view/article/107246 [accessed 5 January 2016].

[121] Guy Hartcup, *The War of Invention: Scientific Developments, 1914–18* (London: Brassey's, 1988), 78; Graeme Gooday, 'Combative Patenting: Military Entrepreneurship in First World War Telecommunications', *Studies in History and Philosophy of Science*, 44 (2013), 252–54.

[122] Priestley, *Work of the Royal Engineers*, 112–13.

[123] 'Overhearing Experiment Using Amplifier Listening Set and Lines Composed of D5 Cable Lying on the Ground', 9 October 1916, X Corps Signal Company War Diary, WO95/876, TNA.

[124] 'Questions Relating to an Initial Attack after Lengthy Preparation', 16 August 1916, X Corps War Diary, WO95/851, TNA.

[125] John William Henry Boon, Interview (1986), 009476/3, Department of Sound Records, IWM.

[126] '1 Corps Instructions No. 5. Signal Communications', 6 April 1917, Signal Instructions, I Corps, HF-95/1, REMA.

signal officer noted after the war, 'observation of the rule was not what it might have been'.[127] Used forward of brigade headquarters, Fuller-phones were in short supply during 1916, but by early 1917 they had become a very familiar and popular means of intercommunication, although restrictions as to their use as a means of voice communication had been firmly established.[128] According to one signaller after the war, Fullerphones were 'a prize instrument... A sort of fetish of the Signal Service, designed for the bafflement of simple soldiers; a contrivance of obscure principles and complicated wiring'.[129] By the end of the war, Fullerphones of improved design were being employed as far back as division headquarters, while later models would form an important part of the British Army's communications system during the Second World War.[130]

The need for 'continuous tactical observation' of the advancing infantry was also to be facilitated by the introduction of kite balloons and contact aeroplanes, which were to keep 'commanders in touch with the situation during offensive operations'.[131] It was noted in May from the experiences of the French at Verdun that 'observation from aeroplanes and balloons may prove of considerable value as one of the means of procuring information on the battlefield regarding the situation of our own and the enemy's troops'.[132] Kite balloons were subsequently allocated to each corps and were to receive messages at night from battalion and brigade headquarters and artillery observation points by electric lamp, and by either lamp or heliograph during the day.[133] Contact aeroplanes were 'intended to establish a supplementary means of direct communication between the frontline and H.Q. of Corps and Divisions'.[134] Each aeroplane was to have a distinctive set of markings which were to be known by all ranks in the infantry. Flying over the frontline

---

[127] Scrivenor, *Brigade Signals*, 75.   [128] Nalder, *Royal Corps of Signals*, 108–9.

[129] 'A Signaller in France 1914–1918', 110, Craven Papers, REMA.

[130] Godfrey, *British Army Communications*, 4.

[131] 'Fourth Army O.A.D. 881', 16 May 1916, Fourth Army Preparations, WO158/233, TNA; E. R. Hooton, *War over the Trenches: Air Power and the Western Front Campaigns 1916–1918* (Hersham: Midland, 2010), 118.

[132] 'Communication between Infantry and the Royal Flying Corps', 26 May 1916, AIR1/2251/209/54/19, TNA.

[133] 'XIII Corps. Plan of Operations', 15 June 1916, XIII Corps War Diary, WO95/895, 'Communication between Infantry and the Royal Flying Corps', 26 May 1916, AIR1/2251/209/54/19, TNA; 'Precis of Conference Held at Fourth Army Headquarters to Discuss the Question of Inter-Communication', 12 May 1916, Fourth Army Records, Vol. 6, IWM.

[134] 'Memorandum on Arrangements for Communications in 10th Corps during Offensive Operations', 12 June 1916, X Corps Signal Company War Diary, WO95/875, TNA.

at previously arranged times,[135] the aeroplanes used Klaxon horns to signal to the infantry that they were ready to receive a message.[136] Red flares, flashing mirrors and flags were to be carried by the advancing infantry and used to indicate their progress to the aeroplanes: 'O' denoted 'barrage'; 'H' indicated that the infantry wanted the artillery to lengthen its range; 'Y' signified that the infantry were short of grenades; 'X' designated 'held up by machineguns'; and 'Z' denoted that the infantry were held up by wire.[137]

Brigade and battalion headquarters were to communicate with the aeroplane by lamp or ground signalling sheet. Once the message was received by the aeroplane, the pilot would then transmit the information by wireless or drop messages and sketches in a bag at corps headquarters.[138] However, it was noted that of the two options available to the pilot 'messages dropped allow of fuller information being given than can be sent by wireless'. This observation had been drawn from recent experiments conducted by the RFC and from the study of German methods of air-to-ground communication.[139] Another major dilemma was that RFC receiving sets were often jammed by ground wireless sets 'being sited so close to them as to prevent reception from aeroplanes when the Short Range Set is sending no matter what the difference in wave lengths of the [two sets]... may be'. In future, better cooperation between the Signal Service and the RFC was required so that the position of all wireless sets was known and 'any moves or proposed moves of sets mutually communicated'.[140] Subsequently, it was agreed that while the RFC would operate on wavelengths up to 300 metres for artillery reconnaissance, the army would use 350-, 450- and 550-metre

---

[135] '7th Division Operation Order No. 81', 12 July 1916, 7 Division War Diary, WO95/ 1631, TNA.

[136] 'Notes on Practice in Communication between Aircraft and Infantry, 12th Sept. 1916', 13 September 1916, Correspondence and Papers of 2 Division Signal Company in WW1, 1915–18, A231.52, REMA.

[137] 'Instructions Regarding Liaison between Infantry and Aircraft. GHQ No. O.B. 1656. Fourth Army No. 170 (G)', 29 May 1916, Liddell Hart Papers 8/64, LHCMA; 32 Division Signal Company War Diary, 1 July 1916, WO95/2384, TNA.

[138] 'Memorandum on Arrangements for Communications in 10th Corps during Offensive Operations', 12 June 1916, X Corps Signal Company War Diary, WO95/875, TNA; 'Fourth Army. Tactical Notes', May 1916, 29–30, Montgomery-Massingberd Papers 7/ 33, LHCMA.

[139] 'Communication between Infantry and the Royal Flying Corps', 26 May 1916; 'Notes on the Study of German Methods in the Observation of Artillery Fire by Aeroplanes and Balloons Fitted with Wireless Telegraph Apparatus', 13 January 1916, AIR1/2251/ 209/54/19, TNA.

[140] 'Director of Army Signals. Circular Memorandum No. 128, Short Range Wireless Sets and RFC Sets with Artillery', 4 August 1916, GHQ Signal Company War Diary, WO95/126, TNA.

wavelengths for general communication purposes.[141] It is worth pointing out, though, that Fourth Army only intended to use contact aeroplanes to 'further supplement existing channels of communication between the troops in the frontline and the higher commands'.[142]

The large-scale introduction of contact aeroplanes during the Somme campaign yielded mixed results. Throughout the period, British commanders looked towards the RFC to help provide them with the earliest possible information as to the progress of a battle.[143] On some occasions, contact aeroplanes proved a most useful aid for command and control. XIII Corps recorded in early August that the metal discs worn on the backs of its infantry 'proved of use to observers in aeroplanes', and that subsequent information pertaining to the progress of attacks and to the disposition of friendly and enemy troops was disseminated to the necessary divisions and brigades as quickly as possible.[144] However, a serious drawback to utilising the contact aeroplane system was identified as early as the end of July, when it was reported that 'cases occurred in which Corps knew more of the tactical situation and of the position of troops than the Brigades to which the troops belonged. This was due to the Corps receiving reports from the Air Service and due to the breakdown of communication between the Brigades and the front line'.[145] As Major-General John Shea, GOC 30 Division, remarked, 'Communication by air via aeroplanes is still in its infancy'.[146] In some cases, airmen complained that 'troops in the front line frequently neglect to show their positions when called on'.[147] This can partly be explained by the unease which many signallers on the ground felt when utilising methods of communication that could easily be viewed by German snipers and pilots, as well.[148] In addition, the task of observing the progress of an attack was made all the more difficult, sometimes impossible,

[141] Priestley, *Work of the Royal Engineers*, 88.
[142] 'Precis of Conference Held at Fourth Army Headquarters to Discuss the Question of Inter-Communication', 12 May 1916, Fourth Army Records, Vol. 6, IWM.
[143] 'Notes of Conference Held at Heilly', 10 September 1916, Fourth Army Records, Vol. 6, IWM.
[144] 'XIII Corps. Lessons Deduced', 6 August 1916, Montgomery-Massingberd Papers 7/3, LHCMA; 'Reports by XIII Corps Signal Company, R.E., on Preparations for the Offensive, and Signals during the Battle of the Somme, August–September 1916', undated, XIII Corps Signal Company War Diary, WO95/906, TNA.
[145] 'IX Corps Notes on Information Collected from Various Sources, Including Troops Who Have Been Engaged in the Recent Fighting', 31 July 1916, Montgomery-Massingberd Papers 7/3, LHCMA.
[146] '30 Division, Preliminary Notes on the Tactical Lessons of the Recent Operations', 10 August 1916, Montgomery-Massingberd Papers 7/3, LHCMA.
[147] 'Notes on Operations of the 56th (London) Division on the Somme, 7/9/16 to 10/10/16', 29 October 1916, 56 Division War Diary, WO95/2932, TNA. See also: Lewis, *Sagittarius Rising*, 104.
[148] Richards, *Old Soldiers Never Die*, 223; Scrivenor, *Brigade Signals*, 69.

by the absence of clear visibility. This was particularly so during the closing weeks of the campaign when rain and low cloud greatly hampered the work of the aircrews. Such was the case on 12 October when five divisions of Fourth Army attacked the German defences of the Transloy Line, south of the Albert-Bapaume Road.[149] A post-battle report identified that one of the primary reasons for the attack's failure was that contact aeroplanes had been 'unable to render as great assistance as they have done in previous attacks'.[150] As Rawlinson noted in his diary, 'the absence of observation from the air has I think been enough to account for our failure'.[151]

From September 1916, British commanders were also confronted with another new signal dilemma, namely, the system of communication required for tanks.[152] Three channels of communication were necessary: first, tank-to-tank communication; second, communication between tanks and the other arms with which they were working, particularly the infantry; and third, communication between tanks and unit headquarters in the rear. Since wireless sets in 1916 did not render reception inside tanks possible, 'owing to noise and engine vibration',[153] the only means of establishing communication between tanks and the supporting infantry and between the tanks themselves was through the use of visual methods of signalling.[154] As Lieutenant Frank Mitchell, 1st Battalion, Tank Corps, recalled after the war:

One of the drawbacks of tanks in battle is the total lack of any means of communication with other tanks. When once inside, with doors bolted, flaps shut and loop holes closed, one can only make signs to a tank very near at hand by taking the great risk of opening the manhole in the roof and waving a handkerchief or a shovel.[155]

Prior to the Battle of Flers-Courcelette on 15 September, Fourth Army issued a memorandum entitled 'Instructions for the Employment of "Tanks"', which stipulated that communication between tanks and the supporting infantry was to be facilitated chiefly by the use of coloured flags. A red flag indicated that the tank was out of

---

[149] Sheffield, *Somme*, 136–43; Prior and Wilson, *Somme*, 261–77.
[150] 'The Causes for the Non-Success of the Fourth Army Attack on the 12th October 1916', 13 October 1916, Fourth Army Records, Vol. 8, IWM.
[151] Rawlinson Diary, 12 October 1916, RWLN 1/7, Rawlinson Papers, CAC.
[152] For additional context, see Hall, 'Development of Tank Communications', 138–42.
[153] Captain B. H. Liddell Hart, *The Tanks: The History of the Royal Tank Regiment, Vol. 1 (1914–1939)* (London: Cassell, 1959), 62.
[154] 'Preliminary Notes on Tactical Employment of Tanks', 16 August 1916, WO158/834, TNA.
[155] F. Mitchell, *Tank Warfare: The Story of the Tanks in the Great War* (London: Thomas Nelson and Sons, 1933), 66.

action, a green flag denoted 'Am on Objective', while all other flags were to be treated as inter-tank signals.[156] Despite these provisions, however, time constraints and the inadequate number of tanks available meant that infantry-tank training prior to the Battle of Flers-Courcelette was both haphazard and restricted, partly explaining why tank-infantry cooperation on the Somme was, on the whole, not a resounding success.[157]

With regards to communication with rear headquarters, a proportion of tanks were provided with two carrier pigeons to serve this purpose. Although the poisonous and sweltering interior conditions within First World War tanks could make the use of carrier pigeons problematic,[158] according to Brigadier-General Christopher Baker-Carr, commanding 1st Tank Brigade (1917–18), the use of carrier pigeons on 15 September was 'found to be the most rapid means of communication from the battle'.[159] Nevertheless, the BEF's tank communication system in 1916 was both ad hoc and experimental in nature. The introduction of tanks into the BEF's order of battle also caused further disruption to the communication networks of other arms. As Sergeant J. Sawers, 2nd New Zealand Brigade Signal Section, recalled after the war, the tanks at Flers-Courcelette 'chewed up' infantry and artillery telephone lines during the course of the battle – 'a historic first for a subsequently far too frequent occurrence'.[160] The result, as III Corps' 'Summary of Operations' noted, was that 'as the attack progressed communication became increasingly difficult and on the right especially, the situation was not definitely known for some time'.[161]

Overall, the Battle of the Somme proved to be a testing ground for a range of communication methods. 'All these means', Walter Congreve stressed, 'have justified their existence and all should, therefore, be used in future attacks'.[162] From the foregoing discussion, however, it is evident that

---

[156] 'Instructions for the Employment of "Tanks"', 11 September 1916, Fourth Army Records, Vol. 8, IWM. See also '41st Division Operation Order No. 42', 13 September 1916, 41 Division War Diary, WO95/2632, TNA.

[157] Christopher Brynley Hammond, 'The Theory and Practice of Tank Co-operation with Other Arms on the Western Front during the First World War' (PhD thesis, University of Birmingham, 2005), 53–9; Trevor Pidgeon, *The Tanks at Flers: An Account of the First Use of Tanks in War at the Battle of Flers-Courcelette, the Somme, 15th September 1916* (Cobham: Fairmile, 1995).

[158] Mitchell, *Tank Warfare*, 102.   [159] Baker-Carr, *From Chauffeur*, 200.

[160] 'Notes: Conversation with Mr J. Sawers', 14 July 1972, Military Histories (General), 914.2, RSMA.

[161] 'Summary of Operations during September, 1916', undated, III Corps War Diary, WO95/674, TNA.

[162] 'XIII Corps. Lessons Deduced', 6 August 1916, Montgomery-Massingberd Papers 7/3, LHCMA.

despite their individual merits, none of the means of communication at the disposal of British commanders between July and November 1916 were infallible. So, just how much impact did these means of communication have upon command and control?

Command and Control

In assessing his performance on the opening day of the battle, the commander of 36 (Ulster) Division, Major-General (later Sir) Oliver Nugent, informed his wife: 'People at home may imagine COs and Generals can alter or change a plan once put in operation. It is impossible. Once troops begin to move under such conditions as the Division encountered on 1st July nothing can be stopped or changed'.[163] Nugent's experience must stand for that of many British commanders that day and indeed throughout the remainder of the Somme campaign. Commanders at all levels experienced the extraordinary difficulty of obtaining prompt and reliable information once an attack commenced, making it very difficult to maintain command and control.

Recalling his experiences around the village of Gueudecourt on 20 October, for example, the brigade-major of the 36th Infantry Brigade (12 Division) informed Edmonds after the war that 'information was inadequate; we had great difficulty in finding out where our own forward troops were and had hardly any detailed knowledge as regards the enemy'.[164] Similarly, at the divisional level, John Shea noted in a report written in mid-August that 'our great difficulty in the Trones Wood fighting and our greater difficulty in the Guillemont fighting was the obtaining of information early enough to act on it with any success'.[165] Even at the highest levels of command, the problem of obtaining speedy and accurate information as to the progress of events at the frontline perplexed Haig and his army commanders. Gough wrote after the war that on 1 July 'information from the front [was] scrappy, disjointed, often inaccurate, or, more often still, [was] lacking altogether'.[166] At a meeting held at Fourth Army headquarters on 9 August, Rawlinson questioned 'the arrangement for obtaining prompt information as to the progress of... attacks' and urged 'some means of keeping better observation and

---

[163] Nugent to His Wife, 11 July 1916, in Perry (ed.), *Major-General Oliver Nugent*, 104.

[164] Brigadier [later Lieutenat-General Sir] Desmond Anderson to Edmonds, 6 April 1936, CAB45/132, TNA.

[165] 'Preliminary Notes on the Tactical Lessons of the Recent Operations, 30 Division', 10 August 1916, Montgomery-Massingberd Papers 7/3, LHCMA.

[166] Gough, *Fifth Army*, 138.

obtaining more accurate information from hour to hour must be found'.[167] Likewise, five days later Haig told Lieutenant-General Claud Jacob, GOC II Corps, that 'information from divisions frequently reaches HQ of corps, armies and GHQ very slowly. Too slowly!' In his diary entry that day Haig recorded: 'I desired Jacob to see that intercommunication between subordinate units in a division and Divisional HQ was sufficiently kept up'.[168]

The breakdown of communication and the subsequent delays in the receipt of information as it filtered up the chain of command made it extremely difficult for British commanders to take full advantage of any successes that presented themselves. On 1 July, for example, although 30 Division had gained the whole of its first objective by 11 a.m., news of this success did not reach Fourth Army headquarters for at least another hour.[169] Similarly, Rawlinson remained blissfully unaware of the true situation on VIII Corps' front, opposite Beaumont Hamel, until a situation report from Hunter-Weston revealed at 2.45 p.m. that the attack had stalled.[170] Although Fourth Army's signal office was inundated with 4,975 telegraph messages that day, the absence of accurate and timely information made it extremely difficult for Rawlinson to have any real influence on the course of the fighting (Figure 5.2).[171] As Rawlinson's chief of staff, Major-General Archibald Montgomery, told Edmonds after the war: 'Lord Rawly being further back did not feel the draught so much and kept on pressing for an advance'.[172]

[167] 'Note of an Interview at Querrieu, at 11 a.m., 9th August, 1916, between General Sir Henry Rawlinson, Lieutenant-General L. E. Kiggell, Major-General Montgomery, and Brigadier-General Davidson', Haig Diary, WO256/12, TNA.

[168] Haig Diary, 14 August 1916, WO256/12, TNA; Sheffield and Bourne (eds.), *Douglas Haig*, 220.

[169] 'XIII Corps Operations on the Somme. July 1st–August 15th 1916', undated, XIII Corps War Diary, WO95/895, 'Summary of Operations', 1 July 1916, Corps Situation Reports to Fourth Army, Compiled from Fourth Army, WO158/322, TNA. In fact, the 89th Infantry Brigade, attacking alongside the French XX Corps, secured its final objective, Dublin Trench, south of Montauban, as early as 8.30 a.m. but was subsequently held up by the neighbouring 21st Infantry Brigade, whose advance had been more gradual on account of stiffer German resistance. See 'Report on Operations, 30th Division, July 1st till 10 a.m. July 5th', undated, 30 Division War Diary, WO95/2310, TNA.

[170] 'Summary of Operations', 1 July 1916, Corps Situation Reports to Fourth Army, Compiled from Fourth Army, WO158/322, TNA; Rawlinson Diary, 1 July 1916, Rawlinson Papers, CAC.

[171] 'Chart Showing Telegraph Traffic – Fourth Army. July 1916', Fourth Army Signal Company War Diary, WO95/493, TNA.

[172] Field Marshal Sir Archibald Montgomery-Massingberd to Edmonds, 7 December 1937, CAB45/136, TNA. See also, Brigadier R. M. Luckock [GSO2, Fourth Army] to Edmonds, 25 January 1931, CAB45/189, TNA.

Telegraph Traffic - Fourth Army, July 1916

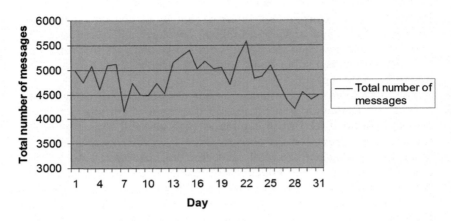

Telegraph Traffic - Fourth Army, August 1916

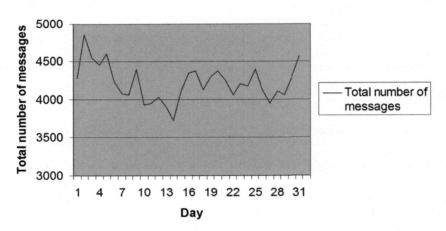

Figure 5.2 Fourth Army signal traffic, July–November 1916

The tenuous means of procuring and transmitting information was not helped by the rather centralised and hierarchical nature of the BEF's command system in 1916.[173] This point was aptly demonstrated on 14 July, when the cavalry arrived 'too little and too late' to exploit the

[173] Travers, *Killing Ground*, chapters 1 and 7; Samuels, *Command or Control?*, 5, 49–51.

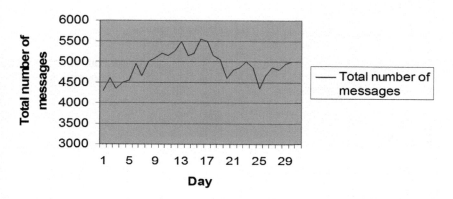

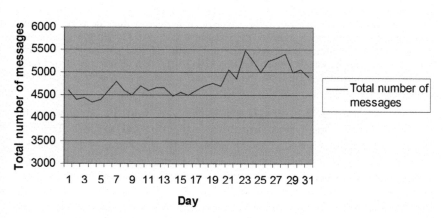

Figure 5.2 (*cont.*)

success of Fourth Army's 'dawn attack'.[174] As Colonel Roderick (Rory) Macleod, an artillery liaison officer, recorded in his diary:

[174] Stephen Badsey, 'Cavalry and the Development of Breakthrough Doctrine', in Griffith (ed.), *British Fighting Methods*, 156–7. For additional context on this controversial episode, see: Stephen Badsey, *Doctrine and Reform in the British Cavalry 1880–1918* (Aldershot: Ashgate, 2008), 273–4; Philpott, *Bloody Victory*, 238–41; and, Kenyon, *Horsemen in No Man's Land*, 59–74.

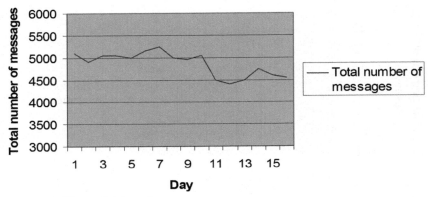

Figure 5.2 (*cont.*)

It was soon reported that Delville Wood and Longueval had been captured, but no word reached us that we could advance. It appeared that the two divisional commanders could not agree, so referred the decision to Corps. Corps said that it was an Army matter and referred to Fourth Army Headquarters. Fourth Army said that the cavalry were the last GHQ reserve and referred it to GHQ. GHQ gave permission and by the time it reached us it was 6 p.m., twelve hours wasted.[175]

As a consequence of both GHQ's decision to hold the cavalry too far back and the 'one-way communication from GHQ and Army to Corps, and from Corps to lower levels', the attack on 14 July quickly degenerated into a protracted and costly struggle.[176] If the BEF's high command was unwilling to delegate responsibility to its inexperienced New Army commanders and staffs in 1916, then, combined with the inadequacies of the means of communication they had at their disposal, British commanders were forced to resolve the dilemma by implementing a variety of solutions to expedite the conveyance of information.

One such solution concerned the distance of headquarters in relation to each other and the frontline. On 1 July, Thomas Morland watched X Corps' attack from the top of an observation tree three miles west of

---

[175] Diary Entry, 14 July 1916, Colonel Roderick (Rory) Macleod Papers 1/2, LHCMA.
[176] Travers, *Killing Ground*, 168; Prior and Wilson, *Somme*, 138.

Thiepval Wood and connected by telephone to his corps headquarters two miles away.[177] Despite such arrangements, however, according to Lieutenant-Colonel William Newton, OC 1/23rd Londons, the Battle of the Somme demonstrated 'the impossibility of trying to control the day-to-day operations of small bodies of men in a shelled trench area from Corps or Division HQ, unless the latter are at least as near to what is going on as Brigade HQ'.[178] In a memorandum issued by Fifth Army in early October 1916, Gough stipulated that it was 'equally important that Divisional Headquarters should be well forward at the outset of an attack'. He further added: 'Any increase of the distance between Divisional Headquarters and brigades adds greatly to the difficulty of communication, whilst an increased distance between Divisional and Corps Headquarters presents little difficulty'.[179] This was chiefly because of the relative strength and security afforded by the trunk line system of cable communications that existed between divisional and corps headquarters and the fact that communications forward of divisional headquarters were subject to the destructive power of German artillery. The focus of the debate concerning the location of headquarters was thus centred upon improving communications forward of brigade headquarters. In mid-September, Fifth Army informed its brigade and battalion commanders that they ought to be in a position so as 'to feel the pulse of the battle, intervene as the situation demands, and miss no opportunities'.[180] The following month, Gough stressed that it was 'essential that Brigadiers should select forward positions whence they can observe the fight from their original Battle Headquarters; then, even if communication fails, they will be able to see what is going on'.[181] Several post-battle reports agreed that brigade and battalion headquarters should 'be best placed as far forward as possible along the main line of communication'.[182] As a result of following this practice,

---

[177] Edmonds, *Military Operations, 1916*, Vol. 1, 406; Morland to Margie, 4 July 1916, in Bill Thompson (ed.), *General Sir Thomas Morland: War Diaries & Letters, 1914–1918* (Kibworth Beauchamp: Matador, 2015), 148–9.

[178] Lieutenant-Colonel William Newton to Edmonds, [?] 1936, CAB45/136, TNA.

[179] 'Memorandum by the Army Commander for the Guidance of Divisional and Infantry Brigade Commanders', 5 October 1916, Fifth Army Notes and Lessons on 1916 Operations, WO158/344, TNA.

[180] 'Fifth Army G.A. 43/0/4', 16 September 1916, Fifth Army Notes and Lessons on 1916 Operations, WO158/344, TNA.

[181] 'Memorandum by the Army Commander for the Guidance of Divisional and Infantry Brigade Commanders', 5 October 1916, Fifth Army Notes and Lessons on 1916 Operations, WO158/344, TNA.

[182] 'Preliminary Notes on the Tactical Lessons of the Recent Operations, 30 Division', 10 August 1916, Montgomery-Massingberd Papers 7/3, LHCMA.

for example, Brigadier-General Cyril Deverell, commanding 20th Infantry Brigade (7 Division), reported that during an attack on High Wood in mid-July, 'complete communication was maintained throughout, and I was able to keep myself personally in touch with the Brigades operating on my right and left'.[183]

However, although IX Corps recommended that brigade headquarters should be situated roughly 2,000 yards from the firing line,[184] the risks involved in being this close to the action were often tragic and devastating, as Brigadier-General Reginald Kentish, GOC 76th Infantry Brigade (3 Division), recalled at the end of July:

Throughout the operations my Headquarters were heavily shelled... Owing to this very heavy shell fire, accompanied as it was by gas and lachrymatory shells, I was compelled to evacuate Headquarters. My Brigade Major was placed hors de combat from the effects of the gas, my Signal Officer was killed and several of my Staff killed and wounded. All my communications were cut.[185]

In addition, with his communication resources stretched to their absolute limit, a battalion commander was forced to contemplate yet another dilemma: 'The difficulty is largely one of communication and it is to be decided whether it is more important for the Battalion Commander to be in touch with his Brigadier and have indifferent communication with his companies or to have good communication with his companies and indifferent communication with his Brigadier'.[186] Overall, it would appear that the attempt to improve the system of communication by situating divisional, brigade and battalion headquarters closer to each other and to the frontline was helpful, but entailed a variety of problems which, arguably, exacerbated the situation and only added to the difficulties of transmitting fast and reliable information up the chain of command.

Another solution to the difficulty of obtaining fast and reliable information from subordinate units was the development of an efficient system of liaison officers, whose task it was to keep 'the superior authority informed of the situation and for verifying the position actually held by the infantry', and to ensure that 'the spirit of the orders of the superior authority is carried out

---

[183] 'Report on Operations of 20th Infantry Brigade, July 11th-20th, 1916', 26 July 1916, 7 Division War Diary, WO95/1631, TNA.
[184] 'IX Corps Notes on Information Collected from Various Sources, Including Troops Who Have Been Engaged in the Recent Fighting', 31 July 1916, Montgomery-Massingberd Papers 7/3, LHCMA.
[185] 'The Situation Which Often Confronts Brigadiers When Headquarters Are Situated Close up to the Front Line', 26 July 1916, Montgomery-Massingberd Papers 7/3, LHCMA.
[186] 'Lessons Learnt from the Recent Operations', 28 November 1916, Fifth Army Notes and Lessons on 1916 Operations, WO158/344, TNA.

Plate 5.2 Emergency telephone post behind the line, October 1916
(Canada. Dept. of National Defence/Library and Archives Canada/
RCSigs.ca, MIKAN no. 3380986)

by lower formations'.[187] As Chapter 4 demonstrated, liaison officers were of paramount importance during the opening weeks of the war, as they were often the only means British commanders had to expedite the transfer of orders and other important messages. By 1916, however, as XIII Corps observed from its experiences in early August, 'more use might, perhaps, be made of the French system of Liaison Officers'.[188] Similarly, in a report entitled 'Artillery Lessons Drawn from the Battle of the Somme', Fourth Army advocated that 'the crux of the whole matter is the vital importance of Senior Officers, Battery Commanders, and Junior Officers of both Field and Heavy Artillery visiting and maintaining the closest relations with the infantry in the line'.[189]

Some units, however, did make good use of liaison officers during the Somme campaign. For example, Major-General Henry Watts, GOC 7 Division, acknowledged that a successful system of liaison with the neighbouring 21 Division had been utilised throughout July to good effect.[190] However, it would appear that this was a rather isolated example. On the whole, the means of procuring information from the 'sharp-end' of the battlefield via an effective system of liaison officers was not standard practice in the BEF in 1916.[191] Whilst this did little to improve the communications system, it also had the negative effect of worsening relations between the staff and the frontline officers and troops.[192] 'We felt', one brigade-major told Edmonds after the war, 'that the Staffs of the higher formations were not taking sufficient trouble to find out the true situation... [They] issued orders and instructions quite inapplicable to the real situation'.[193] According to Major (later Field Marshal Sir) Bernard Montgomery, Brigade-Major of the 104th Infantry Brigade in 1916: 'The higher staffs were out of touch with the regimental officers and with the troops. The former lived in comfort..., and sympathy between the staff and the troops... was often lacking'.[194] Even Haig complained on 14 August: 'I have noticed lately that in many divisions, the Staff does not circulate sufficiently amongst the brigades and battalions when operations are in progress'.[195]

---

[187] 'XIII Corps. Lessons Deduced', 6 August 1916, Montgomery-Massingberd Papers 7/3, LHCMA.

[188] Ibid.

[189] 'Artillery Lessons Drawn from the Battle of the Somme', November 1916, Montgomery-Massingberd Papers 7/3, LHCMA.

[190] 'Notes on Attacks Carried Out by 7th Division in July, 1916', 7 Division War Diary, WO95/1631, TNA.

[191] Robbins, *British Generalship*, 47–48.

[192] Colonel F. W. S. Jourdain, Interview (1990), Department of Sound Records, 011214/6, IWM.

[193] Anderson to Edmonds, 6 April 1936, CAB45/132, TNA.

[194] Montgomery, *Memoirs*, 32–3.   [195] Haig Diary, 14 August 1916, WO256/12, TNA.

Throughout the Somme campaign the breakdown of communications not only affected the conveyance of information up the chain of command, but also had an impact on the flow of information as it filtered down the chain of command. As the Earl of Cavan, GOC XIV Corps, noted in a letter to Edmonds after the war, 'the vital importance of sending information forward' was just as indispensable as the need for information from the frontline.[196] This is perhaps most evident when considering the time it took for orders issued by a corps or divisional commander to reach the frontline. According to one brigade commander after the war, 'no attack could be successful if orders reach attacking troops too late for careful explanations to be given to subordinate commanders and plans to be carefully thought out'.[197] Numerous complaints regarding the time taken for operation orders to reach subordinate commanders with enough time to prepare and carry them out appeared both during and after the Somme. For example, on 1 July, the failure of 32 Division's attack south of Thiepval was partly blamed on the fact that many frontline units 'never got any orders as to the time of attack until 2 hours after it should have been'.[198] Indeed, Major-General William Rycroft, GOC 32 Division, acknowledged that throughout the day 'it had not been possible to get orders to the various units in time'.[199] Likewise, in mid-July, Major-General Tom Bridges, GOC 19 Division, complained that 'in many cases operation orders from higher formations reach Divisional Headquarters 2 hours or less before they have to be acted upon'. As a result, not only was it often 'too late to act on them', but, as Major-General William Furse, GOC 9 Division, observed, the time delays in getting orders forward 'resulted more than once in futile loss of life'.[200] Similarly, with regards to operations in the Gueudecourt area on 20 October, Desmond Anderson recalled that orders 'reach[ed] Brigade Headquarters so late that there was only just time for officers of the Brigade Staff to struggle forward to the battalions in the line and by means of verbal orders try and help them'.[201]

In mid-August Major-General William Walker, GOC 2 Division, stated that in his opinion 'the minimum time for orders to pass from the Corps to Company Commanders', as stipulated in SS. 119, was

[196] Lord Cavan to Edmonds, 28 March 1935, CAB45/132, TNA.
[197] Brigadier-General R. FitzMaurice to Edmonds, 7 November 1936, CAB45/133, TNA.
[198] Brian Bond and Simon Robbins (eds.), Staff Officer: The Diaries of Walter Guinness (First Lord Moyne) 1914–1918 (London: Leo Cooper, 1987), 102.
[199] 'Operations of 32nd Division, 1 July 1916', Fourth Army Records, Vol. 1, IWM.
[200] 'Notes on the Recent Operations, 19 Division', 19 July 1916, '9th (Scottish) Division Report', 26 July 1916, Montgomery-Massingberd Papers 7/3, LHCMA.
[201] Anderson to Edmonds, 6 April 1936, CAB45/132, TNA.

'considerably underestimated'.[202] While Tom Bridges concluded that divisional operation orders 'should be issued 12 hours previously to all concerned', IX Corps recommended six hours and a Fifth Army report in mid-August maintained that five hours was 'the minimum time which is necessary to allow between the time of the receipt of orders for the attack at Divisional Headquarters and the time the assault is due'.[203] However, from his experience, Walter Congreve stated that 'it takes on an average period of at least 24 hours from the time Divisional Operation Orders are issued before the Platoon Commander in the front line is in a position to carry out his part in the attack'.[204]

It appears that two major factors were accountable for the slow transmission and receipt of orders down the chain of command. The first was poor staff work.[205] Like a number of commanders they served, some British staff officers after the war gained a reputation for incompetence and 'hopeless inefficiency'.[206] However, it is worth bearing in mind that in 1916 there was a severe shortage of competent and experienced staff officers in the British Army. One staff officer noted after the war that division, brigade and battalion staff work on the Somme had been poor because even 'the most competent officers were working on a scale and in conditions of which they had no experience, and they had to learn their job'.[207] Even at the highest levels of command, upon his appointment as MGGS Second Army in June 1916, Tim Harington recalled:

I remember being terribly frightened at the task before me. I had never thought in 'Armies'... We never, even in our theory, dealt with, or thought of a force exceeding our Expeditionary Force of six divisions..., but here I was confronted with the staff work of an army which, two or three times in my tenure, exceeded thirty divisions![208]

[202] 'Notes on Experience Gained during the Recent Operations, Compiled from a Conference Held on 15th August and from Reports from Brigadiers, 2nd Division, X Corps', undated, Montgomery-Massingberd Papers 7/3, LHCMA; SS. 119. Preliminary Notes on the Tactical Lessons of the Recent Operations (July 1916) stipulated a time of six hours.

[203] 'Notes on the Recent Operations, 19 Division', 19 July 1916; 'IX Corps Notes on Information Collected from Various Sources, Including Troops Who Have Been Engaged in the Recent Fighting', 31 July 1916, Montgomery-Massingberd Papers 7/3, LHCMA; 'Miscellaneous Notes Gathered from Divisions Who Have Taken Part in Recent Offensive Operations', 17 August 1916, Fifth Army Notes and Lessons on 1916 Operations, WO158/344, TNA.

[204] 'XIII Corps. Lessons Deduced', 6 August 1916, Montgomery-Massingberd Papers 7/3, LHCMA.

[205] For an examination of the development of staff work during the war, see: Robbins, British Generalship, 34–50; and, Harris, 'Men Who Planned the War'.

[206] Gerald Achilles Burgoyne, The Burgoyne Diaries (London: Thomas Harmsworth, 1985), 218.

[207] Captain Pearson Choate to Edmonds, 6 April 1936, CAB45/132, TNA.

[208] General Sir Charles Harington, Tim Harington Looks Back (London: John Murray, 1940), 53.

As Brigadier-General Thomas Shoubridge informed Major-General Ivor - Maxse, GOC 18 Division, in late July 1916, the consequence of this lack of experience was that 'the present staffs' had little idea as to 'how long it takes for an infantry unit to carry out an order and get into position'.[209] Equally, Tom Bridges observed that 'officers of the New Army take more time to digest orders and to pass them on to those who have to act on them. . . It was found that when ample time was not given, attacks failed'.[210]

It must also be stressed that staff officers at all levels of the BEF worked under enormous pressure and for very long hours of the day. As one former corps staff officer wrote: 'It is a fallacy to think the officer with red tabs has a "cushy" job'.[211] Major-General Robert Collins informed Edmonds after the war that, as GSO1 of 17 Division during the Battle of the Somme, he averaged 16 to 18 hours of work per day and 'the pace was terrific'.[212] Similarly, whilst a GSO3(I) at Second Army, Cuthbert Headlam told his wife in a series of letters that staff officers 'are not supposed to go to bed until 11 o'clock at the earliest' and that 'it would be considered curiously slack if I did not spend my whole day at my desk!'[213] With regards to staff work at GHQ, Brigadier-General John Charteris noted that 'there are few, if any, officers who do not do a fourteen-hour day, and who are not to be found at work far into the night'.[214] Thus, through a combination of inexperience and excessive workloads and working hours it is little wonder that errors and mistakes in staff work occurred during the Battle of the Somme. Although the BEF would develop a much more professional and proficient staff system by 1918, in 1916 staff work, like the army's tactical and operational methods, was at its nadir. As such, the process of information transfer as it percolated down the chain of command was often disjointed and slow.

Poor staff work in 1916 was compounded by the tenuous state of the BEF's communications system. As one staff officer wrote in November 1916, 'it takes hours for orders to reach [the] front line, as [telephone] wires [are] invariably cut by shell fire'.[215] It is also worth noting that the

---

[209] Brigadier-General T. H. Shoubridge to Major-General F. I. Maxse, 30 July 1916, Maxse Papers, 69/53/7, IWM.

[210] 'Some Further Notes on the Recent Operations by the Divisional Commander, Major-General Bridges, 19 Division', 9 September 1916, Montgomery-Massingberd Papers 7/3, LHCMA.

[211] Colonel W.N. Nicholson, *Behind the Lines: An Account of Administrative Staff Work in the British Army 1914–1918* (London: Strong Oak Press, 1989), 116.

[212] Major-General R. J. Collins to Edmonds, 7 February 1930, CAB45/132, TNA.

[213] Letters to Beatrice, 12 February and 1 August 1916, in Jim Beach (ed.), *The Military Papers of Lieutenant-Colonel Sir Cuthbert Headlam, 1910–1942* (Stroud: History Press for the Army Records Society, 2010), 116, 132.

[214] Charteris, *At GHQ*, 209.

[215] H. Spencer Clay Diary, 17 November 1916, quoted by H. Spencer Clay to Edmonds, 28 September 1936, CAB45/132, TNA.

standard operating procedures at army, corps and divisional headquarters were often quite different.[216] This included the means of communication each primarily relied upon to pass information to subordinate units. One staff officer, who worked at GHQ, corps and divisional headquarters during the war, recalled that at both GHQ and corps 'we worked by lengthy precisely worded correspondence, whereas in a division we talked on the telephone – and there is a world of difference in the two methods'. With regards to the written form of communication: 'There was a great loss of time, a great loss of the human element and a great loss of driving power'. He concluded: 'A good staff officer... uses his eyes, his memory and his telephone; and rarely needs any foolscap'.[217]

However, as with the difficulties involved in transmitting information up the chain of command, the BEF attempted to introduce a number of measures designed to facilitate the process of communication from the higher command to the frontline. For example, with regards to the issuing of operation orders, Tom Bridges advised that a 'preliminary order' or message should be sent 'to warn all concerned that an operation is about to be initiated, the details following later'.[218] In a similar fashion, Watts acknowledged that 'information of impending orders was always given to Brigadiers as early as possible on the telephone so that they might be able to think out their plans before receipt of written orders'.[219] Subsequently, as Walker concluded, the issuing of preliminary orders did 'much to minimise the difficulties' of ensuring the timely and accurate delivery of information to the regimental officers and their troops at the frontline.[220]

Despite the variety of new methods developed and implemented by the BEF to combat the immense difficulties experienced in obtaining, processing and transmitting information, British commanders throughout the Somme campaign struggled to maintain adequate command and control of their troops in action. A combination of inexperienced staffs, technological shortcomings, the conditions imposed by trench warfare and a rather centralised command structure resulted in the frequent breakdown of communication, which in turn led to huge time constraints in the decision-making process. As a result, many opportunities that

---

[216] Lieutenant-General Sir Philip Neame, Typescript of Interview (1974), 78, Department of Sound Records, 000048, IWM.

[217] Nicholson, *Behind the Lines*, 302–3, 24–5.

[218] 'Notes on the Recent Operations, 19 Division', 19 July 1916, Montgomery-Massingberd Papers 7/3, LHCMA.

[219] 'Notes on Attacks Carried Out by 7th Division in July, 1916', 7 Division War Diary, WO95/1631, TNA.

[220] 'Notes on Experience Gained during the Recent Operations, Compiled from a Conference Held on 15 August 1916 and from Reports from Brigadiers, 2nd Division, X Corps', undated, Montgomery-Massingberd Papers 7/3, LHCMA.

presented themselves were often missed, reserves were committed too late or not at all, confusion spread and lives were lost.

In summary, this chapter has endeavoured to explain how, and with what success, the BEF's communications system developed during the Battle of the Somme. In so doing, it has sought to address three central questions: first, how extensive were the BEF's communication preparations for the battle?; second, what influence did communications have upon the fighting?; and, third, to what extent did the BEF's communications system show signs of improvement over the course of the campaign?

With regards to the first question, it has been shown that, despite having been neglected by historians, the question of communications during the build-up to the Somme was just as important to British commanders as were other key issues, such as logistics and the role of artillery. Overall, the BEF went into battle on 1 July with a variety of methods for communicating information. During the months leading up to the offensive it had devoted a great deal of time and labour to the construction of a deep-buried cable network that was to provide the backbone of the communications system. In addition, a combination of alternative means, such as visual signalling, carrier pigeons, wireless, despatch riders and runners, were to act as supplementary methods of communication in the event of cable communication breaking down. It is evident that British commanders thought long and hard about the issue of communications in the build-up to the battle and that they were clearly well aware of the need for a safe and efficient communications system if they were to maintain command and control. As Lieutenant Joshua Burn, commanding the 36th Infantry Brigade Signal Section, noted after the war, one of the chief lessons to emerge from 1916 was the importance of 'preparing well ahead of the battle'.[221]

In response to the second question, there is no denying that communications had a profound influence on the course of the Somme campaign. From the infamous opening day to the eventual capture of Beaumont Hamel on 13 November, the campaign confirmed to British commanders that one of the chief constraints on the conduct of offensive operations was the lack of an efficient and secure system of 'real-time' communications, and that successful command and control depended upon the receipt of timely and accurate information, without which they were often powerless to co-ordinate the efforts of their forces and, ultimately, influence the fight. While it would be going too far to suggest that poor communications were *the* main cause of British failure on the

---

[221] Typescript Memoir, undated, 69, Lieutenant J. H. Burn Papers, GS0240, LCL.

Somme, it would not be too wrong to argue that the breakdown of communications, whether on 1 July, in the immediate aftermath of the successful 'dawn assault' on 14 July, or during the course of the Battle of Flers-Courcelette in mid-September, had equally adverse implications for these, and other, notable operations as did poor command decisions, inadequate fire support and faulty logistics.[222]

Given its impact on the campaign, therefore, how did British commanders respond to the challenges posed by communications in 1916, and to what extent did the BEF's communications system improve during the course of the year? Certainly the adoption of the Fullerphone and the establishment of the contact aeroplane system demonstrated that British commanders were willing to embrace new technology to combat the problem of communications. However, it is also clear that British commanders realised that improving the communications system required much more than just the implementation of the latest technology. The debates which took place within the BEF with regards to the location of, and distance between, brigade and battalion headquarters, and the time taken for orders to reach the frontline, for example, suggest that British commanders were prepared to modify existing practices in order to improve the BEF's communications system.

However, although inroads were being made, the BEF's machinery for command and control remained in a technical void throughout the Somme campaign. None of the means of communication that British commanders had at their disposal were infallible. Despite the provision of telephones, telegraph, wireless, visual signalling and carrier pigeons, there was still no satisfactory means of ensuring the speedy and reliable transfer of information between the advancing infantry, the other arms that supported them and their commanders to the rear. While the campaign certainly taught the inexperienced New Armies a great deal with regards to the art of communications in modern, industrialised warfare, British commanders in November were still no closer to possessing a war-winning formula that would solve the perennial and intractable problem of communications than they were on 1 July. How the BEF attempted to apply the lessons of the Somme as it sought to refine its communications system in 1917 represents a crucial part of the development of British communications on the Western Front.

---

[222] Travers, *Killing Ground*, 189–90; Prior and Wilson, *Somme*, 303–7; Brown, *British Logistics*, 109–34.

6   1917

In keeping with the attacking disposition of Allied strategy,[1] the BEF launched four major offensives in 1917: the Battle of Arras (9 April-15 May), the Battle of Messines (7-14 June), the Third Battle of Ypres (31 July-10 November) and the Battle of Cambrai (20 November-7 December).[2] Of these, popular and academic attention has almost invariably focused on the controversial Third Ypres, or Passchendaele, campaign, which, alongside the Somme, has become a byword for military incompetence and the supreme embodiment of the supposed futility of the First World War.[3] However, although the offensives of 1917 failed to break the stalemate on the Western Front, a number of historians have argued that these battles did demonstrate the growing tactical and operational sophistication of British fighting methods, most notably at Cambrai with the mass use of tanks.[4] Although frequently mentioned, communications does not take centre stage within this interpretation. This is surprising since, taking into account the lessons learnt from the Somme, considerable ingenuity was applied in attempts to improve the BEF's communications system throughout 1917, though to varying degrees of success. This chapter, therefore, seeks to map the progress

---

[1] On Anglo-French strategy, see: David French, *The Strategy of the Lloyd George Coalition, 1916–1918* (Oxford: Clarendon Press, 1995), 67–147; and, Philpott, *Anglo-French Relations*.

[2] Cyril Falls, *Military Operations, France and Belgium, 1917*, Vol. 1 (London: HMSO, 1940); James Edmonds, *Military Operations, France and Belgium, 1917*, Vol. 2 (London: HMSO, 1948); Wilfred Miles, *Military Operations, France and Belgium, 1917*, Vol. 3 (London: HMSO, 1948).

[3] Brian Bond, 'Passchendaele: Verdicts, Past and Present', in Liddle (ed.), *Passchendaele in Perspective*, 479–88; Prior and Wilson, *Passchendaele*.

[4] See, for example: Griffith, *Battle Tactics*, 84–100; Passingham, *Pillars of Fire*; John Lee, 'Some Lessons of the Somme: The British Infantry in 1917', in Bond et al., *'Look to Your Front'*, 79–88; Sheffield, *Forgotten Victory*, 190–220; Peter Dennis and Jeffrey Grey (eds.), *1917: Tactics, Training and Technology* (Australian History Military Publications, 2007); Hammond, *Cambrai 1917*.

of the BEF's communications system in 1917, examining the impact of communications upon military operations and assessing the extent to which the system was stronger, more flexible and more sophisticated at the end of the year than it had been at the beginning.

Arras

During the winter of 1916–17, as the BEF began to dissect the lessons of the Somme,[5] gradual improvements in tactical and operational methods were beginning to be matched by the quantitative and qualitative output of the British war industry.[6] Consequently, as the official historian noted, 'The divisions of the British Expeditionary Force had in the first half of 1917 reached their highest standard of training since the Force had become a Citizen Army'.[7] The clearest indication that the BEF had learnt lessons from the Somme campaign with regards to communications was the publication of the training manuals *SS. 135.* and, more importantly, *SS. 148.*[8] In support of the French 'Nivelle Offensive', therefore, the Battle of Arras represented the first opportunity for the BEF to put its new communications doctrine to the test.[9]

In light of the vast expenditure of time and effort that had gone into its construction, the deep-buried cable network at the Somme had justified its existence, although certain modifications were required. These modifications led to the creation of the 'grid', which became a key characteristic of the BEF's communications system throughout 1917.[10] The object of this grid was 'to give the necessary communication during the preliminary bombardment and the early stages of the

---

[5] See, for example: Peter Simkins' introduction in Chris McCarthy, *The Somme: The Day-by-Day Account* (London: Arms and Armour Press, 1993), 13; Griffith, *Battle Tactics*, 84–8; Lee, 'Some Lessons of the Somme', 79–88; Sheffield, *Forgotten Victory*, 190–9; and, Simpson, *Directing Operations*, 61–70.

[6] Trevor Wilson, *The Myriad Faces of War: Britain and the Great War, 1914–1918* (Oxford: Politiy Press, 1986), 449.

[7] Falls, *Military Operations, 1917*, Vol. 1, 198.

[8] *SS. 135. Instructions for the Training of Divisions for Offensive Action* (December 1916); *SS. 148. Forward Inter-Communication in Battle* (March 1917). On the importance of the former, see Simpson, *Directing Operations*, 63–5. On the content and significance of the latter, see Chapter 2.

[9] On the Nivelle Offensive, see Elizabeth Greenhalgh, *The French Army and the First World War* (Cambridge: Cambridge University Press, 2014), 170–99.

[10] 'Theoretical Diagram of Main System of Buried Communications in Front of Divisional Headquarters', January 1917, Third Army Signal Company War Diary, WO95/408; 'Signal Notes No. 4', 13 March 1917, Director of Army Signals War Diary, WO95/57, TNA.

operations', and to 'act as a starting point of the forward lines which would have to be laid in the captured trench system'.[11] On each divisional front, one main artery was constructed as far forward as brigade headquarters. Located along the main artery were four principal communication centres (Figure 6.1). Each centre was connected to its corresponding flanking centre by a series of lateral lines and thus a grid was constructed along the whole army front.[12] It was the responsibility of corps to draw up plans for the buried network in front of it and to provide the main corps artery as far forward as brigade headquarters, although they did receive a certain amount of assistance from divisional signal companies.[13] From brigade headquarters, 'one spur per Infantry Brigade was continued to [the] original front line... These spurs terminated in dug outs in the front line, and were used as Brigade Forward Stations'. This work was undertaken by divisions, though once completed, 'the maintenance thereof rested with the Brigade Sections'.[14] Finally, the buried telephone system had to be extended to battalion headquarters and to artillery batteries.[15]

Once an attack was underway, each brigade was to 'concentrate on laying one circuit forward from their respective cable heads' to the Forward Brigade Station. These stations were to be situated 'about half way between the hostile front line and the final objective' and were 'chosen so as to be near to, or coincide with, one of the Battalion Headquarters, and [were] to move forward when these Headquarters move[d]'.[16] A telephone exchange was to be established at the Brigade Forward Station 'to which one Artillery and one Infantry circuit from Advanced Infantry Brigade Headquarters will be connected'.[17] Thus, in an attempt to eliminate what had been a major cause of the slow transmission of information during the Somme campaign, the Brigade Forward Station was to help bridge the all-important communications gap between brigade and battalion headquarters.

[11] 'Notes on Communications during Operations East of Arras', May 1917, 34 Division Signal Company War Diary, WO95/2450, TNA.
[12] 'Theoretical Diagram of Main System of Buried Communications in Front of Divisional Headquarters', January 1917, Third Army Signal Company War Diary, WO95/408, TNA; *SS. 148. Forward Inter-Communication in Battle*, 4–8.
[13] *SS. 148. Forward Inter-Communication in Battle*, 19.
[14] 'Notes on Communications during Operations East of Arras', May 1917, 34 Division Signal Company War Diary, WO95/2450, TNA.
[15] *SS. 148. Forward Inter-Communication in Battle*, 8.
[16] Ibid., 9; '15th Division Instruction No. 3. General Instructions for Forward Communications', 16 March 1917, 15 Division Signal Company War Diary, WO95/1928, TNA.
[17] *SS. 148. Forward Inter-Communication in Battle*, 10.

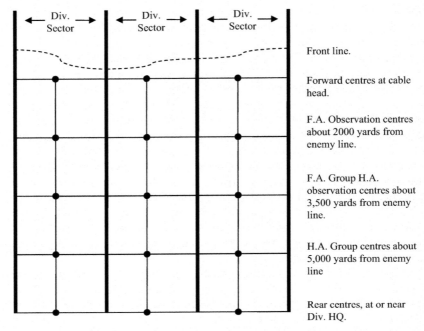

Figure 6.1 Grid system of buried cable communications, January 1917
Source: 'Theoretical Diagram of Main System of Buried Communications in Front of Divisional Headquarters', January 1917, Third Army Signal Company War Diary, WO 95/408, TNA.

On the eve of 9 April, each of the three corps which made up the Third Army attack at Arras had 'laid from three to five buried cable routes', 6 feet deep, up to their respective brigade headquarters.[18] The Arras region was particularly favourable for deep-cable buries since many units were able to lay their cables within the network of deep sewers which ran underneath the sector.[19] The situation was even more promising along the First Army front, where the Canadian Corps, opposite Vimy Ridge, made arrangements for 'the rapid extension of the buried cable system after the attack by utilising subways and enemy tunnels and selected communication trenches'.[20] The extensive mining system which ran

[18] VI Corps (GOC Lieutenant-General James Aylmer Haldane); VII Corps (GOC Lieutenant-General Sir Thomas D'Oyly Snow); and, XVII Corps (GOC Lieutenant-General Sir Charles Fergusson). See Falls, *Military Operations, 1917*, Vol. 1, 193.
[19] 'ZCO, 1914–1919. Narrative by J. H. S. Christian, M.C.', 18, Christian Papers, IWM.
[20] 'Report on Operations of Canadian Corps against Vimy Ridge, April 1917', undated, Canadian Corps War Diary, WO95/1049, TNA.

underneath the Canadian Corps' front was seized upon by the signal companies, who laid their cables within the labyrinth of tunnels up to brigade and battalion headquarters.[21] These tunnels supplemented the deep cable network of the Canadian Corps, which were buried to a depth of '7 feet as a minimum, and 8 feet within 1,000 yards of the frontline', which was considered 'a minimum depth for safety' against direct hits from German artillery.[22] In all, the Canadian Corps constructed 21 miles of cable trenches, with an average of 35 pairs of cable laid per trench. This amounted to 900 miles of buried cable and 1,100 miles of airline to the rear of divisional headquarters.[23] Working predominantly at night over a one-month period, more than 5,000 men alone were employed by 1st Canadian Division to lay its buried cable network. This was success-fully completed one week in advance of the attack 'in order to give the Artillery an opportunity to use it in the preliminary bombardment'.[24] The time and effort which were expended upon the deep-buried cable network on the Canadian Corps' front were in many respects a reflection of the 'careful planning and meticulous attention to detail' which allowed the corps to capture Vimy Ridge on 9 April.[25]

Despite the heavy reliance upon telephones and telegraph, an array of alternative methods were also deemed necessary should the former fail. *SS. 148* listed the means of communication in the order in which they were to be used if all were available. With telephones and telegraph at the top of the pecking order, the next favoured method of communication was wireless.[26] This might seem somewhat surprising given its rather lacklustre performance in 1916, but there is a sense that British com-manders were at last beginning to realise the potential of wireless. John Fowler, for example, acknowledged in May 1917 'the probability that communication by means of simple Wireless gear will in the near future

---

[21] 'Scheme of Communications 4th Canadian Infantry Brigade Offensive No. 3', 23 March 1917, 2 Canadian Division Signal Company War Diary, WO95/3804; 'Communications. 4th Canadian Division, March 5th to May 5th, 1917', undated, 4 Canadian Division Signal Company War Diary, WO95/3891, TNA.

[22] 'Communications. 4th Canadian Division, March 5th to May 5th, 1917', undated, 4 Canadian Division Signal Company War Diary, WO95/3891, TNA; 'Report on Operations Carried Out by the 1st Canadian Division. April 9th–May 5th 1917', June 1917, Currie Papers, MG30, E100/35/160, LAC.

[23] First Army Administrative Report on the Vimy Ridge Operations, October 1917, 26, WO158/900, TNA.

[24] 'Report on Communications. 1st Canadian Division. March 5th–May 5th, 1917', 15 November 1917, 1 Canadian Division Signal Company War Diary, WO95/3751, TNA.

[25] Brown, *British Logistics*, 161. See also: Ian M. Brown, 'Not Glamorous, but Effective: The Canadian Corps and the Set-Piece Attack, 1917–1918', *Journal of Military History*, 58 (1994), 421–44.

[26] *SS. 148. Forward Inter-Communication in Battle*, 19–28.

replace to a greater or less extent the use of other means of communication in front of Brigades'.[27] As this chapter will demonstrate, the
battles of 1917 'added to the laurels of wireless' and much of the preju-
dice and opposition that had been widespread amongst commanders and
staff officers during the first half of the war gradually ended.[28] At Arras,
wireless sets and power buzzers were issued by Corps Wireless Sections
to each attacking division.[29] Two power buzzers per division were to
accompany the headquarters of the assaulting battalions, while one
power buzzer was to be sent forward with each Brigade Forward Station.[30] However, as the instructions issued to the 45th Infantry Brigade
(15 Division) made clear, power buzzers were to be used 'only if cable
communication breaks down', and were 'not [to] be taken into use until
the 2nd objective has been captured'.[31]

The next method of communication that forward units were to utilise,
according to *SS. 148*, was visual signalling. The signal instructions of VII
Corps, issued on 3 April, acknowledged that because of 'a serious shortage of field cable and the difficulties of providing and maintaining telephonic communication in semi-open warfare... it [is] imperative to
supplement the wires by a system of visual signalling'.[32] Similarly, John
Shea, GOC 30 Division, noted that 'owing to the great distances, very
considerable reliance will have to be placed on the visual system', though
adding, 'the nature of the country makes this easy'.[33] A 'Divisional Visual
Signal Scheme' was drawn up in consultation with the corps AD Signals
and arrangements made for signalling to be carried out from the visual
signal stations of battalion forward parties and the Brigade Forward
Stations to the Divisional Central Visual Station.[34] Visual messages
received at the Central Station were then relayed to division headquarters
over the telephone.[35] Brigade and battalion commanders were reassured
that 'as long as they are sent D.D. and slowly the messages will be read

---

[27] 'Communication by Wireless', 27 May 1917, RG9-III-C-5/4440/1/9, LAC.
[28] Schonland, 'W/T. R.E.', 178.   [29] Falls, *Military Operations, 1917*, Vol. 1, 193.
[30] 'Signal Communications', 3 April 1917, VII Corps War Diary, WO95/805, TNA.
[31] '45th Infantry Brigade Instruction No. 5', 21 March 1917, 15 Division Signal Company
War Diary, WO95/1928, TNA.
[32] 'Signal Communications', 3 April 1917, VII Corps War Diary, WO95/805, TNA.
[33] '30th Division Operation Order No. 70 by Major General J. S. M. Shea', 5 April 1917,
'Proposal for Attack. 30th Division', 1 April 1917, 30 Division War Diary, WO95/
2311, TNA.
[34] *SS. 148. Forward Inter-Communication in Battle*, 26.
[35] 'Addendum No. 1 to 15th Division Instruction No. 16', 31 March 1917', 15 Division
Signal Company War Diary, WO95/1928, 'Report on Operations of Canadian Corps
against Vimy Ridge, April 1917', undated, Canadian Corps War Diary, WO95/
1049, TNA.

correctly'.[36] To this end, instructions issued by 15 Division on 16 March stressed that visual messages 'should not be sent at a greater rate than four words per minute'.[37]

Finally, a variety of message carriers were assigned specific roles for the upcoming battle. Information pertaining to the location of the advancing infantry was to be conveyed via contact aeroplanes flying over the front-line at previously arranged times.[38] Aerial observers were also called upon to assist the artillery in counter-battery work, relaying information over wireless to the counter-battery office.[39] Adopting a very similar system to that utilised throughout the Somme campaign, brigade and battalion runners were to be organised along chains of relay posts, roughly covering the same route as the telephone lines and not more than 400 yards apart.[40] In order to speed up this process on the Canadian Corps' front, signposts were set up in the vicinity of principal signal stations in order to help direct runners to their intended destinations.[41] Mounted despatch riders were to be employed between division and brigade headquarters, while each brigade and battalion was to attach an officer or NCO 'to the headquarters of their immediate superior, and to those of the similar units on either flank'.[42] Liaison officers were also to be used as a principal means of communication between the infantry and artillery, with the Heavy Artillery attaching one liaison officer to each attacking infantry brigade headquarters it supported.[43] Finally, 126 carrier pigeons were allotted to XVII Corps, while VI and VII Corps each

---

[36] 'Visual during Coming Operations', 1 May 1917, Correspondence and Papers of 2 Division Signal Company in WW1, A231.52, REMA.

[37] '15th Division Instruction No. 3. General Instruction for Forward Communications', 16 March 1917, Field Marshal Sir John Dill Papers 1/4, LHCMA.

[38] 'VIIth Corps G.C.R. 604/295, File A. No. 26', 5 April 1917, VII Corps War Diary, WO95/805, TNA; SS. 148. Forward Inter-Communication in Battle, 29; '15th Division Instruction No. 3. Communication With Aeroplanes', 25 March 1917, 15 Division Signal Company War Diary, WO95/1928, 'Scheme of Communications 4th Canadian Infantry Brigade Offensive No. 3', 23 March 1917, 2 Canadian Division Signal Company War Diary, WO95/3804, '30th Division Operation Order No. 70 by Major General J. S. M. Shea', 5 April 1917, 30 Division War Diary, WO95/2311, '56th Division Instructions. Contact Aeroplane Signalling Instructions', 4 April 1917, VII Corps War Diary, WO95/805, TNA.

[39] SS. 148. Forward Inter-Communication in Battle, 33; Palazzo, 'The British Army's Counter-Battery Staff Office', 55–74.

[40] '15th Division Instruction No. 3. General Instructions for Forward Communications', 16 March 1917, Dill Papers 1/4, LHCMA.

[41] 'Scheme of Communications. 5th Canadian Infantry Brigade', 23 March 1917, 2 Canadian Division Signal Company War Diary, WO95/3804, TNA.

[42] '30th Division Operation Order No. 70 by Major General J. S. M. Shea', 5 April 1917, 30 Division War Diary, WO95/2311, TNA; SS. 148. Forward Inter-Communication in Battle, 38.

[43] SS. 148. Forward Inter-Communication in Battle, 39.

received 191 birds.[44] Each division decided how best to distribute its quota of pigeons amongst its attacking brigades. In 15 Division, for example, 16 pigeons were provided to each brigade, while in 30 Division, 18 birds were allotted to the 21st and 89th Brigades, and 13 allocated to the 90th Brigade.[45] As at the Somme the previous year, each loft was connected to its respective corps headquarters via a direct telephone link, and although most officers considered carrier pigeons to be a last resort, it was constantly impressed upon them that 'a pigeon message can be long and a great deal of information can be got onto the pigeon message sheets'.[46]

In light of the Canadian Corps' successful capture of Vimy Ridge and the three-and-a-half-mile advance of XVII Corps, the official historian wrote that 'Easter Monday of the year 1917 must be accounted from the British point of view one of the great days of the War'.[47] Indeed, in a letter to his wife the following day, Edmund Allenby described the operation as having 'worked like clockwork'.[48] However, as Cuthbert Headlam, then a staff officer in VIII Corps, which was located farther north in the Ypres Salient, informed his wife on 9 April: 'All these battles are so much alike... So far the news has been very satisfactory, but it always is the first go off. The worry and disappointment begin later when the Boch begins to find his feet again'.[49] By 11 April, just as Headlam predicted, the Germans had done exactly that. There was to be no breakthrough at Arras and the battle degenerated into yet another attritional slogging match.[50] In endeavouring to account for both the successes of the opening day and the failures thereafter, how did the BEF's communications system fare during the battle?

First, the events of 9 April demonstrated that the amount of time and energy expended on the construction of the deep-buried cable

[44] Falls, *Military Operations, 1917*, Vol. 1, 194.
[45] '15th Division Instruction No. 3. General Instructions for Forward Communications', 16 March 1917, Dill Papers 1/4, LHCMA; '30th Division Operation Order No. 70 by Major General J. S. M. Shea', 5 April 1917, 30 Division War Diary, WO95/2311, TNA.
[46] '30th Division Operation Order No. 70 by Major General J. S. M. Shea', 5 April 1917, 30 Division War Diary, WO95/2311, TNA; 'Proposed Draft of Appendix on Signalling for Operation Orders', 12 February 1917, Correspondence and Papers of 2 Division Signal Company in WW1, 1915–18, A231.52, REMA.
[47] Falls, *Military Operations, 1917*, Vol. 1, 201.
[48] General Sir Edmund Allenby to his wife, 10 April 1917, Field Marshal Viscount Allenby Papers 1/8/2, LHCMA.
[49] Letter to Beatrice, 9 April 1917, in Beach (ed.), *The Military Papers of Lieutenant-Colonel Sir Cuthbert Headlam*, 162.
[50] Jonathan Nicholls, *Cheerful Sacrifice: The Battle of Arras 1917* (London: Leo Cooper, 1993), 135–208.

system had been justified. According to the war diary of VI Corps Signal Company, 'not a single circuit was interrupted by enemy fire. Reports came through without intermission and telephone lines were pushed forward successfully everywhere'.[51] The diaries and post-action reports of nearly all the attacking divisions in Third Army further testify to the success of telephonic and telegraphic communication right down to battalion headquarters.[52] The reports from the Canadian divisions at Vimy Ridge also highlighted that 'cable was never cut, no difficulty in maintenance was experienced and communication was never interrupted'.[53] That forward cable communications remained largely intact owed much to the new German defence-in-depth system and to the British set-piece method of attack,[54] the combination of which resulted in a lull in operations which provided signal companies with a brief period in which 'enemy retaliation was feeble and overground lines could be laid and maintained with a fair degree of ease and certainty'.[55] As a report by 34 Division Signal Company noted, the successful maintenance of forward lines 'was no doubt to a large extent due to lack of the enemy's artillery fire'. Furthermore, the limited objectives allotted to the division ensured that the extension of the system into the captured German trenches was made a lot easier, since 'it did not require any

---

[51] VI Corps Signal Company War Diary, 9 April 1917, WO95/793, TNA.

[52] 30 Division Signal Company War Diary, 9 April 1917, WO95/1824, 34 Division Signal Company War Diary, 9 April 1917, WO95/2450, 51 Division Signal Company War Diary, 9 April 1917, WO95/2856, 'Operations of 12th Division from 8th to 13th April, 1917', 20 April 1917, 12 Division War Diary, WO95/1824, 'Notes on Communications during the Recent Offensive 9th–13th April 1917', undated, 14 Division Signal Company War Diary, WO95/1890, TNA.

[53] 'Report on Communications. 3rd Canadian Division. April 9th–May 9th (Vimy Ridge)', 31 May 1917, 3 Canadian Division Signal Company War Diary, WO95/3858, TNA. See also: 'Communications. 4th Canadian Division, March 5th to May 5th, 1917', undated, 4 Canadian Division Signal Company War Diary, WO95/3891, TNA; 'Report on Operations Carried Out by the 1st Canadian Division. April 9th–May 5th 1917', June 1917, Currie Papers, MG30, E100/35/160, LAC.

[54] With regards to the former, in February and March 1917 the Germans had carried out a dramatic withdrawal along a major portion of the Western Front to a newly constructed defensive position, known to the British as the Hindenburg Line. This position was essentially a series of defensive zones rather than a single line, incorporating the principles of flexible defence in depth. A major feature of this system was that the forward defensive zone was lightly held and as such, it could be comparatively easily overrun. However, before assaulting the main defensive position to the rear of this forward zone, the attacker was forced to take a respite in order to consolidate and move forward a considerable portion of artillery ready for the next stage of the attack. At the same time, the Germans were also forced to move their forward artillery to new positions. For a more detailed description of the German defence in depth system, see Samuels, *Command or Control?*, 158–97.

[55] Priestley, *Work of the Royal Engineers*, 174.

great quantity of cable to extend the two pairs of lines originally in use between Division and Brigades to the new Headquarters selected by the Infantry Brigades'.[56]

It must also be noted that in contrast to 1 July 1916, the counter-battery work of the artillery at Arras was much more successful in silencing the enemy guns.[57] As the Canadian Corps commander, Lieutenant-General Sir Julian Byng, noted after the battle, the lack of heavy enemy shelling during the early stages of the attack 'testified to the effectiveness of our artillery preparations and support, to the precision of our counter-battery work and to the well timed and skilful manoeuvre of our troops'.[58] As a result, telephone and telegraph lines remained largely unbroken, enabling the fast and efficient passage of information up and down the chain of command.[59] In 34 Division, for example, once the infantry had established themselves in the enemy's first line system, cable was 'run out by linemen down to a previously selected enemy's communication trench, from the Brigade forward station at the head of the bury... These lines were subsequently continued forward to each successive objective'. Furthermore, 'by a careful distribution of linemen along these cable routes with the Advancing Infantry, it was found possible to maintain practically continuous communication as far forward as the Brigade forward stations'.[60] Elsewhere, in 51 Division the buried system 'stood well and Battalion lines were kept through and pushed forward to advanced Batn. Hqrs. as these went forward'.[61] Likewise, on Vimy Ridge the superimposed cable laid by 3 Canadian Division was 'maintained

---

[56] 'Notes on Communications during Operations East of Arras', May 1917, 34 Division Signal Company War Diary, WO95/2450, TNA.

[57] This was due to a number of factors, such as the superior number of guns and ammunition available, the greater concentration of heavy guns per yard of opposing enemy trench and improvements in the range, accuracy and reliability of artillery pieces. See: Griffith, *Battle Tactics*, 85; Sheffield, *Forgotten Victory*, 191; and, Marble, 'The Infantry Cannot Do with a Gun Less'.

[58] 'Report on Operations of Canadian Corps against Vimy Ridge, April 1917', undated, Canadian Corps War Diary, WO95/1049, TNA. Field Marshal Sir Douglas Haig also recorded in his diary on 12 April the conversation he had with the First Army commander, General Sir Henry Horne, in which the latter stated that 'owing to the amount of artillery and ammunition now available, the frontal attack on a position had become... the easiest task. The difficult matter was to advance later on when the Enemy had organised a defence with machine guns'. See Haig Diary, 12 April 1917, WO256/17, TNA; Sheffield and Bourne (eds.), *Douglas Haig*, 281.

[59] Kelly, *Subaltern's Odyssey*, 153.

[60] 'Notes on Communications during Operations East of Arras', May 1917, 34 Division Signal Company War Diary, WO95/2450, TNA.

[61] 51 Division Signal Company War Diary, 10 April 1917, WO95/2856, TNA.

without any difficulty' and 'further extended on the night of April 9th/10th by a bury of 25 pairs... a distance of 350 yards'.[62]

Nevertheless, some units did experience communication difficulties on 9 April. According to Major-General Cecil Nicholson, GOC 34 Division, following a situation report from the 103rd Infantry Brigade at 10.45 a.m., 'the situation was obscure until about 9 p.m.'.[63] Elsewhere, although the 26th Infantry Brigade (9 Division) acknowledged that telephonic communication with the 8/Black Watch was excellent, in the case of the 7/Seaforth Highlanders, 'the line was cut at once and all communication the HQ of this battalion had, both with its companies and Brigade HQ, was by runner'.[64] Similarly, the failure of communications on the 11th Canadian Brigade's sector (4 Canadian Division) forced Brigadier-General Victor Odlum 'to go forward himself to see what was going on'.[65] It appears, though, that these were the notable exceptions to the successes experienced elsewhere that day. On the whole, cable communications during the initial attack at Arras were a lot more successful than had been the case during the opening day of the Battle of the Somme. The solution to maintaining this success in the days and weeks that followed, however, was to prove once again elusive.

The principal reason for the breakdown of communications after 9 April was the resurgence of German artillery.[66] As early as 10 April, 30 Division Signal Company recorded that its telephone lines to lateral divisions were becoming increasingly difficult to maintain because of the gradual intensification of the enemy's shellfire.[67] Similarly, two days later, the war diary of 12 Division Signal Company reveals that 'great difficulty was experienced in keeping through to adv. Bde. HQ', while on 14 April, 56 Division Signal Company noted its forward lines had been 'severely cut'.[68] By 21 April, Third Army acknowledged that 'the enemy's artillery fire has increased considerably on the VI and XVIII Corps

---

[62] 'Report on Communications. 3rd Canadian Division. April 9th–May 9th (Vimy Ridge)', 31 May 1917, 3 Canadian Division Signal Company War Diary, WO95/3858, TNA.

[63] Diary Entry, 9 April 1917, Major-General Sir Cecil Lothian Nicholson Papers 01/14/1, IWM.

[64] '26th Infantry Brigade Account of the Attack on April 9th 1917', 18 April 1917, 9 Division War Diary, WO95/1738, TNA.

[65] Rawling, 'Communications in the Canadian Corps', 14.

[66] For additional context on German defensive doctrine in 1917, see Robert T. Foley, 'The Other Side of the Wire: The German Army in 1917', in Dennis and Grey (eds.), *1917*, 155–78.

[67] 30 Division Signal Company War Diary, 10 April 1917, WO95/2323, TNA.

[68] 12 Division Signal Company War Diary, 12 April 1917, WO95/1841, 56 Division Signal Company War Diary, 14 April 1917, WO95/2942, TNA.

fronts'.[69] Subsequently, as 51 Division Signal Company reported, 'it was almost impossible to maintain lines from Brigades forward owing to the extreme violence of the enemy shelling and most of the communication was done with the aid of runners'.[70] One week later, Haldane acknowledged that 'since leaving the old trench systems it has been impossible to bury cable so as to ensure good communications'.[71] Indeed, telephonic and telegraphic communication was now 'entirely different from that of the 9th April'. With the whole of the divisional system beyond the buried cable network, communications had become 'more or less of a temporary nature, and not likely to last very long'.[72] As Guy Buckeridge, a sapper in 37 Division, recalled: 'Our 'phone lines rarely lasted more than a quarter-of-an-hour and finally we became too tired and wet to make more effort than would keep one line working forward and one back'.[73] In light of the difficulties of maintaining adequate cable communications after 9 April, to what extent did alternative means of communication alleviate the situation?

In view of the fact that cable communication remained practically intact during the opening day of the battle, numerous divisions reported that virtually no use was made of wireless whatsoever.[74] Nonetheless, as 56 Division Signal Company noted, wireless 'would have relieved pressure on telegraph lines had it been used'.[75] Indeed, the volume of traffic generated throughout the course of the battle was prodigious.[76] Yet, if the experience of 14 Division Signal Company was anything to go by, the

---

[69] 'Third Army No. G. 14/67', 21 April 1917, Third Army Summary of Operations, WO158/230, TNA.

[70] 51 Division Signal Company War Diary, 23 April 1917, WO95/2856, TNA.

[71] 'VI Corps No. G. X. 1/H/140', 30 April 1917, VI Corps War Diary, WO95/770, TNA.

[72] 'Notes on Communications during Operations East of Arras', May 1917, 34 Division Signal Company War Diary, WO95/2450, TNA.

[73] 'Memoirs of his Army Service in the Great War, 1914–18', 27, Buckeridge Papers, IWM.

[74] 'Notes on Communications during Operations East of Arras', May 1917, 34 Division Signal Company War Diary, WO95/2450, 'Report on Communications. 3rd Canadian Division. April 9th–May 9th (Vimy Ridge)', 31 May 1917, 3 Canadian Division Signal Company War Diary, WO95/3858, 'Communications. 4th Canadian Division, March 5th–May 5th, 1917', undated, 4 Canadian Division Signal Company War Diary, WO95/3891, TNA.

[75] 56 Division Signal Company War Diary, 9 April 1917, WO95/2942, TNA.

[76] On 9 April, a total of 4,776 messages – comprising 1,254 DRLS messages and 3,522 telegrams – were dealt with by VI Corps, while 2,385 telegrams and 857 DRLS messages passed through the signal office of XVII Corps. Throughout the remainder of the month, the average daily volume of telegraph traffic at XVII Corps signal office never dropped below 2,200. At the divisional level, 14 Division's signal office averaged 1,000 telegraph messages per day between 9 and 13 April, while at the brigade level the 4th, 5th and 6th Canadian Infantry Brigades handled a daily average of 195, 190 and 347 messages, respectively. See: 'April 1917 General Note', VI Corps Signal Company War Diary,

use of wireless to ease the burden of the cable network might not have
been so straightforward, since encrypting, transmitting and deciphering
the only wireless message sent on 9 April 'took 1 ½ hours to reach the
Divisional Signal Office from the Corps Station'.[77] Even after 9 April, it
was rare for units to rely upon wireless, though there were recorded
instances of its use. For example, on 15 April a BF Trench Set 'kept
communication alive' for the advanced headquarters of the 73rd Infantry
Brigade (24 Division) when all other means had failed.[78] On the whole,
however, despite its growing appeal, the tactical use of wireless at Arras
was still hindered by a combination of technical constraints, the length of
time taken to send and receive coded messages and the fact that sets were
still in rather short supply.[79]

Feedback regarding the newest method of communication tested at
Arras, the power buzzer, was not encouraging. First, its newness
meant there was a lack of experience on the part of the brigade and
battalion signallers, resulting in numerous operator errors which contributed to the inability to send and receive messages correctly.[80]
Second, as 2 Canadian Division Signal Company reported, power
buzzers 'failed to work on account of amplifiers being jammed by
earthed telephone circuits'.[81] Indeed, it was the conclusion of 1 Canadian Division Signal Company that 'this form of communication
would be more suitable for a raid than extensive operations, as earth
return circuits cause so much interference that reception is rendered
difficult'.[82] Third, and finally, difficulties were encountered in transporting the sets. According to 56 Division Signal Company, 'Power
Buzzers and Amplifiers [were] of no value as the amplifiers in the
forward rush when Battalion HQ moved got damaged'.[83] Similarly, a

WO95/793, 'Signal Chart, April 1917', XVII Corps Signal Company War Diary, WO95/
947, 'Notes on Communications during the Offensive 9th–13th April 1917', undated,
14 Division Signal Company War Diary, WO95/1890, 'Traffic Handled through 2nd
Canadian Divisional Report Centre Signal Office, April 1917', 2 Canadian Division
Signal Company War Diary, WO95/3804, TNA.

[77] 'Notes on Communications during the Offensive 9th–13th April 1917', undated,
14 Division Signal Company War Diary, WO95/1890, TNA.

[78] Schonland, 'W/T. R.E.', 178.   [79] Steel, 'Wireless Telegraphy', 458.

[80] 'Notes on Communications during Operations East of Arras', May 1917, 34 Division
Signal Company War Diary, WO95/2450, 'Notes on Communications during the
Offensive 9th–13th April 1917', undated, 14 Division Signal Company War Diary,
WO95/1890, TNA.

[81] 2 Canadian Division Signal Company War Diary, 9 April 1917, WO95/3804, TNA.

[82] 'Report on Communications. 1st Canadian Division. March 5th–May 5th, 1917',
15 November 1917, 1 Canadian Division Signal Company War Diary, WO95/
3751, TNA.

[83] 56 Division Signal Company War Diary, 9 April 1917, WO95/2942, TNA.

report by 34 Division Signal Company stressed that 'unless the weight attached to power buzzers and amplifiers in the shape of accumulators, etc. can be reduced, power buzzer communication will be unsatisfactory in anything like mobile warfare'.[84] Consequently, very little information was sent by power buzzers during the Battle of Arras, although the war diary of 3 Canadian Division Signal Company records that seven messages were received by brigade power buzzers on 10 April.[85] Furthermore, there was some cause for optimism, as a report by 14 Division Signal Company hinted: 'It may be concluded that this means of communication is not suited for work beyond the Trench System, but that within the limits of the Trenches it may prove invaluable, provided the personnel is thoroughly trained'.[86] When given the choice, however, most brigade and battalion commanders preferred to send information by runner rather than power buzzer.[87] Thus, it was the conclusion of one divisional signal officer that during an attack 'it would be well to drop them and concentrate all efforts on cable and visual work'.[88]

A similar situation befell visual communication in that 'had it not been for the fact that wire communication remained on the whole satisfactory, probably much more use would have been made' of it.[89] Visual was of much greater use, however, during the latter stages of the battle when cable communication was subject to continual disruption from the increasing weight of German artillery fire. As on the Somme the previous year, though, visual signalling was hindered to a great extent by the clouds of smoke, dirt and dust thrown up by the battle.[90] An added factor at Arras was the adverse weather conditions.[91] Snow, sleet and hail made it virtually impossible to follow the course of the battle via electric

[84] 'Notes on Communications during Operations East of Arras', May 1917, 34 Division Signal Company War Diary, WO95/2450, TNA.
[85] 3 Canadian Division Signal Company War Diary, 10 April 1917, WO95/3858, TNA.
[86] 'Notes on Communications during the Offensive 9th–13th April 1917', undated, 14 Division Signal Company War Diary, WO95/1890, TNA.
[87] 'Operations of 12th Division from 8th to 13th April, 1917', 20 April 1917, 12 Division War Diary, WO95/1824, 'Notes on Communications during Operations East of Arras', May 1917, 34 Division Signal Company War Diary, WO95/2450, TNA.
[88] Captain George Cline, OC 1st Canadian Division Signal Company, 1917–1918. 'Communications 1st Canadian Division. March 5th–May 5th, 1917', undated, RG9-III-C-5/4438/1/1, LAC.
[89] 'Notes on Communications during Operations East of Arras', May 1917, 34 Division Signal Company War Diary, WO95/2450, TNA.
[90] 'Report on Communications. 3rd Canadian Division. April 9th–May 9th (Vimy Ridge)', 31 May 1917, 3 Canadian Division Signal Company War Diary, WO95/3858, TNA.
[91] 'Operations of 12th Division from 8th to 13th April, 1917', 20 April 1917, 12 Division War Diary, WO95/1824, TNA.

lamps or flags; such was the experience of two signallers of 16/Manchesters, who were 'sent to Divisional HQ for duty on the visual post. They had a wonderful view of the Divisional front from their O.P., but the value of the station was ruined owing to bad visibility'.[92] Human error also played a role. In drawing attention to the system of liaison work carried out by contact aeroplanes, Haldane wrote to his divisional commanders on 13 April citing the 'frequent disregard' by infantry units to light their flares when called upon by the aerial observers to indicate their progress. Haldane made it quite clear just how vital the information provided by contact aeroplanes was, adding, 'If the orders on this subject are not carried out aeroplanes must fly low enough to distinguish the difference between the uniforms of our men and that of the enemy and many unnecessary casualties have been caused to Corps aeroplane squadrons for this reason'.[93]

A fairly negative picture also emerges with regards to the use of carrier pigeons. Because 'several birds homed to lofts which they had occupied many months ago', the report by 1 Canadian Division Signal Company concluded that pigeons were 'hardly worth the trouble expended in looking after them'.[94] Yet the most taxing issue arising from the battle was the time it took for the birds to reach the Corps Loft from the frontline and for the information contained within the message to filter down the chain of command. One report complained that 'the Lofts to which the pigeons returned were not in close enough touch with Divisions which they supplied; the message, on receipt at the Loft, having to be telephoned from there to the Corps, and thence transmitted to the Division'.[95] In 14 Division, 'the pigeons took an average time of 20 minutes to fly back to the Loft, and the messages an average time of 30 minutes from the Loft to the Brigade'.[96] Thus, it took almost an hour for information sent via a carrier pigeon from the frontline to be acted upon by the appropriate level of command. With this in mind, a process of decentralisation began shortly after Arras in which army and corps pigeon lofts were gradually moved forward and attached to divisions, thus helping

---

[92] 'The Signal Section of the 16th Manchesters', 35–6, MRA.

[93] 'GOC VI Corps to Divisional Commanders', 13 April 1917, VI Corps War Diary, WO95/770, TNA. For additional context, see Hooton, *War over the Trenches*, 126–59.

[94] 'Report on Communications. 1st Canadian Division. March 5th–May 5th, 1917', 15 November 1917, 1 Canadian Division Signal Company War Diary, WO95/3751, TNA.

[95] 'Notes on Communications during Operations East of Arras', May 1917, 34 Division Signal Company War Diary, WO95/2450, TNA.

[96] 'Notes on Communications during the Offensive 9th–13th April 1917', undated, 14 Division Signal Company War Diary, WO95/1890, TNA.

reduce the transmission time of messages,[97] a measure that proved popular and ultimately successful.[98]

In sum, communications on the opening day of the Battle of Arras 'proved highly successful',[99] largely on account of the ability of the artillery to neutralise the opposing enemy guns, but also because of the meticulous planning and preparations that had gone into the battle. Consequently, in contrast to 1 July 1916, communications were successfully maintained across 'no-man's-land' as the infantry advanced into the German forward defensive system. However, as the British advance became ever more sluggish over the course of the following days, so too did the system of communications. According to Shea, 'the importance of sending back definite information either positive or negative... was by no means satisfactory, and on many occasions when any information would have been of the highest value, no situation reports were rendered'.[100] The breakdown of this system had serious implications for infantry–artillery cooperation in particular, as a Third Army memorandum on 14 April highlighted: 'Different arms are not always cognisant of each other's position... Instances occurred of Artillery being afraid to open fire, owing to insufficient information regarding [the] position of advanced troops'.[101] The increasing intensity of German resistance after 9 April nullified the advantages afforded by the rather tenuous means of communication available to battalion signallers, with the upshot being that speedy and accurate information as to the progress of the battle became increasingly difficult to come by at brigade, divisional and corps headquarters. Thus, it was the conclusion of the commander of the 6th Canadian Infantry Brigade Signal Company, Lieutenant John Gennet, that 'nothing new in Brigade communications work has developed since the Somme operations, with the exception that this country lends itself better to visual signalling'.[102] Although some inroads had been made, clearly the BEF had much to learn in terms of perfecting communications in semi-open warfare.

---

[97] 'Re-Organisation of the Pigeon Service', 25 June 1917, AWM25/425/3, AWM; Priestley, *Work of the Royal Engineers*, 221–2.

[98] See, for example, 'Supplementary Report on Signal Communications during Offensive against the Messines-Wytschaete Ridge', 21 July 1917, 16 Division Signal Company War Diary, WO95/1966, TNA.

[99] VI Corps Signal Company War Diary, 9 April 1917, WO95/793, TNA.

[100] 'Lessons to Be Learnt from the Operations on the 23rd and 24th April', 25 April 1917, 30 Division War Diary, WO95/2311, TNA.

[101] 'Third Army No. G. 14/57', 14 April 1917, Third Army War Diary, WO95/362, TNA.

[102] 'Report on Communications. 2nd Canadian Division, April 1st–May 15th, 1917', 4 June 1917, 2 Canadian Division Signal Company War Diary, WO95/3804, TNA.

Messines

As the Battle of Arras was winding down, preparations were already underway for a major British offensive in Flanders, the Third Battle of Ypres, more commonly referred to as 'Passchendaele'. The prelude to this infamous campaign was the Battle of Messines, a limited, set-piece operation designed to secure the Messines-Wytschaete Ridge, which overlooked the southern flank of the Ypres Salient.[103] Launched on 7 June with the detonation of 19 underground mines and a meticulous artillery barrage, Messines was one of the BEF's most successful operations of the war and is cited by many historians as evidence of the improving tactical and technical sophistication of British fighting methods.[104] To what extent, though, did Second Army's triumph at Messines owe to better communications?

Preparations for the battle adhered strongly to the principles laid down in SS. 148. Telegraph and telephone lines were buried to a depth of six feet as far forward as battalion headquarters and in accordance with the 'grid' system employed previously at Arras.[105] Wireless sets were issued as far forward as advanced divisional headquarters and were employed between the heavy artillery and its FOOs for counter-battery fire,[106] while 'great reliance' was placed upon power buzzers and amplifiers for communications between divisions and brigade forward stations. Visual signalling, carrier pigeons and runners were also to supplement cable communications, most notably in the forward areas.[107] Much greater emphasis, however, was placed upon balloons and aeroplanes for aerial observation, counter-battery work and infantry contact patrol.[108] Similarly, Second Army detailed a much more thorough and extensive system of liaison officers than in

---

[103] Edmonds, *Military Operations, 1917*, Vol. 2, 32–6.

[104] Prior and Wilson, *Passchendaele*, 55–66; Passingham, *Pillars of Fire*; Brown, *British Logistics*, 162–5; Sheffield, *Forgotten Victory*, 199–204; Simpson, *Directing Operations*, 76–82.

[105] 'Report on Signal Communications during Recent Offensive Operations on IX Corps Front', undated, IX Corps Signal Company War Diary, WO95/845, TNA.

[106] 'Xth Corps Operation Order No. 83. Appendix IV. Signalling Arrangements', 18 May 1917, X Corps War Diary, WO95/852, TNA.

[107] 'Messines Offensive. Instruction No. 1. Signal Communications', 2 May 1917, New Zealand Division War Diary, WO95/3678, TNA; '70th Infantry Brigade Instructions No. 2', 2 June 1917, Military Histories (General) 914.2, RSMA.

[108] 'Xth Corps Instructions. Appendix IV (iii). Signalling to Balloons', 28 May 1917, X Corps War Diary, WO95/852, 'Report on Signal Communications during Recent Offensive Operations on IX Corps Front', undated, IX Corps Signal Company War Diary, WO95/845, TNA; Simpson, *Directing Operations*, 78.

Plate 6.1 Rehearsing signalling to contact aeroplanes for the attack on Messines, 1917 (Henry Armytage Sanders: Alexander Turnbull Library, Wellington, 1/2-013709-G)

any previous British offensive, operating at every level of command and between the infantry and artillery.[109]

At the heart of Second Army's communication preparations, however, was the establishment of a Forward Army Report Centre at Locre.[110] Haig had entertained General Sir Herbert Plumer's proposal for a report centre at an army commanders' conference on 19 May. Written confirmation of GHQ's endorsement was made five days later and work was started to provide the necessary communications for the centre on 28 May.[111] By 2 June, direct telegraph and telephone links had been

---

[109] 'Notes on Liaison Work', 26 May 1917, X Corps War Diary, WO95/852, 'Messines Offensive. Instruction No. 3. Liaison Officers', 3 May 1917, New Zealand Division War Diary, WO95/3678, '19th Divisional Artillery. No. B.M. 174/6. Lessons Learned from the Recent Operations', 15 June 1917, WO158/415, TNA. See also Geoffrey Powell, *Plumer: The Soldiers' General* (Barnsley: Pen and Sword, 2004), 157.

[110] Edmonds, *Military Operations, 1917*, Vol. 2, 43; General Sir Charles Harington, *Plumer of Messines* (London: John Murray, 1935), 101.

[111] 'Appendix III. Second Army G.22', 24 May 1917, WO158/305, TNA.

established not only between the report centre and Second Army head-quarters at Cassel, but also between the centre and the respective head-quarters of the attacking corps (IX, X and II ANZAC), RFC, heavy artillery and anti-aircraft.[112] The purpose of the report centre was:

(1) To enable information from all available sources of the Army to be obtained in the quickest possible manner; (2) To ensure that this information be classified and disseminated with the least delay to the formations to whom it would be most useful (including Army H.Q.); (3) To form a Clearing Station of Information from which the situation could be obtained at any time without interfering with the normal work of Corps or Army Staffs.

A Wireless Interception Section was added and a designated dropping zone for messages from contact aeroplanes established within close proximity to the centre.[113] Each corps also established a report centre of its own, which was connected to the army centre, on the one hand, and to their divisional headquarters, on the other.[114] Thus, the arrange-ments for communications at Messines not only were in keeping with the thorough and meticulous nature of Second Army's preparations as a whole, but were also a reflection of its general desire to learn from earlier practices.[115] In light of the experiences of the Somme and at Arras, Second Army was clearly well aware of the limitations of the BEF's communications system and so introduced a series of measures, some unique, designed to facilitate the rapid, smooth and secure flow of information once the battle commenced.

Indeed, a survey of unit war diaries and after-action reports suggests that 'the extra trouble taken in providing the necessary organisation for quickly disseminating information... seem[ed] to have been fully repaid'.[116] Almost everywhere on 7 June, cable communications during the first phase of the attack were pushed forward as quickly as possible with very few breaks or faults reported.[117] This owed a great deal to

---

[112] Second Army Signal Company War Diary, 28 May–2 June 1917, WO95/288, TNA.
[113] 'Second Army. Report on Army Centre. Battle of Messines, June 1917', 20 June 1917, WO158/305, TNA; Harington, *Plumer of Messines*, 101.
[114] The Report Centres of IX, X and II ANZAC Corps were established at Mont Noir, Reninghelst and Bailleul, respectively. See Edmonds, *Military Operations, 1917*, Vol. 2, 43; 'Second Army Offensive. Xth Corps Instructions. Appendix VII. Corps Advanced Intelligence Report Centre', 27 May 1917, X Corps War Diary, WO95/852, TNA.
[115] Simpson, *Directing Operations*, 80.
[116] 'Report on Signal Communications during Recent Offensive Operations on IX Corps Front', undated, IX Corps Signal Company War Diary, WO95/845, TNA.
[117] 'Report on Signal Communications in the Wytschaete Ridge Offensive', undated, 16 Division Signal Company War Diary, WO95/1966, '25th Divisional Operations MESSINES Ridge, 7 June 1917. Communications', undated, 25 Division Signal Company War Diary, WO95/2238, TNA; Everard Wyrall, *The History of the 19th Division 1914–1918* (London: Edward Arnold, 1932), 93.

the success of Second Army's counter-battery fire and the 'weak enemy barrage' that resulted.[118] Consequently, as a report by 3 Australian Division Signal Company observed, 'Communication throughout worked well, and so far as is ascertainable there was not a single hitch or delay in getting messages through quickly to their destination'.[119] It also meant that 'there was little need to have resource to alternative methods of communication'.[120] This was perhaps just as well because the dust and smoke thrown up by the exploded mines made visual signalling and aerial observation initially very difficult.[121]

Problems with communications began to occur in some sectors during the second phase of the attack, however, once the German frontline had been captured and the crest of the Messines-Wytschaete Ridge assaulted.[122] Both 16 and 23 Divisions (IX and X Corps, respectively) experienced difficulties in keeping in touch with some of their brigade forward stations.[123] In the case of the latter, the 69th Infantry Brigade's forward party 'was practically wiped out going forward', while the 70th Infantry Brigade's Forward Station functioned for just an hour until 'the dug-out was blown in and all the instruments destroyed'. According to a post-battle report: 'This failure was due to the parties attempting to get forward too soon. There does not appear to be any necessity for communications of so elaborate a nature to be pushed forward for about the first hour, provided some observation is possible'.[124] Elsewhere, the brigade forward stations of 41 Division (X Corps) 'worked well from an Infantry and Signal Coy. point of view', but not for the artillery who complained of insufficient telephone facilities for their FOOs.[125] Finally, Brigadier-General Hugh Bethell, GOC 74th Infantry Brigade (25 Division), 'hearing not a syllable' from his advancing battalions, was forced

---

[118] 'Notes on Second Army Offensive, 7 June 1917', undated, Director of Army Signals War Diary, WO95/57, TNA.

[119] 3 Australian Division Signal Company War Diary, 7 June 1917, WO95/3384, TNA.

[120] 'Report on Operations for the Capture of Messines-Wytschaete Ridge. IX Corps', 7 July 1917, WO158/415, TNA.

[121] 'Notes on Second Army Offensive, 7 June 1917', undated, Director of Army Signals War Diary, WO95/57, 'Xth Corps. 41st Div. G.55165/23', 20 June 1917, X Corps War Diary, WO95/852, '25th Divisional Operations MESSINES Ridge, 7 June 1917. Communications', undated, 25 Division Signal Company War Diary, WO95/2238, TNA; Edmonds, *Military Operations, 1917*, Vol. 2, 62; Bond and Robbins (eds.), *Staff Officer*, 156.

[122] Prior and Wilson, *Passchendaele*, 61–2.

[123] 'Report on Signal Communications in the Wytschaete Ridge Offensive', undated, 16 Division Signal Company War Diary, WO95/1966, TNA.

[124] 'Xth Corps. 23rd Divn. S.G.463/1', 18 June 1917, X Corps War Diary, WO95/852, TNA.

[125] 'Xth Corps. 41st Div. G.55165/23', 20 June 1917, X Corps War Diary, WO95/852, TNA.

to send his brigade-major, Walter Guinness, and a group of accompanying runners to find out what had happened.[126]

In spite of these incidents, the meticulous planning and preparations for the battle, combined with the limited objectives assigned to the attacking forces and the success of the counter-battery fire, made for a generally positive picture so far as communications were concerned.[127] Besides the widespread praise given to the system of liaison officers, who furnished commanders and staffs at all levels with timely and accurate information during the course of the battle,[128] the most noteworthy accomplishment at Messines was the performance of the army and corps report centres. The Army Forward Report Centre at Locre kept Second Army headquarters 'informed constantly and promptly of what was taking place, not only on the front, but far behind the enemy's lines', handling a total of 542 messages on 7 June alone.[129] Similarly, a US Army Staff College report in early 1918 noted that the 'Corps Information Centres' at Messines 'reduced [the] duplication of messages and the overloading of Signal Communications, and ensured that information received from all sources [was] summarised and forwarded as soon as possible to all concerned'.[130] In a letter to Archibald Montgomery, MGGS Fourth Army, Plumer's chief of staff, Tim Harington, acknowledged that although 'we got great value from it... we really only gave it a trial at very short notice and it is capable of much improvement'.[131] Fowler, however, was much more optimistic, circulating a memorandum to the other armies which stated that 'a similar system will be required in all future operations on a large scale, and it should be taken into account when planning communications'.[132] Copies of the Second Army report detailing the inner workings of the

---

[126] Having found 'the two advanced Battalions in their final objectives', Guinness 'scribbled a message and sent it back by runner to the General'. Bond and Robbins (eds.), *Staff Officer*, 156.

[127] Lieutenant-Colonel M. Kincaid-Smith, *The 25th Division in France and Flanders* (London: Harrison, 1920), 167; Alan H. Maude, *The 47th (London) Division 1914–1919* (London: Amalgamated Press, 1922), 101–2.

[128] '19th Divisional Artillery. No. B.M. 174/6. Lessons Learned from the Recent Operations', 15 June 1917, WO158/415, 'Xth Corps. 41st Div. G.55165/23', 20 June 1917, X Corps War Diary, WO95/852, TNA.

[129] 'Appendix II. Messages Received and Transmitted during June 7th – Battle of Messines', WO158/305, TNA (emphasis in original).

[130] 'A System in Use by a British Corps for Dealing with Reports', January 1918, AEF Staff College Files, RG120/362/1978, NARA.

[131] 'Harington to Montgomery', 6 July 1917, Montgomery-Massingberd Papers 7/35, LHCMA.

[132] 'Signal Notes No. 8', 15 June 1917, Director of Army Signals War Diary, WO95/57, TNA.

report centre were distributed throughout the BEF.[133] Not only did Second Army make use of the report centre again during its operations in late September, but it would appear that other formations also established similar systems later in the war.[134] Both Third Army and the Australian Corps, for instance, established 'Information Bureaus', based closely on the Messines model, to facilitate command and control during the Battles of Cambrai and Amiens, respectively.[135] In this respect, a case can certainly be made that Second Army's communications system at Messines had an important bearing upon the evolution of the BEF's communications system.

Third Ypres

Six weeks after the success of Messines, the long-awaited Flanders offensive began.[136] Despite thorough training and preparation, the initial attack by Fifth Army on 31 July yielded mixed results. The capture of the Pilckem Ridge on the left and centre of the British line was negated somewhat by the failure to secure the crucial Gheluvelt Plateau on the right.[137] In the unseasonably heavy rainfall that followed, Fifth Army attacked persistently throughout August, making painfully slow progress in atrocious conditions and at horrendous cost.[138] In late August, GHQ handed control of the campaign over to Second Army, who, after meticulous planning and preparation, and benefitting from a period of drier weather, launched a series of relatively successful 'bite and hold' operations in late September and early October that finally drove the Germans off the Gheluvelt Plateau.[139] However, the heavens opened up once more and in appalling conditions three further attacks gradually

---

[133] 'Second Army. Report on Army Centre. Battle of Messines, June 1917', 20 June 1917, Montgomery-Massingberd Papers 7/35, LHCMA; and, Currie Papers MG30, E100/35/160, LAC.

[134] Edmonds, *Military Operations, 1917*, Vol. 2, 248.

[135] 'Distribution of Duties during Operations', 15 November 1917, Cambrai Lessons, WO158/316, TNA; 'Battle Instructions No. 19. Liaison, etc.', 6 August 1918, Dill Papers 1/9, LHCMA.

[136] On the significance of this time delay, compare Prior and Wilson, *Passchendaele*, 49–50, 65–6, with Brown, *British Logistics*, 164.

[137] Prior and Wilson, *Passchendaele*, 86–96.

[138] John Hussey, 'The Flanders Battleground and the Weather in 1917', in Liddle (ed.), *Passchendaele in Perspective*, 140–58.

[139] Officially, these are known as the Battles of Menin Road Ridge (20–25 September), Polygon Wood (26 September–3 October) and Broodseinde (4 October). See Edmonds, *Military Operations, 1917*, Vol. 2, iii; and, Prior and Wilson, *Passchendaele*, 113–39.

inched the British line forward until the campaign was officially brought
to an end on 10 November following the capture of Passchendaele
village.[140] The communication dimension of this infamous campaign
has received rather modest coverage by historians,[141] which is surprising
since communications profoundly influenced the nature and outcome of
the fighting. As will be shown, this in turn forced the BEF to make some
revisions to its communications doctrine.

One of the chief lessons to emerge from the experience of Third
Ypres was the necessity for better camouflage and ever-greater protection for buried cables.[142] A report by Fifth Army Signal Company
in early August noted that 'the enemy is paying very much more
attention to the destruction of cable routes than formerly and has
seriously interfered with digging parties with gas shell'. It had transpired from captured German maps that the majority of these routes
had been plotted from aerial observation. The report recommended
that 'as much use as possible should be made of existing natural
ditches and cover generally, thereby to a great extent escaping the
notice of the enemy'.[143] Evidently, the Germans were well aware of
the importance of communications to the success of the BEF's operations and thus the need to deny them the means of exercising
effective command and control became a top priority. Subsequent
reports from British units confirmed that the Germans were deliberately shelling cable routes and targeting labour parties undertaking
construction work mainly at night.[144] As a result, not only did the
digging parties incur heavy casualties, but sections of the buried
routes remained incomplete, exposed and vulnerable.[145] The conse-
quences of this were twofold.

First, as a report by 51 Division Signal Company in late September
put it, 'where no buried cables exist no amount of foresight will

---

[140] Known as the Battles of Poelcappelle (9 October), First Passchendaele (12
October) and Second Passchendaele (26 October–10 November), respectively.
See Edmonds, *Military Operations, 1917*, Vol. 2, iii; and, Prior and Wilson,
Passchendaele, 159–81.

[141] See, for example, John Lee, 'Command and Control in Battle: British Divisions on the
Menin Road Ridge, 20 September 1917', in Sheffield and Dan Todman (eds.),
Command and Control, 119–39; and, Simpson, *Directing Operations*, 87–113.

[142] Priestley, *Work of the Royal Engineers*, 198.

[143] 'Buried Cables', 4 August 1917, Fifth Army Signal Company War Diary, WO95/
534, TNA.

[144] See, for example, '11th Division. Report on Operations, 8th to 30th August, 1917',
undated, 11 Division War Diary, WO95/1789, TNA.

[145] Priestley, *Work of the Royal Engineers*, 198–9.

ensure telephone speech through a barrage'.[146] This was certainly
the case beyond the buried cable heads, where telephone lines were
laid along the ground, on short poles or stakes or in shallow trenches
and ditches. According to Lionel Harris, in the Westhoek sector in
September it was 'quite impossible. . . to do more than make a ditch
in which to place our cable. Layers of sandbags were built up over
the length concerned to give added protection'.[147] As the campaign
wore on, it became almost standard practice amongst forward signal
units to lay their lines from captured pill-box to pill-box, establishing
test-boxes inside in order to check for faults.[148] Time and again,
however, war diaries and after-action reports testify to the 'endless
trouble' caused by partially buried and unburied cables;[149] to
lines being 'absolutely obliterated by the enemy barrage';[150] and to
a form of communication that was 'ineffective beyond Battalion
Headquarters'.[151] During heavy shelling at Menin Road, the 16/Man-
chesters' telephone lines were likened to 'a spider's web after a big blue-
bottle had torn its way through it'.[152] However, 18 Division found that
even when cables were buried to the recommended depth, 'six feet of
earth cover was not enough to protect them from the tons of metal that
lashed and tore up the dismal stretch of land east of Zillebeke Lake'.[153]
Therefore, since 'enemy shelling was too great to allow of circuits to
Bde. Forward Stations being buried as laid down in SS. 148',[154] the
Director of Army Signals acknowledged that the existing principles
regarding cable communication required some modification.[155] The
revised doctrine, reissued in November as SS. 191. Intercommunication
in the Field, incorporated the technical developments and battlefield
experiences of 1917, making for a more wide-ranging and less-dogmatic

---

[146] 'Report on Communications East of YSER CANAL during the Attack of the 20th
Sept., 1917', 28 September 1917, 51 Division Signal Company War Diary, WO95/
2856, TNA.
[147] Harris, Signal Venture, 41.
[148] Ibid., 40; 'Buried Cable – Test Points', 26 October 1917, RG9-III-C-5/4440/1/6, LAC.
[149] 'Signal Notes No. 14, Dated 19th November, 1917', RG9-III-C-5/4443/7/6, LAC.
[150] 'Report on Operations Carried Out by 2nd Canadian Infantry Brigade against Hill 70.
August 1917', undated, Currie Papers, MG 30, E100/35/161, LAC.
[151] '49th Canadian Battalion Report on the Operations between the Nights October 28/
29th and October 31/November 1st', 4 November 1917, Currie Papers, MG30, E100/
36/162, LAC.
[152] 'Signal Section of the 16th Manchesters', 40, MRA.
[153] Nichols, 18th Division, 203.
[154] 'Notes on SS. 148', 15 August 1917, Fifth Army Signal Company War Diary, WO95/
534, TNA.
[155] 'Signal Notes No. 14. Notes on Second Army Operations of October 1917',
19 November 1917, Director of Army Signals War Diary, WO95/57, TNA.

set of principles which could be adapted by signal officers to suit local conditions and individual circumstances.[156]

A second consequence of the vulnerability of cable communications at Third Ypres was the necessity to rely more than ever upon alternatives. Yet, heavy and persistent enemy shelling, adverse weather and poor terrain made it almost impossible for the BEF to derive any benefits from them.[157] For instance, in spite of the emphasis that had been placed upon them, wireless and power buzzers proved very disappointing for a number of reasons. The first of these was attributed to poor training and inexperienced personnel.[158] Heavy casualties amongst veteran signallers meant that many new operators were not given enough time to adjust to the realities of the conditions they now faced.[159] It was found that unless the operators were sufficiently trained and thoroughly acquainted with their instruments there was 'little prospect of success'.[160] A second explanation for the poor showing of wireless and power buzzers were the limitations imposed by deteriorating weather conditions and unfavourable terrain. Power buzzers, in particular, could not be used effectively because of the shell-torn, uneven and swampy ground, which impeded the transmission of ground signals.[161] It took on average 40 minutes for power buzzer messages to reach brigade headquarters from battalions on 20 September, for example.[162] Third, and finally, the nature of the fighting that transpired at Third Ypres made wireless and power buzzer communication very difficult. The Canadian Corps found it 'impossible for the Brigade BF [wireless] sets to work, as dug-out and pill-box accommodation was too limited and it was quite impossible to keep up aerials in the forward

[156] *SS. 191. Intercommunication in the Field*; Priestley, *Work of the Royal Engineers*, 182.

[157] 'Conference Held at XVIIIth Corps Headquarters', 5 August 1917, 11 Division War Diary, WO95/1789, TNA.

[158] 'Signal Notes No. 15, Dated 21st December, 1917', RG9-III-C-5/4443/7/6, LAC; 'Notes on Conference at Division H.Q. on 2nd September 1917', 3 September 1917, 11 Division War Diary, WO95/1789, TNA.

[159] 'Notes on SS. 148', 15 August 1917, Fifth Army Signal Company War Diary, WO95/534, '148th Bde. G.609', 13 October 1917, 49 Division War Diary, WO95/2768, TNA; '74th Infantry Brigade. Operations 10th, 11th August, 1917', undated, Montgomery-Massingberd Papers 7/35, LHCMA.

[160] 'Signal Notes No. 14, Dated 19th November, 1917', RG9-III-C-5/4443/7/6, LAC.

[161] '11th Division. Report on Operations, 8th to 30th August, 1917', undated, 11 Division War Diary, WO95/1789, TNA; '10th Canadian Infantry Brigade. Report on Operations in the Passchendaele Sector, October 21st to 28th, 1917', 1 November 1917, Currie Papers, MG30, E100/36/162, LAC.

[162] 'Report on Communications East of YSER CANAL during the Attack of the 20th Sept., 1917', 28 September 1917, 51 Division Signal Company War Diary, WO95/2856, TNA.

areas'. The Corps' Directing Station just north of Zonnebeke village, meanwhile, was repeatedly destroyed; it became 'very evident that the enemy was ranging the station by means of a compass set. Whenever the station began sending, the enemy started to shell'.[163] The concussion and vibration caused by heavy shelling also damaged power buzzer valves and amplifier bases,[164] while wireless operators experienced great difficulties from jamming 'owing to the number of stations, both our own and those of the enemy, which [were] crowded into a small area'.[165] Thus, it was the conclusion of a report by 20 Division in late August that 'no attempt should be made to rely directly on these two methods'.[166]

Paradoxically, however, it was with wireless that the BEF made its most important communication development of the campaign. Following the successful use of continuous wave (CW) wireless sets in August to help register the artillery at Hill 70,[167] in October a CW set was employed between a counter-battery observation post and a corps head-quarters, 17 miles apart, generating signals that were 'practically uninter-rupted'.[168] A further experiment, conducted by the Canadian Corps 'in the thick of the fighting' on 7 November,[169] tested the speed of CW wireless against a carrier pigeon. In the event, the wireless message 'was received at C.C.H.A. within 5 minutes of the time it was handed in, in fact, before the pigeon had left the roof of the Pill Box'. Collectively, these successes 'had quite a favourable effect on the general feeling throughout the Army, about the practicability of CW',[170] compelling the high command to place an order for 882 CW sets in December.[171] According to one wireless officer, the use of CW wireless at Third Ypres

---

[163] 'General Report on Wireless Telegraph Communication in the Canadian Corps, Feb. 1915–Dec. 1918', 16 April 1919, RG9-III-D-3/5058/968, LAC.

[164] 'Report on Capture of Hill 70 by 1st Canadian Division. 15th Aug. 1917', undated, Currie Papers, MG30, E100/36/164, LAC; '11th Division. Report on Operations, 8th to 30th August, 1917', undated, 11 Division War Diary, WO95/1789, TNA; '74th Infantry Brigade. Operations 10th, 11th August, 1917', undated, Montgomery-Massingberd Papers 7/35, LHCMA.

[165] 'Signal Notes No. 14, Dated 19th November, 1917', RG9-III-C-5/4443/7/6, LAC.

[166] 'Lessons Learnt from the Recent Operations', 25 August 1917, 20 Division War Diary, WO95/2097, TNA.

[167] Bidwell and Graham, Fire-Power, 142.

[168] 'Signal Notes No. 14. Notes on Second Army Operations of October 1917', 19 November 1917, Director of Army Signals War Diary, WO95/57, TNA.

[169] Moir, History of the Royal Canadian Corps of Signals, 29.

[170] 'General Report on Wireless Telegraph Communication in the Canadian Corps, Feb. 1915–Dec. 1918', 16 April 1919, RG9-III-D-3/5058/968, LAC.

[171] Priestley, Work of the Royal Engineers, 227.

represented 'the turning point in the story of wireless in France, not only in the Canadian Corps but throughout the British Army'.[172]

The same, however, could not be said of visual signalling and aerial observation. On 31 July, poor visibility and the fact that some infantry either forgot, or were too preoccupied, to signal their positions at the designated times, nullified the usefulness of contact aeroplanes.[173] On the ground, while there were many instances when the Lucas daylight signalling lamp proved its value,[174] on the whole smoke, mist and heavy shelling rendered visual signalling a difficult and hazardous undertaking.[175] It was a situation carrier pigeons could do little to ameliorate, with some birds taking between 50 and 60 minutes to fly from the frontline to their lofts.[176] All too often, therefore, it was left to runners to form the sole means of communication beyond brigade headquarters.[177] However, casualties were understandably heavy.[178] As John Lucy related, 'no runner could come through the storm of steel that broke all day to a depth of almost a mile backwards from the front line'.[179] The combination of heavy casualties and runners 'losing their way' led to relay systems' frequently breaking down, 'resulting in unnecessary delay in the transmission of messages'.[180] On 31 July, for example, runners of some of the advancing units in XIX Corps took between one and two hours alone to reach the cable heads in the original front line.[181]

---

[172] Steel, 'Wireless Telegraphy', 462.

[173] Edmonds, *Military Operations, 1917*, Vol. 2, 169; Hooton, *War over the Trenches*, 182.

[174] 'Signal Notes No. 14, Dated 19th November, 1917', RG9-III-C-5/4443/7/6, LAC; MacDonald, *Gun-Fire*, 70.

[175] '11th Division. Report on Operations, 8th to 30th August, 1917', undated, 11 Division War Diary, WO95/1789, TNA; '49th Canadian Battalion Report on the Operations between the Nights October 28/29th and October 31/November 1st', 4 November 1917, Currie Papers, MG30, E100/36/162, LAC; 'Second Army. Comments on Operations, 20 Sept., 1917', 28 September 1917, Montgomery-Massingberd Papers 7/35, LHCMA.

[176] 'Report on Operations Carried out by 2nd Canadian Infantry Brigade against Hill 70. August 1917', undated, Currie Papers, MG30, E100/35/161, LAC; 'Report on Communications East of YSER CANAL during the Attack of the 20th Sept., 1917', 28 September 1917, 51 Division Signal Company War Diary, WO95/2856, TNA.

[177] '49th Canadian Battalion Report on the Operations between the Nights October 28/29th and October 31/November 1st', 4 November 1917, Currie Papers, MG30, E100/36/162, LAC

[178] '10th Canadian Infantry Brigade. Report on Operations in the Passchendaele Sector, October 21st to 28th, 1917', 1 November 1917, Currie Papers, MG30, E100/36/162, LAC; Richards, *Old Soldiers*, 253.

[179] Lucy, *There's a Devil*, 369.

[180] '148th Bde. G.609', 13 October 1917, 49 Division War Diary, WO95/2768, TNA.

[181] Edmonds, *Military Operations, 1917*, Vol. 2, 169.

Plate 6.2 Signaller on a German dugout, Gallipoli Farm, Belgium, 12 October 1917 (Henry Armytage Sanders: Alexander Turnbull Library, Wellington, 1/2-012945-G)

According to both Major-General Albemarie Cator, GOC 58 Division, and Major-General Henry Lukin, GOC 9 Division, communications during the latter stages of the Third Ypres campaign were the worst that they had experienced during the war.[182] The 10th Canadian Infantry Brigade, for instance, reported that during late October information from the frontline was taking as much as three hours to reach brigade headquarters.[183] Yet, the precarious state of communications had had a profound effect upon command and control from the very outset of the campaign. Perhaps most notably, on 31 July a message from a FOO with 45th Infantry Brigade, sent at 11:30 am, warning of German counterattack troops massing behind the Broodseinde-Passchendaele Ridge, did not reach 15 Division headquarters until 12:53 pm. To compound matters, by 1 pm heavy rain had begun to fall. Consequently,

---

[182] Prior and Wilson, *Passchendaele*, 168, 176–7.
[183] '10th Canadian Infantry Brigade. Report on Operations in the Passchendaele Sector, October 21st to 28th, 1917', 1 November 1917, Currie Papers, MG30, E100/36/162, LAC.

'the supporting artillery did not yet know the exact line which had been gained, forward artillery observers lost touch with the batteries, and observers along the second objective could no longer see what was happening ahead'.[184] With no means to call for assistance, the resulting German counterattack forced the leading infantry of 15, 55 and 39 Divisions in the centre of the British line to withdraw from positions that had put them within touching distance of the German third line.[185]

Thus, from the very beginning of the campaign communications acted not only as a 'pipeline', conveying crucial information up and down the chain of command, and between neighbouring and supporting units, but also as a 'lifeline', providing a means of salvation for units that were exposed, vulnerable or isolated.[186] In assessing both of these functions, however, it is clear that the BEF's communications system throughout Third Ypres was woefully inadequate, exacerbating problems with maintaining efficient command and control. Although it had reached a highly developed state, by the second half of 1917 the BEF's communications system was still unable to support operations aimed at securing grandiose objectives in atrocious weather conditions and on unfavourable terrain. This would seem to support Robin Prior and Trevor Wilson's overall judgement that by July 1917 the BEF had both the experience and the methods capable of producing successful results, but only in operations with 'suitably limited objectives'.[187]

Cambrai

The BEF's final undertaking of the year was at Cambrai and a battle that marked a significant departure from the operations that had preceded it. While Messines and Second Army's operations in late September demonstrated the BEF's mastery of the set-piece assault, Cambrai heralded methods which were, in J. F. C. Fuller's words, 'destined to revolutionise the entire theory and practice of land warfare'.[188] The mass use of tanks and, more importantly, the silent registration of the artillery, which allowed the element of surprise to return to the battlefield, not only foreshadowed some of the war-winning techniques employed by the

---

[184] Edmonds, *Military Operations, 1917*, Vol. 2, 170.
[185] Prior and Wilson, *Passchendaele*, 94.
[186] I owe these analogies to Brigadier Philip Pratley, 'Lifeline, Pipeline and Occasional Noose? How the British Army's Communicators Looked Back on World War II', *Mars & Clio*, 22 (Summer 2008), 38–42.
[187] Prior and Wilson, *Passchendaele*, 197.
[188] Major-General J. F. C. Fuller, *Memoirs of an Unconventional Soldier* (London: Ivor Nicholson and Watson, 1936), 169.

BEF in August–November 1918, but also prefigured elements of the initial German campaigns of the Second World War.[189] The object of the Cambrai operation, according to Haig, was 'to break through the enemy's defences by <u>surprise</u> and so to permit the Cavalry Corps to pass through and operate in open country'.[190] As the instructions issued by Lieutenant-General Sir William Pulteney, GOC III Corps, to his divisional commanders stressed: '<u>Secrecy</u> is essential for success, and the most careful precautions regarding it must be taken'.[191] What, therefore, did this entail for communications?

First, a communication 'black-out' was enforced with regards to the use of telephone and telegraph instruments within 3,500 yards of the enemy frontline. This zone was to be 'kept distinct from the remainder and was not used or connected to the back part of the system until Zero hour'.[192] There was to be 'no discussion of the operations or preparations in connection therewith, over the telephone, and all telegrams in any way connected with the movement of troops in connection with the operations [were to] be in code'.[193] All newly arriving infantry brigades were to have 'no communication of any sort by wire before Zero', instead relying solely upon runners. However, in the case of those brigades which already occupied headquarters recently vacated by battalions, cable communication was permitted but only through the use of Fullerphones working towards the rear on the lines of the original system.[194]

Second, and more significantly, since surprise was the essence of the offensive, the digging of trenches for an extensive deep-buried cable network, which had formed the backbone of the BEF's communication system since the Somme, was completely out of the question.[195] In light of the experiences at Third Ypres, any attempt to

---

[189] Marble, 'The Infantry Cannot Do with a Gun Less'; Bailey, *First World War*, 41–2; Travers, *How the War Was Won*, 19–31; Hammond, *Cambrai 1917*. Cambrai is also significant in that the German counterattack on 30 November prefigured the tactics that gave the German Army considerable success during the spring offensives of 1918. See Samuels, *Command or Control?* 230–69.

[190] Haig Diary, 13 November 1917, WO256/24, TNA; Sheffield and Bourne (eds.), *Douglas Haig*, 341–2 (emphasis in original).

[191] 'III Corps Operations. Instruction No. 1', 10 November 1917, III Corps War Diary, WO95/677, TNA (emphasis in original).

[192] 'Lessons Learnt from Recent Operations by the Third Army (November 20th to December 6th, 1917)', undated, Third Army Headquarters, Cambrai Lessons, WO158/316, TNA.

[193] 'III Corps Operations. Instruction No. 3', 11 November 1917, III Corps War Diary, WO95/677, TNA.

[194] 'Third Army No. G.S. 56/17 (a)', 15 November 1917, Third Army Headquarters, Cambrai Lessons, WO158/316, TNA (emphasis in original).

[195] 'Third Army No. G.S. 56/17', 31 October 1917, Third Army Signal Company War Diary, WO95/408, TNA.

construct a deep-buried cable network at Cambrai would not only put the lives of the digging parties in jeopardy but, more importantly, betray the element of surprise. Instead, a main cable route was still provided in each divisional sector up to the frontline, but it was to consist of armoured multi-core cables laid on the ground in the forward area and lead-covered cables slung on poles to the rear.[196]

However, the maintenance of such a system presented an array of difficulties. With regards to the cables laid along the ground in the forward area, suitable cover and camouflage became a necessity. Prior to 20 November, ditches, hedges and existing trenches were all used to provide natural camouflage for ground cables. Although these precautions added greatly to the general secrecy of the operation, the ground cables were left highly vulnerable to routine German shelling. Indeed, at the end of October, Third Army had forewarned that

under these conditions it is obvious that the telephone and telegraph communications will be much less secure than is usually the case in offensive operations, and the difficulty of maintaining them will be so great that the number of circuits provided must be kept to an absolute minimum in order that the efforts of the Signal Service may be concentrated on the maintenance of those circuits which are essential to success.[197]

In the days leading up to the offensive, many of the ground cables in the forward area were cut by enemy shellfire, with the consequence that 'the men who were actually on maintenance of the lines had to be kept working on construction and repairs up to the last moment'.[198] Nevertheless, a post-battle report concluded that, on the whole, the measures introduced prior to 20 November had been most successful and 'the proportion of circuits which were found to be faulty when joined through at Zero was surprisingly small'.[199]

Difficulties were also experienced in the maintenance of the poled cable routes in the rear area. The chief problem here was the damage caused by tanks as they made their way to and from their hiding places and assembly positions.[200] Tanks crushed poles and ripped apart the

[196] Ibid., 'III Corps Operations. Instruction No. 7. Communications', 14 November 1917, III Corps War Diary, WO95/677, TNA; Priestley, *Work of the Royal Engineers*, 232–3.

[197] 'Third Army No. G.S. 56/17', 31 October 1917, Third Army Signal Company War Diary, WO95/408, TNA.

[198] 'Cambrai, Havrincourt-Bourlon Wood Operations, IV Corps Report on Telephone and Telegraph Communications, 20th November–1st December 1917', undated, WO158/383, TNA.

[199] 'Lessons Learnt from Recent Operations by the Third Army (November 20th to December 6th, 1917)', undated, Third Army Headquarters, Cambrai Lessons, WO158/316, TNA.

[200] Hall, 'The Development of Tank Communications', 152–3.

cable, making speech along telephone lines inaudible and Morse code extremely difficult over telegraph lines. In an attempt to remedy this predicament, special crossing places, where tank paths intersected cable routes, were constructed using poles to lift the lines 15 feet off the ground in order for tanks to pass safely underneath them. Tanks fitted with fascines for clearing the wide trenches of the Hindenburg defences required a larger clearance of 20 feet.[201] Unfortunately, labour constraints meant that not enough of these crossings were built. Moreover, many tank units were simply not provided with information from the Signal Service pertaining to the exact location of these crossings. Consequently, one of the principal lessons to emerge from Cambrai was the necessity for much closer liaison between the Signal Service and the Tank Corps in future operations.[202]

Overall, in less than a month Third Army managed to lay 13,000 miles of wire for the upcoming battle.[203] Despite the difficulties imposed by the novel characteristics of the preparation phase, much of the cable system was laid successfully in accordance with the principles advocated in *SS. 191*. The major difference, of course, was the absence of an extensive deep-buried network like those constructed prior to the Battles of the Somme and Arras. However, some divisions were fortunate enough to occupy fronts where a deep-buried cable network already existed. For example, 51 Division, commanded by Major-General (George) Montague Harper, found that by 'using this as the backbone of the system... all necessary communications were provided by Zero [hour]'.[204] In most cases, however, the attacking divisions at Cambrai had to rely upon a system of ground and poled cables. Subsequently, as Major-General William Douglas Smith, GOC 20 Division, instructed his brigade commanders: 'It is therefore essential for commanders to realise that it is impossible for the telephone system to be maintained in the event of heavy hostile shelling behind our lines, and therefore the

[201] 'Lessons Learnt from Recent Operations by the Third Army (November 20th to December 6th, 1917)', undated, Third Army Headquarters, Cambrai Lessons, WO158/316, TNA.

[202] 'Cambrai, Havrincourt-Bourlon Wood Operations, IV Corps Report on Telephone and Telegraph Communications, 20th November–1st December 1917', undated, WO158/383, TNA.

[203] Priestley, *Work of the Royal Engineers*, 233. At the divisional level, for example, 20 Division Signal Company laid 137 miles of armoured cable to various subordinate headquarters before 20 November. See Captain V. E. Inglefield, *The History of the Twentieth (Light) Division* (London: Nisbet, 1921), 180.

[204] '51st (H) Divisional Signal Co. R.E. Report on Communications Between TRESCAULT and FONTAINE during Operations of 20th–24th November 1917', 30 November 1917, 51 Division Signal Company War Diary, WO95/2856, TNA.

arrangements for using wireless, pigeons, visual and runners must be fully understood by all concerned and taken full advantage of.[205] In other words, given the nature of the operation, a much greater reliance was to be placed upon alternative means of communication for the rapid conveyance of orders, reports and other vital information than in any battle the BEF had previously undertaken.

The means of alternative communication available for Cambrai remained much the same as those employed during Third Ypres. In terms of wireless, as well as Army and Corps Directing Stations, Pack Sets for the Cavalry Corps and BF Trench Sets for the infantry divisions and brigades, wireless tanks were also made available to each division. Indeed, of the 476 tanks massed at Cambrai, 9 were fitted with wireless (one per tank battalion) and one carried telephone cable.[206] The wireless tanks could be used by tank, infantry and artillery units, carrying converted Wilson spark transmitters and Mark III receivers, which were to be offloaded and assembled at predetermined sites.[207] However, as a report by the 1st Tank Brigade later noted, 'the sets for these operations were only makeshift and exceedingly clumsy, especially in view of the fact that they were taken in Fighting Tanks'.[208] Furthermore, with so many wireless sets operating within close proximity of each other, Third Army's 'Technical Wireless Instructions', issued on 11 November, warned that a certain amount of interference was going to be inevitable. In an attempt to reduce some of this interference, commanders were cautioned against the 'useless exchange of signals' and wireless operators explicitly told to adhere at all times to the 'correct wireless procedure'.[209] In a novel step taken by the 1st Tank Brigade, the number of forward stations was reduced on account of 'the numerous other Wireless sets likely to be working'.[210] Finally, in accordance with the general

---

[205] '20th (Light) Division Operations. Instructions No. 2. Inter-Communication', 11 November 1917, 20 Division War Diary, WO95/2097, TNA.

[206] Miles, *Military Operations, 1917*, Vol. 3, 28.

[207] 'III Corps Operations. Instruction No. 7. Communications', 14 November 1917, III Corps War Diary, WO95/677, '6th Division Operations. Instructions No. 6. Signal Communications', 17 November 1917, 6 Division War Diary, WO95/1583, '62nd Division. Instructions No. 3. Communications', 15 November 1917, 62 Division War Diary, WO95/3070, TNA; Nalder, *The Royal Corps of Signals*, 138.

[208] 'Report on Communications during Operations 20th November to 23rd November 1917', 9 December 1917, Major-General J. F. C. Fuller Papers 1/4/2, LHCMA.

[209] 'Technical Wireless Instructions', 11 November 1917, Third Army Signal Company War Diary, WO95/408, TNA.

[210] 'Report on Communications during Operations 20th November to 23rd November 1917', 9 December 1917, Fuller Papers 1/4/2, LHCMA.

policy of absolute secrecy, no wireless set was to indicate its presence in any way before 'Z' hour.[211]

Given that speed and mobility were of paramount importance to the success of the operation, the decision to include power buzzers and amplifiers within the array of alternative means available to infantry brigades and battalions seems somewhat puzzling. The foregoing analysis highlighted the relatively poor performance of power buzzers during the Third Ypres campaign. According to one report, the amplifiers were 'too fragile for very forward work. Sending them in front of Brigade Forward Stations is seldom justified'.[212] However, despite a rather inconsistent track record, the decision to utilise power buzzers at Cambrai was based upon the fact that there was an extremely limited supply of carrier pigeons for the upcoming offensive. Only 16 birds were available per division to be distributed amongst the attacking brigades and battalions.[213] Therefore, the 'two-way working of power buzzers [was] to be arranged wherever possible', with two power buzzers and four amplifiers given to each division to distribute between its brigades and battalions.[214]

In addition to wireless and power buzzers, the customary visual signalling scheme was established on each divisional front. For example, in order that 29 Division, in III Corps reserve, received the earliest possible information regarding the capture of the first objectives, 'a Preliminary System of six combined Observation and Visual Signalling Stations' was set up. Once the attacking 6 and 12 Divisions had captured their objectives, they were to signal back 'by repeatedly firing a series of Red Very Lights'. This signal was to be 'repeated by each relay post back to the rear post, and transmitted by them straight to 29th Divisional Headquarters, by every means available'.[215] Finally, arrangements were also made for the employment of despatch riders and runners. In 6 Division the route of the runner relay posts forward of brigade headquarters was to be marked out with white tape so as not only to facilitate the

---

[211] 'Technical Wireless Instructions', 11 November 1917, Third Army Signal Company War Diary, WO95/408, TNA.

[212] 'Notes on SS. 148', 14 August 1917, Fifth Army Signal Company War Diary, WO95/534, TNA.

[213] 'III Corps Operations. Instruction No. 7. Communications', 14 November 1917, III Corps War Diary, WO95/677, '6th Division Operations. Instructions No. 6. Signal Communications', 17 November 1917, 6 Division War Diary, WO95/1583, TNA.

[214] 'Technical Wireless Instructions', 11 November 1917, Third Army Signal Company War Diary, WO95/408, 'III Corps Operations. Instruction No. 7. Communications', 14 November 1917, III Corps War Diary, WO95/677, TNA.

[215] 'III Corps Operations. Instruction No. 8', 16 November 1917, III Corps War Diary, WO95/677, TNA.

location of headquarters but to 'form useful guiding lines for carrying parties and others going forward'.[216]

In sum, the vulnerability of the ground and poled cable network at Cambrai compelled commanders at the divisional, brigade and battalion levels to ensure that an array of alternative means of communication were made readily available and that all ranks were made fully aware of just how important a role they were to play in the upcoming operation. The realisation that cable communication might prove highly unreliable once the battle was underway is illustrated by the signal instructions of 6 Division, which stipulated that 'important messages regarding operations should not be sent by telephone except in cases of extreme urgency. Messages containing orders for operations or information regarding dispositions will be sent by runner or D.R. Such messages should as far as possible be sent in duplicate by two distinct routes'.[217] The need for prompt and accurate information was stressed as never before. As the 'General Instructions' issued by Major-General Walter Braithwaite, GOC 62 Division, made abundantly clear, 'No information is likely to lead to no assistance – therefore, when in a tight place, send back information'.[218]

Overall, the initial phase of Third Army's attack at Cambrai on 20 November was a resounding success, causing church bells to be rung in celebration in Britain. Apart from the difficulties experienced at Flesquières on the front of 51 Division, both the Hindenburg Line and its support line were penetrated in most places to a depth of four to five miles.[219] However, the unprecedented rapidity and depth of this advance created enormous difficulties for command, control and communications. With communications stretched to breaking point, the attack soon lost momentum and over the course of the following days 'the British situation became more and more difficult as German reinforcements began to arrive'.[220] A German counterattack retook nearly all of the British gains on 30 November, much to the embarrassment of the high command. From a communications perspective, the Battle of Cambrai presented the BEF with a number of novel challenges. Chief amongst these were the problems created by the speed and depth of the initial advance and the impact of the large number of

---

[216] '6th Division Operations. Instructions No. 6. Signal Communications', 17 November 1917, 6 Division War Diary, WO95/1583, TNA.

[217] Ibid.

[218] '62nd Division. Instructions No. 4. General Instructions for the Offensive', 15 November 1917, 62 Division War Diary, WO95/3070, TNA.

[219] On the contentious issue of 51 Division's performance on 20 November, see Travers, *How the War Was Won*, 22–3; and, Hammond, *Cambrai 1917*, 177–80.

[220] Miles, *Military Operations, 1917*, Vol. 3, 283.

tanks employed. Although these new challenges were met with varying degrees of success, the experience taught the BEF several important lessons with regards to the conduct of future offensive operations. In fact, many of the lessons learnt from Cambrai were to form the backbone of British communications policy and practice during the 'Hundred Days' campaign in 1918.

Soon after the attack began, the maintenance of telephone communication became highly problematic, since the unusually long lines laid by the Signal Service caused speech to be very faint and often inaudible.[221] It was suggested by 51 Division Signal Company after the battle that

since telephones are a *sine qua non* and the technical difficulties in providing telephones in moving warfare are much greater than those met with in working by vibrator, in future operations which develop into semi-open fighting no attempt should be made to keep touch with units by several separate systems. One main route of three or four poled cables would be run to a succession of previously selected points in the centre of the Divisional Sector and small exchanges established at these points. As soon as an exchange was ready in the forward area Hqrs. of Infantry and Artillery Brigades would be informed and would move to the vicinity of these exchanges.[222]

The problem of maintaining telephonic and telegraphic communication was further exacerbated by the difficulty of supplying attacking units with enough cable. The semi-mobile nature of the offensive and the scarcity and congestion of forward roads made the supply of signal stores very difficult. A report by Third Army complained after the battle that 'signal vehicles should be given as much priority on roads as is permitted by other tactical considerations'.[223] In order to overcome this problem in the future, it was recommended that 'prior to an operation of this sort a large dump of D3 twisted cable on ½ mile drums should be established as near to the front line as possible'.[224] However, even in late 1917, the BEF still did not possess an 'unlimited' supply of cable and other signal

---

[221] 'Lessons Learnt from Recent Operations by the Third Army (November 20th to December 6th, 1917)', undated, Third Army Headquarters, Cambrai Lessons, WO158/316, TNA.

[222] '51st (H) Divisional Signal Co. R.E. Report on Communications Between TRESCAULT and FONTAINE during Operations of 20th–24th November 1917', 30 November 1917, 51 Division Signal Company War Diary, WO95/2856, TNA.

[223] 'Lessons Learnt from Recent Operations by the Third Army (November 20th to December 6th, 1917)', undated, Third Army Headquarters, Cambrai Lessons, WO158/316, TNA.

[224] 62 Division Signal Company War Diary, 30 November 1917, WO95/3076, TNA. Twisting D3 cable was found to be a successful preventative measure to combat enemy overhearing. The drawback, however, was that only 5 miles of twisted cable could be wound around a drum instead of 10 miles for non-twisted cable. See Priestley, *Work of the Royal Engineers*, 238–9.

equipment. This was made clear in a memorandum issued by the Director of Army Signals, in which he pointed out 'the urgent need for economy in the expenditure of Signal Service stores... as a matter of the gravest national importance'.[225]

To compound matters, the movement of tanks and cavalry did extensive damage to cable communications.[226] It was generally found that communication was much more successfully maintained when cables were poled rather than simply laid along the ground. According to the war diary of 62 Division Signal Company: 'When Brigades moved forward a line was laid from Cable Head in each sector to their new HQ. The line on the right sector was poled and held well, but that on the left sector was not poled and was continuously broken when the 185th and 186th Brigades moved forward into GRAINCOURT'.[227] However, even when cable was elevated off the ground and poled, 'the poles... chosen on account of lightness for easy transport, were very easily broken. They should... have been longer, to raise the cable high enough to clear the Tanks'.[228] Several suggestions as how best to overcome this problem in future operations were provided after the battle. Major-General Douglas Smith, for instance, believed that 'routes for returning Tanks should be laid down and marked back to the original front line' in order to guide tank commanders away from vulnerable telephone lines.[229] Third Army went so far as to suggest that 'special tanks, capable of carrying about 10 tons, and cutting a trench about 3 inches wide and 1 foot deep', should be provided for use by the Signal Service. Such tanks were to 'be fitted with a means of paying out multi-core cable from drums through a hawse pipe into the trench as it is cut', and 'all the apparatus for using the Tank as a Signal Office should also be provided'.[230] Some units also resorted to more ingenious methods of preserving cable communications. On 51 Division's front, for example, the 153rd Brigade made 'considerable use of German overhead lines east of Flesquières' on 21 November, while the

---

[225] 'Director of Army Signals. Circular Memorandum No. 220', 19 December 1917, Director of Army Signals War Diary, WO95/57, TNA.

[226] 'Notes on the Operations Which Began on November 20th 1917 in Front of Cambrai', 7 December 1917, 62 Division War Diary, WO95/3070, TNA.

[227] 62 Division Signal Company War Diary, 20 November 1917, WO95/3076, TNA.

[228] 'Cambrai, Havrincourt-Bourlon Wood Operations, IV Corps Report on Telephone and Telegraph Communications, 20th November–1st December 1917', undated, WO158/383, TNA.

[229] 'Experiences Gained in the Recent Operations, 20th and 21st November, 1917', 10 December 1917, 20 Division War Diary, WO95/2097, TNA.

[230] 'Lessons Learnt from Recent Operations by the Third Army (November 20th to December 6th, 1917)', undated, Third Army Headquarters, Cambrai Lessons, WO158/316, TNA.

OC 36 Division Signal Company, Major Thomas Vigers, opened up telephone communication with the infantry brigades on 20 November utilising the bed of the Canal du Nord to lay its wires.[231]

Owing to the damage done to telephone and telegraph cables by the passage of tanks and the high capacity of the long lines laid during the advance, which caused speech over the circuits to be very faint, the conveyance of orders, reports and other information was subject to long delays, exacerbating efforts to maintain command and control. As Oliver Nugent informed his wife in a series of letters written during the course of the battle: 'information is hard to get when fighting is on... Once the orders have been given there is nothing more one can do but wait for results... I can't get information as quick as I should like'.[232] Indeed, the lack of timely information arriving at 29 Division's headquarters on the morning of 20 November forced its commander, Major-General (Henry de) Beauvoir De Lisle, to use his initiative and issue the order for his brigades to move forward much earlier than planned. As De Lisle recollected after the war: 'My own orders were to wait until the leading Divisions had secured the Hindenburg lines before I moved, but as the capture of the Outpost line was not reported at my HQ for two hours after the event, I knew it would be fatal to success if I waited for definite news of the capture of the 3rd objective'.[233] Thus, despite its novel characteristics, the Battle of Cambrai still presented British commanders with the all-too-familiar difficulties of procuring timely and accurate information once the fighting was underway.

The situation was also not helped by the fact that the 'HQ of formations did not always go to places where communication either existed or could be easily obtained'.[234] Major-General Braithwaite complained of the 'delay in the delivery of important orders' as a result of the 'unexpected and unnotified moves' of some battalion headquarters.[235]

---

[231] '51st (H) Divisional Signal Co. R.E. Report on Communications Between TRESCAULT and FONTAINE during Operations of 20th–24th November 1917', 30 November 1917, 51 Division Signal Company War Diary, WO95/2856, TNA; Cyril Falls, *The History of the 36th (Ulster) Division* (London: McCaw, Stevenson and Orr, 1922), 155.

[232] Nugent to his wife, 20, 22 and 23 November 1917, in Perry (ed.), *Major-General Oliver Nugent*, 198–201.

[233] 'My Narrative of the Great German War, Vol. 2', 55, De Lisle Papers 3/2, LHCMA.

[234] 'Lessons Learnt from Recent Operations by the Third Army (November 20th to December 6th, 1917)', undated, Third Army Headquarters, Cambrai Lessons, WO158/316, TNA.

[235] 'Notes on the Operations which Began on November 20th 1917 in Front of Cambrai', 7 December 1917, 62 Division War Diary, WO95/3070, TNA.

Likewise, 51 Division Signal Company noted that 'it did not appear to be sufficiently realised in all cases that the decisive factor in the movement and position of Headquarters ought to be communications'.[236] This was particularly the case on 21 November, when 'the tactical situation forced some brigades to move away from the main line system'.[237] The frequent and uninformed movement of some brigade and battalion headquarters greatly increased the difficulties of communication and made it impossible for divisional and corps commanders to direct the battle. By the end of the first day, many divisional commanders were uncertain as to the exact whereabouts of their attacking troops. When Haig convened an army commander's conference at Doullens on 7 December, the position of commanders and their headquarters and the system of divisional control were cited as key reasons why Cambrai was not more successful.[238]

The volume of telephonic and telegraphic communication generated during the course of the battle also added to the difficulties of command and control. The simple and fragile nature of the cable network laid immediately prior to and during the initial period of the attack resulted in corps, divisional and brigade lines becoming 'very much congested'.[239] III Corps Signal Office handled 2,497 telegrams alone on 20 November, while the average daily number of messages dealt with at IV Corps Signal Office during the course of November was 3,397, as opposed to 1,908 messages in October and 1,436 messages in December.[240] At the divisional level, the signal office of 20 Division processed 2,000 messages per day during the battle, a volume which 'severely taxed the powers of the Signal Company'.[241] Thus, by reducing the complexity of the forward cable network prior to the battle, the BEF was able to maintain the elements of secrecy and surprise. However, the principal drawback to this was that once the battle was underway, the system became severely overloaded on account of the sheer weight of messages

[236] '51st (H) Divisional Signal Co. R.E. Report on Communications Between TRESCAULT and FONTAINE during Operations of 20th–24th November 1917', 30 November 1917, 51 Division Signal Company War Diary, WO95/2856, TNA.

[237] 'Cambrai, Havrincourt-Bourlon Wood Operations, IV Corps Report on Telephone and Telegraph Communications, 20th November–1st December 1917', undated, WO158/383, TNA.

[238] Miles, *Military Operations, 1917*, Vol. 3, 94, 284.

[239] 'Report on Communications during Operations 20th November to 23rd November 1917', 9 December 1917, Fuller Papers 1/4/2, LHCMA.

[240] 'Total and Daily Average Traffic at CCO for Month of November, 1917', III Corps Signal Company War Diary, WO95/701, IV Corps Signal Company War Diary, November 1917, WO 95/737, TNA.

[241] Inglefield, *History of the Twentieth (Light) Division*, 180.

being transmitted.[242] In light of this, to what extent did the alternative methods of communication relieve the pressure of the telephone and telegraph lines?

The vulnerability and overloading of the cable network at Cambrai forced many commanders to seek alternative means of communication. Wireless was used on a far greater scale than in any previous British offensive. Not only were wireless sets available in greater numbers, but confidence in their use throughout the BEF as a whole by late 1917 was at an all-time high.[243] A memorandum issued by I ANZAC Corps in August stressed that 'not less than one hour daily' should be spent by operators enciphering and deciphering messages in order to improve wireless procedure.[244] Similarly, by late September VI Corps had established a process whereby each wireless set in the corps area transmitted two to three messages to its neighbouring formation every night after sunset in order to 'add to the efficiency of the wireless personnel, enable valuable information to be obtained regarding the efficiency of the instruments, and give opportunities to Commanders of formations concerned to keep in close touch'.[245] At Cambrai, numerous divisions reported very favourable results. For example, 51 Division Signal Company noted that 'over 80 messages were sent and received during three days' working', while 62 Division Signal Company recorded that 16 of the 18 messages sent by a wireless set at Graincourt on 21 November were successfully received at the division's headquarters.[246] Similarly, Major-General Frederick Dudgeon, GOC 56 Division, reported after the battle that 'Trench Wireless Sets were used with success from positions within 200 yards of the Germans, being erected only at night and dismantled by day'.[247]

However, although the work done by wireless proved invaluable, it was acknowledged that perhaps a far greater proportion of messages could

---

[242] For an interesting discussion of the problems of complexity and overload in contemporary intelligence systems, see Peter Gill and Mark Phythian, *Intelligence in an Insecure World* (Cambridge: Polity Press, 2006), 82–102.

[243] Hall, 'British Army and Wireless', 306–9.

[244] 'Training of Wireless Operators in Divisions', 3 August 1917, AWM25/425/23, AWM.

[245] 'VI Corps. GX 779/24', 27 September 1917, 914.2, Military Histories (General), 914.2, RSMA.

[246] '51st (H) Divisional Signal Co. R.E. Report on Communications Between TRESCAULT and FONTAINE during Operations of 20th–24th November 1917', 30 November 1917, 51 Division Signal Company War Diary, WO95/2856, 62 Division Signal Company War Diary, 21 November 1917, WO95/3076, TNA.

[247] 'Report on Operations in Third Army from 20th November to 3rd December 1917', 15 December 1917, Major-General F.A. Dudgeon Papers 86/51/1, IWM.

have been sent by this means.[248] Nevertheless, there were still many instances when wireless communication proved extremely difficult to establish under more mobile circumstances. A report by the 1st Tank Brigade, for instance, noted that the use of wireless in fighting tanks proved 'most unsatisfactory'. It cited one occasion when the wireless apparatus was divided between two tanks and one of the tanks broke down, rendering the set useless. In another incident, the apparatus was again split between two fighting tanks, but before it could be utilised one of the tanks was 'knocked out' by enemy shellfire.[249] A faulty wireless set, 'owing to a pole breaking when moving across rough ground', was also blamed for the slow transmission of information between 2 Cavalry Division and Cavalry Corps headquarters on the afternoon of 20 November.[250] The fluidity of the attack had a similarly detrimental impact on the use of power buzzers and amplifiers. Although each brigade forward party and one of the two battalions of the second wave of the attack carried them forward, the depth of the initial advance created 'distances which were too great to allow for adequate communication' between the operators of power buzzers and amplifiers.[251] The shortness of their range coupled with the bulky nature of the apparatus made them a highly inappropriate means of communication in semi-mobile warfare.[252] Overall, in spite of the favourable results obtained by the more widespread use of wireless and power buzzers at Cambrai, the difficulties of utilising the sets under more fluid conditions remained far from resolved.

The fortunes of visual signalling fared little better. The initial assault on the morning of 20 November took place under dull and misty

---

[248] 'Cambrai, Havrincourt-Bourlon Wood Operations, IV Corps Report on Telephone and Telegraph Communications, 20th November–1st December 1917', undated, WO158/383, TNA.

[249] 'Report on Communications during Operations 20th November to 23rd November 1917', 9 December 1917, Fuller Papers 1/4/2, LHCMA. The latter incident is also recorded in the memoirs of Major E. F. Churchill, who served as a signal officer in the 1st Tank Brigade at the time. See 'Memories 1914–1919 by a Signal Officer', 29, Churchill Papers, IWM.

[250] 'Cavalry Corps. Report on Operations Commencing 20th Nov. 1917', 13 December 1917, Third Army Headquarters, Cambrai Lessons, WO158/316, TNA. For additional context, see Kenyon, *Horsemen*, 154–5.

[251] 'Experiences Gained in the Recent Operations, 20th and 21st November, 1917', 10 December 1917, 20 Division War Diary, WO95/2097, TNA.

[252] 'Lessons Learnt from Recent Operations by the Third Army (November 20th to December 6th, 1917)', undated, Third Army Headquarters, Cambrai Lessons, WO158/316, '51st (H) Divisional Signal Co. R.E. Report on Communications Between TRESCAULT and FONTAINE during Operations of 20th–24th November 1917', 30 November 1917, 51 Division Signal Company War Diary, WO95/2856, TNA; 'Report on Operations in Third Army from 20th November to 3rd December 1917', 15 December 1917, Dudgeon Papers, IWM.

conditions with very little visibility.[253] As a result, 'visual signalling from ground stations was impossible, or very uncertain, and little could be seen from the air'.[254] Nevertheless, once the mist cleared, the open nature of the terrain favoured the use of visual communication.[255] Signalling by Lucas Lamp, in particular, was 'in full use between Companies, Battalions and Infantry Brigades and between FOOs, Field Batteries and Artillery Brigades'.[256] In some sectors, 'the disorganisation and demoralisation of the enemy' made it possible to establish two-way working between visual stations safely.[257] However, the deterioration of the weather during the latter stages of the operation made communication by visual signalling much more problematic. This was aptly demonstrated when the Germans launched their counterattack on 30 November. Although the success of the German counterattack has been ascribed to numerous factors, including the command and intelligence failings of the BEF and the innovative use of 'storm troop' tactics by the Germans,[258] the situation from the British point of view was not helped by the fact that mist and fog obscured the frontline infantry's SOS signals for urgent and immediate assistance from the artillery.[259]

Finally, in terms of message carriers, pigeons were of limited utility throughout the battle, partly on account of the lack of birds made available, but also on account of the poor weather conditions.[260] It was found that 'under semi-mobile conditions the distribution of birds is very

[253] Nugent to his wife, 20 November 1917, in Perry (ed.), *Major-General Oliver Nugent*, 198.

[254] Miles, *Military Operations, 1917*, Vol. 3, 62.

[255] 'Cambrai, Havrincourt-Bourlon Wood Operations, IV Corps Report on Telephone and Telegraph Communications, 20th November–1st December 1917', undated, WO158/383, TNA.

[256] '51st (H) Divisional Signal Co. R.E. Report on Communications Between TRESCAULT and FONTAINE during Operations of 20th–24th November 1917', 30 November 1917, 51 Division Signal Company War Diary, WO95/2856, TNA.

[257] Priestley, *Work of the Royal Engineers*, 62.

[258] Travers, *How the War Was Won*, 27–31; Simpson, *Directing Operations*, 124–6; Beach, *Haig's Intelligence*, 262–72.

[259] 'A Report Written by Lieutenant-General Sir T. D'O. Snow, Who Commanded the VII Corps in the Battle of Cambrai, 30th November 1917, Together with Evidence Collected as to the Gallant Behaviour of the 55th Division in That Battle', 16 April 1927, CAB45/118, TNA; Miles, *Military Operations, 1917*, Vol. 3, 172.

[260] 'Cambrai, Havrincourt-Bourlon Wood Operations, IV Corps Report on Telephone and Telegraph Communications, 20th November–1st December 1917', undated, WO158/383, '51st (H) Divisional Signal Co. R.E. Report on Communications Between TRESCAULT and FONTAINE during Operations of 20th–24th November 1917', 30 November 1917, 51 Division Signal Company War Diary, WO95/2856, TNA; 'Report on Operations in Third Army from 20th November to 3rd December 1917', 15 December 1917, Dudgeon Papers, IWM.

Plate 6.3 A runner leaves the dugout at company headquarters to deliver an important message, November 1917 (Henry Armytage Sanders: Alexander Turnbull Library, Wellington, 1/2-012996-G)

difficult and requires careful organisation'.[261] The one notable exception, however, was with the 1st Tank Brigade, where it was noted after the battle that 'although the weather conditions were very adverse, fairly good results were obtained on the first day... From the loft, messages were telephoned to the 1st Brigade Headquarters and a Despatch Rider brought in the originals every half hour'.[262] Meanwhile, runners performed their usual heroics in front of brigade headquarters, furnishing commanders with invaluable information, though inevitably sustaining heavy casualties in the process.[263]

[261] 'Lessons Learnt from Recent Operations by the Third Army (November 20th to December 6th, 1917)', undated, Third Army Headquarters, Cambrai Lessons, WO158/316, TNA.

[262] 'Report on Communications during Operations 20th November to 23rd November 1917', 9 December 1917, Fuller Papers 1/4/2, LHCMA.

[263] 'Experiences Gained in the Recent Operations, 20th and 21st November, 1917', 10 December 1917, 20 Division War Diary, WO95/2097, '51st (H) Divisional Signal Co. R.E. Report on Communications Between TRESCAULT and FONTAINE during Operations of 20th–24th November 1917', 30 November 1917, 51 Division Signal Company War Diary, WO95/2856, 62 Division Signal Company War Diary, 30 November 1917, WO95/3076, TNA.

In sum, the air of secrecy that surrounded the Battle of Cambrai, and the unique combination of a mass tank assault and the silent registration of the artillery, meant that the nature of the BEF's communications system was fundamentally different from that of the battles that preceded it. Third Army could not depend upon an elaborate maze of deep-buried telephone cables, and instead had to make greater use of the alternative means of communication. The unprecedented speed and depth of the initial advance created novel challenges, some of which were successfully overcome, while others proved much more problematic. Despite the novelty of the operation, the deterioration of communications following the spectacular successes of the opening day closely adhered to the all-too-familiar pattern of previous British offensives on the Western Front. Because of the breakdown of communications and the stiffening of German resistance, the difficulty of maintaining the momentum of the initial attack resurfaced and the battle degenerated into stalemate once again. Significantly, however, the experience of maintaining a communications system under the mobile conditions of the first day provided important lessons from which the BEF would develop a template for communications during the summer and autumn of 1918.

In conclusion, it is clear from the foregoing examination of the BEF's operations in 1917 that for communications to perform well and to have a positive influence, three preconditions were necessary: first, meticulous planning and preparation. This included thorough training of signal personnel according to the principles advocated in training manuals, most notably *SS. 148* and later *SS. 191*, and the provision of all available means of communication and the supporting infrastructure, such as deep-buried cable networks and report centres; second, the support of effective counter-battery fire, neutralising the opposing enemy guns, ensured that communications, particularly cable based and wireless, survived long enough to facilitate command and control during the critical opening stages of an attack; third, and perhaps most significantly, the operation in question had to be aimed at securing strictly limited objectives so as not to stretch communications above and beyond their capabilities. When these prerequisites were met, such as on the opening day of the Battle of Arras and at Messines in June, the communications system played an integral part in the BEF's success. However, when these preconditions were absent, notably at Arras after 9 April, at Ypres in August and October–November and at Cambrai from the afternoon of 20 November onwards, communications invariably broke down, exacerbating efforts to maintain command and control, which inevitably resulted in failure.

Thus, upon first reflection it would appear that by the end of 1917 communications had not made any significant progress since the Battle of the Somme the previous year. Indeed, despite three years of trench warfare, communications forward of battalion headquarters were but little more effective at Cambrai than they had been at the Battle of Neuve Chapelle in March 1915. Telephone and telegraph lines were routinely destroyed by enemy artillery fire, visual signalling was hindered by a variety of obstacles, both natural and man-made, information from carrier pigeons remained a very slow process and there was still no light-weight and fool-proof wireless set available in adequate numbers for frontline infantry. Power buzzers, despite showing some initial promise, were unsuited to the conditions of semi-mobile operations, which, more often than not, left runners as the sole method of communication.

Nevertheless, although significant problems remained – and indeed, new dilemmas presented themselves during the course of the fighting at Cambrai – the BEF's communications system did show signs of being stronger and more flexible and sophisticated at the close of 1917 than it had been at the beginning of the year. Improvements in signals practice and organisation had led to a more proficient system of collecting, processing and disseminating information. Invaluable lessons had also been drawn from each battle and new methods and techniques developed as a result. New technologies, most notably CW wireless, had demonstrated their potential and had been incorporated into the communications system by the end of the year. In fact, wireless communication as a whole had grown in terms of its value and popularity, cementing its place as the most important of the BEF's alternative methods of communication.

Finally, and perhaps most importantly, the battles of 1917 were the first to incorporate the principles laid down in *SS. 148*, the BEF's first authoritative communications manual. On the basis of the lessons of 1916, *SS. 148* furnished the BEF with a universal set of guidelines governing communication policy, practice and organisation, demonstrating that British commanders had clearly grasped the importance of communications in modern warfare and were actively taking steps to improve the communications system. The principles advocated in *SS. 148*, modified and updated on the basis of the experiences and technological developments of the year and reissued in November as *SS.191*, would serve the BEF well for the remainder of the war. However, there was one glaring omission: it failed to address the issue of communications in a retreat. As the events of early 1918 were to show, it was an omission that nearly cost the BEF dearly.

7 1918

The fighting on the Western Front in 1918 fell into two distinct phases. In the first phase, March to July, the German Army launched a series of offensives against the BEF and the Allies, inflicting heavy losses and forcing them to retreat some 40 miles in the process. However, despite throwing everything that they had against them, the Germans were unable to achieve a decisive victory. With the German Army practically exhausted, from August the war in 1918 entered its second phase, with the Allies mounting a series of successful offensives of their own, known collectively as the 'Hundred Days' campaign, which eventually compelled the Germans to seek armistice terms from the Allies.[1] Explaining how, and why, the war on the Western Front ended in 1918 has always been contentious and controversial, not least because of the link to the 'stab-in-the-back' myth and its effect upon interwar German politics.[2] Some historians have argued that the German Army effectively defeated itself as a result of the failings of its own offensives.[3] Others have argued that after four years of attrition, the Germans were eventually overwhelmed by the weight of superior Allied manpower and resources.[4] These explanations are closely related to the works of a third group of historians, who have emphasised the role played by morale in bringing

[1] For the British official histories, see J. E. Edmonds, *Military Operations, France and Belgium, 1918*, 5 Vols. (London: HMSO, 1935–47).

[2] Richard Bessel, *Germany after the First World War* (Oxford: Clarendon Press, 1993), 254–84; Wilhelm Deist, 'The Military Collapse of the German Empire: The Reality behind the Stab-in-the-Back Myth', *War in History*, 3 (1996), 186–207; Scott Stephenson, *The Final Battle: Soldiers of the Western Front and the German Revolution of 1918* (Cambridge: Cambridge University Press, 2009).

[3] Travers, *How the War Was Won*, 179; Holger H. Herwig, *The First World War: Germany and Austria-Hungary, 1914–1918* (London: Arnold, 1997), 433; Martin Kitchen, *The German Offensives of 1918* (Stroud: Tempus, 2001), 233–7; David Stevenson, *With our Backs to the Wall: Victory and Defeat in 1918* (London: Allen Lane, 2011), 539.

[4] Avner Offer, *The First World War: An Agrarian Interpretation* (Oxford: Clarendon Press, 1989), 76–8; Stephen Broadberry and Mark Harrison, 'The Economics of World War I: An Overview', in Stephen Broadberry and Mark Harrison (eds.), *The Economics of World War I* (Cambridge: Cambridge University Press, 2005), 3–40.

about the German Army's collapse.[5] Finally, a growing number of historians have argued that the Allies, and in particular the BEF, won the war in 1918 through the application of new technology and better tactical and operational methods, though they disagree as to how these methods came about and how consistently they were applied.[6]

Despite this copious amount of scholarship, very few of these studies have offered any detailed assessment of the role played by communications. This is an important omission, because an analysis of the influence that communications had upon the BEF's operations can provide fresh insight into many of the debates concerning the course and outcome of the war on the Western Front in 1918. Therefore, this chapter seeks to answer three main questions: first, what bearing did communications have upon the BEF's military performance in 1918, both on the defensive during the first half of the year and then on the offensive during the Hundred Days? Second, did British commanders make the most of the communications technology available to them during this period? Third, and finally, what can a study of communications reveal about the nature of command and control within the BEF in 1918?

German Offensives

Like the Somme and Third Battle of Ypres, the German offensives of 1918 have generated considerable debate within the historiography. Between 21 March and 29 April, the main weight of the German attacks, Operations *Michael* and *Georgette,* respectively, fell principally upon the BEF.[7] Although historians have attributed the BEF's poor performance during this time to a variety of factors, including the shortage of available manpower,[8] flawed British command structure,[9] and the BEF's misunderstanding and misapplication of defence-in-depth methods,[10]

[5] Hew Strachan, 'The Morale of the German Army, 1917–18', in Hugh Cecil and Peter H. Liddle (eds.), *Facing Armageddon: The First World War Experienced* (London: Leo Cooper, 1996), 383–98; Alexander Watson, *Enduring the Great War: Combat, Morale and Collapse in the German and British Armies, 1914–1918* (Cambridge: Cambridge University Press, 2008); Stephenson, *Final Battle,* 17–66.

[6] Prior and Wilson, *Command on the Western Front,* 305–9; Harris with Barr, *Amiens to the Armistice,* 287–301; Simpson, *Directing Operations,* 155–80; Boff, *Winning and Losing;* Gary Sheffield and Peter Gray (eds.), *Changing War: The British Army, the Hundred Days Campaign and the Birth of the Royal Air Force, 1918* (London: Bloomsbury, 2013).

[7] Kitchen, *German Offensives,* 66–136; David T. Zabecki, *The German 1918 Offensives: A Case Study in the Operational Level of War* (London: Routledge, 2006), 113–205.

[8] Simpson, *Directing Operations,* 131–54.   [9] Travers, *How the War Was Won,* 50–109.

[10] Samuels, *Command or Control?* 198–269.

communications does not occupy a central position in their analyses. A more thorough investigation, however, reveals that communications had a major bearing upon the BEF's fortunes throughout this turbulent period.

Throughout the winter of 1917–18 the BEF began the construction of a defence-in-depth system, based upon the German model, consisting of three zones: forward, battle and rear.[11] It has been argued that this system was neither fully complete nor properly understood when the Germans attacked on 21 March.[12] What is often overlooked, however, is that the same was also true of the scheme of communications which was to support this defensive system. The experience of the German counterattack at Cambrai in November 1917 had demonstrated the necessity for an efficient and reliable system for communicating information whilst on the defensive.[13] Lieutenant-General Sir Ivor Maxse, GOC XVIII Corps, reiterated this need at a conference in February 1918, in which he urged those present 'to perfect your arrangements for getting information back so that we shall have time to man the battle zone before the Boche gets into it'.[14] Despite this awareness, SS. 191 was not updated to include communications in a retreat. Without any formal doctrinal guidance, therefore, British commanders began to modify their communications systems to suit local conditions, thus supporting Andy Simpson's argument that regional variations undoubtedly existed in the British defences.[15] Although every method of communication was to be employed, the main focus was on the establishment of a deep-buried cable network on each corps front.[16] However, there appeared a clear north–south divide in the state and preparedness of these deep-buried cable networks. The situation was much more favourable to the north of Arras, held principally by the First and Second Armies, than to the south of the British line, which was held by the Third and Fifth Armies,[17] and there appear to be two explanations for this discrepancy.

---

[11] Edmonds, *Military Operations, 1918*, Vol. 1, 41–2.

[12] Samuels, *Command or Control?* 198–229; Travers, *How the War Was Won*, 50.

[13] 'Action Fought South of Cambrai, 30 November 1917. Court of Enquiry. Appendix L', February 1918, WO158/53, TNA.

[14] 'Corps Commander's Conference. Lecture by Lieutenant-General Sir Ivor Maxse, Commanding XVIII Corps. "Lessons from Cambrai", 19 February 1918', Maxse Papers 69/53/12, File 40, IWM.

[15] Simpson, *Directing Operations*, 133.

[16] 'XVIII Corps Instructions for Defence', 10 January 1918, XVIII Corps War Diary, WO95/953, TNA.

[17] Priestley, *Work of the Royal Engineers*, 258.

First, the BEF in early 1918 was suffering from an acute shortage of manpower.[18] Between January and March the strength of infantry divisions was reduced from 12 battalions to 9.[19] As the official historian observed, this meant that 'never before had the British line been held with so few men and so few guns to the mile'.[20] From the point of view of communications, it meant that the Signal Service had to compete with the other branches of the army for the use of the limited number of working parties available. It was therefore deprived of the sufficient number of men required to complete the digging and filling in of cable trenches.[21] Moreover, since Haig and GHQ anticipated the main weight of the German attack to fall against Third Army and only the northern third of the Fifth Army front,[22] the majority of the corps and divisional signal companies in the latter were much more affected by the shortage of labour than their counterparts to the north.

Second, with Haig having reluctantly agreed to a 28-mile extension of the British right flank in January, a move which further thinned the BEF's defences,[23] the Fifth Army formations taking up residency in this area, which had previously been occupied by the French, found it to be almost completely devoid of deep-buried cable. The reason for this, according to a British liaison officer attached to the French XIV Corps, was that whereas the BEF was 'a firm believer in buried cable... the French ran all their communications over-ground'.[24] Although this claim is somewhat exaggerated, an American signal officer observed in December 1917 that the British were nonetheless 'outdoing the French in the matter of buried cable'.[25] Consequently, having less than two months in which to establish comprehensive communications systems, the corps' deep-buried cable

---

[18] For additional context, see: David Woodward, 'Did Lloyd George Starve the British Army of Men Prior to the German Offensive of 21 March 1918?', *The Historical Journal*, 27 (1984), 241–52; Keith Grieves, *The Politics of Manpower, 1914–18* (Manchester: Manchester University Press, 1988), 181–201; and, Elizabeth Greenhalgh, 'David Lloyd George, Georges Clemenceau, and the 1918 Manpower Crisis', *Historical Journal*, 50 (2007), 397–421.

[19] Haig Diary, 10 January 1918, WO256/26, TNA; Sheffield and Bourne (eds.), *Douglas Haig*, 371.

[20] Edmonds, *Military Operations, 1918*, Vol. 1, 254.   [21] Portway, *Memoirs*, 117.

[22] Beach, *Haig's Intelligence*, 280–1.

[23] Haig Diary, 7, 10, 14 and 29 January 1918, WO256/26, TNA; Sheffield and Bourne (eds.), *Douglas Haig*, 370–6; Elizabeth Greenhalgh, 'Myth and Memory: Sir Douglas Haig and the Imposition of Allied Unified Command in March 1918', *Journal of Military History*, 68 (2004), 784–6; Greenhalgh, 'David Lloyd George', 400–2.

[24] 'Memoirs of 1914–1918' (1935), 49, Wallace Papers, IWM.

[25] Colonel George S. Gibbs (Chief Signal Officer of the AEF Zone of Advance), in 'History of the Signal Corps, American Expeditionary Forces, 1917–19, Vol. 1', 36, RG120/2041/42, NARA. Further evidence of the differing British and French cable-laying practices is provided by David Kelly, who, as the intelligence officer of the 110th

networks in the southern portion of the British line were 'at best, partial and, at worst, absent altogether' when the German attack began on 21 March.[26] A report by 25 Division Signal Company, for example, noted that the buried cable system on IV Corps' front was 'good in the first system of defence and every effort was being made to bring this system back through the second and third line system but the battle opened before the work was in any way complete'.[27] Likewise, upon taking command of the 110th Infantry Brigade (21 Division) on 18 March, Hanway Cumming observed that the 'main routes of telephone communication had been buried but were by no means complete'.[28]

In contrast, the corps deep-buried cable networks to the north were much better prepared. At Arras, a report by Frederick Dudgeon, GOC 56 Division, noted that on 28–29 March 'the Corps buried cable system was invaluable and communication was maintained to forward battalions until they had to leave their HQ'.[29] Similarly, due to a considerable amount of construction work that had taken place along the First and Second Army fronts, the corps' buried cable systems also fared much better than their Third and Fifth Army counterparts when *Georgette* began on 9 April.[30] At Armentieres, for instance, an intricate system of buried cables had been laid in cellars and sewers 'so that any section of a route could easily be tested and any required connections made'.[31] According to Lieutenant-Colonel H. W. Edwards, AD Signals IX Corps, 'the buried cable system withstood the shelling splendidly and telephone communication was maintained uninterrupted from Corps Headquarters down to Battalions in the line'.[32]

Infantry Brigade, noted that when 21 Division relieved the French 74th Division on the Aisne in May 1918, 'one of the first things I noticed was that the telephone wires were merely carried along the trenches, instead of being buried as was our usual practice'. D. V. Kelly, *39 Months with the 'Tigers', 1915–1918* (first published 1930; new ed., Uckfield: Naval and Military Press Ltd., 2006), 122–3.

[26] Priestley, *Work of the Royal Engineers*, 258.

[27] 'Lessons to Be Learnt from the Operations 21st to 27th of March, 1918', 8 April 1918, 25 Division Signal Company War Diary, WO95/2238, TNA.

[28] Hanway R. Cumming, *A Brigadier in France 1917–1918* (London: Jonathan Cape, 1922), 94.

[29] 'Report on the Operations of 56th Division in the Vicinity of Oppy and Gavrelle, 28th and 29th March 1918', 4 April 1918, Dudgeon Papers, IWM. See also 'Narrative of Artillery Operations in Connection with the German Attack on Gavrelle-Oppy Sector, March 28th, 1918', undated, XIII Corps War Diary, WO95/897, TNA.

[30] 'XXII Corps – Buried Cable System. Instructions No. 7 and 8', 19 January 1918, XXII Corps Signal Company War Diary, WO95/978, XI Corps Signal Company War Diary, 25 March 1918, WO95/890, TNA.

[31] Scrivenor, *Brigade Signals*, 45.

[32] Lieutenant-Colonel H. W. Edwards to James Edmonds, 7 February 1933, CAB45/122, TNA.

Plate 7.1 Canadian signallers repairing wire in communication trench, February 1918 (Canada. Dept. of National Defence/Library and Archives Canada/RCSigs.ca, MIKAN no. 3405811)

The combination of the shortage of working parties and the absence of a thorough deep-buried cable network along much of the Fifth Army front in particular meant that there were severe weaknesses in the BEF's communications system on 21 March. According to the history of the Signal Section of the 16/Manchesters (30 Division), as a result of the German bombardment 'it was impossible to know what was happening in front as all wires were broken'.[33] The intensity of the German artillery fire was matched by its accuracy.[34] An officer of 14 Division (III Corps) informed Sir James Edmonds after the war that the division's incomplete deep-buried cable system 'had been photographed from the air by the Germans with the result that they fired at the junctions... and everyone was disconnected in a few minutes'.[35] Likewise, Oliver Nugent, GOC 36 Division, informed his wife in a letter on 21 March that 'all the lines to the front are... cut and we have to depend on runners and byke [sic] orderlies, a very slow process when as in this case the Germans are

---

[33] 'Signal Section of the 16th Manchesters', 38, MRA.
[34] Edmonds, *Military Operations, 1918*, Vol. 1, 162.
[35] Quoted in Travers, *How the War Was Won*, 55.

shelling all the roads'.[36] All along the Fifth Army front confusion and disorganisation ensued, with information in and behind the battle zone often reduced to rumour as exposed and vulnerable telephone and telegraph cables were obliterated by German shellfire.[37] The reports reaching Fifth Army Headquarters at Nesle, for example, were 'meagre and scrappy, and did not enable either Corps or Army Headquarters to be absolutely sure of the true course of events'.[38]

The breakdown of the deep-buried cable networks was matched by the inability to utilise fully alternative means of communication. The thick early morning mist which masked the initial German assault impaired visual signalling and runners, as well as preventing the use of carrier pigeons and aerial observation.[39] According to the history of the King's (Liverpool) Regiment (14 Division):

From the outpost line and the front line SOS signals soared up into the murky sky – they were useless, the fog blotted them out and blinded the gunners who, seeing nothing, could only fire on targets already registered... Visual signalling and lamp signals were alike impossible. The gas shelling made the wearing of gas masks essential, and in the fog no runner could be expected to find his way.[40]

The nature of the German attack and the subsequent retreat also created several dilemmas for the practical utility of wireless. Not only were a large number of wireless sets destroyed by German shellfire, but many wireless messages that were transmitted were difficult to read on account of the success of German Field Stations in jamming the signals.[41] Furthermore, the novelty of being on the defensive, combined with 'the previous calm on the front, and the experience gained by divisions in attack', meant that many units had placed their wireless sets too far forward. Subsequently, when the Germans overran the BEF's forward defensive position, many

---

[36] Nugent to his wife, 21 March 1918, in Perry (ed.), *Major-General Oliver Nugent*, 227.

[37] 'The German Attack on the XVIII Corps Front, from 21st March–27th March, 1918', undated, XVIII Corps War Diary, WO95/953, 'Communications of XIXth Corps during Operations March 21st–April 4th, 1918', undated, XIX Corps Signal Company War Diary, WO95/970, TNA; 'Manuscript Recollections of the 1918 Retreat', undated, Sir James Hunter Blair Papers GS0820, LCL; Edmonds, *Military Operations, 1918*, Vol. 1, 164.

[38] Gough, *Fifth Army*, 262.

[39] 'A Signaller in France 1914–1918', 186, Craven Papers, REMA; Edmonds, *Military Operations, 1918*, Vol. 1, 164; Cumming, *A Brigadier*, 103. From 1 p.m., however, most of the fog had cleared, making aerial observation possible. See Gough, *Fifth Army*, 264.

[40] Everard Wyrall, *The History of the King's Regiment (Liverpool) 1914–1919*, Vol. 3 (London: Edward Arnold, 1933), 617.

[41] 'Communications of XIXth Corps during Operations March 21st–April 4th, 1918', undated, XIX Corps Signal Company War Diary, WO95/970, TNA.

units simply did not have the time to dismantle their sets and thus had to abandon their wireless equipment.[42]

The consequence of the German offensive was the almost-complete paralysis of the BEF's command and control system. The density and accuracy of the German bombardment, combined with the weaknesses of the BEF's defensive doctrine and the fragility of its communication networks, severed the army's nervous system to the point that 'to send news or to circulate orders became impossible'.[43] The 'perpetual shifting of Headquarters' also added to the difficulties of communication.[44] A report by 25 Division Signal Company stated that lateral communication with neighbouring units was 'rarely obtainable... due to ignorance of one another's line of retirement'.[45] Similarly, Major-General Cecil Pereira, GOC 2 Division, recorded in his diary on 24 March how it was 'getting increasingly difficult to keep touch with the Corps and the neighbouring Divns. We sent out D.Rs and Staff Officers at times to flanking Divisions giving them our dispositions and finding out theirs, but they are not always particular in advising us of their change of Divl. Hqrs. and this delayed most important information'.[46] Even Haig noted in his official despatch of 20 July 1918 that 'the frequent changes of headquarters and the shifting of the line' entailed significant problems in the maintenance of communication.[47] Many commanders, though, felt that they simply had no other option. Oliver Nugent, for instance, informed his wife that he had been forced to move his headquarters on the night of 21–2 March 'as it was getting dangerous and disturbing owing to the shelling'.[48]

Nonetheless, despite the enormous pressure that the BEF's command, control and communications system was put under during the spring of

---

[42] 'Wireless Communication in Fifth Army. 21st March to 2nd April, 1918', undated, Fifth Army Signal Company War Diary, WO95/534, 'Notes of a Conference Held by Third Army Commander 4th May 1918', undated, 17 Division War Diary, WO95/1984, TNA.

[43] Edmonds, *Military Operations, 1918*, Vol. 1, 164.

[44] 'The German Attack on the XVIII Corps Front, from 21st March–27th March, 1918', undated, XVIII Corps War Diary, WO95/953, TNA. See also: 'Communications of XIXth Corps during Operations March 21st–April 4th, 1918', undated, XIX Corps Signal Company War Diary, WO95/970, TNA.

[45] 'Lessons to Be Learnt from the Operations 21st to 27th of March, 1918', 8 April 1918, 25 Division Signal Company War Diary, WO95/2238, TNA.

[46] 'Private Diary of Major-General C. E. Pereira, Vol. III, 1917 & 1918', 2 Division War Diary, WO95/1289, TNA. See also 'Summary of Points Brought to Notice during Recent Operations', undated [March/April 1918], XIII Corps War Diary, WO95/897, TNA.

[47] Boraston (ed.), *Sir Douglas Haig's Despatches*, 238.

[48] Nugent to his wife, 22–24 March 1918, in Perry (ed.), *Major-General Oliver Nugent*, 228–31.

1918, it did not, contrary to some historians, break down completely.[49] Given the half-finished state of the British defensive and communication systems, the acute shortage of manpower and the intensity and accuracy of the German bombardment, it is remarkable that the BEF was able to function at all. According to Tim Travers, 'the German army defeated itself through its own offensives from March to July, because these offensives led to excessive casualties due to poor tactics, and because OHL employed an unwise strategy that did not maintain its objectives'.[50] While the German Army undoubtedly contributed to its own misfortune, the BEF also deserves some credit for its ability to recover from the setbacks of the opening days of the German offensive and prevent the enemy breaking through.[51] If anything, the issue of communications demonstrates the BEF's capacity to adapt to a major shift in its environment – one of the key characteristics of a 'learning organisation'.[52] Neither SS. 148 nor its successor SS. 191 had laid down any guidance with regards to communications in a retreat. Three years of trench warfare and a predominantly offensive strategy had resulted in 'a certain rigidity in the conception of communications'.[53] Thus, from 21 March the BEF was faced with the challenge of having to uphold a communications system whilst in a large-scale retreat and without any formal doctrinal guidance.

However, instead of completely disintegrating, the BEF's communications system, through ad hoc improvisation, pragmatic initiative and the dissemination of lessons learnt, soon began to adapt to the task at hand. As Gary Sheffield has noted, the 're-emergence of open warfare left the BEF no choice but to shake off some of their trench-bound habits'.[54] Admittedly, some of these habits were difficult to leave behind. It was noted at a Third Army conference that after three years of trench warfare 'many

---

[49] Travers, How the War Was Won, 50–90.   [50] Ibid., 175.

[51] Sheffield, Forgotten Victory, 221–37. Although he argues that the absence of clearly defined strategic and operational objectives doomed the German offensives from the start, David Zabecki also acknowledges that 'it is impossible to ignore completely the responses of the Allied forces and commanders in contributing to the German defeat'. Zabecki, German 1918 Offensives, 311–28.

[52] The concept of a 'learning organisation' was first popularised by Peter M. Senge in The Fifth Discipline: The Art and Practice of the Learning Organisation (London: Transworld, 1990). See also: Mark Easterby-Smith, John Burgoyne and Luis Araujo (eds.), Organizational Learning and Learning Organizations: Developments in Theory and Practice (London: SAGE, 1999). For an examination of the problems that military organisations confront when attempting to adapt in war, see Murray, Military Adaptation in War.

[53] Nalder, Royal Corps of Signals, 144.

[54] Gary Sheffield, 'The Indispensable Factor: The Performance of British Troops in 1918', in Peter Dennis and Jeffrey Grey (eds.), 1918: Defining Victory (Canberra: Army History Unit, 1999), 93–4.

commanders appear to be lost when separated from their telephones'.[55] The Director of Army Signals concurred: 'Trench warfare, and the constant use of the telephone... has resulted in a lack of foresight required for giving written orders for transmission by means other than the telephone, with the consequence that when telephone communication has failed, there is at once the cry that signal communication is impossible'.[56] In late April GHQ concluded that since telephonic communication 'cannot be extensively maintained in warfare of movement..., units must accustom themselves to rely entirely upon other methods of communication'.[57] Similarly, in a report detailing some of the major lessons observed during recent fighting, Maxse stated in May that 'officers must learn to discard the "telephone habit" as soon as open warfare commences and concentrate on alternative methods of communication'.[58]

Indeed, speedier and more efficient methods of conveying information were considered essential if the BEF was to get to grips with the difficulties of fighting whilst on the move and achieve a higher rate of tempo than the Germans.[59] This involved officers' not only 'organising and using communications to which they were not accustomed in trench warfare', but also having to get used to working with a more elementary and less rigid communications system.[60] A GHQ memorandum in April advised that 'in warfare of movement... it is necessary for headquarters to be prepared to dispense with heavy paraphernalia, to send away such officers and personnel as are not immediately necessary to the conduct of battle, and to work as far as possible with a message book only'.[61] Although many commanders and staff officers initially found it difficult to break free from their reliance on the telephone, by April there was

---

[55] 'Notes of a Conference Held by Third Army Commander, 4th May 1918', 17 Division War Diary, WO95/1984, TNA.

[56] 'Signal Communication', 13 April 1918, RG9-III-C-5/4440/1/9, LAC.

[57] 'Notes on Recent Fighting No. 8. Issued by the British General Staff, April 28, 1918', 30 April 1918, Miscellaneous Summaries of Information, 1917–19, General Headquarters, General Staff, G-5 Schools, Langres, Army Signal School, RG120/403/91/1, NARA.

[58] 'Lessons from the Recent Operations of the XVIII Corps', 16 May 1918, Notes on British Operations, April–October 1918, WO158/406, TNA.

[59] 'Tempo' is defined as 'the rate or rhythm of activity relative to the enemy'. See John Kiszely, 'The British Army and Approaches to Warfare since 1945', in Brian Holden Reid (ed.), *Military Power: Land Warfare in Theory and Practice* (London: Frank Cass, 1997), 180.

[60] 'Lessons from the Recent Operations of the XVIII Corps', 16 May 1918, Notes on British Operations, April–October 1918, WO158/406, TNA. See also: Lieutenant-Colonel J. S. Yule, 'Signals with Carey's Force: An Episode of the March Retreat, 1918', *Royal Signals Quarterly Journal*, 5 (1937), 158.

[61] 'Notes on Recent Fighting No. 4', 13 April 1918, Lieutenant-Colonel Charles Mitchell Papers, MG30-E61/31, LAC.

widespread evidence that more and more commanders were making greater use of alternative means of communication, if only because the surviving telephone and telegraph services were severely 'over-taxed and rapid-intercommunication impeded'.[62]

The inevitable loss of cable stores during the course of the retreat also forced British commanders and their staff to utilise alternative methods in order to facilitate the conveyance of information. The strict conservation of cable stores not only compelled headquarters to retire along existing cable routes, but also left commanders with little choice but to make greater use of wireless, despatch riders and liaison officers.[63] Some divisions handled between 100 and 120 wireless messages per day, far exceeding the average daily number of messages transmitted during the operations of 1916–17.[64] A report by Major Edward Bradley, OC 25 Division Signal Company, stated that wireless 'was used extensively' down to brigade headquarters and was 'to a great extent responsible for keeping the General Staff posted as to the trend of events along the whole [corps] front'.[65] A report by Fifth Army Signal Company argued that a better supply of wireless sets 'would have been invaluable to turn heavy guns on to fleeting targets, when in many cases the only means of communication was Despatch Rider who arrived far too late'.[66] In the aftermath of the Lys offensive, a report by Lieutenant-General Sir Alexander Hamilton Gordon, GOC IX Corps, also testified to the growing importance of wireless as an essential method of communication.[67] Although the use of wireless was still fraught with technical difficulties, its value over the telephone as a means of communication in mobile warfare could no longer be ignored.[68] As a Third

[62] 'Third Army No.G.34/659', 4 June 1918, RG9-III-C-5/4443/7/6, LAC. See also: 'Notes on Methods of Effecting Economies in the Volume of Traffic in the Signal Service', 29 May 1918, AWM27/311/13, AWM.

[63] 'Communications of XIXth Corps during Operations March 21st–April 4th, 1918', undated, XIX Corps Signal Company War Diary, WO95/970, 'Private Diary of Major-General C. E. Pereira, Vol. III, 1917 & 1918', 24 March 1918, 2 Division War Diary, WO95/1289, TNA; 'Signal Communication', 13 April 1918, RG9-III-C-5/4440/1/9, LAC; MacGregor and Welti (ed.), Signals from the Great War, 62.

[64] Nalder, Royal Corps of Signals, 143.

[65] 'Communications of 25th Divisional Signal Coy. in the Operations – 21st to 28th March 1918', 8 April 1918, 25 Division Signal Company War Diary, WO95/2238, TNA; Kincaid-Smith, 25th Division, 167.

[66] 'Wireless Communication in Fifth Army. 21st March to 2nd April, 1918', undated, Fifth Army Signal Company War Diary, WO95/534, TNA.

[67] 'Report on Operations Undertaken by IX Corps between 9th and 21st April 1918', 20 May 1918, IX Corps War Diary, WO95/836, TNA.

[68] 'Reference G.S. 781', 16 April 1918, 55 Division Signal Company War Diary, WO95/2916, TNA.

Army report in early May made clear: 'Wireless Telegraphy... must be exploited to the full'.[69]

In summary, communications profoundly affected the BEF's military performance during the spring of 1918, much more so than historians have hitherto acknowledged. The breakdown of communications in the wake of the initial German attack on 21 March exacerbated efforts to maintain command and control at every level, hampering the BEF's ability to regain the initiative from the Germans. The chief explanation for these communication difficulties was the unfinished state of the deep-buried cable networks, particularly along much of the Fifth Army front. However, the evidence presented here suggests that even if the buried cable system had been completed in time, the numerical manpower advantage held by the attacker, as well as the accuracy and concentration of his artillery bombardment, would have compelled the BEF to fall back anyway. Nevertheless, a more thorough and complete buried cable network might have helped the BEF to regain its composure much sooner and thus have prevented the Germans from penetrating as far as they did, as was demonstrated during the German Lys offensive in April. Here, the BEF's communications system performed much better, largely as a result of an extensive buried cable system that had been completed before the German onslaught. Indeed, in the broader context, the experiences of March–April afforded invaluable lessons regarding the nature of communications in more mobile operations. Although the BEF was on the defensive, the lessons learnt and the techniques devised during this period could equally be applied to the offensive. Thus, an examination of communications during the war-winning battles of the Hundred Days cannot ignore the lessons the BEF had drawn from its experiences during the first half of 1918.

Amiens

Often remembered because of Erich von Ludendorff's post-war assessment as 'the black day of the German army', the Battle of Amiens was one of the BEF's greatest successes of the war.[70] The battle represented a watershed for the BEF, demonstrating its tactical and operational effectiveness and

---

[69] 'Notes of a Conference Held by Third Army Commander 4th May 1918', undated, 17 Division War Diary, WO95/1984, TNA. For further evidence of the BEF's growing appreciation of wireless, see 'General Staff Circular No. 29. Wireless Communications', 26 June 1918, AWM25/425/26, AWM.
[70] General Erich Ludendorff, *My War Memories 1914–1918*, Vol. II (London: Hutchinson & Co., 1920), 679.

marking the beginning of the Allied Hundred Days offensives.[71] Amiens also provides a suitable case study with which to examine the British communications system at the start of the Hundred Days, in terms of both its growing flexibility and sophistication, and the challenges that it now faced in the transition from static to semi-mobile warfare. Indeed, many of the lessons learnt between 8 and 11 August were to form the basis of the BEF's communications practice for the remainder of the year.

In the summer of 1918, the important rail hub of Amiens was chosen by Haig as the ideal place from which to strike a major blow against the German Army.[72] Henry Rawlinson, GOC Fourth Army, was entrusted with the operation and submitted his plan of attack to GHQ on 17 July. In it, he stressed that success at Amiens would 'depend to a very large extent... on effecting a complete surprise'.[73] Secrecy was therefore of paramount importance and information pertaining to the attack was gradually released on a strict need-to-know basis.[74] The concealment of the movement and build-up of forces in the area were also high priorities. As well as ensuring that all troop and transport movements took place at night, the BEF organised a highly effective deception plan aimed at keeping the Germans second-guessing as to where the British attack would be launched. A key element of this plan involved the use of 'dummy wireless stations' near Arras to conceal the redeployment of the Canadian Corps to the Amiens sector.[75] Furthermore, in order not to give the game away, instructions were issued to all frontline units insisting that communication traffic 'should remain absolutely normal before impending operations'.[76] The combination of these factors, as well as the fact that there was to be no preliminary artillery bombardment, meant that, in essence, Fourth Army was adhering to the very principles that had brought about such initial success at Cambrai the previous November.

---

[71] Prior and Wilson, *Command on the Western Front*, 316–36; Harris with Barr, *Amiens to the Armistice*, 87–117; Sheffield, *Forgotten Victory*, 237–41.

[72] For British intelligence estimates on the state and preparedness of German forces prior to the battle, see Beach, *Haig's Intelligence*, 304–5.

[73] 'General Staff, Headquarters, Fourth Army, 220 (G)', 17 July 1918, Rawlinson Papers, RWLN 1/12, CAC.

[74] 'Fourth Army No. 32 (G). General Instructions', 31 July 1918, Fourth Army War Diary, WO95/437, TNA.

[75] Prior and Wilson, *Command on the Western Front*, 304; Rawling, 'Communications in the Canadian Corps', 17. For additional context, see John Ferris, '"FORTITUDE" in Context: The Evolution of British Military Deception in Two World Wars, 1914–1945', in Richard Betts and Thomas Mahnken (eds.), *Paradoxes of Strategic Intelligence* (London: Frank Cass, 2003), 117–65.

[76] '18th Division Instructions No. 5. Communications', 5 August 1918, 18 Division War Diary, WO95/2017, TNA.

Plate 7.2 A signaller in a tree mending lines broken by shellfire,
April 1918 (Henry Armytage Sanders: Alexander Turnbull Library,
Wellington, 1/2-013090-G)

From the point of view of communications, the preparation phase for Amiens was also somewhat similar to that of Cambrai. Given the need for secrecy, 'it was neither advisable nor possible to make any large or obvious preparations for communications to follow upon advance'.[77] Thus, the digging of deep-buried cable trenches was completely out of the question. The attacking infantry divisions of III Corps, Australian Corps and Canadian Corps were therefore required to make do with what little buried cable existed in their areas.[78] According to instructions issued by 18 Division, 'the Buried Cable System is at present in a bad state and wants thoroughly overhauling. . . it would be unwise to place too much reliance on the Buried Cable Routes remaining under a heavy bombardment'.[79] With this in mind, all efforts were concentrated upon extending cable communications once the attack was underway. According to Major (later Lieutenant-Colonel) Stan Watson, OC 2 Australian Division Signal Company:

At the Signal Conference it had been decided that. . . it was essential to construct a poled cable route down the centre of the [divisional] sector to the final objective, and that such construction would follow the attacking infantry. . . The provision of test points for junctions, maintenance and testing, manned by signals personnel, would be essential to enable moving units to obtain brief or lengthy contact as the battle proceeded. . . Subsequent to the infantry's moving off after zero hour, the cable detachments. . . would commence laying multi-pairs of lines on a route as close to the centre of the sector as possible. . . Immediately following, cable detachments with supplies of hop poles and cross-arms would proceed and pole the route.[80]

Within three hours of zero, the brigade station parties were expected to have 'connected to their respective cable heads by two pairs of cable to their advanced Brigade Exchange'.[81] This method was deemed 'the most reliable and flexible communication system practicable', as it 'formed a quick and efficient method of construction, well suited to the conditions of the moment'.[82] However, until the brigade forward

---

[77] 'Communications during Fourth Army Operations Commencing August 8th 1918', 22 August 1918, Fourth Army Signal Company War Diary, WO95/494, TNA.

[78] 'Communications for Offensive Action', 3 August 1918, 3 Australian Division Signal Company War Diary, WO95/3385, 'Report on Communications', 22 August 1918, 2 Australian Division Signal Company War Diary, WO95/3296, TNA; '1st Canadian Division. Preliminary Instructions', 4 August 1918, Maxse Papers, PP/MCR/C42, File 51, IWM.

[79] '18th Division Instructions No. 5. Communications', 5 August 1918, 18 Division War Diary, WO95/2017, TNA.

[80] 'Typescript of an Interview with Peter Liddle (1974)', 44, Watson Papers, LCL.

[81] 'Signal Communication Orders, Part 1', 3 August 1918, 2 Australian Division Signal Company War Diary, WO95/3296, TNA.

[82] 'Typescript of an Interview with Peter Liddle (1974)', 44, Watson Papers, LCL; Harris, *Signal Venture*, 52.

stations could be established and connected to the cable head, there would exist a two-to-three-hour telephonic 'blackout'. Given this predicament, all possible arrangements were to be made to maintain communication by wireless, visual and despatch riders until telephonic and telegraphic communication could be re-established.[83]

The experiences of March–April had convinced many officers as to the importance of wireless. Throughout the early summer many units observed 'silent days', whereby all but the most urgent priority telephonic and telegraphic messages were forbidden in an effort to cultivate more familiarity with, and greater reliance upon, wireless and other alternative methods.[84] Although wireless was still some way from attaining the same level of status as cable communication,[85] the feelings of anxiety, scepticism and mistrust that it once generated had now been replaced by a more general mood of confidence, reliance and expectation.[86] Thus, as the battle instructions issued by the Australian Corps to its divisions made clear, the employment of wireless at Amiens was to be 'exploited to the full'.[87] By the summer of 1918 British divisions were issued with four BF trench sets: one at division headquarters, one at advanced division headquarters and the others at the two leading infantry brigade headquarters. Brigades were also equipped with five Loop Sets, one of which went forward with the brigade forward stations and the others with the battalions.[88] Even more significant was the use of CW sets for directing artillery fire from forward observation posts, and for anti-aircraft, tank and RAF ground station signals.[89]

---

[83] 'Fourth Army No. 32 (G). General Instructions', 31 July 1918, Fourth Army War Diary, WO95/437, 'L.C. Instructions No. 2', 4 August 1918, Canadian Corps War Diary, WO95/1053, TNA.

[84] Priestley, *Work of the Royal Engineers*, 289; 'General Report on Wireless Telegraph Communication in the Canadian Corps, Feb. 1915–Dec. 1918', 16 April 1919, RG9-III-D-3/5058/968, LAC.

[85] See, for example, 'Communications. 4 Canadian Division Signal Company from 7th to 14th August 1918', undated, RG9-III-D-3/5005/693, LAC.

[86] This is clearly evident when analysing *SS. 135. The Division in the Attack* (November 1918), which, despite not having any direct influence upon the BEF's operations during the Hundred Days, did represent British practice at the time. See Jim Beach's introduction in *SS. 135. The Division in the Attack – 1918* (Strategic and Combat Studies Institute, The Occasional, No. 53, 2008), 3–5.

[87] 'Battle Instructions No. 3. Communications and Headquarters', 1 August 1918, Dill Papers 1/9, LHCMA.

[88] 'III Corps. No. G.S. 31. Communications', 4 August 1918, III Corps War Diary, WO95/680, 'Signal Communication Orders, Part 1', 3 August 1918, 2 Australian Division Signal Company War Diary, WO95/3296, 'L.C. Instructions No. 2', 4 August 1918, Canadian Corps War Diary, WO95/1053, TNA.

[89] 'Instructions No. 10. Signal Arrangements', 4 August 1918, 2 Australian Division War Diary, WO95/3259, TNA; Schonland, 'W/T. R.E.', 396–7.

All wireless activity was to be monitored and controlled by the corps directing stations.[90]

In addition to wireless, the open nature of the Amiens countryside favoured the use of visual signalling. A chain of visual stations was to be established forward of brigade headquarters and infantry equipped with Very lights, red and white flares and smoke rockets for SOS signals and calls for barrage lifts.[91] Meanwhile, infantry were to indicate their position to contact aeroplanes at designated times using red flares and reflective metal discs and by laying three rifles parallel to one another across the top of a trench.[92] Dropping stations were provided at corps and divisional headquarters where aeroplanes could drop maps and other information.[93] Nearly 600 carrier pigeons were made available to corps, who then distributed them amongst their divisions,[94] while infantry brigades and battalions and artillery groups were also issued with message carrying rockets, which had a maximum range of 2,300 yards.[95] Finally, repeated emphasis was placed upon the value of despatch riders, mounted orderlies, liaison officers and runners. Despatch riders were to operate chiefly between divisional and brigade headquarters,[96] whereas mounted orderlies and runners were to perform the main message carrying duties forward of brigade

---

[90] 'III Corps. No. G.S. 31. Communications', 4 August 1918, III Corps War Diary, WO95/680, TNA.

[91] 'Fourth Army No. 32 (G). General Instructions (Continued)', 2 August 1918, Fourth Army War Diary, WO95/437, 'III Corps. No. G.S. 31. Communications', 4 August 1918, III Corps War Diary, WO95/680, 'Instructions No. 10. Signal Arrangements', 4 August 1918, 2 Australian Division War Diary, WO95/3259, TNA; 'Battle Instructions No. 9. Light Signals, Message Rockets, Smoke', 3 August 1918, Dill Papers 1/9, LHCMA.

[92] 'Arrangements for Signalling to Aeroplanes with Reference to 12th Division Order No. 271', 6 August 1918, 12 Division War Diary, WO95/1827, TNA; 'Battle Instructions No. 11. Co-Operation of Infantry and Aircraft', 3 August 1918, Dill Papers 1/9, LHCMA.

[93] 'III Corps. No. G.S. 31. Communications', 4 August 1918, III Corps War Diary, WO95/680, TNA.

[94] 'General Instructions. Fourth Army No. 32 (G). General Instructions (Continued)', 4 August 1918, Fourth Army Records, Vol. 44, IWM.

[95] Priestley, *Work of the Royal Engineers*, 152–3; 'Third Australian Division – Signal Instructions No. 1', 6 August 1918, 3 Australian Division Signal Company War Diary, WO95/3385, TNA; 'Battle Instructions No. 9. Light Signals, Message Rockets, Smoke', 3 August 1918, Dill Papers 1/9, LHCMA.

[96] Pre-arranged timetables for despatch rider runs were formulated prior to the offensive. In 18 Division, for example, the despatch riders operating between divisional headquarters and divisional report centre would leave the latter at 7.30 a.m., 1 p.m., 5 p.m. and 9 p.m., whereas the despatch riders operating between the divisional report centre and the brigade headquarters would leave at 7 a.m., 12.30 p.m., 5 p.m. and 8 p.m. See '18th Division Instructions No. 5. Communications', 5 August 1918, 18 Division War Diary, WO95/2017, TNA.

headquarters.[97] Liaison officers were to operate at every level of command in order to achieve the best possible cooperation among neighbouring and subordinate units,[98] and among the different arms.[99]

In summary, careful planning and meticulous attention to detail characterised the communication preparations for Amiens. Communications had been 'carefully organised to ensure the maintenance of communication throughout the advance and after its conclusion'.[100] Given the anticipated advance, more reliance than ever before was placed upon alternative means of communication, particularly wireless, in order to facilitate the rapid transfer of information once the battle was underway. Additionally, arrangements had been made prior to the battle for the efficient maintenance and functioning of corps and divisional signal offices. A new and larger telephone switchboard was installed and extra lines laid to the Australian Corps' report centre. By the end of July, the Australian Corps Signal Company had 81 subscribers on its telephone exchange, averaging 237 telephone calls per hour.[101] To cope with this influx of information, not only did the Australian Corps Signal Company manage to lay 232 miles of new lines between 2 and 7 August, but the total number of personnel working at the signal office was increased from 60 to 90.[102] Overall, as Lionel Harris later recalled, 'Preparations were made with extreme speed and secrecy, complete in every detail and entirely on the assumption of success... We were passing into a new and very different era of the war'.[103]

The exploits of Fourth Army on 8 August have been well documented.[104] By the end of the day the attackers had managed to

[97] 'Signal Communication Orders Part 1', 3 August 1918, 2 Australian Division Signal Company War Diary, WO95/3296, 'Communications for Offensive Action', 3 August 1918, 3 Australian Division Signal Company War Diary, WO95/3385, TNA; '1st Canadian Division. Preliminary Instructions', 4 August 1918, Maxse Papers, PP/MCR/C42, File 51, IWM.

[98] 'Battle Instructions No. 19. Liaison, etc.', 6 August 1918, Dill Papers 1/9, LHCMA; 'Instructions No. 8. Liaison Officers', 4 August 1918, 2 Australian Division War Diary, WO95/3259, TNA.

[99] 'L.C. Instructions No. 2', 4 August 1918, Canadian Corps War Diary, WO95/1053, TNA.

[100] 'Battle Instructions No. 3. Communications and Headquarters', 1 August 1918, Dill Papers 1/9, LHCMA.

[101] 'Report by O.C., Company', 31 July 1918, Australian Corps Signal Company War Diary, WO95/1011, TNA.

[102] 'Report on Communications of Australian Corps during Operations of 8th August, 1918', undated, 'War Diary. Month of August 1918. Headquarters Section, Australian Corps Signal Company', Australian Corps Signal Company War Diary, WO95/1011, TNA. Details of the functioning of the Canadian Corps' report centre can be found in 'L.C. Instructions No. 6', 7 August 1918, Canadian Corps War Diary, WO95/1053, TNA.

[103] Harris, *Signal Venture*, 51.

[104] Travers, *How the War Was Won*, 115–38; Prior and Wilson, *Command on the Western Front*, 316–26.

advance up to eight miles on a 15,000-yard front, inflict 27,000 enemy casualties – of whom 12,000 were taken prisoner – and capture 400 guns.[105] As Haig wrote to his wife that day: 'Who would have believed this possible even 2 months ago? How much easier it is to attack, than to stand and await an enemy's attack!'[106] Despite this success, however, events during the course of the following days adhered to the all-too-familiar pattern of British attacks on the Western Front. With British troops growing ever wearier in the face of mounting German resistance, by 11 August 'the sting had gone out of the Fourth Army offensive'.[107] Nevertheless, the Battle of Amiens represented the BEF's greatest victory of the war. How, and to what extent, did communications contribute to this success?

The sudden switch to semi-mobile conditions on 8 August found the Signal Service in 'a thoroughly prepared state'.[108] All along the Fourth Army front cable was pushed forward rapidly by the brigade forward parties and within the space of two hours telephonic and telegraphic communication had been established between most brigade and battalion headquarters.[109] In the case of 2 Canadian Division, 'these lines... held for over two hours, allowing much valuable information to be sent back'.[110] Just as at Messines and on the opening days of the Battles of Arras and Cambrai the previous year, the successful construction and maintenance of these cable routes 'proved to be far more reliable than is generally conceded, owing no doubt to the fact that the enemy artillery was neutralised from the outset'.[111] However, by the early afternoon problems were beginning to surface. As at Cambrai, although hostile artillery fire was still light and sporadic, the main difficulty in maintaining telephonic and telegraphic communication was the damage caused by the heavy traffic of tanks, cavalry, transport and troops.[112] Tanks, in particular, 'tore cable lines to pieces' and 'carried away most lines that

---

[105] Edmonds, *Military Operations, 1918*, Vol. IV, 84–5.
[106] Haig to Lady Haig, 8 August 1918, in Sheffield and Bourne (eds.), *Douglas Haig*, 440.
[107] Harris with Barr, *Amiens to the Armistice*, 113.
[108] 'O.C.'s Report', 31 August 1918, 3 Australian Division Signal Company War Diary, WO95/3385, TNA.
[109] 'Report on Communications', 22 August 1918, 2 Australian Division Signal Company War Diary, WO95/3296, 3 Australian Division Signal Company War Diary, 8 August 1918, WO95/3385, TNA; 'Report on Operations of III Corps from July 1918 to October 1st. 1918', 11 November 1918, Fourth Army Records, Vol. 63, IWM.
[110] 2 Canadian Division Signal Company War Diary, 8 August 1918, WO95/3804, TNA.
[111] 'Notes on Operations of 2nd Aust. Div. on 8th August, and Succeeding Days', 5 September 1918, 2 Australian Division Signal Company War Diary, WO95/3259, TNA.
[112] 2 Canadian Division Signal Company War Diary, 8 August 1918, WO95/3804, TNA; 4 Canadian Division Signal Company War Diary, 8 August 1918, WO95/3891, TNA.

they cross[ed]'.[113] From 10 a.m., communication between 2 Canadian Division and its brigades 'became very difficult, such lines as had been laid being frequently broken by transport, by field artillery and by Tanks'.[114] Although Fourth Army later stated that co-operation between the various arms 'contributed in no small degree to the success of the operation',[115] it would appear that in the mobile conditions that prevailed on 8 August there was very little that could be done to prevent damage to newly laid cables by 'tanks roaming about in search of targets'.[116]

A second issue that presented itself during the course of the battle was the difficulty of maintaining telephonic communication over the considerable advances that were made. A report by 1 Canadian Division stated that 'as a result of the long distances of 5–8 miles that were experienced, telephonic communication was much interfered with'. The rubber insulation on the cable proved 'very brittle and unreliable'.[117] Similarly, it was found that upon reaching Cayeux-en-Santerre, the speaking distance of the cable laid between the advancing cavalry divisions and Cavalry Corps headquarters had been outranged. Fortunately, telegraphic communication was eventually established.[118] The unprecedented advances that were made on 8 August also created profound difficulties for the laying of cable communication in general. The Canadian Corps complained that the construction of new lines 'could not keep pace with [the] advance'.[119] Likewise, a report by Lieutenant-General Charles Kavanagh, GOC Cavalry Corps, stressed that 'although the cable was laid at a rapid rate, Divisional H.Q. at times moved too fast for the cable to keep pace with them'.[120] Artillery communications were also hampered as a result of the speed of the advance. 'The necessary length of line, the subsequent maintenance, the number of lines and the

[113] Canadian Corps Signal Company War Diary, 8 August 1918, WO95/1072, '174th Infantry Brigade Report on Signal Communications during Operations 8th to 12th August 1918', 21 August 1918, 58 Division War Diary, WO95/2990, TNA. See also: '3rd Cdn. Inf. Bde. Report on Operations. August 3rd to 20th. 1918', 20 August 1918, Currie Papers, MG30, E100/37/167, LAC.
[114] 'Operations of 2nd Canadian Division, 1918. Battle of Amiens', undated, Fourth Army Records, Vol. 65, IWM.
[115] 'Summary of Operations, 8th August 1918', Fourth Army Records, Vol. 44, IWM.
[116] Edmonds, *Military Operations, 1918*, Vol. IV, 57.
[117] 'Report on Amiens Operations, Aug. 8th–20th Inclusive, 1918', undated, Maxse Papers, PP/MCR/C42, File 51, IWM.
[118] 'Summary of Lessons from Recent Operations No. 6. Cavalry Corps G.X. 444/11', 24 August 1918, Fourth Army Records, Vol. 65, IWM.
[119] Canadian Corps Signal Company War Diary, 9 August 1918, WO95/1072, TNA.
[120] 'Summary of Lessons from Recent Operations No. 6. Cavalry Corps G.X. 444/11', 24 August 1918, Fourth Army Records, Vol. 65, IWM. For additional context on the cavalry at Amiens, see Kenyon, *Horsemen*, 204–14.

small number of linesmen available', 4 Australian Division Signal Company remarked, rendered it 'impossible to keep all Brigades of Artillery in direct touch with D.A.H.Q. by telephone whilst Brigades are moving'.[121] As will be shown, these were problems that were to cause commanders repeated headaches throughout the Hundred Days.

The final difficulty experienced at Amiens with regards to cable communication was a more familiar one. After 8 August, the increasing weight of German artillery fire caused significant problems in the maintenance of forward lines.[122] On 10 August, 2 Australian Division Signal Company recorded that 'a good deal of shell fire by day and bombs by night caused a great deal of trouble with lines both with Artillery and Infantry Brigades. Linemen were out almost continuously replacing breaks'.[123] On the following day, Fourth Army noted that 'harassing fire against our communications and battery areas was more pronounced',[124] while the lines laid by the advancing cavalry divisions 'were heavily damaged by bombing, and telegraphic traffic had to be dealt with by W/T'.[125] As Lionel Harris later observed, although the signal companies at Amiens were at last able to utilise cable wagons to lay lines to advancing units, 'a cable wagon with its six-horse team makes a conspicuous target, and we soon found it necessary to take advantage of the cover of hedges and woods to escape strafing from aircraft and shelling from the guns of the enemy rear guard'.[126] Nevertheless, although the importance of maintaining cable communications could not be 'too strongly impressed upon',[127] considerable emphasis was also placed on the utility of alternative means of communication in order to ensure the conveyance of orders, reports and other information.

Wireless, for example, proved at long last that it deserved recognition as the most prominent of the BEF's alternative methods of communication. This was particularly true of events during the initial hours of the attack, when brigade forward parties were preoccupied with laying and connecting their lines to their respective cable heads. Numerous unit war diaries testify to the 'good work' and 'invaluable assistance' rendered by

---

[121] 'Lessons Learned from Communications during Operations Commencing 8/8/18', 21 August 1918, 4 Australian Division Signal Company War Diary, WO95/3475, TNA.

[122] Rawlinson Diary, 10 August 1918, RWLN 1/11, CAC.

[123] 2 Australian Division Signal Company, 10 August 1918, WO95/3296, TNA.

[124] 'Summary of Operations, 11th August 1918', Fourth Army Records, Vol. 44, IWM.

[125] 'ZCO, 1914–1919', 24, Christian Papers, IWM.   [126] Harris, *Signal Venture*, 54.

[127] '4th Canadian Division Narrative of Operations, Battle of Amiens. August 8th to August 13th, 1918', 10 September 1918, Fourth Army Records, Vol. 65, IWM.

wireless communication during this period.[128] The experience of the
Cavalry Corps, who came to rely almost entirely upon wireless on 8–9
August,[129] led to the conclusion that wireless 'must be looked on as the
first means of getting into touch after a move'.[130] Likewise, when information could not be transmitted via telephone or telegraph as a result of
tanks destroying cables, wireless in the Canadian Corps was often the
first means commanders turned to in order to rectify the situation.[131]
However, the most noteworthy admiration of wireless communication
was given to CW. According to a report by 4 Australian Division Signal
Company, CW wireless 'has become a most important method of communication in Field Artillery – especially during recent operations in
which Brigades were constantly moving and with only one cable wagon
available to lay lines it meant that without wireless, Brigades were out of
touch for some considerable time after each move'.[132] The CW sets of
1 Canadian Division's artillery were also 'very successful... From the 9th
to the 11th inclusive, they handled 50 messages, 28 being in cipher and
22 in clear'.[133] For artillery fire to be directed both effectively and
quickly, artillery commanders had to be 'furnished with information
from all available sources with the least possible delay'.[134] CW wireless
proved an indispensable means to this end.[135] As Lieutenant-Colonel
Elroy Forde, AD Signals Canadian Corps, noted, 'It has been proved
that flash spotting by wireless is not only possible, but that better results
can be obtained than by the use of telephone'.[136] Similarly, the 3rd Tank
Brigade testified to the importance of CW, reporting that at one point
during the battle, 'a communication from Advanced H.Q. Tank Corps,

---

[128] I ANZAC Corps Wireless Section War Diary, 8 August 1918, WO95/1010, 'Report on
Communications', 22 August 1918, 2 Australian Division Signal Company War Diary,
WO95/3296, 2 Canadian Division Signal Company War Diary, 8 August 1918, WO95/
3804, 4 Canadian Division Signal Company War Diary, 8 August 1918, WO95/
3891, TNA.
[129] Cavalry Corps Signal Company War Diary, 8–9 August 1918, WO95/584, TNA.
[130] 'Summary of Lessons from Recent Operations No. 6. Cavalry Corps G.X. 444/11',
24 August 1918, Fourth Army Records, Vol. 65, IWM.
[131] Canadian Corps Signal Company War Diary, 8 August 1918, WO95/1072, TNA.
[132] 'Reference: Charging of Accumulators for C.W. Wireless Sets', 19 August 1918,
4 Australian Division Signal Company War Diary, WO95/3475, TNA.
[133] 'Report on Amiens Operations, Aug. 8th–20th Inclusive, 1918 – Appendix "G". Signal
Communications', undated, Maxse Papers PP/MCR/C42, File 51, IWM.
[134] SS. 135. The Training and Employment of Divisions, 1918 (January 1918), 25.
[135] 'Artillery Notes on Attack by Canadian Corps August 8th 1918', 24 August 1918, RG9-
III-D-3/4957/ 504, LAC.
[136] 'Operations. Amiens (Report on Wireless Communications) 8-8-18 to 22-8-18. Cdn.
Corps Heavy Arty', 29 August 1918, RG9-III-C-1/3923/10/6, LAC. For flash spotting
within the context of intelligence, see Beach, Haig's Intelligence, 93–4.

sent by Wireless, Wire, and by D[espatch].R[ider]. arrived – by Wireless
1 hour before the Wire, and 1 ¼ hours before the D.R.'.[137]

Although it was being used on a greater scale and yielding impressive
results, wireless was still prone to a number of technical constraints and
practical complications that ensured its use was not uniform throughout
the BEF.[138] This was particularly the case with regards to the use of
wireless forward of brigade headquarters. According to 4 Canadian
Division, the difficulties experienced between 8 and 11 August owed
much to the fact that 'wireless instruments had only been in use with
Brigades and Battalions a short time and were not properly adjusted'.[139]
Similarly, while a report by 4 Australian Division Signal Company
acknowledged that 'personnel still require training, especially in erecting
stations quickly', the war diary of 3 Australian Division Signal Company
records that the 42nd AIF Battalion took a Loop Set forward on 8 August
but 'efforts made to get it working were of no avail as the range of the Left
Bde. Forward Station was too great'.[140] Several units also experienced
difficulties in transporting their wireless equipment over the long
distances covered. For instance, 4 Australian Divisional Artillery found
it 'absolutely impossible to keep up a working supply of charged accumulators for C.W. Wireless Sets'.[141] During the afternoon of 8 August,
2 Canadian Division experienced difficulties with wireless communication to its brigades 'owing to the jamming of the numerous other sets on
the front and the large amount of business done by Corps to some of the
Divisional Stations'.[142] Some of the artillery's CW sets were also jammed
by the infantry's spark sets.[143] Finally, a post-action report by the 4th
Tank Brigade stated that three out of the four wireless tanks that were
allotted to the brigade 'had engine trouble at some point during the
operations... [and] were not fast enough for the pace of the advance'.

[137] 'Report on Operations – 8th to 12th August 1918', 8 September 1918, 3rd Tank
Brigade War Diary, WO95/105, TNA.
[138] For a comparison of the Australian, Canadian and British employment of wireless at
Amiens, see Andrew Powell, 'The Use of Wireless at the Battle of Amiens, 8–11 August
1918' (MA Dissertation, University of Birmingham, 2013).
[139] '4th Canadian Division Narrative of Operations, Battle of Amiens. August 8th to
August 13th, 1918', 10 September 1918, Fourth Army Records, Vol. 65, IWM.
[140] 'Lessons Learned from Communications during Operations Commencing 8/8/18',
21 August 1918, 4 Australian Division Signal Company War Diary, WO95/3475,
3 Australian Division Signal Company War Diary, 8 August 1918, WO95/3385, TNA.
[141] 'Reference: Charging of Accumulators for C.W. Wireless Sets', 19 August 1918,
4 Australian Division Signal Company War Diary, WO95/3475, TNA.
[142] 2 Canadian Division Signal Company War Diary, 8 August 1918, WO95/3804, TNA.
[143] 'Signals   Fourth   Australian   Divisional   Artillery.   Lessons   Learned   from
Communications during Operations Commencing 8/8/18', 21 August 1918, AWM4/
22/14/30, AWM.

Despite acknowledging that wireless communication 'proved very satisfactory', the report concluded that by the end of 8 August 'the distance
over which they were working was too great, and the directing stations
were moved forward... and an additional station was erected'.[144]

Thus, although wireless communication proved an indispensable asset
for many units during the Battle of Amiens, the transition from static to
semi-mobile warfare also served once more to highlight its limitations,
resulting in a general desire amongst commanders to re-establish cable
communications as soon as possible. Wireless constituted less than 5 per
cent of the total number of messages handled by 4 Canadian Division
Signal Company between 8 and 15 August.[145] This caused some advocates of wireless, such as the Cavalry Corps and the 5th Tank Brigade, to
argue that the potential of its use within the BEF was 'not as yet fully
realised' and that 'it might have been used more with advantage'.[146]
However, circumstances dictated that some units, particularly the more
mobile cavalry and Tank Corps, were able to make greater use of wireless
than others. Generally speaking, the overall impression gained from
surveying the after-action reports and war diaries concerning wireless
communication at Amiens is certainly more positive than those that were
written during the battles of 1916 and 1917. According to the ANZAC
signallers, wireless had demonstrated its value 'both as an emergency and
normal method of signalling'.[147] As 4 Canadian Division concluded in
early September, 'there is no doubt that Wireless forms a very important
communication between units and Division, and will be used to a far
greater extent in future operations'.[148]

Compared to wireless communication, the results obtained from
visual signalling proved more mixed. The initial attack on the morning
of 8 August began under a thick blanket of mist, which, although
assisting the infantry's advance, rendered visual signalling and aerial
observation 'worse than useless'.[149] The smoke and dust generated by

---

[144] '4th Tank Brigade Report on Operations August 8th to 11th 1918', 24 August 1918,
Fuller Papers 1/7, LHCMA.
[145] 'Communications: 4 Canadian Division Signal Company from 7th to 14th August
1918', RG9-III-D-3/5005/693, LAC.
[146] 'Summary of Lessons from Recent Operations No. 6. Cavalry Corps G.X. 444/11',
24 August 1918, Fourth Army Records, Vol. 65, IWM; 'Report on Communications of
the 5th Tank Brigade during the Operations Commencing August 8th 1918', 23 August
1918, Fuller Papers 1/7, LHCMA.
[147] I ANZAC Corps Wireless Section War Diary, 26 August 1918, WO95/1010, TNA.
[148] '4th Canadian Division Narrative of Operations, Battle of Amiens. August 8th to
August 13th, 1918', 10 September 1918, Fourth Army Records, Vol. 65, IWM.
[149] C. E. W. Bean, *Official History of Australia in the War of 1914–18*, Vol. VI: *The Australian
Imperial Force in France during the Allied Offensive, 1918* (Sydney: Angus and Robertson,
1942), 545.

the artillery barrage also compounded efforts to follow the course of the battle and obtain information by visual methods.[150] At 7 a.m., for example, a situation report received at Fourth Army headquarters from Sir John Monash, GOC Australian Corps, made specific reference to the delay of information received from the frontline as a result of the heavy ground mist.[151] According to 3 Canadian Division Signal Company, visual signalling did not become effective until late morning 'after the settling of the dust and the clearing of heavy smoke'.[152] Yet on 2 Australian Division's front, 'heat, haze, dust and the flat nature of the ground' continued to cause problems for visual methods of communication well into the afternoon.[153] Once the early morning mist had cleared, however, aerial observation provided a rich source of information. According to Archibald Montgomery, 'observation balloons were pushed well forward with the greatest rapidity. They obtained much useful information and performed valuable service in directing the fire of the mobile artillery'.[154] Of even more significance were the aerial observers of the RAF, whose wireless messages were 'the quickest and often the only means of discovering the enemy's artillery positions'.[155] According to 58 Division, 'contact aeroplanes constantly reported the arrival of our men on the final objective'.[156] Similarly, a report by 2 Australian Division stated that 'after sunrise the tin discs carried by the Infantry materially assisted our planes in picking up our positions'.[157] Indeed, it was later acknowledged that the assistance the RAF afforded the other arms as a means of communication was 'of equal or greater importance than [the] direct offensive action of [the] aircraft'.[158]

[150] 2 Australian Division Signal Company War Diary, 8 August 1918, WO95/3296, 2 Canadian Division Signal Company War Diary, 8 August 1918, WO95/3804, TNA; '3rd Cdn. Inf. Bde. Report on Operations. August 3rd to 20th. 1918', 20 August 1918, Currie Papers, MG30, E100/37/167, LAC.

[151] 'Operation Messages Received and Issued', 8 August 1918, Fourth Army War Diary, WO95/437, TNA.

[152] 3 Canadian Division Signal Company War Diary, 8 August 1918, WO95/3858, TNA.

[153] 'Report on Communications', 22 August 1918, 2 Australian Division Signal Company War Diary, WO95/3296, TNA.

[154] Major-General Sir Archibald Montgomery, *The Story of the Fourth Army in the Battles of the Hundred Days, August 8th to November 11th 1918* (London: Hodder and Stoughton, 1919), 50.

[155] 'Notes on Corps Squadron Work during the Somme Offensive, August 1918', Artillery Observation by RAF, AIR1/725/97/2, TNA.

[156] '58th Division. Narrative of Operations. Period 8th to 13th August 1918', undated, Fourth Army Records, Vol. 63, IWM.

[157] 'Notes on Operations of 2nd Aust. Div. on 8th August, and Succeeding Days', 5 September 1918, 2 Australian Division War Diary, WO95/3259, TNA.

[158] J. C. Nerney, 'The Western Front Air Operations, May–November 1918', 159, AIR1/677/21/13/1887, TNA.

While contact aeroplanes provided a steady flow of information from the battlefield, the same cannot be said of power buzzers and carrier pigeons. The former were found to be 'useless' on account of their weight and insufficient range, as well as 'the great amount of interference due to earth return lines'.[159] With regards to the latter, little use was actually made of pigeons on account of the mist and the success of other methods. Even when they were employed, a report by the 4th Tank Brigade noted that the quickest that a carrier pigeon message reached the brigade headquarters from a front line tank was 49 minutes, while the longest time recorded was 3 hours and 52 minutes.[160] By comparison, according to 2 Australian Division Signal Company, 'messages were delivered at Brigade Headquarters by Battalion runners 20 minutes after being handed in at the Signal Office of the Battalion'.[161] Despite being much faster than carrier pigeons, however, 'relay chains of runners, cyclists and horsemen established in some divisions could not compete in time and reliability with wires and cables'.[162] The distances with which they had to contend only added to their journey times. As Monash related after the war, 'The retransmission of such messages, in succession, by Battalions, Brigades and Divisions only prolongs the delay', a process 'far too dilatory for the exigencies of actual battle control'.[163] Similarly, although they were of 'inestimable value in carrying despatches between Brigades and Divisional Headquarters',[164] motorcycle despatch riders were 'taxed very heavily during the operations' owing to the distance between headquarters and also 'by the abnormal number of special D.R.L.S. required'.[165] The build-up of heavy road traffic throughout the battle further impeded the flow of information carried by despatch riders.[166]

---

[159] 'Operations. Amiens (Report on Wireless Communications) 8-8-18 to 22-8-18. Cdn. Corps Heavy Arty', 29 August 1918, RG9-III-C-1/3923/10/6, LAC; 2 Canadian Division Signal Company War Diary, 8 August 1918, WO95/3804, TNA.

[160] '4th Tank Brigade Report on Operations August 8th to 11th 1918', 24 August 1918, Fuller Papers 1/7, LHCMA.

[161] 2 Australian Division Signal Company War Diary, 12 August 1918, WO95/3296, TNA.

[162] Edmonds, *Military Operations, 1918*, Vol. IV, 93.

[163] Monash, *Australian Victories*, 124.

[164] 'Report on Communications', 22 August 1918, 2 Australian Division Signal Company War Diary, WO95/3296, TNA. Other positive reports can be found in: 'Operations of the 58th Division from 8–13 August 1918', 15 August 1918, III Corps War Diary, WO95/680, TNA; '4th Tank Brigade Report on Operations August 8th to 11th 1918', 24 August 1918, Fuller Papers 1/7, LHCMA.

[165] 'Report on Communications of Australian Corps during Operations of 8th August, 1918', undated, Australian Corps Signal Company War Diary, WO95/1011, TNA.

[166] Edmonds, *Military Operations, 1918*, Vol. IV, 157; 3 Canadian Division Signal Company War Diary, 9 August 1918, WO95/3858, TNA.

The change from static to semi-open warfare also presented a variety of other, related challenges for British commanders to contend with. The issue surrounding the location and distance between unit headquarters, although it had been a topic of discussion since the Somme campaign, was now of paramount importance in light of the considerable advance that had occurred on 8 August, most notably on the Australian and Canadian Corps' fronts. Events overnight and on the following day demonstrated that efficient communication depended very largely on co-ordination among the various levels of command and the location of all unit headquarters at suitable places. The advance that had occurred opened up large distances among divisional, brigade and battalion headquarters. The communication links connecting these headquarters had not been sufficiently catered for when corps received their orders from Fourth Army on the night of 8–9 August to renew the offensive the following morning. Subsequently, Australian and Canadian divisional headquarters did not receive these instructions until the early hours of 9 August, upon which they then had to be re-drafted and transmitted to brigade headquarters via an overextended communications system. In these circumstances many frontline units received their orders with less than seven hours to make the necessary preparations for the attack.[167] Even in 58 Division, 'owing to the shortness of notice received, verbal instructions had to be conveyed to all commanders concerned'.[168]

As a result, the attacks made by Fourth Army on 9 August were disjointed, poorly co-ordinated and lacked surprise.[169] According to Charles Bean, it was 'a classic example of how *not* to follow up a great attack'.[170] The depth of the advance on the previous day had profound implications for the BEF's command and control system and, in particular, for the ability of the high command to furnish frontline units with timely information. Both the British and Australian official historians were apt to point out that the time taken for orders to be conferred, explained and transmitted to the battalions in the frontline was greatly underestimated by the high command.[171] Indeed, *SS. 135*, published in January, had stated explicitly that 'not less than 24 hours should elapse between the time the order leaves Divisional Headquarters and the hour fixed for the operation, otherwise Company and Platoon Commanders

[167] Prior and Wilson, *Command on the Western Front*, 328–30; Schreiber, *Shock Army*, 52.
[168] 'History of the 58th Division. The Battle on August 8th', undated, 58 Division War Diary, WO95/2990, TNA.
[169] Moir, *History of the Royal Canadian Corps of Signals*, 32.
[170] Bean, *Official History of Australia*, Vol. 6, 684.
[171] Edmonds, *Military Operations, 1918*, Vol. 5, 578; Bean, *Official History of Australia*, Vol. 6, 683.

will have great difficulty in completing their arrangements on time'.[172] As a report by 4 Canadian Division maintained: 'Brigades must choose their Report Centre so as to facilitate their own communication being open to Battalions. In the same way, Divisional Report Centre should be selected in order to facilitate communication with Brigades'.[173] Despite these instructions, it would appear that the system for transmitting information forward was still rather sluggish.[174]

As a result of the large advance made on 8 August, the difficulties of communication during the subsequent day's fighting induced a strange sense of déjà vu. According to Major Leigh Mallory, Commanding 8 (Tank Contact) Squadron, 'It became practically impossible to communicate with the Tank Battalions, and very difficult to get in touch with the Brigades. Distances were great, the roads were bad, and blocked with traffic, and it was naturally impossible to communicate by phone'.[175] Thus, as at Cambrai in 1917, the breakdown of communications in the follow-up phase at Amiens meant that the operational tempo and achievements of the opening day were neither repeated nor capitalised upon. According to Shane Schreiber, this is proof that the BEF's 'signals capabilities had failed their first test in conditions of "open warfare"'.[176] While there is an element of truth in this assessment, it does seem rather harsh given the successes of 8 August. Monash was adamant that despite the early morning mist and the long distances over which reports had to travel, 'the stream of information which reached me, by telegraph, telephone, pigeon and aeroplane was so full and ample that I was not left for a moment out of touch with the situation'.[177] Monash found himself in a position which had eluded all the corps commanders on the Somme in 1916. In many respects this was evidence of the growing flexibility and sophistication of the BEF's communications system during the latter stages of the war. Nevertheless, although Monash was the beneficiary of a communication system at Amiens that a corps

---

[172] SS. 135. The Training and Employment of Divisions, 1918, 14. Interestingly, the November edition of SS. 135 increased this time to 36 hours. SS. 135. The Division in the Attack – November 1918, 39.

[173] '4th Canadian Division Narrative of Operations, Battle of Amiens. August 8th to August 13th, 1918', 10 September 1918, Fourth Army Records, Vol. 65, IWM.

[174] This problem was not just confined to the BEF. In early August, Ludendorff complained that 'an order issued at midnight by a division, with supplementary instructions added by lower formations, does not reach a company commander, let alone a section commander, until 6 a.m.' See 'Translation of a German Document', 10 August 1918, GHQ War Diary, WO95/21, TNA.

[175] 'History of Tank and Aeroplane Cooperation', 31 January 1919, AIR1/1671/204/109/26, TNA.

[176] Schreiber, Shock Army, 52.   [177] Monash, Australian Victories, 122–3.

commander in 1916 could only dream of, the events of 9–11 August suggest that poor communications were still undermining the tempo of the BEF's operations. This is significant because according to some historians the success of the BEF during the Hundred Days owed a great deal to the high tempo of its operations, which was achieved as a result of several important factors, such as the devolution of command, the employment of a combined-arms 'weapons system' and improvements to logistics and staff work at all levels.[178] Did the communications system contribute to the BEF's high operational tempo during this period, or was it more of a hindrance?

Communications in the Hundred Days

Writing to British GHQ on 16 June 1918, Ferdinand Foch offered some personal reflections on the nature of command.[179] According to the Allied Generalissimo: 'As soon as battle commences it is the duty of the command to <u>conduct the battle</u> by quickly obtaining information of its development and by utilising its available resources at the right time'.[180] However, despite Foch's emphasis on the importance of acquiring rapid information, a report by 63 Division Signal Company following the Battle of the Canal du Nord, four months later, noted that 'the most difficult problem to be faced is [still] the maintenance of communication during the first hour of the battle'.[181] Throughout the Hundred Days, even though the BEF was employing a much more robust, flexible and sophisticated communications system than it had ever done before, tenuous communications were still having a detrimental impact on its operations. These problems stemmed largely from the conditions of semi-open warfare which characterised the battles of late 1918. As Haig's chief artillery advisor later remarked, the possibilities of command in war 'are limited by the capacity of one man's brain, the facilities for communication and the degree of movement that is going on. The more mobile the fighting, the fewer will be the units that can be controlled by one

---

[178] Simpson, *Directing Operations*, 175; Andy Simpson, 'British Corps Command on the Western Front, 1914–1918', in Sheffield and Todman (eds.), *Command and Control*, 115.

[179] Elizabeth Greenhalgh, *Foch in Command: The Forging of a First World War General* (Cambridge: Cambridge University Press, 2011).

[180] 'Translation of Note No. 1459, dated 16 June 1918, by General Foch', General Information by GHQ to Army Commanders, April 1917–November 1918, WO158/ 311, TNA.

[181] 'Notes on Signal Communications 63rd (RN) Division during Operations – 27th September to 2nd October 1918', 15 October 1918, 63 Division Signal Company War Diary, WO95/3104, TNA.

commander, and the greater will be the difficulty of communicating orders'.[182] Although numerous attempts were made to resolve the communication difficulties experienced, some of which proved successful, on the whole the BEF never found a permanent solution to the problem of ensuring that commanders were furnished with timely and accurate information as to the progress of an operation.

Throughout the last months of the war there was growing recognition amongst British officers that cable communications were not ideally suited to the conditions of mobile warfare. For example, Major-General Philip Robertson, GOC 17 Division, noted at a conference in September that 'too much reliance is being placed on the telephone' and that this 'excessive use must stop'.[183] Likewise, in reflecting on the lessons learnt during October and November, Major-General Henry Jackson, GOC 50 Division, observed that 'the trench warfare methods of laying telephone lines to everyone must be recognised to be impossible'.[184] In spite of these protestations, however, large sections of the BEF had become too reliant on the static telephone system of the previous three and a half years, resulting in a general demand throughout the summer and autumn of 1918 for telephone communications on a scale experienced during trench warfare.[185]

The mobile nature of operations and the advances made 'necessitated cables of abnormal length'.[186] Standard practice was for brigade, division and corps headquarters to advance along 'one main pre-ordained route' which was 'fully advertised well in advance and changed as little as possible'.[187] Brigades would establish their headquarters in advance of the cable head when they moved forward, while divisions would usually locate their advanced headquarters on the cable heads and connect themselves to the brigades via a network of over-ground cables, preferably poled. Advanced divisional headquarters were connected to divisional headquarters by three circuits, 'which were found to be sufficient

---

[182] Lieutenant-General Sir Noel Birch, 'Artillery Development in the Great War', *The Army Quarterly*, 1 (1920), 83.

[183] 'Notes for Conference, September 1918', undated, 17 Division War Diary, WO95/1985, TNA.

[184] 'Lessons Learnt during Recent Operations', 14 November 1918, Fourth Army Records, Vol. 64, IWM.

[185] 'Information as to HQs of Formations and Signals – Notes from Lt. Col. C. J. Aston, 38th Div. Sigs., V Corps, from 21st Aug. 1918', 3 October 1937, CAB45/184, 'Communications 42nd Division, by Lieut-Col. S. Gordon Johnson, Late O.C. Signals 42nd Division', 30 September 1937, CAB45/186, TNA.

[186] 'General Remarks on August Operations', undated, 5 Australian Division Signal Company War Diary, WO95/3596, TNA.

[187] Priestley, *Work of the Royal Engineers*, 311.

Plate 7.3 An observation post on Westhoek Ridge, Ypres, 3
February 1918 (Henry Armytage Sanders: Alexander Turnbull Library,
Wellington, 1/2-013049-G)

to carry the traffic between Divisional Headquarters and their advanced
exchange'. With regards to corps headquarters, 'when it appeared certain
that a considerable advance was likely to take place, it was decided to
push forward two main trunks of open wire, one in each half of the Corps
area. Each of these forward routes consisted of 16 wires'.[188] Often,
divisions found themselves connected to corps by a single cable which
was laid mainly at night when units halted.[189]

The Signal Service did everything possible to speed up the construction
of cable routes. During the course of the fighting at Arras in late September and early October, the Motor Airline Sections of the Canadian Corps
Signal Company 'built 35 miles of 6-pair semi-permanent route and
rewired 15 miles of German route'.[190] Throughout the Hundred Days
extensive use was made of existing German and civilian lines.[191] Captain

[188] 'Report on Operations of III Corps from July 1918 to October 1st. 1918', 11 November
1918, Fourth Army Records, Vol. 63, IWM.
[189] Edmonds, *Military Operations, 1918*, Vol. 5, 577–8.
[190] 'General Remarks', 30 September 1918, Canadian Corps Signal Company War Diary,
WO95/1072, TNA.
[191] XXII Corps Signal Company War Diary, 28 September 1918, WO 95/978, 'Addendum
No. 3 to V Corps O.O. No. 239. Dated 1/11/1918. Signal Communications',
2 November 1918, V Corps War Diary, WO95/752, TNA. On the employment of
German POWs for reeling up and 'disentangling mixed-up coils of wire', see diary

Wallace noted after the war that many of the German and civilian routes that were re-conditioned and adapted to suit the communication needs of the Allied forces 'had been left almost intact' by the retreating German Army.[192] According to the Fourth Army Signal Company war diary at the end of October: 'These [lines] proved quite useful except for the confusion which arose owing to diverse methods of maintaining these routes'.[193] Similarly, of the French and Belgian 'underground long distance telegraph circuits', it was noted that 'special attention' was to be paid to these routes upon their capture. Accordingly, 'as soon as the situation permits, they should be sought for, dug up and cut... The ends will be most carefully insulated with compound and protected by wooden boxes. The trench should then be filled in, and the point marked with a permanent marker'.[194] That orders were being issued for signal units to economise on cable supplies and to make every endeavour to salvage and then use captured German and civilian lines[195] supports the argument of historians such as Jonathan Boff that the material superiority of the BEF during the Hundred Days was perhaps not so overwhelming as has often been suggested.[196]

A range of methods were also employed in the construction and maintenance of cable routes forward of divisional headquarters. Horse-drawn cable wagons were widely employed for laying lines in forward areas, while there was repeated emphasis on the need to make use of captured reels of German cable.[197] During the Battle of the Sambre (4–6 November), a signal tank 'proved of the greatest value' to 50 Division by 'laying two lines over very difficult country to Advanced Brigade Head-quarters'. The tank was able to carry 50 miles of cable, issuing it to brigades, battalions and artillery en route.[198] Newly laid cables were also

entry, 28 October 1918, in Jim Beach (ed.), *The Diary of Corporal Vince Schürhoff, 1914–1918* (Stroud: Army Records Society, 2015), 295.

[192] 'Memoirs of 1914–1918', 86, Wallace Papers, IWM. See also: R. E. Priestley, *Breaking the Hindenburg Line: The Story of the 46th (North Midland) Division* (London: Unwin Fisher, 1919), 168.

[193] 'October 1918. General Notes', 31 October 1918, Fourth Army Signal Company War Diary, WO95/494, TNA.

[194] 'Signalling Special Instructions No. 1', 7 October 1918, Fifth Army Signal Company War Diary, WO95/559, TNA.

[195] 'General Staff Circular No. 35. Economy in use of Signal Cable', 4 September 1918, AWM4/22/1/28, AWM.

[196] Boff, *Winning and Losing*, 74–91.

[197] MacGregor and Welti (ed.), *Signals from the Great War*, 96; Scrivenor, *Brigade Signals*, 109.

[198] 'Lessons Learnt during Recent Operations', 14 November 1918, Fourth Army Records, Vol. 64, IWM.

poled or raised off the ground onto trees in order to prevent damage from tanks, cavalry and infantry units.[199] Such measures often proved invaluable. During the Battle of the Canal du Nord, the trunk lines of 1 Canadian Division 'were poled most of the way... and good telephone communication was maintained'.[200] Similarly, the successful maintenance of 1 Division's cables throughout Fourth Army's attack on the Hindenburg Line in late September was 'ascribed to the fact that these were laid always well away from roads and across country'.[201] Finally, the poled cable routes constructed by the signal company of 2 Australian Division during the successful capture of Montbrehain in early October ensured that 'telephone communication [with the brigades] was kept almost continuously throughout the operations'.[202]

Despite these measures, the rapidity with which new headquarters and communications had to be established created problems which often defied practical solutions. One brigade signal officer, for instance, described his work throughout the summer and autumn of 1918 as 'one long struggle to maintain communications with battalions over long distances, laying miles of cable and taking it up again if possible', which was made all the more difficult by the fact that battalion headquarters 'would not keep still'.[203] While some brigade headquarters found themselves as far back as four miles from their battalions,[204] it was not uncommon for corps to be as much as 10–20 miles behind divisional headquarters following a rapid advance and, as a result, speech over the long telephone lines that connected the two headquarters was almost inaudible.[205] The length of the lines laid between 2 Australian Division and its advancing brigades in early October also caused very faint and intermittent speech, resulting in the employment of runners to compensate.[206] It was found that laying field cables on wet ground also impeded

[199] 'General Remarks on August Operations', undated, 5 Australian Division Signal Company War Diary, WO95/3596, 3 Canadian Division Signal Company War Diary, 1 September 1918, WO95/3858, 'Report on Communications – 62nd (W.R.) Division. 24th August, 1918–3rd September, 1918', 6 September 1918, 62 Division Signal Company War Diary, WO95/3076, 'Signal Instructions', 29 September 1918, 2 Australian Division Signal Company War Diary, WO95/3296, TNA.
[200] 1 Canadian Division Signal Company War Diary, 27 September 1918, WO95/3751, TNA.
[201] 1 Division Signal Company War Diary, 30 September 1918, WO95/1255, TNA.
[202] 'Report on Communications during Period 2nd to 6th October, 1918', 16 October 1918, 2 Australian Division Signal Company War Diary, WO95/3296, TNA.
[203] Scrivenor, *Brigade Signals*, 113, 110.   [204] Ibid., 54.
[205] Priestley, *Work of the Royal Engineers*, 310; Priestley, *Breaking the Hindenburg Line*, 168.
[206] 'Report on Communications during Period 2nd to 6th October, 1918', 16 October 1918, 2 Australian Division Signal Company War Diary, WO95/3296, TNA.

telephone communication over long distances.[207] In addition, cables remained highly vulnerable to damage from tanks and shellfire from German rear guards.[208] As a report by the signal company of 63 Division in mid-October observed: 'Brigade Headquarters are now invariably situated in dugout systems well known to the enemy, and therefore a certain target for the enemy's artillery'.[209] However, the BEF's telephone and telegraph lines were not just under threat from German artillery fire. According to a British liaison officer, 'The Major succinctly outlined my job as being nominally that of assisting the French but actually that of preserving British signal routes from pillage and ruin at the hands of our happy go luck[y] Allies'. The reason for this, as the officer explained, perhaps lay in the perceived superiority of British telecommunication equipment:

I had two 50-line switchboards full of such subscribers as Delousing Stations, Laundry Offices and, of course, the more usual "Q" Staff offices, such as railheads – provision and ammunition dumps, etc. The French on the other hand, for all the communications of an Army Corps, had one ancient "Hughes" Telegraphic Writer working to Army H.Q. and one 50-line switchboard. Any English Corps has at least one and probably two "Wheatstone" high speed machines working Duplex to Army H.Q., Duplex Morse Sounders to all Divisions and Artillery and anything up to 200 lines on the switchboard.[210]

Overall, despite the variety of problems that the more mobile operations of late 1918 posed for line-based communications, the BEF still placed considerable emphasis on the importance of telephonic and telegraphic communication. To some extent this was understandable given the trench-bound communication habits of three and a half years of static warfare and the drawbacks of the alternative means of communication. As a report by the 188th Infantry Brigade in early September admitted: 'Accustomed as we are to the telephone, when removed from it we become somewhat helpless'.[211] However, the lavish scale and complicated

[207] 'Summary of Important Points (Not Specially Emphasised in Reports on Previous Operations) Brought Out during the Advance from the Trinquis and Sensee Rivers, between October 11th and 22nd 1918', 6 November 1918, RG9-III-C-5/4438/1/1, LAC.

[208] '3rd Cdn. Inf. Bde. Report on Operations. Aug. 26th-Sep. 3rd. 1918', 6 September 1918, Currie Papers, MG30, E100/37/168, LAC; 32 Division Signal Company War Diary, 29 September 1918, WO95/2384, 'Report on Operations from 27th September. 2nd Signal Co. R.E.', 6 October 1918, 2 Division Signal Company War Diary, WO95/1333, TNA; 'Report on Operations. 4th Tank Brigade, September 27th to October 17th 1918', 27 October 1918, Fuller Papers 1/7, LHCMA.

[209] 'Notes on Signal Communications 63rd (RN) Division during Operations – 27th September to 2nd October 1918', 15 October 1918, 63 Division Signal Company War Diary, WO95/3104, TNA.

[210] 'Memoirs of 1914–1918', 79, Wallace Papers, IWM.

[211] Quoted in Boff, *Winning and Losing*, 184.

nature of the cable networks constructed during the period of trench warfare were now things of the past.[212] Although this gave headquarters a degree of freedom and mobility that they lacked during the battles of 1915–17, the nature of the operations between August and November 1918 meant that it was 'only possible to provide a very simple and limited system of lines'.[213] Consequently, commanders and staff at all levels were forced to make increasing use of the alternative methods of communication in order to 'ease pressure on lines' and 'to economise cable wherever [possible]'.[214]

The only alternative to telephonic and telegraphic communication which had any appreciable use during the Hundred Days was wireless. Although 'the efficiency of the wireless system improved greatly in the latter phases of the operations',[215] it was noted as early as the end of August that wireless was proving 'a useful means of communication when cables have for a time been cut, and also to relieve the lines when traffic has been heavy'.[216] Similarly, a report by 4 Canadian Division Signal Company in September stressed that wireless was 'proving to be a most valuable, vital and reliable supplementary method of communication and it is hoped that all Staffs will be persuaded to appreciate its value and utilise it as much as possible'.[217] As Major E. F. Churchill, a signal officer with the 1st Tank Brigade, noted, 'Communications [during the Hundred Days] were stretching a tremendous distance and if it had not been for wireless we could not have maintained them'.[218]

The control of all wireless communication within a corps sector was still maintained with the use of a Wilson set by the wireless section at the corps directing station.[219] However, apart from in the Canadian Corps, wireless communication between corps and divisional headquarters only

---

[212] Lieutenant J. R. Byrne, *New Zealand Artillery in the Field: 1914–18* (Auckland: Whitcombe and Tombs, 1922), 258.

[213] 'Notes on Communications during Recent Operations', 7 September 1918, 18 Division Signal Company War Diary, WO95/2028, TNA.

[214] '34th Division General Staff Instructions No. 7. Notes on Forthcoming Operations', 23 September 1918, 34 Division War Diary, WO95/2437, 'G.S. 3550', 13 October 1918, 58 Division Signal Company War Diary, WO95/2996, TNA.

[215] 'Report on Communications during Recent Operations', 5 October 1918, 52 Division Signal Company War Diary, WO95/2893, TNA.

[216] 'General Remarks on August Operations', 5 Australian Division Signal Company War Diary, WO95/3596, TNA. See also: 'Report by 1st Canadian Divisional Signal Company, C.E., Bourlon Wood Operations', October 1918, RG9-III-C-5/1/1, LAC.

[217] 'Communications. 4th Canadian Divisional Signal Coy. From the 1st to 5th September, 1918', 9 September 1918, 4 Canadian Division Signal Company War Diary, WO95/3891, TNA.

[218] 'Memories 1914–1919', 36, Churchill Papers, IWM.

[219] Nalder, *Royal Corps of Signals*, 148–9.

constituted a very small percentage of the total information exchanged between the two levels of command. In the case of III Corps, this was because the service offered by telephone, telegraph and despatch riders proved more than adequate.[220] At the divisional level, a Wilson set was kept at advanced division headquarters for controlling and monitoring forward communications and 'acting as a transmitting and receiving station to and from the Bde. Stations and the station allotted to the Divisional Observation Officer'.[221] In addition, four trench sets were employed at the headquarters of division, advanced division and the two leading brigades.[222] Finally, Loop sets were made readily available to infantry brigades, some of which were issued to battalions.[223]

The success of this wireless system varied according to the level of command. Generally speaking, the further down the chain of command the more difficult wireless communication became. There were plenty of instances which highlighted the value of wireless between division and brigade headquarters. For example, on the night of 28/29 September, during Second Army's Flanders offensive, wireless kept communication alive between 41 Division and its brigades after all other methods had failed.[224] Similarly, during Fourth Army's assault on the Beaurevoir Line, 2 Australian Division lost all telephonic and telegraphic communication with its brigades on the afternoon of 2 October as a result of heavy enemy shellfire. Nevertheless, as a post-battle report highlighted, 'During this period 5th and 7th A.I. Bdes. [Trench] sets disposed of eight priority messages'. It was noted that wireless communication proved more efficient than ever, 'no doubt due to Brigade Staffs, and Brigade Signal Officers taking more interest in this method of communication, and employing it to a greater extent'.[225] These successes contrasted strongly with the poor results obtained by power buzzers.[226] The technology was considered 'useless, being too heavy and of too short a

[220] 'Report on Operations of III Corps from July 1918 to October 1st. 1918', 11 November 1918, Fourth Army Records, Vol. 63, IWM.

[221] '46th Divisional Signal Company. General Instructions for Communication in Battle', undated, 46 Division Signal Company War Diary, WO95/2678, TNA.

[222] 'Notes on Communications during Recent Operations', 7 September 1918, 18 Division Signal Company War Diary, WO95/2028, TNA.

[223] 'Report on Operations of III Corps from July 1918 to October 1st. 1918', 11 November 1918, Fourth Army Records, Vol. 63, IWM.

[224] 41 Division Signal Company War Diary, 28 September 1918, WO95/2627, TNA.

[225] 'Report on Communications during Period 2nd to 6th October 1918', 16 October 1918, 2 Australian Division Signal Company War Diary, WO95/3296, TNA.

[226] 'Notes on Communications during Recent Operations', 7 September 1918, 18 Division Signal Company War Diary, WO95/2028, 'Report on Communications during Recent Operations', 5 October 1918, 52 Division Signal Company War Diary, WO95/2893, 'Notes on Signal Communications 63rd (RN) Division during Operations – 27th

range' for the operations the BEF was now conducting.[227] It was noted that the brigade signal officers in 1 Canadian Division 'consider they secure better results by employing the men of the Power Buzzer Pool on maintaining telephone lines'.[228] Further, since power buzzers were 'found to be of little use during operations of a more or less mobile nature', many divisional and brigade signal officers had suggested their abolition in favour of more Trench wireless sets, which had proven of much greater value.[229]

Indeed, successful results were obtained from the use of Loop sets between brigades and battalions. Wireless proved 'of the utmost value' to 51 Division's operations on 11–12 October, for instance, with battalions 'in touch with brigades throughout by wireless and several messages... sent without delay'.[230] However, wireless communication forward of brigade headquarters was fraught with difficulties. Its use within such close proximity of the enemy meant that security restrictions were sometimes vigorously enforced.[231] The experience of 4 Canadian Division during the Battle of the Drocourt-Quéant Line in early September led it to advocate afterwards that 'urgent operation priority messages should not be sent by wireless, on account of the dangers of interception'.[232] Yet as one signal officer related after the war, 'in the stress of battle cipher and code are slow and often had to be dispensed with and messages sent in clear'.[233] Some wireless operators were given permission to send messages in clear once operations became mobile.[234] Yet this practice

September to 2nd October 1918', 15 October 1918, 63 Division Signal Company War Diary, WO95/3104, TNA.

[227] 'Operations. Amiens (Report on Wireless Communications) 8-8-18 to 22-8-18. Cdn. Corps Heavy Arty', 29 August 1918, RG9-III-C-1/3923/10/6, LAC.

[228] 'Report on Wireless Communication during the Operations at Arras, Aug. 26th–Sept. 10th, 1918. 1st Canadian Division', undated, RG9-III-C-1/3928/11/3, LAC.

[229] 'Report on Operations of III Corps from July 1918 to October 1st. 1918', 11 November 1918, Lieutenant-General Sir Richard Butler Papers 69/10/1, IWM.

[230] 'Report on Communications during Operations between 11th/12th October', undated, 51 Division Signal Company War Diary, WO95/2856, TNA. See also: 14 Division Signal Company War Diary, 28 September 1918, WO95/1890, 1 Division Signal Company War Diary, 30 October 1918, WO95/1255, TNA; 'Lessons Learnt during Recent Operations', 14 November 1918, Fourth Army Records, Vol. 64, IWM.

[231] Brigadier Harry Hopthrow, Interview (1990), 011581/17, Department of Sound Records, IWM.

[232] 'Communications. 4th Canadian Divisional Signal Coy. From the 1st to 5th September, 1918', 9 September 1918, 4 Canadian Division Signal Company War Diary, WO95/3891, TNA.

[233] 'Information as to HQs of Formations and Signals – Notes from Lt. Col. C. J. Aston, 38th Div. Sigs., V Corps, from 21st Aug. 1918', 3 October 1937, CAB45/184, TNA.

[234] See, for example: Australian Corps Signal Company War Diary, 24 September 1918, WO95/1011, TNA; 'Summary of Lessons from Recent Operations No. 6. Cavalry Corps G.X. 444/11', 24 August 1918, Fourth Army Records, Vol. 65, IWM.

was not universal and there is much to suggest that fears concerning wireless insecurity contributed significantly to the fall to negligible proportions of the amount of traffic generated by Loop sets as the campaign wore on.[235] The value of Loop sets was also discounted by a dearth of highly trained operators at the brigade and battalion levels.[236] As one report concluded, 'where good operators manned the sets, it was possible to get through a large amount of traffic, but poor operators were helplessly lost', clearly highlighting the need for better and more consistent training at the lower levels.[237]

Above all, the fact remains that the environment that lay beyond brigade headquarters was still not conducive to the widespread and effective use of the wireless technology of the era. The aerials of Loop sets were too conspicuous and thus 'vulnerable under concentrated shelling'.[238] Even if they managed to avoid damage from German shell and machine gun fire, 'the distance of Battalion Headquarters from Brigades was usually greater than the efficient range for these sets'.[239] Finally, as one artillery signal officer observed, even in 1918 spark wireless sets 'were very cumbersome contraptions, very difficult to tune in and keep in adjustment. Such signals as did come through were almost impossible to read'.[240] Since the mainstay of the BEF's wireless communication system rested on the employment of spark sets, the limited choice of frequencies that such sets offered, combined with their use in ever-greater numbers, meant that mutual interference was often inevitable.[241] Even if precautions were taken, the deliberate jamming of wireless messages by the enemy could not be prevented.[242]

By contrast, the artillery's use of CW wireless for counter-battery work proved to be 'a technical triumph for the British'(see Figure 7.1).[243] CW

---

[235] 'Report on Communications during Recent Operations' 5 October 1918, 52 Division Signal Company War Diary, WO95/2893, TNA.

[236] 'Notes on Communications during Recent Operations', 7 September 1918, 18 Division Signal Company War Diary, WO95/2028, TNA.

[237] 'Operations. Amiens (Report on Wireless Communications) 8-8-18 to 22-8-18. Cdn. Corps Heavy Arty', 29 August 1918, RG9-III-C-1/3923/10/6, LAC.

[238] 'Notes on Signal Communications 63rd (RN) Division during Operations – 27th September to 2nd October 1918', 15 October 1918, 63 Division Signal Company War Diary, WO95/3104, TNA.

[239] 'Report on Communications during Recent Operations', 5 October 1918, 52 Division Signal Company War Diary, WO95/2893, TNA. See also: 'Report on Communications – Battle of Arras – 2nd/4th-9-18', 14 September 1918, Currie Papers, MG30, E100/37/168, LAC.

[240] 'A Signaller in France 1914–1918', 186, Craven Papers, REMA.

[241] Australian Corps Signal Company War Diary, 24 September 1918, WO95/1011, TNA.

[242] See, for example, 1 Australian Division Signal Company War Diary, 29 September 1918, WO95/3198, TNA.

[243] Bidwell and Graham, Fire-Power, 142.

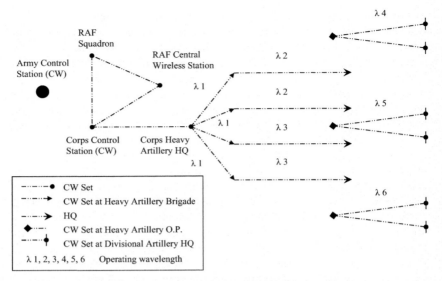

Figure 7.1 A typical Army Corps CW wireless system, August–November 1918

sets were less conspicuous that their spark counterparts, operated on a wider range of frequencies, and gave little trouble from jamming.[244] As one artillery officer recorded in his diary in mid-August:

The CW Wireless as a means of communication between mobile artillery units and Arty Hdqrs has shown itself to be the only one dependable for open warfare. These sets can be put into action within 15 minutes and therefore send back location of artillery units and special information within 30 minutes of taking up a new position.[245]

According to a Canadian Heavy Artillery report, flash spotting by CW wireless produced 'better results [than] can be obtained... by the use of

[244] 'Notes on Communications during Recent Operations', 7 September 1918, 18 Division Signal Company War Diary, WO95/2028, 'Communications. 4th Canadian Divisional Signal Coy. From the 1st to 5th September, 1918', 9 September 1918, 4 Canadian Division Signal Company War Diary, WO95/3891, 'Notes on Signal Communications 63rd (RN) Division during Operations – 27th September to 2nd October 1918', 15 October 1918, 63 Division Signal Company War Diary, WO95/3104, TNA; 'Report on Operations of III Corps from July 1918 to October 1st. 1918', 11 November 1918, Fourth Army Records, Vol. 63, IWM.
[245] Major Arthur Hardie Bick and Peter Hardie Bick (ed.), *The Diary of an Artillery Officer: The 1st Canadian Divisional Artillery on the Western Front* (Stroud: Amberley, 2011), 111.

telephone'.[246] The CRA, 4 Canadian Division, concurred, remarking after the fighting around Arras in early September that 'he would not go into action again without these sets'.[247] Indeed, during the last two months of the war cable communication was practically 'non-existent, in so far as the Divisional Artillery was concerned'.[248] CW operators were subsequently kept very busy, with some units averaging 80 messages per day.[249]

CW was also employed within the Tank Corps, where, according to one officer, 'although the distances were far greater than the set was intended to work, the signals were quite clear'.[250] CW also allowed the Allies to develop and experiment with wireless telephony further. At a conference held at RAF headquarters on 18 July, not only was the issue of wireless telephony between aeroplanes discussed, but it was also recognised that there was 'a large field of usefulness for wireless telephones from air to ground principally in connection with reconnaissance, counter attack patrol work, and co-operation with Tanks'.[251] However, at the close of the war only two squadrons had been equipped with wireless telephones, and they were forbidden to fly over enemy lines for fear of being shot down and the sets captured.[252] At the same time, tests involving wireless telephony between tanks and between tanks and aircraft had revealed that communication was practicable, but the operational range was limited to just 500 yards.[253] Thus, wireless telephony remained at a basic, experimental stage when the war ended.[254]

Compared to that of CW wireless, the performance of the other means of communication during the last four months of the war varied from satisfactory to very poor. Visual signalling was employed to good effect during the initial stages of the campaign but became increasingly less relevant from late September onwards because of the unaccommodating autumnal weather. The reports of both 18 and 32 Divisions in early

---

[246] 'Operations. Amiens (Report on Wireless Communications) 8-8-18 to 22-8-18. Cdn. Corps Heavy Arty', 29 August 1918, RG9-III-C-1/3923/10/6, LAC.

[247] 'Report on Wireless Communication during the Operations at Arras, Aug. 26th–Sept. 10th, 1918, 4th Canadian Division', RG9-III-C-1/3923/11/3, LAC.

[248] Steel, 'Wireless Telegraphy', 542.

[249] 'Report on Wireless Communications during the Operations at Arras, Aug. 26th–Sept. 10th, 1918', 24 September 1918, RG9-III-C-1/3923/11/3, LAC.

[250] 'Memories 1914–1919', 35, Churchill Papers, IWM. For more detail, see Hall, 'Development of Tank Communications', 159–60.

[251] 'Minutes of a Meeting to Discuss the Tactical Use of Wireless Telephony in the R.A.F., Held at H.Q., R.A.F.', 18 July 1918, AIR1/32/15/1/169, TNA.

[252] Hartcup, War of Invention, 154–5.

[253] 'Experimental Work on Radio-Telephony', undated [summer 1918], 1st Tank Brigade Signal Company War Diary, WO95/100, TNA.

[254] Priestley, Work of the Royal Engineers, 248.

September testified to 'the value of visual between brigades and battalions and between the latter and the frontline' during a rapid advance in open warfare. Heliographs and lamps were found to be invaluable since 'the country was admirably suited, the weather good and there was little shell fire'.[255] By late September, however, the full use of visual methods was not always possible because attacks usually took place in the early hours of the morning 'when mist and smoke interfered seriously with visibility'.[256] According to a signaller with the 21st Battery, Canadian Field Artillery, during the Battle of the Canal du Nord

the weather turned chilly and rainy and there was a mist which totally obscured our gun position, making communication with them next to impossible. It was well that we had no important messages to send as they could only have been delivered by our riding back [across the canal] to deliver them in person.[257]

In addition to the restrictions imposed by the unfavourable weather conditions,[258] although visual signalling 'provided a much useful means of relieving traffic on telephone lines',[259] it was noted in a report by 2 Australian Division Signal Company that 'the disposal of traffic by visual is slow, particularly so when passing through a series of transmitting stations. Even with first class signallers, the traffic could not be handled as rapidly and efficiently as by W/T, or by wire'.[260]

As the utility of visual signalling declined during the course of the Hundred Days so too did that of carrier pigeons. Although the British Army was operating 150 pigeon lofts on the Western and Italian fronts in 1918, the speed of the BEF's advance on the former rendered the use of carrier pigeons impractical.[261] According to Richard Butler: 'In the latter stages of the operations, when the lofts were a considerable distance from

[255] 'Notes on Communications during Recent Operations', 7 September 1918, 18 Division Signal Company War Diary, WO95/2028, 'Some Lessons from Recent Fighting. 8th to 11th Aug., 18th to 12th Sept. 1918', 12 September 1918, 32 Division War Diary, WO95/2372, TNA.

[256] 'Report on Operations of III Corps from July 1918 to October 1st. 1918', 11 November 1918, Butler Papers, IWM. See also: 'Account of the Part Taken by the 46th Division in the Battle of Bellenglise on the 29th September, 1918', undated, Fourth Army Records, Vol. 63, IWM; 1 Canadian Division Signal Company War Diary, 27 September 1918, WO95/3751, TNA.

[257] Ogilvie, Umty-Iddy-Umty, 51.

[258] 'Report by 1st Canadian Divisional Signal Company, C.E., Bourlon Wood Operations', October 1918, RG9-III-C-5/4438/1/1, LAC.

[259] 'Report on Signal Communications during Operations. 1st September 1918 to 5th September 1918', 12 September 1918, 63 Division Signal Company War Diary, WO95/3104, TNA.

[260] 'Report on Communications during Period 2nd to 6th October, 1918', 16 October 1918, 2 Australian Division Signal Company War Diary, WO95/3296, TNA.

[261] Osman, Pigeons in the Great War, 6.

the line and the birds were taking anything from an hour to an hour and a half to fly from the frontline to the lofts', the messages received by this means 'proved absolutely valueless' as a result of the time delay.[262] During 2 Division's attack over the Canal du Nord, the average time taken for pigeon messages to reach divisional headquarters from the frontline was two hours.[263] Lofts could be moved closer to the frontline, but it then took at least three weeks of training for the birds to become accustomed to the new location.[264] As a consequence of these many drawbacks, a report by the 2nd Tank Brigade in November concluded that 'it will never be possible to count on this form of communication' in mobile warfare.[265]

The unreliability of visual signalling and carrier pigeons meant that a heavy burden of responsibility for the conveyance of orders, reports and other information fell on the shoulders of other message carriers. Weather permitting, contact aeroplanes provided a steady flow of information from the battlefield to rear headquarters. Such was the case during the 3rd Tank Brigade's attack on the Drocourt-Quéant Line on 2 September, when messages delivered by aeroplanes at the rallying point 'were received at the Brigade Signal Office at the very satisfactory average time of 20 minutes after being dropped'.[266] However, in scenes reminiscent of 1914, it was despatch riders and runners who provided the backbone of the BEF's forward communications system during the closing months of the war. Heavy duties, very long runs and the difficulty of locating headquarters in unfamiliar country became part and parcel of the despatch rider's routine once again.[267] On account of their greater speed of delivery, 'motorcyclists were used whenever road conditions made it possible'.[268] In fact, an examination of various divisional signal

[262] 'Report on Operations of III Corps from July 1918 to October 1st. 1918', 11 November 1918, Butler Papers, IWM.
[263] 'Report on Operations from 27th September. 2nd Signal Co. R.E.', 6 October 1918, 2 Division Signal Company War Diary, WO95/1333, TNA.
[264] 'Outstanding Features of the Recent Offensive. Signal-Communications', 18 October 1918, Assistant Director of Signals, 1st ANZAC Corps War Diary, AWM4/22/1/29, AWM.
[265] '2nd Tank Brigade. Report on Operations: 4th November, 1918', 20 November 1918, Fourth Army Records, Vol. 65, IWM.
[266] '3rd Tank Brigade. Report on Operations with Canadian Corps – 2nd September 1918', 18 September 1918, 3rd Tank Brigade War Diary, WO95/105, TNA.
[267] 'General Remarks on August Operations', undated, 5 Australian Division Signal Company War Diary, WO95/3596, 'Notes on Communications during Recent Operations', 7 September 1918, 18 Division Signal Company War Diary, WO95/2028, TNA.
[268] 'Communications. 4th Canadian Divisional Signal Coy. From the 1st to 5th September, 1918', 9 September 1918, 4 Canadian Division Signal Company War Diary, WO95/3891, TNA.

company war diaries during this period reveals just how much reliance was placed upon despatch riders. Throughout September, for example, 1 Australian Division Signal Company handled daily an average of 426 DRLS 'packets', compared with 185 telegrams and just 7 wireless messages.[269] However, as the campaign wore on they could not always adhere to delivery timetables as a result of 'exceptionally bad roads and more than ordinary congestion of traffic'.[270]

Runners, meanwhile, continued to be vexed by the same difficulties that hindered their efficiency during the years of static warfare. In mid-September the 187th Infantry Brigade noted that runners were taking as much as three hours to deliver messages between battalion and company headquarters.[271] Nonetheless, there were also occasions when runners were the only option available. Following receipt of a telephone message from divisional headquarters that a pre-arranged attack for 27 August was to be cancelled, the commander of the 110th Infantry Brigade was forced to send 'his Brigade-Major and another officer to run and stop the two leading regiments', as there 'was no other means of communicating'.[272] Thus, it was the opinion of one commander that, in spite of their drawbacks, despatch riders, liaison officers and runners were an essential ingredient to the BEF's success in open warfare.[273]

Command and Control in the Hundred Days

The efficiency of the BEF's communications system during the Hundred Days did not just depend upon the performance of the various means of communication employed. One of the most profound challenges confronting British officers regarded the location of, and the distance between, headquarters. These difficulties had a huge bearing upon command and control, and were to surface repeatedly throughout the campaign. In a report detailing the lessons learnt during the operations of late August and early September, Lieutenant-General Sir Charles Fergusson, GOC XVII Corps, stated:

---

[269] 'Graph Showing Signal Office Traffic. Month of September 1918', 1 Australian Division Signal Company War Diary, AWM4/22/11/40, AWM.

[270] 'O.C's Report', 30 September 1918, 3 Australian Division Signal Company War Diary, WO95/3385, TNA.

[271] 'Narrative of Operations, 11–15 September, 1918', 187th Infantry Brigade War Diary, WO95/3089, TNA. I am indebted to Dr Jonathan Boff for pointing out this reference to me.

[272] Cumming, *Brigadier*, 222.

[273] 'Report on Operations of III Corps from July 1918 to October 1st. 1918', 11 November 1918, Butler Papers, IWM.

Divisional, brigade and battalion commanders must be right up where they can see the fluctuations of the battle and command. To command by the telephone – basing action on the reports of junior commanders – is a crime. It is better to be cut off communication with the rear than to be out of direct touch with the front.[274]

Fergusson's view was shared by other commanders, such as Major-General Cecil Nicholson, GOC 34 Division, who issued a set of 'General Staff Instructions' on 23 October which stipulated:

Headquarters of Infantry and Artillery Brigades and of Battalion Commanders must be further forward than is the case in trench warfare. This does not mean that every Battalion and Brigade Commander should be in a position whence he can control the movements of every unit under his command, but he should be so located with reference to the troops engaged and the positions of reserves, that he can influence the progress and action of the fight by the use of his reserves and auxiliary weapons.[275]

The positioning of headquarters in relation to each other profoundly affected communications during the last months of the war. Before any operation, great emphasis was laid on 'the advisability of before-hand information of proposed new headquarters. Such information [is] very essential to the efficiency and prompt arrangement of signal services'.[276] Both before a move of his headquarters and upon the immediate arrival at the new headquarters, a commander had to inform his superior and those commanders on either flank of the new location of his headquarters; 'failure to do this means the miscarriage of orders, delays, etc., and may lead to a failure of an operation'.[277] Furthermore, the new position of his headquarters was to 'be clearly marked by distinguishing flags', in order to assist runners and liaison officers.[278]

Battalion and brigade headquarters had to move rapidly in order to keep in touch with the action and each other. The best practice for brigades was for them to 'move as close together as possible and along a pre-arranged route so that Signals only have to maintain one forward route'. With regards to battalion headquarters, it was deemed essential that they moved forward with their reserve companies. It was found that

---

[274] 'Lessons Learnt during the Operations from 21st August to 7th September', undated, XVII Corps War Diary, WO95/936, TNA.

[275] '34th Division. General Staff Instructions No. 15', 23 October 1918, 34 Division War Diary, WO95/2437, TNA.

[276] 3 Canadian Division Signal Company War Diary, 2 September 1918, WO95/3858, TNA.

[277] SS. 135. The Division in the Attack – 1918, 64–5.

[278] 'Instructions for Operations. Fourth Army No. 273 (G)', 23 September 1918, Fourth Army Records, Vol. 45, IWM.

those battalion commanders who remained at their report centres 'were not able to keep in close touch with the situation owing to the rapidity of the advance, and were not able to take charge of their Battalions when the advance was checked'.[279] Thus, in 5 Australian Division in early September, although the 14th AIF Brigade headquarters was roughly 5,000 yards behind its battalions, the brigade forward station would reduce the distance to 2,000 yards.[280] To simplify and speed up communications further, and to ensure greater co-ordination between brigades and battalions, headquarters were regularly grouped together, or in the case of infantry brigade and artillery group headquarters, located in very close proximity.[281] Subsequently, as the 'General Instructions' issued by 46 Division Signal Company prior to the division's successful breach of the Hindenburg Line in late September made clear, if brigades could be located in the same headquarters, 'Brigade Section Officers will keep close liaison and... will arrange to economise personnel by running a common Signal Office for both Brigades'.[282] Meanwhile, at division headquarters, the divisional commander and CRA 'were able to control the whole situation from a central point, where they could each consult the other as Artillery support was needed or Infantry dispositions were changed'.[283] Such measures to improve command and control proved highly effective and were subsequently incorporated into *SS. 135*, published in November.[284]

With regards to division headquarters, a report by Henry Jackson noted that while in previous battles 'it may have been better for Divisional Headquarters to be stationary as earlier information as to the situation was received by Pigeon, Aeroplanes, Telephone, etc.', in the conditions which prevailed in the autumn of 1918 'the only way of keeping touch with the situation is by constantly moving forward and

---

[279] 'Lessons Learnt during Recent Operations', 14 November 1918, Fourth Army Records, Vol. 64, IWM.

[280] 'Report upon Signal Communications during Operations Extending from 31st August 1918 to 3rd September 1918', 18 September 1918, 5 Australian Division Signal Company War Diary, AWM4/22/15/33, AWM.

[281] '42nd Division. Battle Instructions No. 1. Signal Communications', 25 September 1918, 42 Division Signal Company War Diary, WO95/2651, 'Report on Communications during Operations between 11th/12th October', undated, 51 Division Signal Company War Diary, WO95/2856, 'Information as to HQs of Formations and Signals – Notes from Lt. Col. C. J. Aston, 38th Div. Sigs., V Corps, from 21st Aug. 1918', 3 October 1937, CAB45/184, TNA; 'Report on Operations. 4th Tank Brigade September 27th to October 17th 1918', 27 October 1918, Fuller Papers 1/7, LHCMA.

[282] '46th Divisional Signal Company. General Instructions for Communication in Battle', undated, 46 Division Signal Company War Diary, WO95/2678, TNA.

[283] Priestley, *Breaking the Hindenburg Line*, 95.

[284] *SS. 135. The Division in the Attack – 1918*, 64–5.

Plate 7.4 Canadian Signal Section laying cable. Advance East of Arras, September 1918 (Canada. Dept. of National Defence/Library and Archives Canada/ RCSigs.ca, MIKAN no. 3405814)

being sufficiently close to keep personal touch with the Brigadiers'.[285] Similarly, 18 Division Signal Company stressed that the farther forward divisional headquarters was placed, 'the shorter will be the length of the forward communications, thereby increasing the speaking efficiency of field cable and decreasing the length of important lines to be maintained'.[286] In XIII Corps, divisional headquarters often moved either late in the evening or in the early morning on an almost-daily basis in order to keep in contact with their brigades.[287] However, in spite of these moves, divisional headquarters could sometimes find themselves as much as 6 to 12 miles behind their brigades, as was the case for 5 Australian Division in late August and early September.[288]

---

[285] 'Lessons Learnt during Recent Operations', 14 November 1918, Fourth Army Records, Vol. 64, IWM.

[286] 'Notes on Communications during Recent Operations', 7 September 1918, 18 Division Signal Company War Diary, WO95/2028, TNA.

[287] 'Lessons Learnt during Recent Operations', 14 November 1918, Fourth Army Records, Vol. 64, IWM.

[288] 'Report upon Length of Communications between Division and Brigades during Recent Operations', 19 September 1918, 5 Australian Division Signal Company War Diary, AWM4/22/15/33, AWM.

With divisional headquarters often moving on a daily basis, the distance between the latter and corps headquarters resulted in a number of complications. Writing to his wife on 11 September, Monash explained: 'If my headquarters thereby falls back more than five or six miles behind the division, the maintenance of communication by telegraph and telephone becomes very difficult'.[289] Similarly, in his diary on 9 October Major-General Reginald Pinney, GOC 33 Division, noted: 'Our wires are very bad and touch with Corps (thank God) is almost impossible'.[290] Beside the problem of attenuation with telephonic communication, the extensive distance between corps and divisional headquarters affected telegraphic communication. For instance, 50 Division's headquarters moved a total of six times between 4 and 10 November, whereas XIII Corps headquarters moved just once. The end result was that the gap between the two headquarters was extended from 13 to 18 miles. According to a post-action report by the divisional commander, 'From a Division point of view, it is not so great a drawback to be cut off from the Corps as it is to be cut off from the fighting troops'.[291] From the point of view of Lieutenant-General Sir Thomas Morland, GOC XIII Corps, however, it was a major inconvenience. On 8 November, Morland issued a memorandum to his divisional commanders outlining his frustration with the fact that since 'priority telegrams [between corps and divisional headquarters] are taking as much as 5 ½ hours in transmission..., the situation as known at Corps Headquarters is bound to be somewhat vague'.[292]

Thus, the large distances between corps and divisional headquarters made it increasingly difficult for corps commanders to obtain real-time information as to the progress of operations. This may partly explain why a general process of decentralisation occurred throughout the BEF during the Hundred Days. While by 1918 commanders and their staffs were much more experienced than they had been in 1916,[293] and subsequently much greater confidence was placed in their abilities, the

---

[289] Letter from Monash to his wife, 11 September 1918, in F. M. Cutlack (ed.), *War Letters of General Sir John Monash* (Sydney: Angus and Robertson, 1935), 266.

[290] Diary entry, 9 October 1918, Major-General Sir Reginald Pinney Papers 66/257/1, IWM. The corps referred to was V Corps, whose commander, Lieutenant-General Cameron Shute, Pinney did not get on well with. See Robbins, *British Generalship*, 32; and, Boff, *Winning and Losing*, 224.

[291] 'Lessons Learnt during Recent Operations', 14 November 1918, Fourth Army Records, Vol. 64, IWM.

[292] 'XIII Corps 1451/61. G.A.', 8 November 1918, Fourth Army Records, Vol. 64, IWM. On the movement and location of XIII Corps headquarters during this period, see diary entries, 4–11 November 1918, in Thompson (ed.), *General Sir Thomas Morland*, 294–6.

[293] See, for example, the assessment of Kelly, *39 Months*, 137–8.

difficulties of communications which resulted from the conditions of mobility necessitated a more decentralised system of command.[294] As one officer remarked after the war, in 1918 'decentralization occurred everywhere... Control became limited to what the controlling authorities could arrange before the battle... The individuality of subordinate officers came again into play'.[295] Although the BEF possessed a more flexible and sophisticated communications system, it had still not solved the problem of how to bridge the communication gap between the front-line troops and the commanders to the rear. Since there was no permanent technical solution to this dilemma, if the BEF was to maintain the initiative it had to delegate more responsibility to divisional, brigade and even battalion commanders. Otherwise, the decision cycle would have been far too slow to allow for a higher level of tempo.[296]

Indeed, with the conditions of mobility clearly affecting the higher echelons of command, although the bulk of GHQ remained at Montreuil during the Hundred Days, Haig established his advanced headquarters on a special train closer to the frontline.[297] By placing himself in this capacity, Haig clearly anticipated the degree of mobility which was to characterise the BEF's operations from then on. Far from being the remote commander so often portrayed in some First World War historiography, Haig's advanced GHQ train placed him much closer to the action, allowing him to maintain regular, personal contact with his army, corps and divisional commanders.[298] Indeed, the signal office at Advanced GHQ handled 209 telegrams and 153 telephone calls per day (Figure 7.2).[299] At the army and corps levels, the moves of headquarters became a standard procedure during the Hundred Days. Army headquarters, which had remained static for the best part of the war, moved

---

[294] In a letter to Sir Henry Wilson on 20 September, for example, Haig admitted that the BEF had 'a surprisingly large number of *very capable* generals'. See Sheffield and Bourne (eds.), *Douglas Haig*, 462.

[295] Lieutenant-Colonel W. H. F. Weber, 'The Development of Mobile Artillery, 1914–1918', *Journal of the Royal United Service Institution*, 64 (1919), 56.

[296] However, this does not mean that decentralisation was applied uniformly throughout the BEF. See Jonathan Boff, 'Command Culture and Complexity: Third Army during the Hundred Days, August–November 1918', in Sheffield and Gray (eds.), *Changing War*, 19–35.

[297] Haig Diary, 7 August 1918, WO256/34, TNA; Edmonds, *Military Operations, 1918*, Vol. IV, 157.

[298] Peter Simkins, 'Haig and the Army Commanders', in Brian Bond and Nigel Cave (eds.), *Haig: A Reappraisal 70 Years On* (Barnsley: Leo Cooper, 1999), 96.

[299] These figures take into account the fact that Advanced GHQ closed at Boubers-sur-Canche on 5 September and did not re-open until 25 September at Gouy. See 'GHQ and Advanced GHQ Signal Offices, August–November 1918', GHQ Signal Company War Diary, WO95/127, TNA.

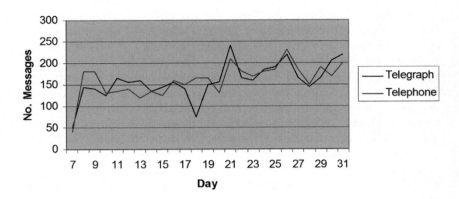

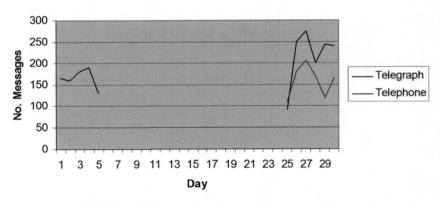

Figure 7.2 Advanced GHQ signal traffic, August–November 1918
Source: GHQ Signal Company War Diary, WO95/127, TNA.

two or three times during this period, while the moves of corps headquarters were even more frequent. Indeed, when corps headquarters relocated, it was not uncommon for them to move in bounds of 15 to 20 miles at a time.[300]

[300] Priestley, *Work of the Royal Engineers*, 307–10.

Adv. GHQ Telegraph and Telephone Traffic, October 1918

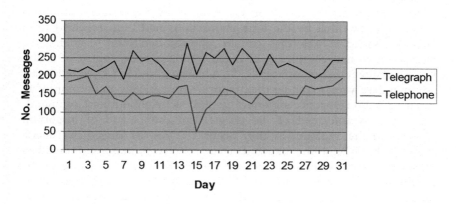

Adv. GHQ Telegraph and Telephone Traffic, 1-11 November 1918

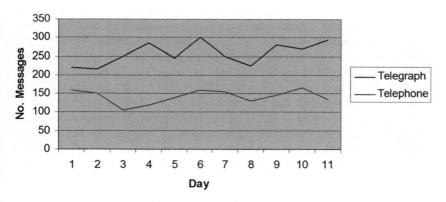

Figure 7.2 (*cont.*)

Although greater initiative was allowed to the commanders at lower levels, it would be inaccurate to claim that the last three months of the war was a period of untainted success for the BEF. Tenuous communications continued to hamper operations. For example, during the Battle of Epéhy on 18 September, the communication system forward of divisional headquarters was completely reliant upon a reliable but slow service of runners. Subsequently, 'it was hours after events had happened at the front that they became known to divisional headquarters, and the direction of the battle lagged even more than ordinarily'.[301] Similarly, Lieutenant-Colonel J. L. Ralston, CO 8th Canadian Infantry Battalion, stated that during the attack on Cambrai on 29 September, 'situations changed so fast that by the time instructions had been received from Brigade, issued in view of a certain reported condition of affairs, the circumstance had completely changed, rendering the course of action proposed altogether inapplicable'.[302] According to *SS. 135*, subordinate commanders were 'to render their reports automatically and promptly' in order to 'keep respective superiors, as well as neighbouring Commanders, regularly informed of the progress of events and of important changes in the situation as they occur'.[303] Yet, as Brigadier-General James Jack, GOC 28th Infantry Brigade, observed, junior commanders were 'far too busy to write messages until there [was] a pause in the operations'.[304] Subsequently, as 18 Division Artillery experienced, information concerning the progress of events at the frontline was often 'very scarce and slow in arriving'.[305] As Richard Butler complained: 'Information from the front is never too abundant, and Officers should be instructed to forward detailed information of their position, and to repeat their messages'.[306]

The difficulty of maintaining high tempo during the operations of August–November – stemming in no small measure from the breakdown of real-time communications – forced many commanders to search for alternative ways of acquiring information. James Jack noted on 28 September that 'in action the first reports of progress – or failure – usually come from wounded'.[307] Likewise, while GSO2 of 66 Division, Walter Guinness revealed that during the Battle of the Selle in mid-October, 'The only news I could... get as to the progress of the attack of the 50th Division was from their walking wounded',[308] often, the information obtained from returning wounded soldiers proved invaluable. During the Battle of the St. Quentin Canal, information acquired from the

---

[301] Edmonds, *Military Operations, 1918*, Vol. 4, 478.
[302] 'Fourth Canadian Division Report on Operations around Cambrai, 27 September–1 October 1918', undated, 4 Canadian Division War Diary, WO95/3882, TNA.
[303] *SS.135. The Training and Employment of Divisions*, 47.
[304] John Terraine (ed.), *General Jack's Diary: The Trench Diary of Brigadier-General J. L. Jack, D.S.O.* (London: Cassell, 2001), 272.
[305] '18th Divisional Artillery Operation Order No. 147', 7 October 1918, Fourth Army Records, Vol. 64, IWM.
[306] 'Report on Operations of III Corps from July 1918 to October 1st. 1918', 11 November 1918, Fourth Army Records, Vol. 63, IWM.
[307] Terraine (ed.), *General Jack's Diary*, 272.
[308] Bond and Robbins (eds.), *Staff Officer*, 236.

questioning of wounded troops and German prisoners enabled 46 Division to ascertain that its leading infantry units had successfully crossed the canal. Subsequently, 'on this information orders were issued for 139th and 138th Infantry Brigades to push straight across the Canal up to the barrage, and move directly on the objectives assigned to them'.[309]

Paradoxically, while commanders continued to be vexed by the lack of timely and accurate information, the battles of the Hundred Days generated the largest volume of signal traffic within the BEF of any period in the war. Monash, for instance, noted that on the morning of 29 September, 'the stream of messages pouring into my Headquarters Office... exceeded in volume and import anything that I had met with in my previous war experience'.[310] During the Somme campaign in 1916, III Corps signal office had dealt with a daily average of 1,730 telegrams and 1,446 despatch rider messages. Throughout August 1918, however, it handled an average of 2,077 telegrams and 2,144 despatch rider messages per day.[311] Divisional signal offices in 1918 were handling almost the same amount of correspondence as army signal offices had done in 1915. At Amiens, 5 Australian Division signal office processed 2,180 messages, while 2 Canadian Division dealt with 1,500 telegrams and 1,188 despatch rider letters.[312] At the brigade level, in August 1918 the 9th, 10th and 11th AIF Brigades each dealt with an average of 3,166 messages, while in September the 1st Tank Brigade's signal traffic amounted to 284 telegrams, 251 despatch rider messages, 216 telephone calls and 27 wireless messages per day.[313] Unsurprisingly, the sheer volume of information passing over the BEF's communications system created further difficulties for command and control. According to a report by 18 Division Signal Company in early September, the 'limited scale of forward communications' resulted in 'a certain amount of

---

[309] 'Account of the Part Taken by the 46th Division in the Battle of Bellenglise on the 29th September, 1918', undated, Fourth Army Records, Vol. 63, IWM.

[310] Monash, *Australian Victories*, 260–1.

[311] 'Total and Daily Average of Traffic at C.C.O., July–December 1916', 'Total, Daily Average and Heaviest Day Traffic at III Corps Signal Office, August–September 1918', III Corps Signal Company War Diary, WO95/701, TNA.

[312] 'Signal Office Diary', 8–11 August 1918, 5 Australian Division Signal Company War Diary, WO95/3596, 'Traffic – 2nd Canadian Divnl. Signal Office – CYB – August, 1918', 2 Canadian Division Signal Company War Diary, WO95/3804, TNA. At Neuve Chapelle in 1915, First Army's signal office sent and received 1,390 and 1,010 messages, respectively. 'Traffic Chart 1st Army HQRS. Signal Office, March 1915', First Army Signal Company War Diary, WO95/199, TNA.

[313] 'August 1918. Graph Showing Daily Number of A, B and C Messages, 3rd Aust. Divl. Signal Company', 3 Australian Division Signal Company War Diary, WO95/3385, TNA; 'Memories 1914–1919 by a Signal Officer', 34, Churchill Papers, IWM.

congestion owing to the heavy traffic due to active operations'. The only way to reduce this pressure was 'by a judicious use of the lines, both for telephone calls and number and length of telegrams'.[314] Similarly, on several occasions during 2 Australian Division's operations in early October, the telephone and telegraph circuits 'became "choked" resulting in delays to "Urgent Operation" and "Priority" messages'.[315]

In summary, this chapter has endeavoured to provide a more thorough understanding of the role and influence of communications upon the BEF's operations in 1918 than has so far been presented in the historiography. In order to achieve this, it has sought to provide answers to three principal questions: first, what bearing did communications have upon the BEF's military performance in 1918, both on the defensive during the first half of the year and then on the offensive during the Hundred Days? Second, did British commanders make the most of the communications technology available to them during this period? Third, and finally, what can a study of communications reveal about the nature of command and control within the BEF in 1918?

With regards to the first question, it is clear that the communication difficulties that had plagued the BEF's operations since the beginning of the war remained a constant thorn in the side of British commanders throughout 1918. This was particularly evident during the German spring offensive, when the breakdown of communications created an atmosphere of confusion and uncertainty which exacerbated 'one of the most acute crises of the entire war'.[316] While the BEF lacked any formal doctrinal guidance as to communications in a retreat, the situation was made worse on Fifth Army's front by the absence of a thorough, deep-buried cable network. This factor, which has so far been overlooked by historians, partly explains why the breakdown of communications was generally much more severe in Fifth Army in March than along the First and Second Army front in the Lys sector during the German *Georgette* offensive in April, since the latter had had plenty of time to complete the installation of an extensive buried cable system.

Turning to the Hundred Days, it can certainly be argued that communications played an important role in the BEF's successes. Building upon the experiences of Cambrai and the lessons learnt during the first half of 1918, commanders at all levels made extensive use of a variety of

---

[314] 'Notes on Communications during Recent Operations', 7 September 1918, 18 Division Signal Company War Diary, WO95/2028, TNA.

[315] 'Report on Communications during Period 2nd to 6th October 1918', 16 October 1918, 2 Australian Division Signal Company War Diary, WO95/3296, TNA.

[316] Harris, *Douglas Haig*, 451.

means of communication to expedite the conveyance of information. The co-ordination of the combined-arms battle, involving infantry, artillery, tanks and aeroplanes, required a flexible and sophisticated communications system, without which the BEF would have simply consisted of a collection of unconnected, and therefore relatively useless, pieces of equipment. It is difficult to see how the BEF would have managed to achieve what it did during the Hundred Days without the support of the communications system it employed. However, the transition from static to semi-mobile warfare introduced a whole host of communication problems which, when combined, served to undermine the tempo of the BEF's operations. Although the British made impressive gains during this period, there was never a shortage of complaints regarding the meagre and untimely receipt of information from the frontline. While the BEF managed to achieve a high tempo of operations during the last months of the war, contrary to Priestley's assessment, the tactical and operational limitations of communications acted as a barrier to potentially even greater success.[317] Nevertheless, in favouring the less glamorous, though much more effective, approach of limited objective, set-piece attacks, thereby not seeking to secure a decisive breakthrough as it had done earlier in the war,[318] the BEF in 1918 was able to reduce the severity of the impact that the breakdown of communications inevitably caused during the heat of battle. Moreover, as recent historians have observed, tempo is a relative concept; so long as the BEF's operational tempo was greater than that of the German Army, as during the Hundred Days it appears it was, the former held the upper hand.[319]

In answering the second question, the evidence presented within this chapter would seem to suggest that, in general, British commanders did make the most of the communications technology available to them during the Hundred Days. However, it is also clear that some units, such as the Canadian Corps, were more successful than others when it came to integrating newer technology into their communication systems. Fighting under semi-mobile conditions in the spring of 1918 forced British commanders and their staff to embrace a variety of alternative means of communication, since they could no longer rely upon the luxury afforded by telephones and telegraph. Although many officers

---

[317] 'An inefficient intercommunication service might undoubtedly have proved the limiting factor to the advance ... This never was the case, never even nearly the case ... '. R. E. Priestley, 'The Evolution of Intercommunication in France, 1914–1918', *Royal Engineers Journal*, 34 (1921), 275.
[318] Brown, *British Logistics*, 198–202.   [319] Boff, *Winning and Losing*, 191.

found it difficult to change their 'trench-bound' communication habits, by the beginning of the summer there was widespread recognition at all levels of the value of alternative means of communication. The shining example was wireless. Although, given the shortage of available sets, its technical limitations and vulnerability beyond brigade headquarters, wireless did not resolve the BEF's communication problems, it is difficult to see how British commanders could have made greater use of it. BF trench sets and Loop Sets were in operation as far forward as battalion headquarters during the last months of the war – something that British commanders on the Somme in 1916 would almost certainly not have foreseen. The use of CW wireless for artillery, tank and RAF communications was even more significant, particularly since the German Army, having never developed CW during the course of the war, issued special instructions in June 1918 'to salve enemy wireless equipment of this description'.[320] Thus, from the perspective of communications, it is difficult to agree with the view that the BEF in 1918 did not exploit the technologies available to their full military potential.[321]

Finally, in addressing the third question, the return of mobility to British operations in 1918 meant that the high command could no longer rely principally upon the rigid and inflexible system of line-based communications which had acted as a mechanism for maintaining centralised control over the BEF during the years of trench warfare. Such a system was ideal for dealing with repetitive tasks within an inexperienced organisation trapped within a static environment.[322] However, as Robin Prior and Trevor Wilson have noted, by the summer of 1918 'the British army at every level [had become] a more complex, sophisticated, and above all specialist organisation'.[323] This, combined with the shift to a more fluid environment, meant that it was neither necessary nor possible for the BEF to continue to employ the communications system it had developed and utilised between 1915 and 1917. The BEF's circumstances in 1918 had changed and to a certain extent so too had its communications system. Decentralisation of command and control within the BEF in the second half of 1918 helped relieve Haig and his army commanders of information overload by placing decision making in the hands of those commanders who were closer to the action and who knew more about

---

[320] 'Translation of a German Document', 1 June 1918, AIR1/2217/209/33/6, TNA.
[321] Travers, *How the War Was Won*, 175–82; Bullock and Lyons, *Missed Signals*, 192–4.
[322] For an overview of the nature of communications within centralised and decentralised organisations, see Fisher, *Communication in Organizations*, 68–97.
[323] Prior and Wilson, *Command on the Western Front*, 305.

the situation. As the 'decision to action time'[324] was made faster, since information did not have to travel to the very top of the command hierarchy and back down again, the communications system which emerged during the Hundred Days facilitated creativity and spontaneity, to varying degrees, thus enabling the BEF to reach its full potential as it sought to maximise its operational tempo.

---

[324] Also referred to as the 'flash to bang' time. See McCarthy, 'Queen of the Battlefield', 191.

Conclusion

This book has sought to scrutinise British military operations on the Western Front during the First World War through the lens of the BEF's communications system, offering assessments, first, of the key components that constituted the BEF's communications system and how these evolved during the course of the war, and, second, of the role and contribution of this communications system to the principal military operations undertaken by the BEF. In so doing, it has sought to answer one key question: how, and to what extent, did communications influence British military operations on the Western Front between 1914 and 1918?

The conventional response to this question is perhaps best summed up by Paddy Griffith, who argued that the fallibility of early twentieth-century battlefield communications was 'probably sufficient in itself to explain the generalised failure of any Great War attack to produce a decisive breakout'.[1] While communications cannot be considered a catch-all explanation for the failings of the BEF, the analysis in this study would support the broad truth of Griffith's judgement. From the BEF's opening encounter with the German Army at Mons in August 1914 to its last major attack on the Sambre in November 1918, tenuous communications imposed profound restrictions on the ability of British commanders to exercise efficient command and control during the heat of battle. Indeed, this was one of the principal findings in the final report of 'the Committee on the Lessons of the Great War' in October 1932 when highlighting the inherent difficulty that the BEF had had in attempting to convert the *break-in* into a *breakthrough*. The destruction of telephone and telegraph lines, and the fragility of wireless, visual signalling and message carriers meant that 'once the battle was joined the higher command ceased to influence it'. In the absence of the smooth and rapid transfer of accurate information, vital decisions, such as committing

---

[1] Griffith, *Battle Tactics*, 175.

298

reserves, were often made too late or not at all. As a result, the momentum of the attacking forces slowly ground to a halt as opportunities to exploit any initial successes were lost and the Germans given ample time to call up their reserves and shore up their defences.[2]

However, although communications adversely affected the BEF's military performance, undoubtedly contributing to the prolongation of trench stalemate between 1915 and 1917, they were also a precondition for the successes of 1918. This latter point has not been sufficiently emphasised by historians, who have instead preferred to focus on the exploits of the more 'lethal' elements of the BEF's combined-arms system during the Hundred Days.[3] As this book has demonstrated, it was communications that held these 'lethal' elements together. Although far from perfect, communications were nonetheless critical in enabling British commanders to co-ordinate the movement of their forces in semi-mobile operations. By 1918, not only was the BEF generally more proficient in the art of waging modern warfare, but it also possessed a more robust, flexible and sophisticated communications system capable of supporting these advances. Thus in many respects, communications acted as a doubled-edged sword: on the one hand, the technical shortcomings and vulnerabilities of the various means of communication employed undermined the BEF's attempts at achieving a high level of tactical mobility and operational tempo; yet, on the other hand, an improved communications system facilitated the degree of inter-arm co-operation that played an important part in enabling the BEF to defeat the German Army in the summer and autumn of 1918.

Given, then, that communications posed one of the most fundamental challenges to waging war on the Western Front, any attempt to secure victory on the battlefield had to address this issue. As this study has shown, the BEF clearly recognised at an early stage in the war the necessity of good communications for conducting successful operations and subsequently began the process of adapting its communications system to meet the demands of modern, industrialised warfare. Understanding the evolutionary development of the key components that constituted the BEF's communications system, therefore, is crucial when assessing its influence upon operations. Organisationally, the size and complexity of the communications system grew in conjunction with the

---

[2] 'Report of the Committee on the Lessons of the Great War (The Kirke Report), October 1932', WO32/3116, TNA.

[3] Robin Prior and Trevor Wilson, for example, acknowledge that communications were part of a war-winning 'weapons system' employed by the BEF during the Hundred Days, but devote nearly all their attention to the exploits of the artillery, infantry, tanks and aeroplanes. See Prior and Wilson, *Command on the Western Front*, 309–91.

rest of the BEF. During the first half of the war, the BEF's communications machinery was small and lacked sufficient control, direction and co-ordination. However, over the course of the second half of the war it changed significantly, marked in particular by two important milestones: first, the appointment in 1916 of DD Signals and AD Signals at army and corps, respectively; and, second, the absorption of artillery signals into the Signal Service's jurisdiction in the winter of 1916/17. As a result of these, and other, changes, by 1918 the BEF had in the Signal Service an organisation that was more than capable of meeting the voracious communication needs of the army.

Successfully adapting the BEF's communications system to the novel conditions on the Western Front required major organisational changes that depended crucially upon the pragmatic nature of the British officer corps and, in particular, upon its readiness to utilise civilian expertise, methods and equipment. Having already forged strong personal and professional ties before 1914, the Signal Service brilliantly exploited its relationship with the GPO throughout the war to ensure not only the supply of much-needed and improved signal stores and technical equipment, but also the staffing of the BEF's communications system, to a large extent, by skilled individuals from the civilian communications sector. This 'civilianisation' of one of the army's most important support services goes some way in explaining how the BEF's communications system became increasingly more sophisticated, innovative and professionalised during the course of the war, lending further support to the argument that the inherent pragmatism of the British Army of the period should be viewed as a strength, rather than a weakness.[4]

In spite of these achievements, however, the means of communication available to the BEF constituted the weakest component of the communications system. The chief explanation for this lay in the deficiencies of the communications technology of the era, which had simply not reached the same level of maturity as had the weapon systems they supported. British commanders were well aware of this, however, and sought to overcome the shortcomings inherent in each of the existing means of communication by designing a communications system with 'built-in redundancy' as one of its governing features.[5] From the onset of trench stalemate in the winter of 1914–15, the BEF set about increasing the reliability of its communications system by duplicating the number of telegraph and telephone lines laid and by ensuring multiple means of communication were made available so that, should

---

[4] See, for example: Brown, *British Logistics*, 231–40; Boff, *Winning and Losing*, 249.
[5] Downer, 'When Failure Is an Option', 1–24.

one method fail, there was always a back-up that could take over. While this safety mechanism went some way in reducing the chances of the BEF's communications system breaking down completely, it added to the ever-growing complexity of the system and, as evidenced in the operations examined in this book, often made it vulnerable, prone to accidents and human error.[6]

Thus, the narrow technological and organisational focus on the Signal Service that has so far prevailed in the historiography has generally distracted attention from the complex and all-pervading nature of communications. Taken as a whole, the overlapping and mutually reinforcing components that constituted the BEF's communications system made it qualitatively and quantitatively superior to anything the British Army had previously possessed. In order to elaborate upon this point, this book also articulated a number of sub-questions that can now be addressed: first, how, and to what extent, did the BEF's communications system show signs of adaptability during the course of the war? Second, with specific reference to communications, how successful were British commanders at recognising the utility of new technologies and exploiting their full military potential? Third, what evidence is there to suggest that the BEF developed a communications doctrine during the war? Fourth, and finally, what does an examination of communications tell us about the nature of learning within the BEF?

With regards to the first sub-question, the BEF's communications system can be measured according to four key criteria: speed, integrity, capacity and security. Throughout the war, all of these factors created problems which served to undermine the efficiency of the communications system, which in turn prejudiced British military operations. While the absence of suitable 'real-time' communications, a dilemma shared by all the armies on the Western Front, made it extremely difficult to convey information rapidly during the heat of battle, human error was also partly to blame for many instances when commanders were the recipients of confusing and disjointed information. In addition, the exponential growth of the BEF and the increase in the power of modern artillery resulted in a huge demand for telephonic and telegraphic communication, which in turn led to a massive increase in the volume of information passing over the communication channels. All too often, as the battles examined in this study demonstrate, the system broke down at critical moments under the sheer weight of messages being carried. Furthermore, the security of the BEF's communications system, particularly

---

[6] Scott D. Sagan, 'Learning from *Normal Accidents*', *Organisation & Environment*, 17 (2004), 15–19.

during the first half of the war, was often negated by a combination of British complacency and German success.

British commanders made continuous efforts to resolve these problems by implementing a wide range of solutions. Some of the most notable of these included the grouping of brigade and battalion headquarters closer to each other in order to expedite the conveyance of information; the introduction of a much more thorough system of liaison officers from 1917 so as to preserve the integrity of the information being relayed over the communications system; the promotion of alternative means of communication to improve the system's capacity at critical moments; and tighter restrictions on the use of telephones within close proximity of the frontline and the introduction of formal voice procedures in order to enhance communication security. Again, these measures add further weight to the argument that much of the BEF's ability to overcome the obstacles of fighting on the Western Front rested on the pragmatic nature of the British officer corps and its willingness to implement new solutions to problems as and when they presented themselves.

Improving the BEF's communications system also depended upon the willingness of British commanders to embrace the latest communication technologies and to exploit their full military potential. In response to the second sub-question, therefore, it can be concluded that contrary to the argument of some historians that British commanders failed to make the best use of some of the technology that was available to them,[7] this study has shown that, in their desperation to plug the communications gap, British commanders displayed a readiness to embrace new and alternative means of communication. The use of the Fullerphone, contact aeroplanes and power buzzers, for example, offers plenty of evidence to support the argument that British commanders were receptive to new forms of communication. However, the interaction between the BEF and the newest communication methods is best illustrated by the army's relationship with wireless. According to one recent study, the 'significant institutional bias', or 'lack of vision and will', of the British high command towards wireless communication prevented it being employed both earlier and to its fullest extent.[8] While there is no doubting that there were individuals within the BEF who remained sceptical as to the practical utility of wireless for communications, by 1918 such individuals were very much in the minority. The personal diaries of Haig and Rawlinson, for example, reveal that both men were keen advocates of the development of wireless

---

[7] See, for example: Travers, *How the War Was Won*, 175–82.
[8] Bullock and Lyons, *Missed Signals*, 192–4.

communication during the war. As Haig stated in a letter to the Marconi Company in late 1918, 'The good services performed by the wireless telegraphists throughout the war... has been one of great and increasing importance, and the zeal and efficiency with which it has been carried out has been of great value to their country'.[9] Indeed, the ability of the BEF to exploit CW wireless during the last year of the war, especially with regards to counter-battery, RAF and Tank Corps communications, was a remarkable achievement, certainly when considering the German Army did not employ such technology. Above all, it was the constraints imposed by the unique battlefield environment which existed on the Western Front – an unfavourable force-to-space ratio, lack of open flanks for manoeuvre and the overwhelming concentration of enemy artillery fire – combined with the scientific and technical limitations of the sets of the era which hindered the widespread and more effective use of wireless within the BEF, certainly until the resumption of semi-mobile operations in 1918.[10] But even then, as Chapter 7 revealed, wireless, even CW wireless, did not fully resolve the BEF's communications dilemma.

Improving the BEF's communications system was not just a matter of employing the newest communication devices, but of using them in the most effective way possible. To this end, and in response to the third sub-question posed in this book, the BEF did eventually develop and apply what amounted to a 'communications doctrine' in all but name. *SS. 148. Forward Inter-Communication in Battle*, published in March 1917, was the BEF's first authoritative communications manual, which laid down the principles of best communications policy and practice based on the lessons learnt from the experiences of 1916. Not only did it codify a universal set of communication principles, aimed at improving signal training and communications in battle, but it also helped promote a mutual understanding between the Signal Service and the rest of the BEF, particularly between the Signal Service and the General Staff. As a result of further experience, the manual was subsequently modified and reissued in November 1917 as *SS. 191. Intercommunication in the Field*. This revised publication was found to be much more flexible in its application, with a wider-ranging and less-dogmatic set of principles which could be adapted by signal officers to suit local conditions and individual circumstances.[11]

---

[9] Field Marshal Douglas Haig to the Wireless Press Ltd., 1 December 1918, Marconi Papers 358, Bodleian Library, Oxford (BLO).
[10] Analysis of British military operations in Africa and the Middle East during the war lends further support to this argument. See: Hall, 'Technological Adaptation', 37–71.
[11] Priestley, *Work of the Royal Engineers*, 182.

Although it was not perfect – the omission of guidelines for establishing and maintaining communications during a retreat, for instance, had a major bearing upon the BEF's poor performance during the spring of 1918 – *SS. 191* served the BEF well for the remainder of the war. It also reinforces the argument that the British Army of the period was more than able to develop and refine its doctrine on the basis of a 'cult of pragmatism, flexibility and an empirical approach'.[12]

With regards to the fourth, and final, sub-question, an examination of the BEF's communications system draws attention to the 'learning curve' debate. 'Learning curve' is a term commonly used to describe how long it takes for a learner to acquire knowledge, an attitude or a skill, in order to overcome a certain level of difficulty. Crucially, it implies a steady and constant rate of development on the part of the learner. The argument that emerges from this study with regards to communications suggests that the BEF underwent a 'learning process' or 'learning experience', rather than a 'learning curve'. As has been demonstrated, while definite improvements to the communications system were made, these were not constant and incremental. Instead, the development of the BEF's communications system was a long and painful process of trial and error, which included almost as many failures as there were successes. Indeed, the dilemma posed by the inadequacy of 'real-time' communications was something that would not begin to be rectified until the developments in wireless telephony during the interwar period, which, alongside the rise of armour, played a major part in ensuring that the tactical and operational stalemate experienced on the Western Front did not prevail during the Second World War.[13]

Nevertheless, although it did not undergo a 'learning curve' during the war, the Signal Service, and the BEF as a whole, displayed many of the characteristics of a 'learning organisation' – that is, 'an organisation which facilitates the learning of all its members and continuously transforms itself'.[14] While mistakes and setbacks are 'elemental features of development and learning', it is 'the way in which organisations

---

[12] Gary Sheffield, 'Doctrine and Command in the British Army: An Historical Overview', E-2, in *Army Doctrine Publication (ADP). Operations* (2010), www.gov.uk/government/uploads/system/uploads/attachment_data/file/33695/ADPOperationsDec10.pdf (Accessed 15 January 2016).

[13] This did not mean, however, that the British Army did not experience communication difficulties during the Second World War. See Godfrey, *British Army Communications*.

[14] Michael Muller-Camen, Richard Croucher and Susan Leigh, *Human Resource Management: A Case Study Approach* (London: Chartered Institute of Personnel and Development, 2008), 457.

respond' to challenges and 'the lessons that are learnt from the experience' that qualify them for the title 'learning organisation'.[15] As this study has shown, throughout the war the BEF continuously strove to improve its communications system by making changes to it as and when problems arose and by seeking the advice of experts both within and outside the organisation. Although not all of these modifications were successful, by the summer and autumn of 1918 the communications system was good enough to enable British commanders to mount limited-objective operations that were certainly less ambitious than those in 1916 and 1917, but far more effective.[16] Thus, like the development of the tank and the overhaul of the BEF's logistical network, the transformation of the communications system between 1914 and 1918 seems to provide another clear-cut example of the British Army's preference for 'non-formal' learning processes. However, the manner in which SS. 148 and its successor SS. 191 were developed demonstrates that the BEF was also capable of embracing more 'formal' learning methods as well.[17]

Clearly, 5the answers to these four sub-questions have important implications with regards to the much wider debate on the supposed RMA. Although some historians view the transformation of the character of war between 1914 and 1918 as revolutionary in effect,[18] they have failed to emphasise sufficiently the fact that the demands of fighting a modern, industrialised war necessitated a communications system of far greater significance than in any previous conflict. As the report of 'the Committee on the Lessons of the Great War' acknowledged, 'the extent to which the value of communications was realised in the war [was] reflected in the labour and energy displayed in their provision'.[19] By 1918, British commanders at all levels, and in all arms, realised that their success depended upon the efficiency of their communications system. The success of three-dimensional, indirect artillery fire, the most important feature of the modern battlefield, necessitated a comprehensive communications system linking FOOs with their batteries in the rear. The aeroplanes of the newly formed RAF, crucial to the effectiveness of counter-battery work, depended upon an efficient wireless

---

[15] Dale, 'Learning Organisations', 22.
[16] Todman and Sheffield, 'Command and Control', 8–9.
[17] Foley, 'Dumb Donkeys', 279–98.
[18] Bailey, *The First World War*, 3; Gray, *Strategy for Chaos*, 170–221; Sheffield and Gray (eds.), *Changing War*.
[19] 'Report on the Lessons of the Great War on the Western Front, by Major-General A. E. McNamara', in 'Report of the Committee on the Lessons of the Great War: Appendix 1, The War Office 1932', WO32/3116, TNA.

system for communicating with the ground, while the success of the infantry and of tanks also relied upon the existence of a more robust, flexible and sophisticated communications system integrating them into the framework. In essence, if communications were a precondition of the combined-arms successes of 1918, then they were undoubtedly a crucial component of the 'Modern Style of Warfare'. With this in mind, it is plausible to suggest that the First World War also laid the foundations for the modern military communications system, be it at the early stages of its development. The communications system employed by the BEF in the summer and autumn of 1918 contained nearly all the necessary components – organisational, doctrinal and technical – to facilitate the conveyance of information in modern battle. Indeed, during the Second World War, apart from the notable addition of wireless telephony, British commanders still found that the most flexible and efficient communications system was one that utilised a combination of cable, wireless and despatch riders – almost identical to the system employed by the BEF during the war-winning battles of 1918.[20] In short, the 'Modern Style of Warfare' that evolved during the First World War depended heavily upon its communications and information components to succeed.

In sum, this study has sought to provide much-needed correction and clarification to our understanding of a support service that had a major bearing upon the fortunes of British military operations on the Western Front during the First World War. It has concluded that, despite not having been prepared in 1914 for the difficulties of modern, industrialised warfare, the BEF's communications system did improve during the course of the war and made an important contribution to the final victory of the BEF over its German opponent in 1918. In other words, not only did communications help shape the static nature of the fighting on the Western Front between 1915 and 1917, it also played an important part in overcoming the superiority of the defence and the stalemate of trench warfare in 1918. Although this study has drawn some comparisons with the communication systems of the other armies on the Western Front, a similar assessment of the German, French or American system would offer conclusive proof as to whether or not the BEF's communications system was more efficient and thus gave it a significant advantage. However, it is worth bearing in mind that neither the BEF's opponents nor its allies were able to find a definitive solution to the intractable

---

[20] Godfrey, *British Army Communications*, 213–28.

problems posed by tenuous battlefield communications. What can be said with more certainty is that the communications system pioneered by the British during the First World War pointed the way towards possibilities in the future, laying the groundwork for the signals systems of modern armies. Indeed, the creation of the Royal Corps of Signals in 1920 was the ultimate recognition by the British Army of the importance of communications in modern war.

Appendix 1   AD Signals, BEF, 1916–1918[1]

Cavalry Corps	20 November 1916 24 May 1917 1 March 1918	L. W. De V. Sadleir-Jackson R. Chenevix-Trench J. B. Wheeler
I Corps	20 November 1916 26 November 1916 30 December 1917	W. L. De M. Carey E. F. W. Barker M. T. Porter
II Corps	20 November 1916 4 February 1917 29 December 1917 27 August 1918	J. Day A. St. J. Yates C. V. Monier-Williams E. De W. H. Bradley
III Corps	20 November 1916 20 August 1917 8 October 1918	A. B. Cunningham A. C. Allan N .F. Hitchins
IV Corps	20 November 1916 29 January 1918	J. C. M. Kerr J. Stevenson
V Corps	20 November 1916	J. W. Danielsen
VI Corps	20 November 1916 August 1918	H. Lee Wright P. R. Bald
VII Corps	20 November 1916 8 June 1918 16 August 1918 October 1918	D. C. Jones C. H. Walsh Captain H. F. Dallison (acting) Captain A. McK. Johnson (acting)
VIII Corps	20 November 1916 1 February 1917 4 May 1918 2 July 1918 16 September 1918	R. V. Doherty Holwell J. W. Cohen J. A. F. Mair W. L. De M. Carey M. G. Platts

[1] All Lieutenant-Colonel, unless otherwise stated. Compiled from Becke (Comp.), *History of the Great War*, 123–268; and, Nalder, *The Royal Corps of Signals*, 503–80.

(cont.)

IX Corps	20 November 1916 18 January 1918	R. H. Willan H. W. Edwards
X Corps	20 November 1916 December 1916 27 December 1916 7 February 1917 12 May 1918	R. M. Powell F. A. Iles Major A. Yates (acting) F. A. Iles R. F. B. Naylor
XI Corps	20 November 1916 15 January 1917 13 June 1917 15 February 1918 14 May 1918	G. E. B. Dobbs A. H. French Captain J. W. Orange-Bromhead (acting) Major Orange-Bromhead (acting) J. A. F. Mair
XIII Corps	20 November 1916 18 January 1918	P. R. Bald T. W. Vigers
XIV Corps	20 November 1916 25 October 1918	O. C. Mordaunt J. A. Arrowsmith-Brown
XV Corps	20 November 1916	N. Harrison
XVII Corps	20 November 1916 20 January 1917 2 October 1917 7 November 1917 15 December 1917 18 August 1918	F. V. Yeats-Brown H. C. Smith A. C. Cameron Major J. Stevenson (acting) A. C. Cameron C. H. Walsh
XVIII Corps	15 January 1917 21 June 1917	G. E. B. Dobbs W. L. De M. Carey
XIX Corps	4 February 1917 26 June 1917	F. V. Yeats-Brown J. F. M. Stratton
XXII Corps	20 November 1916 6 April 1918 8 November 1918	W. T. Dodd H. C. Smith C. W. M. Firth
Tank Corps	27 August 1917	J. D. N. Molesworth

Appendix 2 Principal Wireless Sets in the BEF, 1914–1918[1]

Type	Year Introduced	Mode	Purpose	Sending Frequency	Receiving Frequency	Power	Range	Notes
Wagon Set	1910	Spark	Transportable field station	550–1,000 metres	300–1,500 metres	1.5 kW	100 miles	Complete station (3 tons); Aerial (2 x 70 ft)
Motor Lorry Set	1912	Spark	Transportable station (mainly GHQ)	700–1,200 metres	300–1,500 metres	1.5 kW	100 miles	Aerial (2 x 70 ft); Number of sets produced (13)
Pack Set	1914 (earlier designs c. 1911)	Spark	Light transportable station (mainly cavalry)	500–750 metres	300–1,300 metres	0.5 kW	25–30 miles	Complete station (600 lb); Aerial (2 x 30 ft); Number of sets produced (156)
No.1 Aircraft Transmitter	1914	Spark	RFC; Artillery Spotting	100–260 metres	-	30 watt	-	Set (10 lb); Aerial (100–200 ft); Number of sets produced (3,958)
Wilson Set	1915	Spark	Corps-Division (Corps Directing Station)	350, 450 or 550 metres	Transmitter only; required Mk. III Short Wave receiver (100–700 metres)	130 watt	Approx. 5 miles	Set (40.5 lb); Accumulator (33 lb); Aerial (30 ft); Number of sets produced (765)

[1] Compiled from *SS. 100. Notes on Wireless* (January 1916); and, Louis Meulstee, *Wireless for the Warrior: Compendium 1. Spark to Larkspur (Wireless sets 1910–1948)* (Groenlo: Emaus Uitgeverij, 2009), 19–92.

Type	Year Introduced	Mode	Purpose	Sending Frequency	Receiving Frequency	Power	Range	Notes
British Field (BF) Trench Set	1915	Spark	Division-Brigade	350, 450 or 550 metres	350–600 metres	50 watt	Approx. 2 miles	Set (31 lb), plus three loads of 25, 25.5 and 31 lb for the rest of the station; Aerial (15 ft); Number of sets produced (1,245)
Power Buzzer and Amplifier	1916	Earth Induction Telegraphy	Brigade-Battalion	-	-	10 volt	Approx. 1 mile (2.5 miles in very favourable circumstances)	Number of sets produced (1,534)
Loop Set	1917	Spark	Brigade-Battalion	65 or 80 metres	65 or 80 metres	20 watt	Approx. 1 mile	Rear station (82 lb); Front station (74 lb); Number of transmitters produced (4,670); Number of receivers produced (3,842)
W/T Trench Set Mk. I	1917	Continuous Wave	Artillery; RFC/RAF; Tank Corps	500–1,400 metres	500–1,400 metres	30 watt	5 miles	Aerial (15 ft); Number of sets produced (199)
W/T Trench Set Mk. II	1917	Continuous Wave	Artillery; RFC/RAF; Tank Corps	340–1,850 metres	340–1,850 metres	30 watt	5 miles	Aerial (2 x 4 ft, or single 15 ft); Number of sets produced (133)
W/T Trench Set Mk. III	1917	Continuous Wave	Artillery; RFC/RAF; Tank Corps	450–1,450 metres	450–1,450 metres	30 watt	2–5 miles	Receiver (17 lb); Transmitter (18.5 lb); Aerial (2 x 4 ft, or single 15 ft); Number of transmitters produced (2,853); Number of receivers produced (2,650)
Telephone Wireless Aircraft Mk. II	1918	Continuous Wave (wireless telephony)	RFC/RAF	400 metres	400 metres		2 miles (air-to-air); 15 miles (air-to-ground); both one-way speech only	Transmitter (45 lb); Receiver (25 lb); Aerial (120 ft); Number of sets produced (621)

Bibliography

UNPUBLISHED PRIMARY SOURCES

I. GOVERNMENT PAPERS

Australian War Memorial
AWM4/25/27   Australian Imperial Force

Library and Archives Canada
RG9   Canadian Expeditionary Force

National Archives and Records Administration, United States
RG120   American Expeditionary Force

National Archives, United Kingdom
AIR   Air Ministry
CAB   Cabinet
MUN   Ministry of Munitions
PRO   Public Record Office
T   Treasury Board
WO   War Office

II. ORAL SOURCES

Imperial War Museum, London
John William Henry Boon (1986)
Lieutenant-Colonel Arthur Hemsley (1987)
Brigadier Harry Hopthrow (1990)
Colonel F. W. S. Jourdain (1990)
Mr Lambert (1985)
Lieutenant-General Sir Philip Neame (1974)
Bertram Neyland (1974)

III. PRIVATE PAPERS

Bodleian Library, Oxford
Marconi Papers

British Library, London
Lieutenant-General Sir Aylmer Gould Hunter Weston Papers

BT Archives, London
POST30 Post Office: Registered Files, Minuted Papers (England and Wales) 1792- 1952

Churchill Archives Centre, Cambridge
Leopold Amery Papers
General Sir Charles Bonham-Carter Papers
General Lord Rawlinson Papers

Imperial War Museum, London
Guy Buckeridge Papers
Lieutenant-General Sir Richard Butler Papers
Captain J. H. Christian Papers
Major E. F. Churchill Papers
Major-General F. A. Dudgeon Papers
Lieutenant W. H. Foster Papers
Fourth Army Records
Field Marshal Sir John French Papers
Major F. S. Garwood Papers
Second Lieutenant H. A. J. Lamb Papers
General Sir Ivor Maxse Papers
Major Sir Owen Morshead Papers
Major-General Sir Cecil Lothian Nicholson Papers
Sir Henry Norman Papers
Orders, Maps and Papers Relating to the Service of Signal Companies of 2nd and 20th Division during the Great War
General Sir Horace Smith-Dorrien Papers
Lieutenant-General Sir Thomas D'Oyly Snow Papers
Arthur Surfleet Papers
Captain W. G. Wallace Papers
Field Marshal Sir Henry Wilson Papers
Arthur E. Wrench Papers

Library and Archives Canada
Sir Arthur Currie Papers
Lieutenant-Colonel Charles Mitchell Papers

Liddle Collection, University of Leeds
Sir James Hunter Blair Papers
Lieutenant J. H. Burn Papers
Sergeant J. C. Dart Papers
Brigadier H. E. Hopthrow Papers
W. George Mead Papers
M. J. Millie Papers
Raymond Priestley Papers
Sergeant W. M. Rumsey Papers
Lieutenant-Colonel S. H. Watson Papers

Liddell Hart Centre for Military Archives, King's College, London
Field Marshal Viscount Allenby Papers
Captain Sir Basil Liddell Hart Papers
General Sir Beauvoir De Lisle Papers
Field Marshal Sir John Dill Papers
Major-General William Dimoline Papers
Major-General J. F. C. Fuller Papers
Brigadier Harry Ewart Hopthrow Papers
Colonel Roderick (Rory) Macleod Papers
Field Marshal Sir Archibald Montgomery-Massingberd Papers
Field Marshal Sir William Robertson Papers
Major-General Sir Edward Spears Papers

Manchester Regiment Archive, Tameside
MR 1/3/1/50 The Signal Section of the 16th Manchesters: A Record of its
Activities, 1914–18 by ex-Sgt. T. E. Pennington, 1937

Royal Engineers Museum, Gillingham
Captain J. C. Craven Papers
Correspondence and Papers of 2 Division Signal Company in WW1
Historical Memoranda of the Army Postal Services in World War I
Organisation and Work of Signals in WW1 – Papers on Various Subjects
Signal Instructions, I Corps, 1914–18

Royal Mail Archive, London
POST30 Post Office: Registered Files, Minuted Papers (England and
Wales) 1792–1952
POST47 Post Office: Army Postal History 1888–1975
POST56 Post Office: War and Civil Emergencies 1859–1969

Royal Signals Museum, Blandford
History of Military Signalling
Military Histories (General)

PUBLISHED PRIMARY SOURCES

I. OFFICIAL SOURCES

Army Doctrine Publication (ADP). Operations. Prepared under the Direction of the
Chief of the General Staff (2010).
Bean, C. E. W., *Official History of Australia in the War of 1914–18*, Vol. VI: *The
Australian Imperial Force in France during the Allied Offensive, 1918*. Sydney:
Angus and Robertson, 1942.
Becke, Major A. F. (Comp.), *History of the Great War: Order of Battle of Divisions,
Part 4*. London: HMSO, 1945.
Edmonds, Brigadier-General J. E., *Military Operations: France and Belgium, 1914*,
Vol. 1. London: HMSO, 1922.
Military Operations: France and Belgium, 1914, Vol. 2. London: HMSO, 1925.

Military Operations: France and Belgium, 1915, Vol. 2. London: HMSO, 1928.
Military Operations, France and Belgium, 1916, Vol. 1. London: HMSO, 1932.
Military Operations, France and Belgium, 1917, Vol. 2. London: HMSO, 1948.
Military Operations, France and Belgium, 1918, Vols. 1–5. London: HMSO, 1935–47.

Edmonds, J. E. and Wynne, G. C., *Military Operations: France and Belgium, 1915*, Vol. 1. London: HMSO, 1927.

Falls, Cyril, *Military Operations, France and Belgium, 1917*, Vol. 1. London: HMSO, 1940.

General Staff, War Office, *Field Service Manual, 1914 Infantry Battalion, Expeditionary Force.* London, HMSO, 1914.

Field Service Pocket Book. 1914 (Reprinted, with Amendments, 1916). London: HMSO, 1917.

Field Service Regulations, Part I: *Operations (1909)* (Reprinted, with Amendments, October 1914). London: HMSO, 1914.

Field Service Regulations, Part II: *Organisation and Administration (1909)* (Reprinted, with Amendments, October 1914). London: HMSO, 1914.

Instruction in Army Telegraphy and Telephony, Vol. 1: *Instruments.* London: HMSO, 1914.

Manual of Army Signal Service – War (Provisional). 1914. London: HMSO, 1914.

Quarterly Army List for the Quarter Ending 31st December 1919, Vol. 2. London: HMSO, 1920.

Signal Service (France). Technical Instructions No. 1. W/T Sets, Forward, Spark, 20 Watts, B., Front and Rear ("Loop" Set) (May 1917).

SS. 100. Notes on Wireless (January 1916).

SS. 109. Training of Divisions for Offensive Action (May 1916).

SS. 119. Preliminary Notes on the Tactical Lessons of the Recent Operations (July 1916).

SS. 123. Notes on the Use of Carrier Pigeons (August 1916).

SS. 135. Instructions for the Training of Divisions for Offensive Action (December 1916).

SS. 135. The Training and Employment of Divisions, 1918 (January 1918).

SS. 148. Forward Inter-Communication in Battle (March 1917).

SS. 152. Instructions for the Training of the British Armies in France (January 1918).

SS. 191. Intercommunication in the Field (November 1917).

SS. 537. Summary of Recent Information Regarding the German Army and its Methods (January 1917).

SS. 713. The German Wireless System (March 1917).

Training Manual – Signalling. Part II. London: HMSO, 1914.

Hart's Annual Army List, Special Reserve List, and Territorial Force List, for 1914. London: John Murray, 1914.

Jones, H. A., *The War in the Air: Being the Story of the Part Played in the Great War by the Royal Air Force*, Vol. 2. Oxford: The Clarendon Press, 1928.

Miles, W., *Military Operations, France and Belgium, 1916*, Vol. 2. London: HMSO, 1938.

Military Operations, France and Belgium, 1917, Vol. 3. London: HMSO, 1948.

Perrott, H. C. (comp.), *The War Office List. 1917.* London: HMSO, 1917.
Raleigh, Walter, *The War in the Air, Vol. 1: The Part Played in the Great War by the Royal Air Force.* Oxford: The Clarendon Press, 1922.
Signalling: Imperial Army Series, Based on Training Manual – Signalling, Part II. 1914. London: John Murray, 1914.
Tank Corps Headquarters, *Instructions for the Training of the Tank Corps in France* (December 1917).
The New Annual Army List, Militia List, and Yeomanry Cavalry List, for 1900. London: John Murray, 1900.
United Kingdom Glossary of Joint and Multinational Terms and Definitions, Joint Doctrine Publication 0–01.1 (June 2006).
Wade, J. R. (comp.), *The War Office List. 1918.* London: HMSO, 1918.
War Office, *Statistics of the Military Effort of the British Empire, 1914–1920.* London: HMSO, 1922.

II. OTHER CONTEMPORANEOUS SOURCES, DIARIES AND MEMOIRS

An Ex-Staff Officer, 'Some Staff Duties'. *Journal of the Royal United Service Institution,* 68 (1923), 601–7.
Anonymous., 'Communication on the Battlefield. Translated by Permission from La Revue d'Infanterie'. *Journal of the Royal United Services Institution,* 53 (1909), 357–69.
'Complimentary Dinner to Sir Andrew Ogilvie'. *The Post Office Electrical Engineers' Journal,* 13 (1920–21), 66–75.
'Colonel/Air Commodore L. F. Blandy, CB, DSO'. *The Royal Engineers Journal,* 78 (1964), 340.
'Memoir: Col. E. C. Seaman'. *The Royal Engineers Journal,* 30 (1919), 139–42.
'Memoir: Lieutenant-General Sir John Fowler'. *The Royal Engineers Journal,* 53 (1939), 580–3.
Nature: International Weekly Journal of Science, 130 (10 December 1932), 874.
'Naval and Military. Official Appointments and Notices'. *The Times,* 5 November 1923, 24.
'Obituaries: Lieut.-Gen. Sir John Fowler. Development of Army "Signals"'. *The Times,* 21 September 1939, 10.
'Obituary. Colonel Sir (Arthur) Stanley Angwin, KCMG, KBE, DSO, MC, 1883–1959'. *ICE Proceedings,* 14 (1959), 224–5.
'Obituary. Major-General Sir R. S. Curtis', *The Times,* 12 January 1922.
'Obituary Notices. Arthur Henry Bagnold'. *Monthly Notices of the Royal Astronomical Society,* 104 (1944), 86.
'Profile: Sir Lionel Harris: Leader of the Post Office's Engineers'. *The New Scientist,* 4 (September 1958), 856–7.
'Recollections of a R. E. Sapper-Signaller, 1914–1918'. *Mercury: The Journal of the Royal Signals Amateur Radio Society,* 32 (1970), 5.
'The Service of Communication in the Light of the Experience of the Russo-Japanese War'. *Journal of the Royal United Services Institution,* 52 (1908), 968–70.

'Trench Signaling [sic] becomes a Fine Art: British Officer Writes of Difficulties Overcome on the Western Front'. *The New York Times*, 12 August 1917, 5.

'With a Signal Company on Service: A Short Account of the Doings of the 5th Signal Company, R. E., since Leaving Carlow for the War'. *The Sapper*, 21 (February 1916), 174.

'Wireless Telegraphy and Telephony'. *Journal of the Royal United Services Institution*, 56 (1912), 1004–5.

Atkinson, C. T., *The Seventh Division 1914–1918*. Uckfield: The Naval and Military Press, 2012; first published 1926.

Baker-Carr, Brigadier-General C. D., *From Chauffeur to Brigadier*. London: Ernest Benn, 1930.

Barnes, Ronald Gorell, 'A Citizen Army from Within, II – Ease and Unconcern'. *The Times*, 1 December 1916.

Beach, Jim (ed.), *The Military Papers of Lieutenant-Colonel Sir Cuthbert Headlam, 1910–1942*. Stroud: History Press for the Army Records Society, 2010.

(ed.), *SS. 135. The Division in the Attack – 1918*. Strategic and Combat Studies Institute, The Occasional, No. 53, 2008.

(ed.), *The Diary of Corporal Vince Schürhoff, 1914–1918*. Stroud: Army Records Society, 2015.

Beckett, Ian F. W. (ed.), *The Judgement of History: Sir Horace Smith-Dorrien, Lord French and 1914*. London: Tom Donovan, 1993.

Beresford, R. E., Major C. F. C., 'The Field Telegraph: Its Use in the War and Its Employment in the Late Expeditions in the Soudan and South Africa'. *Journal of the Royal United Service Institution*, 30 (1886), 573–601.

'The Telephone at Home and in the Field', *Journal of the Royal United Service Institution*, 36 (1892), 347–68.

Bick, Major Arthur Hardie and Bick, Peter Hardie (eds.), *The Diary of an Artillery Officer: The 1st Canadian Divisional Artillery on the Western Front*. Stroud: Amberley, 2011.

Birch, Lieutenant-General Sir Noel, 'Artillery Development in the Great War'. *The Army Quarterly*, 1 (1920), 79–89.

Bond, Brian and Robbins, Simon (eds.), *Staff Officer: The Diaries of Walter Guinness (First Lord Moyne) 1914–1918*. London: Leo Cooper, 1987.

Boraston, Lieutenant-Colonel J. H. (ed.), *Sir Douglas Haig's Despatches*. London: Dent, 1920.

Brown, Brigadier-General W. Baker, *History of the Corps of Royal Engineers*, Vol. 4. Chatham: The Institute of Royal Engineers, 1952.

'Hints from History (Part II). The Supply of Engineer Stores and Equipment'. *The Royal Engineers Journal*, 56 (1942), 282–3.

Bull, Stephen (comp.), *An Officer's Manual of the Western Front 1914–1918*. London: Conway, 2008.

Burgoyne, Gerald Achilles, *The Burgoyne Diaries*. London: Thomas Harmsworth, 1985.

Byrne, Lieutenant J. R., *New Zealand Artillery in the Field: 1914–18*. Auckland: Whitcombe and Tombs, 1922.

Callwell, Major-General Sir C. E., Field-Marshal Sir Henry Wilson: His Life and Diaries, *Vol. I.* London: Cassell, 1927.

Cane, Colonel Hubert du (trans.), *The War in South Africa: The Advance to Pretoria after Paardeberg, the Upper Tugela Campaign, etc. Prepared in the Historical Section of the Great General Staff, Berlin.* London: John Murray, 1906.

Capper, Batt.-Col. J. E., 'Information on the Battlefield'. *The Royal Engineers Journal*, 6 (July 1907), 27–43.

Carrington, Charles, *Soldier from the Wars Returning.* London: Hutchinson, 1965.

Carus-Wilson, Captain L. C., 'Earth-Current Telegraphy'. *The Royal Engineers Journal*, 31 (1920), 1–12.

Chadwick, James, 'Frederick John Marrian Stratton, 1881–1960'. *Biographical Memoirs of Fellows of the Royal Society*, 7 (1961), 280–93.

Charteris, Brigadier-General John, *At GHQ.* London: Cassell, 1931.

Chenevix-Trench, Major R., 'Signal Communications in War'. *Journal of the Royal United Service Institution*, 72 (1927), 295–313.

Chenevix-Trench, Lieutenant-Colonel R., 'The Technical Officer in the Field'. *Journal of the Royal United Services Institution*, 75 (1930), 516–23.

Chenevix-Trench, Brigadier R., 'A Signal Officer in North Russia, 1918–1919'. *Journal of the Royal United Services Institution*, 104 (1959), 341–8.

Clutterbuck, Lieutenant-Colonel C. A. (ed.), *The Bond of Sacrifice: A Biographical Record of all British Officers who Fell in the Great War,* Vol. 1: *Aug-Dec. 1914.* London: The Cranford Press, 1917.

Coleman, Frederic, *From Mons to Ypres with French.* London: Marston., 1916.

Collins, Major G. R. N., *Military Organization and Administration.* London: Hugh Rees, 1918.

Corcoran, Captain A. P., 'Wireless in the Trenches'. *Popular Science Monthly,* May 1917, 795.

Corcoran, Austin Patrick, *The Daredevil of the Army: A Motorcycle Despatch Rider and 'Buzzer' in the British Army during the First World War.* Milton Keynes: Leonaur, 2011; first published 1919.

Creagh, Sir O'Moore and Humphris, E. M. (eds.), *The V.C. and D.S.O.,* Vols. 1–3. London: Standard Art Book Company, 1924.

Cumming, Hanway R., *A Brigadier in France 1917–1918.* London: Jonathan Cape, 1922.

Curtis, Colonel R. S., 'The Work of Signal Units in War'. *The Royal Engineers Journal*, 18 (1913), 267–76.

Cutlack, F. M. (ed.), *War Letters of General Sir John Monash.* Sydney: Angus and Robertson, 1935.

Davies, C. B., Colonel F. J., 'The Communications of a Division in the Field'. *Journal of the Royal United Service Institution*, 53 (1909), 885–900.

Davey, R.E., Captain Norman, 'The Telephone at the Front'. *The Journal of the Royal Signals Institution*, 24 (2010), 11 [reprinted from *Punch*, 17 November 1915].

Dopson, F. W., *The 48th Divisional Signal Company in the Great War.* Bristol: J. W. Arrowsmith, 1938.

Dunn, Captain J. C., *The War the Infantry Knew 1914–1919.* London: Abacus, 1998; first published 1938.

Eaton, Gertrude and Waddell, Marion Gates (eds.), *With the Signallers in France: The Diary of a WAAC*. London: First Choice Books, 2010.

Emden, Richard van (ed.), *Sapper Martin: The Secret Great War Diary of Jack Martin*. London: Bloomsbury, 2010.

Evans, Paul W., 'Strategic Signal Communication: A Study of Signal Communication as Applied to Large Field Forces, Based upon the Operations of the German Signal Corps during the March on Paris in 1914'. *Signal Corps Bulletin*, 82 (1935), 24–58.

Falls, Cyril, *The History of the 36th (Ulster) Division*. London: McCaw, Stevenson and Orr, 1922.

Ferris, John (ed.), *The British Army and Signals Intelligence during the First World War*. Stroud: Alan Sutton, 1992.

French, Field Marshal Viscount, *The Despatches of Lord French*. London: Chapman and Hall, 1917.

1914. London: Constable, 1919.

F. S. M. [Frank Stanley Morgan], 'Signals and Mechanization'. *The Army Quarterly*, 16 (1928), 386–92.

Fuller, J. F. C., *Tanks in the Great War 1914–1918*. New York: E. P. Dutton, 1920.

Memoirs of an Unconventional Soldier. London: Ivor Nicholson and Watson, 1936.

General Post Office, *Post Office Circular*. Wednesday, 26 August, 1914. No. 2178.

Post Office Circular. Tuesday, 29 September, 1914, No. 2187.

Post Office Circular. Tuesday, 22 December, 1914. No. 2203.

Post Office Circular. Tuesday, 16 January 1916, No. 2332.

Post Office Circular. Tuesday, 22 January 1917, No. 2333.

Post Office Circular. Tuesday, 13 February 1917, No. 2337.

Post Office Circular. Tuesday, 26 June 1917, No. 2357.

G. G. R., 'Memoirs: Brigadier-General E. G. Godfrey-Faussett'. *The Royal Engineers Journal*, 56 (1942), 331.

Godfrey-Faussett, Major E. G., 'Studies on the Use of Field Telegraphs in South Africa'. *The Royal Engineers Journal*, 8 (1908), 24–9, 81–5, 137–42, 249–52, 289–92.

Gough, General Sir Hubert, *The Fifth Army*. London: Hodder and Stoughton, 1931.

Griffith, Llewelyn Wyn, *Up to Mametz and Beyond*. Barnsley: Pen & Sword, 2010; first published 1931.

Gwilliam, R. E. and Lieutenant W. J., 'A Signal Master on Active Service'. *The Post Office Electrical Engineers' Journal*, 8 (1915–16), 262–3, 332–4.

Gwilliam, R. E. and Captain W. J., 'Transmission of Messages by Carrier Pigeons'. *The Post Office Electrical Engineers' Journal*, 11 (1918–19), 203–6.

Hamilton, R. E. and Lieutenant-Colonel A. C., 'Our Field Telegraph: Its Work in Recent Campaigns, and Its Present Organisation'. *Journal of the Royal United Service Institution*, 28 (1884), 329–55.

Hammond, Captain R. C., 'Communication in the Field'. *The Royal Engineers Journal*, 7 (1908), 139–52.

Hanson, J. Ivor and Wakefield, Alan (eds.), *Plough and Scatter: The Diary-Journal of a First World War Gunner*. Yeovil: Haynes, 2009.

Harington, General Sir Charles, *Plumer of Messines*. London: John Murray, 1935.
Tim Harington Looks Back. London: John Murray, 1940.
Harris, Brigadier L. H., *Signal Venture*. Aldershot: Gale and Polden, 1951.
Hay, Ian [John Hay Beith], *Carrying On – After the First Hundred Thousand*.
Edinburgh: William Blackwood and Sons, 1917.
Hildebrand, Brigadier-General Arthur, 'Recollections of Sir Horace Smith-Dorrien at Le Cateau, August 1914'. *The Army Quarterly*, 21 (October 1930), 15–19.
'Second Army Signals, 1914: From the Personal Diary of Brigadier-General A. B. R. Hildebrand'. *The Royal Signals Quarterly Journal*, 6 (July 1938), 129–41.
Hines, R. E., Captain J. G., 'The Training of Permanent Linemen in the Army Signal Service'. *The Post Office Electrical Engineers' Journal*, 12 (1919–20), 21–3.
Hurst, Gerald B., *With Manchesters in the East*. Manchester: Manchester University Press, 1918.
Closed Chapters. Manchester: Manchester University Press, 1942.
Inglefield, Captain V. E., *The History of the Twentieth (Light) Division*. London: Nisbet, 1921.
Jayne, R. E., Lieutenant A. A., 'Telegraphing in the Field: Arrangements at Headquarters'. *The Times*, 31 December 1914.
Kelly, D. V., *39 Months with the "Tigers", 1915–1918*. Uckfield: Naval and Military Press, 2006; first published 1930.
Kelly, R. B. *Talbot, A Subaltern's Odyssey: A Memoir of the Great War 1915–17*. London: William Kimber, 1980.
Kincaid-Smith, Lieutenant-Colonel M., *The 25th Division in France and Flanders*. London: Harrison, 1920.
Laws, Felicity Jane (ed.), *War on Two Wheels: A Diary of Overseas Service British Expeditionary Force France, 1915–1918, David Winder Small, Royal Engineers Signals*. Raleigh, NC: Lulu Press, 2010.
Lewis, Cecil, *Sagittarius Rising*. London: Frontline Books, 2013; first published 1936.
Lloyd George, David, *War Memoirs*, 2 Vols. London: Odhams Press, 1938.
Longley, Cecil, *Battery Flashes*. New York: E. P. Dutton, 1916.
Lucy, J. F., *There's a Devil in the Drum*. London: Faber and Faber, 1938.
Ludendorff, General Erich, *My War Memories 1914–1918*, Vol. II. London: Hutchinson, 1920.
Lynch, E. P. F, *Somme Mud: The Experiences of an Infantryman in France, 1916–1919*. London: Bantam Books, 2008.
MacDonald, Lieutenant J. A., *Gun-Fire: An Historical Narrative of the 4th Brigade C.F.A. 1914–1918*. Uckfield: Naval and Military Press, 2004; first published 1929.
MacGregor, Archibald Gordon and Welti, Anna (eds.), *Signals from the Great War: The Experiences of a Signals Officer on the Western Front as Told Through his War Diaries 1917–1919*. Brighton: Reveille Press, 2014.
Mackworth, Major A. W., 'The Field Telegraph Corps in Egypt'. *The Royal Engineers Journal*, 12 (1882), 269–72.

Maude, Alan H., *The 47th (London) Division 1914–1919*. London: Amalgamated Press, 1922.

Maurice, Major-General Sir Frederick (ed.), *The Life of General Lord Rawlinson of Trent*. London: Cassell, 1928.

Milne, Lieutenant A. A., 'Communications: Signalling Officer's Work'. *The Evening Post*, 11 September 1918, 8.

Milne, A. A., *It's Too Late Now: The Autobiography of a Writer*. London: Methuen, 1939.

Mitchell, F., *Tank Warfare: The Story of the Tanks in the Great War*. London: Thomas Nelson and Sons, 1933.

Moir, John S., *History of the Royal Canadian Corps of Signals 1903–1961*. Ottawa: Royal Canadian Corps of Signals, 1962.

Monash, Lieutenant-General Sir John, *The Australian Victories in France in 1918*. London: Battery Press, 1993; first published 1920.

Montgomery, Major-General Sir Archibald, *The Story of the Fourth Army in the Battles of the Hundred Days, August 8th to November 11th 1918*. London: Hodder and Stoughton, 1919.

Montgomery, Field Marshal Viscount, *The Memoirs of Field-Marshal the Viscount Montgomery of Alamein*. London: Collins, 1958.

Morgan, Captain F. S., 'The Development of Communication and Command'. *Journal of the Royal United Services Institution*, 76 (1931), 128–36.

'Modern Communications and Command'. *Journal of the Royal United Services Institution*, 76 (1931), 411–19.

Nalder, Major-General R. F. H., *The Royal Corps of Signals: A History of Its Antecedents and Development, 1800–1955*. London: Royal Signals Institution, 1958.

Nichols, G. H. F., *The 18th Division in the Great War*. Edinburgh: Blackwood, 1922.

Nicholson, Colonel W. N., *Behind the Lines: An Account of Administrative Staff Work in the British Army 1914–1918*. London: Strong Oak Press, 1989.

Ogilvie, William G., *Umty-Iddy-Umty: The Story of a Canadian Signaller in the First World War*. Ontario: Boston Mills Press, 1982.

O'Meara, Major W. A. J., 'The Various Systems of Multiplex Telegraphy'. *The Royal Engineers Journal*, 14 (1911), 353–64.

Osman, Lieutenant-Colonel A. H., *Pigeons in the Great War: A Complete History of the Carrier Pigeon Service during the Great War, 1914 to 1918*. London: Racing Pigeon, 1928.

Perry, Nicholas (ed.), *Major-General Oliver Nugent and the Ulster Division 1915–1918*. Stroud: Sutton for the Army Records Society, 2007.

Pinsent, R. E., Lieutenant J. R., 'The Diary of a Cable Section Officer from August to November, 1914'. *The Royal Signals Quarterly Journal*, 3 (1935), 16–23.

Portway, Donald, *Memoirs of an Academic Old Contemptible*. London: Leo Cooper, 1971.

Powell, Colonel R. M., 'Divisional Signals in 1914'. *The Royal Signals Quarterly Journal*, 7 (1940), 339–59.

Priestley, Raymond, *Breaking the Hindenburg Line: The Story of the 46th (North Midland) Division*. London: Unwin Fisher, 1919.

Work of the Royal Engineers in the European War, 1914–19: The Signal Service (France). Uckfield: The Naval and Military Press, 2006; first published 1921.

'The Evolution of Intercommunication in France, 1914–1918'. *The Royal Engineers Journal*, 34 (1921), 269–75.

Prince, Major C. E., 'Wireless Telephony on Aeroplanes'. *Journal of the Institution of Electrical Engineers*, 58 (1920), 377–84.

Pritchard, Major-General H. L. (ed.), *History of the Corps of Royal Engineers*, Vol. V: *The Home Front, France, Flanders and Italy in the First World War*. Chatham: The Institution of Royal Engineers, 1952.

Purves, T. F., 'Trench Telephones'. *The Post Office Electrical Engineers' Journal*, 8 (1915–16), 95–9.

Rawlinson, A., *Adventures on the Western Front, August 1914 to June 1915*. London: Andrew Melrose, 1925.

Reid, Miles, *Into Colditz*. London: Michael Russell, 1983.

Richards, Frank, *Old Soldiers Never Die*. Eastbourne: Antony Rowe, 1933.

Old Soldier Sahib. Uckfield: The Naval and Military Press Ltd., 2003; first published 1936.

Richardson, Lieutenant-Colonel E. H., *British War Dogs: Their Training and Psychology*. London: Skeffington and Son, 1920.

Robertson, Sir William, *Soldiers and Statesmen 1914–1918*, Vol. 1. London: Cassell, 1926.

Schonland, Captain B. F. J., 'W/T. R.E.: An Account of the Work and Development of Field Wireless Sets with the Armies in France'. *The Wireless World*, 7 (July 1919), 124–8, 261–7, 394–7, 452–5.

Scott, Peter T. (ed.), 'The View From GHQ: The Second and Third Parts of the War Diary of General Sir Charles Deedes, KCB, CMG, DSO'. *Stand To! The Journal of the Western Front Association*, 11, no. 12 (1984), 6–17, 28–33.

Scrivenor, J. B., *Brigade Signals*. Oxford: Basil Blackwell, 1932.

Sheffield, Gary and Bourne, John (eds.), *Douglas Haig: War Diaries and Letters 1914–1918*. London: Weidenfeld and Nicolson, 2005.

Singleton-Gates, G. R., *Bolos and Barishynas: Being an Account of the Doings of the Sadleir-Jackson Brigade, and Altham Flotilla, on the North Dvina during the Summer, 1919*. Aldershot: Gale & Polden, 1920.

Smith-Dorrien, General Sir Horace, *Memories of Forty-Eight Years' Service*. London: John Murray, 1925.

Snape, Michael (ed.), 'Archbishop Davidson's Visit to the Western Front, May 1916', in Barber, Melanie and Taylor, Stephen, with Sewell, Gabriel (eds.), *From the Reformation to the Permissive Society: A Miscellany in Celebration of the 400th Anniversary of Lambeth Palace Library*. Woodbridge: Church of England Record Society, 2010, 455–520.

Snow, Dan and Pottle, Mark (eds.), *The Confusion of Command: The War Memoirs of Lieutenant General Sir Thomas D'Oyly Snow, 1914–1915*. London: Frontline Books, 2011.

Spears, Brigadier-General E. L., *Liaison 1914: A Narrative of the Great Retreat*. London: William Heinemann, 1930.

Speight, R. E., Captain A., 'GHQ Signal Office, France'. *The Post Office Electrical Engineers' Journal*, 13 (1920–21), 52–5.

Staniforth, J. H. M. and Grayson, Richard S. (ed.), *At War with the 16th Irish Division 1914–1918: The Staniforth Letters*. Barnsley: Pen and Sword, 2012.

Steel, Major W. Arthur, 'Wireless Telegraphy in the Canadian Corps in France'. *Canadian Defence Quarterly*, 6–8 (1929–1931), 443–61, 45–52, 365–75, 458–67, 84–93, 387–99, 536–46.

Stevens, Lieutenant E. J., *Field Telephones for Army Use: Including an Elementary Course in Electricity and Magnetism*. London: Crosby Lockwood & Son, 1908.

Swinton, Major-General Sir Ernest D., *Eyewitness*. London: Hodder and Stoughton, 1932.

Terraine, John (ed.), *General Jack's Diary: The Trench Diary of Brigadier-General J. L. Jack, D.S.O.* London: Cassell, 2001.

Thompson, Bill (ed.), *General Sir Thomas Morland: War Diaries and Letters, 1914–1918*. Kibworth Beauchamp: Matador, 2015.

Venner, David (ed.), *Despatch Rider on the Western Front: The Diary of Sergeant Albert Simpkin MM*. Barnsley: Pen and Sword, 2015.

Wächter, Dr Frederic, Communicated by Major A. H. Bagnold, R. E., 'Visual Signalling'. *Journal of the Royal United Services Institution*, 40 (1896), 149–64.

Watson, Captain W. H. L., *Adventures of a Motorcycle Despatch Rider during the First World War*. Liskeard: Diggory Press, 2006; first published 1915.

Wavell, General Sir Archibald, *Allenby: A Study in Greatness*. London: George G. Harrap, 1940.

W. B. B., 'Memoir: Colonel A. H. Bagnold'. *The Royal Engineers Journal*, 58 (1944), 131–2.

Weber, Lieutenant-Colonel W. H. F., 'The Development of Mobile Artillery, 1914–1918'. *The Journal of the Royal United Service Institution*, 64 (1919), 49–58.

Wheeler, Victor W., *The 50th Battalion in No Man's Land*. Ontario: CEF Books, 2000.

Williams, Captain Basil, *Raising and Training the New Armies*. London: Constable, 1918.

Woodward, David R. (ed.), *The Military Correspondence of Field-Marshal Sir William Robertson, Chief of the Imperial General Staff, December 1915-February 1918*. Army Records Society: The Bodley Head, 1989.

Wyrall, Everard, *The History of the 19th Division 1914–1918*. London: Edward Arnold, 1932.

The History of the King's Regiment (Liverpool) 1914–1919, Vol. 3. London: Edward Arnold, 1933.

Yule, Lieutenant-Colonel J. S., 'Signals with Carey's Force: An Episode of the March Retreat, 1918'. *The Royal Signals Quarterly Journal*, 5 (1937), 157–65.

SECONDARY SOURCES

I. BOOKS

Ackroyd, Stephen, *The Organisation of Business: Applying Organisational Theory to Contemporary Change*. Oxford: Oxford University Press, 2002.

Alberts, David S. and Hayes, Richard E., *Understanding Command and Control*. Washington, DC: CCRP, 2006.

Ascoli, David, *The Mons Star*. London: George Harrap, 1981.

Austin, Brian, *Schonland: Scientist and Soldier: From Lightning on the Veld to Nuclear Power at Harwell: The Life of Field Marshal Montgomery's Scientific Adviser.* London: IOP Press, 2001.

Badsey, Stephen, *Doctrine and Reform in the British Cavalry 1880–1918.* Aldershot: Ashgate, 2008.

Bailey, Jonathan, *The First World War and the Birth of the Modern Style of Warfare,* Occasional Papers 22. Camberley: Strategic and Combat Studies Institute, Staff College, 1996.

Baker, W. J., *A History of the Marconi Company.* London: Routledge, 1970.

Beach, Jim, *Haig's Intelligence: GHQ and the German Army, 1916–1918.* Cambridge: Cambridge University Press, 2013.

Beckett, Ian F. W., *Johnnie Gough, V. C.* London: Tom Donovan, 1989.

The First World War: The Essential Guide to Sources in the UK National Archives. London: Public Record Office, 2002.

Ypres: The British Army and the Battle for Flanders, 1914. London: Longman, 2004.

Beckett, Ian and Simpson, Keith (eds.), *A Nation in Arms.* Manchester: Manchester University Press, 1985.

Bessel, Richard, *Germany after the First World War.* Oxford: Clarendon Press, 1993.

Bidwell, Shelford and Graham, Dominick, *Fire-Power: The British Army Weapons and Theories of War 1904–45.* London: Allen and Unwin, 1982.

Coalitions, Politicians and Generals: Some Aspects of Command in Two World Wars. London: Brassey's, 1993.

Boff, Jonathan, *Winning and Losing on the Western Front: The British Third Army and the Defeat of Germany in 1918.* Cambridge: Cambridge University Press, 2012.

Bond, Brian, *The Victorian Army and the Staff College 1854–1914.* London: Eyre Methuen, 1972.

(ed.), *The First World War and British Military History.* Oxford: Clarendon Press, 1991.

et al., *'Look to Your Front': Studies in the First World War by The British Commission for Military History.* Staplehurst: Spellmount, 1999.

The Unquiet Western Front: Britain's Role in Literature and History. Cambridge: Cambridge University Press, 2002.

Survivors of a Kind: Memoirs of the Western Front. London: Continuum, 2008.

Bowman, Timothy and Connelly, Mark, *The Edwardian Army: Recruiting, Training, and Deploying the British Army, 1902–1914.* Oxford: Oxford University Press, 2012.

Bray, John, *The Communications Miracle: The Telecommunication Pioneers from Morse to the Information Superhighway.* London: Plenum Press, 1995.

Brown, Ian Malcolm, *British Logistics on the Western Front 1914–1919.* Westport, CT: Praeger, 1998.

Brown, Malcolm, *The Imperial War Museum Book of 1914.* London: Sidgwick and Jackson, 2004.

Builder, Carl H., Bankes, Steven C. and Nordin, Richard, *Command Concepts: A Theory Derived From the Practice of Command and Control*. Washington, DC: Rand National Defence Research Institute, 1999.

Bullock, Mike and Lyons, Laurence A., *Missed Signals on the Western Front: How the Slow Adoption of Wireless Restricted British Strategy and Operations in World War I*. Jefferson, NC: McFarland, 2010.

Campbell-Smith, Duncan, *Masters of the Post: The Authorised History of the Royal Mail*. London: Penguin Books, 2012.

Clark, Alan, *The Donkeys*. London: Hutchinson, 1961.

Clark, Ronald, *Sir Edward Appleton G.B.E., K.C.B., F.R.S.* Oxford: Pergamon Press, 1971.

Clausewitz, Carl von, *On War*, ed. and trans. Michael Howard and Peter Paret, Princeton, NJ: Princeton University Press, 1976.

Coakley, Thomas P., *Command and Control for War and Peace*. Washington, DC: National Defence University Press, 1992.

Creveld, Martin van, *Command in War*. Cambridge, MA: Harvard University Press, 1985.

Davies, Frank and Maddocks, Graham, *Bloody Red Tabs: General Officer Casualties of the Great War, 1914–1918*. London: Leo Cooper, 1995.

DeGroot, Gerard J., *Blighty: British Society in the Era of the Great War*. London: Longman, 1996.

Dennis, Peter and Grey, Jeffrey (eds.), *1917: Tactics, Training and Technology*. Canberra: Australian History Military Publications, 2007.

Downer, John, 'When Failure is an Option: Redundancy, Reliability and Regulation in Complex Technical Systems', *Discussion Paper No. 53, Centre for Analysis of Risk and Regulation at the London School of Economics and Political Science*. London: Kube, 2009.

Easterby-Smith, Mark, Burgoyne, John and Araujo, Luis (eds.), *Organizational Learning and Learning Organizations: Developments in Theory and Practice*. London: Sage, 1999.

Fang, Irving, *A History of Mass Communication: Six Information Revolutions*. Oxford: Focal Press, 1997.

Fisher, Dalmar, *Communication in Organizations*. New York: West, 1993.

Frater, Michael R. and Ryan, Michael, *Electronic Warfare for the Digitised Battlefield*. London: Artech House, 2001.

French, David, *The Strategy of the Lloyd George Coalition, 1916–1918*. Oxford: Clarendon Press, 1995.

Raising Churchill's Army: The British Army and the War Against Germany 1919–1945. Oxford: Oxford University Press, 2000.

Military Identities: The Regimental System, the British Army, and the British People c. 1870–2000. Oxford: Oxford University Press, 2005.

Fussell, Paul, *The Great War and Modern Memory*. Oxford: Oxford University Press, 1977.

Gardiner, Juliet, *The Animals' War: Animals in Wartime from the First World War to the Present Day*. London: Portrait, 2006.

Gardner, Nikolas, *Trial by Fire: Command and the British Expeditionary Force in 1914*. Westport, CT: Praeger, 2003.

Garth, John, *Tolkien and the Great War: The Threshold of Middle-Earth*. London: HarperCollins, 2004.

Gill, Peter and Phythian, Mark, *Intelligence in an Insecure World*. Cambridge: Polity Press, 2006.

Godfrey, Simon, *British Army Communications in the Second World War: Lifting the Fog of Battle*. London: Bloomsbury, 2013.

Goldman, Emily O. (ed.), *Information and Revolutions in Military Affairs*. London: Routledge, 2005.

Gongora, Thierry and Riekhoff, Harald von (eds.), *Towards a Revolution in Military Affairs? Defence and Security at the Dawn of the Twenty-First Century*. Westport, CT: Greenwood Press, 2000.

Gray, Colin S., *Strategy for Chaos: Revolutions in Military Affairs and the Evidence of History*. London: Routledge, 2004.

Another Bloody Century: Future Warfare. London: Weidenfeld and Nicolson, 2005.

Green, Andrew, *Writing the Great War: Sir James Edmonds and the Official Histories 1915–1948*. London: Frank Cass, 2003.

Greenhalgh, Elizabeth, *Victory through Coalition: Britain and France during the First World War*. Cambridge: Cambridge University Press, 2006.

Foch in Command: The Forging of a First World War General. Cambridge: Cambridge University Press, 2011.

The French Army and the First World War. Cambridge: Cambridge University Press, 2014.

Gregory, Adrian, *The Last Great War: British Society and the First World War*. Cambridge: Cambridge University Press, 2008.

Grieves, Keith, *The Politics of Manpower, 1914–18*. Manchester: Manchester University Press, 1988.

Griffith, Paddy, *Battle Tactics of the Western Front: The British Army's Art of Attack 1916–18*. New Haven, CT: Yale University Press, 1994.

(ed.), *British Fighting Methods in the Great War*. London: Frank Cass, 1996.

Hammond, Bryn, *Cambrai 1917: The Myth of the First Great Tank Battle*. London: Weidenfeld and Nicolson, 2008.

Hannagan, Tim, *Management Concepts and Practices*. London: FT Prentice Hall, 2005.

Harris, C. J. (ed.), *Application of Artificial Intelligence to Command and Control Systems*. London: Peter Peregrinus, 1988.

Harris, C. J. and White, I. (eds.), *Advances in Command, Control and Communications Systems*. London: Peter Peregrinus, 1987.

Harris, J. P., *Men, Ideas, and Tanks: British Military Thought and Armoured Forces, 1903–1939*. Manchester: Manchester University Press, 1995.

Douglas Haig and the First World War. Cambridge: Cambridge University Press, 2008.

Harris, J. P. with Barr, Niall, *Amiens to the Armistice: The BEF in the One Hundred Days' Campaign, 8 August–11 November 1918*. London: Brassey's, 1998.

Hartcup, Guy, *The War of Invention: Scientific Developments, 1914–18*. London: Brassey's, 1988.

Headrick, Daniel R., *The Invisible Weapon: Telecommunications and International Politics 1851–1945*. Oxford: Oxford University Press, 1991.

Herwig, Holger H., *The First World War: Germany and Austria-Hungary, 1914–1918*. London: Arnold, 1997.

The Marne, 1914: The Opening of World War I and the Battle That Changed the World. New York: Random House, 2009.

Hinton, Matthew (ed.), *Introducing Information Management: The Business Approach*. Oxford: Butterworth-Heinemann, 2005.

Holmes, Richard, *Riding the Retreat: Mons to the Marne 1914 Revisited*. London: Cape, 1995.

The Little Field Marshal: A Life of Sir John French. London: Weidenfeld and Nicolson, 2004.

Hong, Sungook, *Wireless: From Marconi's Black-Box to the Audion*. Cambridge, MA: MIT Press, 2001.

Hooton, E. R., *War over the Trenches: Air Power and the Western Front Campaigns 1916–1918*. Hersham: Midland, 2010.

Hugill, Peter J., *Global Communications Since 1844: Geopolitics and Technology*. Baltimore and London: The John Hopkins University Press, 1999.

Jones, Heather, *Violence against Prisoners of War in the First World War: Britain, France and Germany, 1914–1920*. Cambridge: Cambridge University Press, 2011.

Jones, Spencer, *From Boer War to World War: Tactical Reform of the British Army, 1902–1914*. Oklahoma: University of Oklahoma Press, 2012.

(ed.), *Stemming the Tide: Officers and Leadership in the British Expeditionary Force 1914*. Solihull: Helion, 2013.

(ed.), *Courage without Glory: The British Army on the Western Front 1915*. Solihull: Helion, 2015.

Kenyon, David, *Horsemen in No Man's Land: British Cavalry and Trench Warfare 1914–1918*. Barnsley: Pen and Sword, 2011.

Kitchen, Martin, *The German Offensives of 1918*. Stroud: Tempus, 2001.

Krause, Jonathan, *Early Trench Tactics in the French Army: The Second Battle of Artois, May-June 1915*. Farnham: Ashgate, 2013.

Laffin, John, *British Butchers and Bunglers of World War One*. London: Bramley Books, 1988.

Liddell Hart, Basil, *The Real War, 1914–1918*. London: Faber and Faber, 1930.

Liddle, Peter H., (ed.), *Passchendaele in Perspective: The Third Battle of Ypres*. Barnsley: Pen and Sword, 1997.

Lloyd, Nick, *Loos 1915*. Stroud: Tempus, 2006.

Lord, Cliff and Watson, Graham, *The Royal Corps of Signals: Unit Histories of the Corps (1920–2001) and its Antecedents*. Solihull: Helion, 2004.

Luttwak, Edward N., *Strategy: The Logic of War and Peace*. Cambridge, MA: Harvard University Press, 2003.

Mattelart, Armand, *Mapping World Communication: War, Progress, Culture*. Minneapolis: University of Minnesota Press, 1994.

McCarthy, Chris, *The Somme: The Day-by-Day Account*. London: Arms and Armour Press, 1993.

McCrery, Nigel, *Into Touch: Rugby Internationals Killed in the Great War*. Barnsley: Pen and Sword, 2014.

Messenger, Charles, *Call to Arms: The British Army 1914–18*. London: Weidenfeld & Nicolson, 2005.

Meulstee, Louis, *Wireless for the Warrior: Compendium*. 1: *Spark to Larkspur (Wireless Sets 1910–1948)*. Groenlo: Emaus Uitgeverij, 2009.

Middlebrook, Martin, *The First Day on the Somme*. London: Allen Lane, 1971.

Miller, Steven E., Lynn-Jones, Sean M. and Evera, Stephen Van (eds.), *Military Strategy and the Origins of the First World War: An International Security Reader*. Princeton, NJ: Princeton University Press, 1991.

Mitchinson, K. W., *England's Last Hope: The Territorial Force, 1908–14*. London: Palgrave, 2008.

Pioneer Battalions in the Great War: Organised and Intelligent Labour. Barnsley: Pen and Sword, 2013.

Mosier, John, *The Myth of the Great War: A New Military History of World War One*. London: Profile Books, 2001.

Muller-Camen, Michael, Croucher, Richard and Leigh, Susan, *Human Resource Management: A Case Study Approach*. London: Chartered Institute of Personnel and Development, 2008.

Murray, Williamson, *Military Adaptation in War: With Fear of Change*. Cambridge: Cambridge University Press, 2011.

Nejat, A., Evrendilek, Cem, Wilhelmsen, Dag and Gezer, Fadil, *Planning and Architectural Design of Modern Command Control Communications and Information Systems*. London: Kluwer Academic, 1997.

Nicholls, Jonathan, *Cheerful Sacrifice: The Battle of Arras 1917*. London: Leo Cooper, 1993.

Noakes, Lucy, *Women in the British Army: War and the Gentle Sex, 1907–1948*. London: Routledge, 2006.

Noakes, Vivien, *Voices of Silence: The Alternative Book of First World War Poetry*. Stroud: Sutton, 2006.

Offer, Avner, *The First World War: An Agrarian Interpretation*. Oxford: Clarendon Press, 1989.

Palazzo, Albert, *Seeking Victory on the Western Front: The British Army and Chemical Warfare in World War One*, Lincoln: University of Nebraska Press, 2000.

Passingham, Ian, *Pillars of Fire: The Battle of Messines Ridge June 1917*. Stroud: Sutton, 1998.

Philpott, William, *Anglo-French Relations and Strategy on the Western Front, 1914–18*. London: Macmillan, 1996.

Bloody Victory: The Sacrifice on the Somme and the Making of the Twentieth Century. London: Little Brown, 2009.

Pidgeon, Trevor, *The Tanks at Flers: An Account of the First Use of Tanks in War at the Battle of Flers-Courcelette, The Somme, 15th September 1916*. Cobham: Fairmile, 1995.

Poole, Ian, *Newnes Guide to Radio and Communications Technology*. Oxford: Newnes, 2003.

Powell, Geoffrey, *Plumer: The Soldiers' General*. Barnsley: Pen and Sword, 2004.

Prior, Robin and Wilson, Trevor, *Command on the Western Front: The Military Career of Sir Henry Rawlinson, 1914–1918*. Oxford: Blackwell, 1992.

Passchendaele: The Untold Story. London: Yale University Press, 1996.

The Somme. New Haven, CT: Yale University Press, 2005.

Pugsley, Christopher, *We Have Been Here Before: The Evolution of the Doctrine of Decentralised Command in the British Army 1905–1989*, Sandhurst Occasional Papers No. 9. Camberley: The Royal Military Academy Sandhurst, 2011.

Rawling, Bill, *Surviving Trench Warfare: Technology and the Canadian Corps 1914–1918*. Toronto: University of Toronto Press, 1992.

Reid, Brian Holden, *A Doctrinal Perspective 1988–98*. The Strategic and Combat Institute: The Occasional, No. 33, May 1998.

Rice, M. A. and Sammes, A. J., *Communications and Information Systems for Battlefield Command and Control*. London: Brassey's, 1989.

Robbins, Simon, *British Generalship on the Western Front, 1914–18: Defeat into Victory*. London: Frank Cass, 2004.

Samuels, Martin, *Command or Control? Command, Training and Tactics in the British and German Armies, 1888–1918*. London: Frank Cass, 1995.

Schreiber, Shane B., *Shock Army of the British Empire: The Canadian Corps in the Last 100 Days of the Great War*. Westport, CT: Praeger, 1997.

Senge, Peter M., *The Fifth Discipline: The Art and Practice of the Learning Organisation*. London: Transworld, 1990.

Shamir, Eitan, *Transforming Command: The Pursuit of Mission Command in the US, British and Israeli Armed Forces*. Stanford, CA: Stanford University Press, 2011.

Sheffield, Gary, *Forgotten Victory: The First World War – Myths and Realities*. London: Headline, 2001.

The Somme. London: Cassell, 2003.

The Chief: Douglas Haig and the British Army. London: Aurum Press, 2011.

Sheffield, Gary and Todman, Dan (eds.), *Command and Control on the Western Front: The British Army's Experience 1914–18*. Staplehurst: Spellmount, 2004.

Sheffield, Gary and Gray, Peter (eds.), *Changing War: The British Army, the Hundred Days Campaign and the Birth of the Royal Air Force, 1918*. London: Bloomsbury, 2013.

Simkins, Peter, *Kitchener's Army: The Raising of the New Armies 1914–1916*. Manchester: Manchester University Press, 1988.

Simpson, Andy, *The Evolution of Victory: British Battles on the Western Front 1914–1918*. London: Tom Donovan, 1995.

Directing Operations: British Corps Command on the Western Front 1914–18. Stroud: Spellmount, 2006.

Solymar, Laszlo, *Getting the Message: A History of Communications*. Oxford: Oxford University Press, 1999.

Standage, Tom, *The Victorian Internet*. London: Weidenfeld and Nicolson, 1998.

Stephenson, Scott, *The Final Battle: Soldiers of the Western Front and the German Revolution of 1918*. Cambridge: Cambridge University Press, 2009.

Stevenson, David, *With Our Backs to the Wall: Victory and Defeat in 1918*. London: Allen Lane, 2011.

Strachan, Hew, *The First World War*, Vol. 1: *To Arms*. Oxford: Oxford University Press, 2001.

Taylor, A. J. P., *The First World War: An Illustrated History*. London: Hamish Hamilton, 1963.

Terraine, John, *Mons: The Retreat to Victory*. Ware: Wordsworth, 2002; first published 1960.

Douglas Haig: The Educated Soldier. London: Hutchinson, 1963.

The Road to Passchendaele: The Flanders Offensive of 1917: A Study in Inevitability. London: Leo Cooper, 1977.

To Win a War: 1918, the Year of Victory. London: Sidgewick and Jackson, 1978.

White Heat: The New Warfare, 1914–1918. London: Sidgewick and Jackson, 1982.

The Smoke and the Fire: Myths and Anti-Myths of War 1861–1945. Barnsley: Leo Cooper, 1992.

Thompson, Paul, *The Edwardians: The Remaking of British Society*. London: Routledge, 1992.

Thwaite, Ann, *A. A. Milne: His Life*. London: Faber and Faber, 1990.

Todman, Dan, *The Great War: Myth and Memory*. London: Hambledon, 2005.

Torrington, Derek and Weightman, Jane, *Effective Management: People and Organization*. Hemel Hempstead: Prentice Hall, 1994.

Travers, Tim, *The Killing Ground: The British Army, the Western Front and the Emergence of Modern War 1900–1918*. London: Unwin Hyman, 1987.

How the War Was Won: Command and Technology in the British Army on the Western Front 1917–1918. London: Routledge, 1992.

Waltz, Edward, *Information Warfare: Principles and Operations*. London: Artech House, 1998.

Watson, Alexander, *Enduring the Great War: Combat, Morale and Collapse in the German and British Armies, 1914–1918*. Cambridge: Cambridge University Press, 2008.

Weatherly, Leslie A., *Human Capital – the Elusive Asset: Measuring and Managing Human Capital: A Strategic Imperative for HR*. Alexandria: Society for Human Resource Management, 2003.

Wilson, Trevor, *The Myriad Faces of War: Britain and the Great War, 1914–1918*. Oxford: Politiy Press, 1986.

Winter, Denis, *Haig's Command: A Reassessment*. London: Viking Press, 1991.

Yates, JoAnne, *Control through Communication: The Rise of System in American Management*. Baltimore: Johns Hopkins University Press, 1993.

Yates, JoAnne and Maanen, John Van (eds.), *Information Technology and Organisational Transformation: History, Rhetoric, and Practice*. London: Sage, 2001.

Zabecki, David T., *The German 1918 Offensives: A Case Study in the Operational Level of War*. London: Routledge, 2006.

II. CHAPTERS AND ARTICLES

Afflerbach, Holger and Sheffield, Gary, 'Waging Total War: Learning Curve or Bleeding Curve?' in Winter, Jay (ed.), *The Legacy of the Great War: Ninety Years On*. Missouri: University of Missouri Press, 2009, 61–90.

Allibone, T. E., 'Cockcroft, Sir John Douglas (1897–1967)', in *Oxford Dictionary of National Biography*, www.oxforddnb.com/view/article/32473 [accessed 20 March 2015].

'Schonland, Sir Basil Ferdinand Jamieson (1896–1972)', in *Oxford Dictionary of National Biography*, www.oxforddnb.com/view/article/31659 [accessed 6 March 2015].

Athans, Michael, 'Command and Control (C²) Theory: A Challenge to Control Science'. *IEEE Transactions on Automatic Control*, 32 (1987), 286–93.

Badsey, Stephen, 'Cavalry and the Development of Breakthrough Doctrine', in Griffith, Paddy (ed.), *British Fighting Methods in the Great War*. London: Frank Cass, 1996, 138–74.

'Ninety Years On: Recent and Changing Views on the Military History of the First World War', in Ekins, Ashley (ed.), *1918 Year of Victory: The End of the Great War and the Shaping of History*. Auckland: Exisle, 2010, 360–86.

Bailey, Jonathan, 'British Artillery in the Great War', in Griffith, Paddy (ed.), *British Fighting Methods in the Great War*. London: Frank Cass, 1998, 23–49.

'The First World War and the Birth of Modern Warfare', in Knox, MacGregor and Murray, Williamson (eds.), *The Dynamics of Military Revolution 1300–2050*. Cambridge: Cambridge University Press, 2001, 132–53.

Barr, Niall, 'Command in the Transition from Mobile to Static Warfare, August 1914 to March 1915', in Sheffield, Gary and Todman, Dan (eds.), *Command and Control on the Western Front: The British Army's Experience 1914–18*. Staplehurst: Spellmount, 2004, 13–38.

Beach, Jim, 'Mosier's Myths' (review essay of John Mosier, *The Myth of the Great War*, 2001). *British Army Review*, 142 (2007), 90–4.

'"Intelligent Civilians in Uniform": The British Expeditionary Force's Intelligence Corps Officers, 1914–1918'. *War & Society*, 27 (2008), 1–22.

'Issued by the General Staff: Doctrine Writing at British GHQ, 1917–1918'. *War in History*, 19 (2012), 464–91.

Beckett, Ian F. W., 'The Territorial Force', in Beckett, Ian F. W. and Simpson, Keith (eds.), *A Nation in Arms*. Manchester: Manchester University Press, 1985), 127–63.

'Wood, Sir (Henry) Evelyn (1838–1919)', in *Oxford Dictionary of National Biography*, www.oxforddnb.com/view/article/37000 [accessed 18 December 2015].

Black, Alastair and Brunt, Rodney, 'Information Management in Business, Libraries and British Military Intelligence: Towards a History of Information Management'. *Journal of Documentation*, 55 (1999), 361–74.

Boff, Jonathan, 'Air/Land Integration in the Hundred Days: The Case of Third Army'. *Air Power Review*, 12 (2009), 77–88.

'Command Culture and Complexity: Third Army during the Hundred Days, August–November 1918', in Sheffield, Gary and Gray, Peter (eds.),

Changing War: The British Army, the Hundred Days Campaign and the Birth of the Royal Air Force, 1918. London: Bloomsbury, 2013, 19–35.

Bond, Brian, 'Passchendaele: Verdicts, Past and Present', in Liddle, Peter H. (ed.), *Passchendaele in Perspective: The Third Battle of Ypres*. Barnsley: Leo Cooper, 1997, 479–88.

Bourne, John, 'Goodbye to All That? Recent Writing on the Great War'. *Twentieth Century British History*, 1 (1990), 87–8.

'British Generals in the First World War', in Sheffield, G. D. (ed.), *Leadership and Command: The Anglo-American Military Experience Since 1861*. London: Brassey's, 2002, 93–116.

Bowman, Timothy, 'Officering Kitchener's Armies: A Case Study of the 36th (Ulster) Division'. *War in History*, 16 (2009), 189–212.

Boyd, John R., 'Organic Design for Command and Control' (US Air Force Academy, 1987), www.ausairpower.net/JRB/c&c.pdf [Accessed 27 August 2014].

Broadberry, Stephen and Harrison, Mark, 'The Economics of World War I: An Overview', in Broadberry, Stephen and Harrison, Mark (eds.), *The Economics of World War I*. Cambridge: Cambridge University Press, 2005, 3–40.

Brown, Ian M., 'Not Glamorous, but Effective: The Canadian Corps and the Set-Piece Attack, 1917–1918'. *Journal of Military History*, 58 (1994), 421–44.

Bruton, Elizabeth and Gooday, Graeme J. N., 'Fuller, Algernon Clement (1885–1970)', in *Oxford Dictionary of National Biography*, www.oxforddnb.com/view/article/107246 [accessed 5 January 2016].

Bryson, Richard, 'The Once and Future Army', in Bond, Brian et al., *'Look to Your Front': Studies in the First World War by the British Commission for Military History*. Spellmount: Staplehurst, 1999, 25–62.

Burkett, Lieutenant-Colonel Jack, 'Dynamic Management of US Army Doctrine'. *Military Review*, 71 (February 1991), 81–4.

Carragher, Michael, '"Amateurs at a Professional Game": The Despatch Rider Corps in 1914', in Jones, Spencer (ed.), *Stemming the Tide: Officers and Leadership in the British Expeditionary Force 1914*. Solihull: Helion, 2013, 332–49.

Clapp G. and Sworder, D., 'Command, Control, and Communications (C³)', in Richard C. Dorf (ed.), *The Electrical Engineering Handbook*. London: CRC Press, 1993, 2211–18.

Crawshaw, Michael, 'The Impact of Technology on the BEF and its Commander', in Bond, Brian and Cave, Nigel (eds.), *Haig: A Reappraisal 70 Years On*. Barnsley: Leo Cooper, 1999, 155–75.

Daft, Richard L. and Lengel, Robert H., 'Organisational Information Requirements, Media Richness and Structural Design'. *Management Science*, 32 (1986), 554–71.

Dale, Margaret, 'Learning Organisations', in Mabey, Christopher and Iles, Paul (eds.), *Managing Learning*. London, 1994, 22–33.

Danchev, Alex, '"Bunking" and Debunking: The Controversies of the 1960s', in Bond, Brian (ed.), *The First World War and British Military History*. Oxford: Clarendon Press, 1991, 263–88.

Deist, Wilhelm, 'The Military Collapse of the German Empire: The Reality behind the Stab-in-the-Back Myth'. *War in History*, 3 (1996), 186–207.

Echevarria II, A. J., 'The "Cult of the Offensive" Revisited: Confronting Technological Change before the Great War'. *Journal of Strategic Studies*, 25 (2002), 199–214.

Edmonds, J. E., 'Murray, Sir Archibald James (1860–1945)', rev. Martin Bunton, in *Oxford Dictionary of National Biography*, www.oxforddnb.com/view/article/35155 [accessed 18 December 2015].

Everett, Oliver, 'Morshead, Sir Owen Frederick (1893–1977)', in *Oxford Dictionary of National Biography*, www.oxforddnb.com/view/article/66332 [accessed 4 January 2016].

Ferris, John, 'The British Army and Signals Intelligence in the Field during the First World War'. *Intelligence and National Security*, 3 (1988), 23–48.

'"FORTITUDE" in Context: The Evolution of British Military Deception in Two World Wars, 1914–1945', in Betts, Richard and Mahnken, Thomas (eds.), *Paradoxes of Strategic Intelligence*. London: Frank Cass, 2003, 117–65.

Foley, Robert T., 'The Other Side of the Wire: The German Army in 1917', in Dennis, Peter and Grey, Jeffrey (eds.), *1917: Tactics, Training and Technology*. Canberra: Australian History Military Publications, 2007, 155–78.

'Dumb Donkeys or Cunning Foxes? Learning in the British and German Armies during the Great War'. *International Affairs*, 90 (2014), 279–98.

French, David, '"Official but not History"? Sir James Edmonds and the Official History of the Great War'. *Journal of the Royal United Services Institute for Defence Studies*, 131 (1986), 58–63.

'Doctrine and Organization in the British Army, 1919–1932'. *The Historical Journal*, 44 (2001), 497–515.

Gardner, Nikolas, 'Command in Crisis: The British Expeditionary Force and the Forest of Mormal, August 1914'. *War & Society*, 16 (1998), 13–32.

Goldman, Emily O., 'Introduction: Information Resources and Military Performance'. *Journal of Strategic Studies*, 27 (2004), 195–219.

Gooday, Graeme, 'Combative Patenting: Military Entrepreneurship in First World War Telecommunications'. *Studies in History and Philosophy of Science*, 44 (2013), 247–58.

Gordon, Andrew, 'Rat Catchers and Regulators at the Battle of Jutland', in Sheffield, Gary and Till, Geoffrey (eds.), *The Challenges of High Command: The British Experience*. London: Palgrave Macmillan, 2003, 26–33.

Gray, Peter, 'The Air Ministry and the Formation of the Royal Air Force', in Sheffield, Gary and Gray, Peter (eds.), *Changing War: The Hundred Days Campaign and the Birth of the Royal Air Force, 1918*. London: Bloomsbury, 2013, 135–48.

Grayson, Richard S., 'Military History from the Street: New Methods for Researching First World War Service in the British Military'. *War in History*, 21 (2014), 465–95.

Greenhalgh, Elizabeth, 'Why the British Were on the Somme in 1916'. *War in History*, 6 (1999), 147–73.

'Flames over the Somme: A Retort to William Philpott'. *War in History*, 10 (2003), 335–42.

'Myth and Memory: Sir Douglas Haig and the Imposition of Allied Unified Command in March 1918'. *Journal of Military History*, 68 (2004), 771–820.

'David Lloyd George, Georges Clemenceau, and the 1918 Manpower Crisis'. *The Historical Journal*, 50 (2007), 397–421.

Hall, Brian N., 'The "Life-Blood" of Command? The British Army, Communications and the Telephone, 1877–1914'. *War & Society*, 27 (October 2008), 43–65.

'The British Army and Wireless Communication, 1896–1918'. *War in History*, 19 (2012), 290–321.

'Technological Adaptation in a Global Conflict: The British Army and Communications beyond the Western Front, 1914–1918'. *Journal of Military History*, 78 (2014), 37–71.

'Letters to the Editor', *Journal of Military History*, 78 (2014), 1208–13.

'The Development of Tank Communications in the British Expeditionary Force, 1916–1918', in Searle, Alaric (ed.), *Genesis, Employment, Aftermath: First World War Tanks and the New Warfare, 1900–1945*. Solihull: Helion, 2015, 136–62.

Harfield, Alan, 'Lieutenant-General Sir John Sharman Fowler, KCB, KCMG'. DSO'. *Journal of the Society for Army Historical Research*, 70 (1992), 67–70.

Harris, J. P., 'The Rise of Armour', in Griffith, Paddy (ed.), *British Fighting Methods in the Great War*. London: Frank Cass, 1996, 113–37.

Harris, J. P. and Marble, Sanders, 'The "Step-by-Step" Approach: British Military Thought and Operational Method on the Western Front 1915–17'. *War in History*, 15 (2008), 17–42.

Holley Jr., I. B. Major-General, 'The Doctrinal Process: Some Suggested Steps'. *Military Review*, 59 (April 1979), 2–13.

Howard, Michael, 'Men Against Fire: The Doctrine of the Offensive in 1914', in Paret, Peter (ed.), *Makers of Modern Strategy from Machiavelli to the Nuclear Age*. Princeton, NJ: Princeton University Press, 1986, 510–26.

Hughes, Clive, 'The New Armies', in Beckett, Ian F. W. and Simpson, Keith (eds.), *A Nation in Arms: The British Army in the First World War*. Manchester: Manchester University Press, 1985), 99–126.

Hussey, John, 'The Flanders Battleground and the Weather in 1917', in Liddle, Peter H. (ed.), *Passchendaele in Perspective: The Third Battle of Ypres*. Barnsley: Pen and Sword, 1997, 140–58.

Juniper, Dean, 'The First World War and Radio Development'. *Royal United Services Institute Journal*, 148 (2003), 84–9.

Kennedy, P. M., 'Imperial Cable Communications and Strategy, 1870–1914'. *English Historical Review*, 86 (1971), 728–52.

Kiszely, John, 'The British Army and Approaches to Warfare Since 1945', in Reid, Brian Holden (ed.), *Military Power: Land Warfare in Theory and Practice*. London: Frank Cass, 1997, 179–206.

Lawson J. S., Jr., 'Command Control as a Process'. *IEEE Control Systems Magazine*, 1 (1981), 5–11.

Lee, John, 'Some Lessons of the Somme: The British Infantry in 1917', in Bond, Brian et al. (eds.), *'Look to Your Front'. Studies in the First World War by the British Commission for Military History*. Spellmount: Staplehurst, 1999, 79–88.

'Command and Control in Battle: British Divisions on the Menin Road Ridge, 20 September 1917', in Sheffield, Gary and Todman, Dan (eds.), *Command*

and Control on the Western Front: The British Army's Experience 1914–18. Staplehurst: Spellmount, 2004, 119–39.

Lloyd, Nick, '"With Faith and without Fear": Sir Douglas Haig's Command of First Army during 1915'. *The Journal of Military History*, 71 (2007), 1051–76.

McCarthy, Chris, 'Queen of the Battlefield: The Development of Command, Organisation and Tactics in the British Infantry Battalion during the Great War', in Sheffield, Gary and Todman, Dan (eds.), *Command and Control on the Western Front: The British Army's Experience 1914–18*. Staplehurst: Spellmount, 2004, 173–94.

McRandle, James and and Quirk, James, 'The Blood Test Revisited: A New Look at German Casualty Counts in World War I'. *Journal of Military History*, 70 (2006), 667–701.

Mews, Stuart, 'Davidson, Randall Thomas, Baron Davidson of Lambeth (1848–1930)', in *Oxford Dictionary of National Biography*, www.oxforddnb.com/view/article/32733, [accessed 19 February 2015].

Millett, Allan R., Murray, Williamson and Watman, Kenneth H., 'The Effectiveness of Military Organizations', in Millett, Allan R. and Murray, Williamson (eds.), *Military Effectiveness*, Volume I: *The First World War, New Edition*. Cambridge: Cambridge University Press, 2010, 1–30.

Milne, Graeme J., 'British Business and the Telephone, 1878–1911'. *Business History*, 49 (2007), 163–85.

Moffat, J., 'Representing the Command and Control Process in Simulation Models of Conflict'. *Journal of the Operational Research Society*, 51 (2000), 431–9.

Moffat, J. and Witty, S., 'Bayesian Decision Making and Military Command and Control'. *Journal of the Operational Research Society*, 5 (2002), 709–18.

Murray-Smith, S., 'Priestley, Sir Raymond Edward (1886–1974)', in *Australian Dictionary of Biography*, National Centre of Biography, Australian National University, http://adb.anu.edu.au/biography/priestley-sir-raymond-edward-8116/text14173 [Accessed 1 September 2014].

Palazzo, Albert P., 'The British Army's Counter-Battery Staff Office and Control of the Enemy in World War 1'. *Journal of Military History*, 63 (1999), 55–74.

Perry, Charles R., 'The British Experience 1876–1912: The Impact of the Telephone during the Years of Delay', in Pool, Ithiel de Sola (ed.), *The Social Impact of the Telephone*. Cambridge, MA: MIT Press, 1977), 68–96.

Philpott, William, 'Why the British Were Really on the Somme: A Reply to Elizabeth Greenhalgh'. *War in History*, 9 (2002), 446–71.

'Beyond the "Learning Curve": The British Army's Military Transformation in the First World War', 10 November 2009, www.rusi.org/analysis/commentary/ref:C4AF97CF94AC8B/ [Accessed 27 August 2014].

Pratley, Brigadier Philip, 'Lifeline, Pipeline and Occasional Noose? How the British Army's Communicators Looked Back on World War II'. *Mars & Clio*, 22 (Summer 2008), 38–42.

Prior, Robin and Wilson, Trevor, 'Review of *Haig's Command: A Reassessment*, by Denis Winter'. *Australian War Memorial Journal*, 23 (1993), 57.

Radley, Gordon, 'Angwin, Sir (Arthur) Stanley (1883–1959)', in *Oxford Dictionary of National Biography*, www.oxforddnb.com/view/article/30421, [accessed 6 March 2015].

Radner, Roy, 'The Organisation of Decentralised Information Processing'. *Econometrica*, 61 (1993), 1109–46.

Rawling, Bill, 'Communications in the Canadian Corps, 1915–1918: Wartime Technological Progress Revisited'. *Canadian Military History*, 3 (1994), 6–21.

Redman, R. O., 'Stratton, Frederick John Marrian (1881–1960)', in *Oxford Dictionary of National Biography*, www.oxforddnb.com/view/article/36346, [accessed 20 February 2015].

R.M.A., 'Esto Pernox: A Story of Lieutenant-General Sir John Fowler, KCB, KCMG, DSO'. *Journal of the Royal Signals Institution*, 7 (1966), 177–84.

Sagan, Scott D., 'Learning from *Normal Accidents*'. *Organisation & Environment*, 17 (2004), 15–19.

Shapiro, Jeremy, 'Information and War: Is It a Revolution?', in Khalilzad, Zalmay M. and White, John P. (eds.), *Strategic Appraisal: The Changing Role of Information in Warfare*. Washington, DC: RAND Corporation, 1999, 113–53.

Shaw, Diana, 'The Forgotten Army of Women: The Overseas Service of Queen Mary's Army Auxiliary Corps with the British Forces, 1917–1921', in Cecil, Hugh and Liddle, Peter H. (eds.), *Facing Armageddon: The First World War Experienced*. London: Leo Cooper, 1996), 365–79.

Sheffield, Gary, 'The Indispensable Factor: The Performance of British Troops in 1918', in Dennis, Peter and Grey, Jeffrey (eds.), *1918: Defining Victory*. Canberra: Army History Unit, 1999, 72–95.

'British High Command in the First World War: An Overview', in Sheffield, Gary and Till, Geoffrey (eds.), *The Challenges of High Command: The British Experience*. London: Palgrave Macmillan, 2003, 15–25.

'John Terraine as a Military Historian'. *Journal of the Royal United Services Institute*, 149 (2004), 70–5.

'Doctrine and Command in the British Army: An Historical Overview', E-2, in *Army Doctrine Publication (ADP). Operations* (2010), www.gov.uk/government/uploads/system/uploads/attachment_data/file/33695/ADPOperationsDec10.pdf (Accessed 15 January 2016).

Sheffield, Gary and Jordan, David, 'Douglas Haig and Airpower', in Gray, Peter W. and Cox, Sebastian (eds.), *Air Power Leadership: Theory and Practice*. London: The Stationary Office, 2002, 264–82.

Simkins, Peter, 'Haig and the Army Commanders', in Bond, Brian and Cave, Nigel (eds.), *Haig: A Reappraisal 70 Years On*. Barnsley: Leo Cooper, 1999, 78–106.

'"Building Blocks": Aspects of Command and Control at Brigade Level in the BEF's Offensive Operations, 1916–1918', in Sheffield, Gary and Todman, Dan (eds.), *Command and Control on the Western Front: The British Army's Experience 1914–1918*. Staplehurst: Spellmount, 2004, 141–72.

Simpson, Andy, 'British Corps Command on the Western Front, 1914–1918', in Sheffield, Gary and Todman, Dan (eds.), *Command and Control on the Western Front: The British Army's Experience 1914–18*. Staplehurst: Spellmount, 2004, 97–118.

Simpson, Keith, 'The Officers', in Beckett, Ian F. W. and Simpson, Keith (eds.), *A Nation in Arms: The British Army in the First World War*. Manchester: Manchester University Press, 1985), 63–98.

Skyttner, Lars, 'Systems Theory and the Science of Military Command and Control'. *Kybernetes Journal*, 34 (2005), 1240–60.

Spiers, Edward, 'The Late Victorian Army 1868–1914', in Chandler, David and Beckett, Ian F. W. (eds.), *The Oxford History of the British Army*. Oxford: Oxford University Press, 1996, 187–210.

Strachan, Hew, 'Review of *Command or Control? Command, Training and Tactics in the British and German Armies, 1888–1918*, by Martin Samuels'. *Journal of Military History*, 60 (1996), 778–9.

'The Morale of the German Army, 1917–18', in Cecil, Hugh and Liddle, Peter H. (eds.), *Facing Armageddon: The First World War Experienced*. London: Leo Cooper, 1996, 383–98.

'The Battle of the Somme and British Strategy'. *Journal of Strategic Studies*, 21 (1998), 79–95.

'Back to the Trenches: Why Can't British Historians Be Less Insular about the First World War?', *The Times Literary Supplement*, 5 November 2008.

Todman, Dan and Sheffield, Gary, 'Command and Control in the British Army on the Western Front', in Sheffield, Gary and Todman, Dan (eds.), *Command and Control on the Western Front: The British Army's Experience 1914–18*. Staplehurst: Spellmount, 2004, 1–11.

Torpy, Air Chief Marshal Sir Glen, 'Effective Air Command and Control'. *RUSI Defence Systems*, 9 (2006–7), 54–6.

Travers, Tim, 'The Offensive and the Problem of Innovation in British Military Thought, 1870–1915'. *Journal of Contemporary History*, 13 (1978), 531–53.

'Technology, Tactics, and Morale: Jean de Bloch, the Boer War, and British Military Theory, 1900–1914'. *Journal of Modern History*, 51 (1979), 264–86.

'Could the Tanks of 1918 Have Been War-Winners for the British Expeditionary Force?'. *Journal of Contemporary History*, 27 (1992), 389–406.

Wallace, Lietenant-General William S., 'Network-Enabled Battle Command'. *RUSI Defence Systems*, 7 (Spring 2005), 20–2.

Wetherell, David, 'Strong, Philip Nigel (1899–1983)', in *Australian Dictionary of Biography*, National Centre of Biography, Australian National University, http://adb.anu.edu.au/biography/strong-philip-nigel-15782/text26974 [accessed 7 March 2015].

Whitmarsh, Andrew, 'British Army Manoeuvres and the Development of Military Aviation, 1910–1913'. *War in History*, 14 (2007), 325–46.

Wohl, Joseph G., 'Force Management Decision Requirements for Air Force Tactical Command and Control'. *IEEE Transactions on Systems, Man, and Cybernetics*, 11 (1981), 618–39.

Woodward, David, 'Did Lloyd George Starve the British Army of Men Prior to the German Offensive of 21 March 1918?'. *The Historical Journal*, 27 (1984), 241–52.

III. THESES

Fox-Godden, Aimée, '"Putting Knowledge in Power": Learning and Innovation in the British Army of the First World War'. PhD Thesis. University of Birmingham, 2015.

Harris, Paul, 'The Men Who Planned the War: A Study of the Staff of the British Army on the Western Front, 1914–18'. PhD Thesis. King's College London, 2013.

Jordan, David, 'The Army Co-Operation Missions of the Royal Flying Corps/ Royal Air Force 1914–1918'. PhD Thesis. University of Birmingham, 1997.

Hammond, Christopher Brynley, 'The Theory and Practice of Tank Co-Operation with Other Arms on the Western Front during the First World War'. PhD Thesis. University of Birmingham, 2005.

Marble, William Sanders, '"The Infantry Cannot Do with a Gun Less": The Place of Artillery in the BEF, 1914–1918'. PhD Thesis. King's College London, 1998.

Mitchell, Stuart, 'An Inter-Disciplinary Study of Learning in the 32nd Division on the Western Front, 1916–1918'. PhD Thesis. University of Birmingham, 2013.

Powell, Andrew, 'The Use of Wireless at the Battle of Amiens, 8–11 August 1918'. MA Dissertation. University of Birmingham, 2013.

Index

Printed by Printforce, United Kingdom